THE COMPLETE RESULTS & LINE-UPS OF THE UEFA CHAMPIONS LEAGUE 2018-2021

Dirk Karsdorp

British Library Cataloguing in Publication Data
A catalogue record for this book is available from the British Library

ISBN: 978-1-86223-471-0

Copyright © 2021, SOCCER BOOKS LIMITED (01472 696226)
72 St. Peter's Avenue, Cleethorpes, N.E. Lincolnshire, DN35 8HU, England
Web site   www.soccer-books.co.uk
e-mail   info@soccer-books.co.uk

All rights are reserved. No part of this publication may be reproduced, stored in a retrieval system or transmitted, in any form or by any means, electronic, mechanical, photocopying, recording, or otherwise, without the prior written permission of Soccer Books Limited.

Printed in the UK by 4edge Ltd.

FOREWORD

'Hail Wolves – Champions of the World', screamed the headlines one grey December morning in 1954. Wolverhampton Wanderers had recovered from a two-goal deficit to beat Honvéd of Budapest, a significant event maybe, but hardly justifying such a headline.

Much of the euphoria stemmed from the make-up of the Hungarian team. Puskas, Kocsis and four others had been in national side, which had twice beaten England in the previous 13 months, scoring 13 goals in the process. But Wolves had been favoured by the conditions, had more incentive than their opponents (who were simply on a European jaunt), and had survived a number of goalmouth escapes earlier in the game. While English eyes viewed the result through rose-tinted spectacles, more objectivity was revealed elsewhere in Europe.

The most far-sighted reaction came from France. In the daily sports paper *L'Equipe*, the editor Gabriel Hannot decried the overreaction of the English. He wrote: 'We must wait for Wolves to visit Moscow or Budapest before we proclaim their invincibility. There are other clubs of international prowess, notably Milan and Real Madrid to name but two...'

Hannot's opinion was not baseless. The next day the paper devoted much space to outline plans for a European tournament, in which patriotic boasts could be put to the test. It was not an original idea; there had already been international competitions like the Mitropa Cup before the Second World War, which featured the leading club sides in Austria, Czechoslovakia, Hungary, Yugoslavia and later Switzerland, Italy and Romania. After the War, France, Italy, Spain and Portugal played one another for the Latin Cup. But L'Equipe's plan provided for the whole of Europe, and Gabriel Hannot called for the support of UEFA.

This campaign from France originated an entirely new era in football. Not only did UEFA accept the proposal except for the name (UEFA preferred European Champion Clubs' Cup to Hannot's European Cup, which they wanted to keep for a national team competition), but in their acceptance they took a step which certainly cracked and even broke down much of the traditional insularity of top class club football. Aided by the parallel development of floodlighting, which made practicable the extra fixtures which had to be played in midweek, the European Champion Club's Cup became a tremendous success – though officials might have been a little peeved that their lengthy nomenclature was immediately shortened into the European Cup by the media and most other commentators.

As the European dream became reality, the commercial prospects of international club competition were not lost on the continent's leading participants. Before the end of the decade, the European Cup Winners' Cup had been instituted as a spin-off tournament, while in 1958 the first official contest between national sides, the European Nations' Cup, began its life span. Oddly enough, the actual name European Cup has never been utilised.

The first 'European Cup' tie was played on 4th September 1955, between Sporting Club de Portugal from Lisbon and Partizan of Belgrade; just four days later Real Madrid set out on an astounding run during which they would not lose an aggregate tie for five years!

This first competition comprised 16 entrants, 8 of whom were not actually the reigning champions of their countries at the time. Over the years the number of entrants increased until there were regularly 32 teams competing for the trophy. Between the years of 1955 and 1991 each tie was played on a knock-out basis over two legs and a sister title to our books covering the Champions League, *The Complete Results and Line-ups of the European Champion Clubs' Cup 1955-1991 – The Knockout Years*, is also available from Soccer Books Ltd. This contains full statistics for every game played in the competition during this period.

The 1991-92 season saw the beginning of a new era with the start of the so-called "Champions League", a money-spinning format which saw entrants grouped in Leagues of four teams in certain stages of the competition. Together with a gradual increase in entrants this led to a huge rise in the number of lucrative matches to be played meaning qualification for the Champions League is now vitally important for Europe's major teams.

Sister titles to this book containing full statistics for every game played in the European Champions League from 1991-2004, from 2004-2009, from 2009-2012, from 2012-2015 and from 2015-2018 are also available from Soccer Books Ltd as are other books containing full statistics for a variety of European football competitions (including the UEFA Cup, Fairs Cup, Europa League and Mitropa Cup), and other World competitions. Further details of these titles can be found on the back cover.

We have endeavoured to make the contents of this book as accurate as possible but often, checking two different sources leads to different information for the same match. In cases such as this we have used the most trustworthy information we could find.

Throughout this book, rather than use English spellings, we have used the correct spelling of Club names and places as used in the country of origin. For example, Rome is Roma, Copenhagen is København etc.

UEFA CHAMPIONS LEAGUE
2018-2019

PRELIMINARY ROUND
SEMI-FINAL ROUND

26.06.18   Victoria Stadium, Gibraltar:
           FC Santa Coloma – FC Drita 0-2 (0-0, 0-0) (a.e.t.)
FC Santa Coloma: Eloy Casals, Ildefons Lima, Marc Rebés, Andreu Ramos, Víctor Rodríguez (86' Albert Mercadé), Moisés San Nicolás, Yago Pérez, Loren Burón (105+1' Cédric Fauré), Aleix Cistero (84' Jaime Noguerol), Gabi Riera (62' Juli Sánchez), Juanma Torres.
Coach: Marc Rodriguez Rebull.
FC Drita: Leutrim Rexhepi, Liridon Leci, Fidan Gërbeshi, Viktor Kuka, Ardian Limani, Haxhi Neziraj (112' Denis Haliti), Drilon Musaj (98' Arbër Shala), Bujar Shabani, Xhevdet Shabani, Endrit Krasniqi, Leotrim Kryeziu (85' Përparim Livoreka). Coach: Bekim Isufi.
Goals: 99' Xhevdet Shabani 0-1, 105+3' Fidan Gërbashi 0-2 (p).
Referee: Paul McLaughlin (IRL)   Attendance: 288.

FC Drita won after extra time.

26.06.18   Victoria Stadium, Gibraltar:
           S.P. La Fiorita – Lincoln Red Imps FC 0-2 (0-1)
S.P. La Fiorita: Gianluca Vivan, Samuele Olivi, Roberto Di Maio, Marco Gasperoni, Riccardo Mezzadri, Damiano Tommasi, Simone Loiodice (69' Luca Righini), Ivan Buonocunto (89' Alessandro Cattelan), Armando Amati, Danilo Rinaldi (75' Andy Selva), Emiliano Olcese.
Coach: Gianluca Procopio.
Lincoln Red Imps FC: Lolo Soler, Joseph Chipolina, Oliver "Oli" (74' Sykes Garro), Bernardo Lopes, Jean Garcia, Calderón, Diego Gámiz, "Álex" Moreno (69' Ryan Casciaro), Juan Montesinos, Juanma Ortiz (61' Lee Casciaro), Anthony Hernandez.
Coach: Diego Perez Jimenez "Yiyi".
Goals: 2' Anthony Hernandez 0-1, 51' "Álex" Moreno 0-2.
Referee: Jørgen Burchardt (DEN)   Attendance: 840.

PRELIMINARY ROUND
FINAL ROUND

29.06.18   Victoria Stadium, Gibraltar:
   Lincoln Red Imps FC – FC Drita 1-4 (0-1, 1-1) (a.e.t.)
Lincoln Red Imps FC: Lolo Soler, Joseph Chipolina (105' Jean Garcia), Oliver "Oli", Bernardo Lopes, Calderón (46' Pedro Corral), Diego Gámiz, "Álex" Moreno, Juan Montesinos (46' André dos Santos), Juanma Ortiz (72' Falu Aranda), Anthony Hernandez, Lee Casciaro.
Coach: Diego Perez Jimenez "Yiyi".
FC Drita: Leutrim Rexhepi, Liridon Leci, Fidan Gërbeshi, Viktor Kuka, Ardian Limani, Haxhi Neziraj, Drilon Musaj (68' Arbër Shala), Bujar Shabani, Xhevdet Shabani (120+3' Adonis Ruhani), Endrit Krasniqi (120+2' Denis Haliti), Leotrim Kryeziu (73' Përparim Livoreka).
Coach: Bekim Isufi.
Goals: 2' Liridon Leci 0-1, 61' Pedro Corral 1-1, 105+3' Liridon Leci 1-2 (p), 120' Xhevdet Shabani 1-3, 120+4' Haxhi Neziraj 1-4.
Referee: Manfredas Lukjancukas (LTU)   Attendance: 468.
Sent off: 101' Fidan Gërbeshi, 105+2' Bernardo Lopes.

FC Drita won after extra time.

FIRST QUALIFYING ROUND

10.07.18   Ramaz Shengelias Sakhelobis Stadioni, Kutaisi:
   Torpedo Kutaisi – FC Sheriff Tiraspol 2-1 (1-1)
Torpedo Kutaisi: Roin Kvaskhvadze, Manuka Kobakhidze (82' Davit Khurtsilava), Giorgi Kimadze (77' Beka Tughushi), Levan Gegetchkori, Oleksandr Azatskyi, Lazar Marin, Grigol Dolidze (62' Arfang Daffé), Levan Kutalia, Giorgi Kukhianidze, Marek Hlinka, Mate Tsintsadze. Coach: Kakhaber Chkhetiani.
FC Sheriff Tiraspol: Zvonimir Mikulic, Ante Kulusic, Mateo Susic, Vladimir Kovacevic, Cristiano, Antun Palic, Yuri Kendysh, Rifet Kapic (66' Joálisson), Ziguy Badibanga, Al-Hadji Kamara, Gerson Rodrigues (78' Alexandru Boiciuc). Coach: Goran Sablic.
Goals: 14' Ziguy Badibanga 0-1, 24' Giorgi Kimadze 1-1, 64' Giorgi Kukhianidze 2-1 (p).
Referee: Aleksandrs Golubevs (LAT)   Attendance: 7,251.

10.07.18   A. Le Coq Arena, Tallinn: FC Flora Tallinn – Hapoel Be'er Sheva 1-4 (0-2)
FC Flora Tallinn: Mait Toom, Gert Kams, Joseph Saliste (57' Kevin Aloe), Jürgen Lorenz, Madis Vihmann, Aleksandr Dmitrijev, Zakaria Beglarishvili (71' Markus Poom), Mihkel Ainsalu, Rauno Alliku, Rauno Sappinen, Frank Liivak (66' Maksim Gussev).
Coach: Arno Pijpers.
Hapoel Be'er Sheva: David Goresh, Ben Bitton, Loai Taha, Shir Tzedek, Oren Bitton, Hen Ezra, Maor Melikson, Hanan Maman (61' Niv Zrihan), Daniel Einbinder, Marwan Kabha (48' Vladimir Brown), Ben Sahar (79' Tomás Pekhart). Coach: Bachar Bakhar.
Goals: 18' Ben Sahar 0-1, 36' Shir Tzedek 0-2 (p), 53' Hanan Maman 0-3, 73' Rauno Sappinen 1-3 (p), 85' Hen Ezra 1-4.
Referee: Erik Lambrechts (BEL)   Attendance: 1,106.

10.07.18 Stade Jos Nosbaum, Dudelange: F91 Dudelange – MOL Vidi FC 1-1 (0-1)
F91 Dudelange: Jonathan Joubert, Tom Schnell, Jerry Prempeh, Bryan Mélisse, Marc-André Kruska, Stélvio (46' Patrick Stumpf, 74' Jordann Yéyé), Dominik Stolz (90' Sanel Ibrahimovic), Edisson Jordanov, Clément Couturier, Danel Sinani, David Turpel.
Coach: Dino Toppmöller.
MOL Vidi FC: Ádam Kovácsik, Attila Fiola, Loïc Négo, Paulo Vinícius, Stopira, Szabolcs Huszti (79' Stefan Scepovic), Anel Hadzic, Máté Pátkai, István Kovács (69' Boban Nikolov), Danko Lazovic, Marko Scepovic. Coach: Marko Nikolic.
Goals: 42' Szabolcs Huszti 0-1, 58' Bryan Mélisse 1-1.
Referee: Zaven Hovhannisyan (ARM)   Attendance: 1,057.

10.07.18 Vazgen Sargsyan anvan Hanrapetakan Marzadasht, Yerevan:
       FC Alashkert – Celtic FC 0-3 (0-1)
FC Alashkert: Ognjen Cancarevic, Gagik Daghbashyan, Artak Yedigaryan, Oliver Práznovsky, Taron Voskanyan, Artur Yedigaryan (82' Mihran Manasyan), Artak Dashyan, Danilo Sekulic, Jefferson (85' Artem Simonyan), Artak Grigoryan, Uros Nenadovic (55' César Romero).
Coach: Varuzhan Sukiasyan.
Celtic FC: Craig Gordon, Jozo Simunovic, Kieran Tierney, Kristoffer Ajer, Jack Hendry, Scott Brown, James Forrest, Callum McGregor, Olivier Ntcham (68' Kouassi Eboue), Moussa Dembélé (68' Scott Sinclair), Odsonne Édouard (77' Lewis Morgan).
Coach: Brendan Rodgers.
Goals: 45+2' Odsonne Édouard 0-1, 81' James Forrest 0-2, 90' Callum McGregor 0-3.
Referee: Danilo Grujic (SRB)   Attendance: 4,948.

(FC Alashkert played their home match at Vazgen Sargsyan anvam Hanrapetakan Marzadasht instead of their regular stadium, Alashkert Stadium).

10.07.18 Svangaskard, Toftir: Víkingur Gøta – HJK Helsinki 1-2 (0-2)
Víkingur Gøta: Elias Rasmussen, Atli Gregersen, Hans Djurhuus (59' Dennis Nieblas), Hanus Jacobsen, Adrian Cascaval, Gunnar Vatnhamar (89' Hans Jákup Lervig), Elias Jóhannesson Lervig, Sølvi Vatnhamar, Hedin Hansen (74' Karl Løkin), Filip Djordjevic, Adeshina Lawal.
Coach: Sigfríður Clementsen.
HJK Helsinki: Maksim Rudakov, Rafinha, Hannu Patronen, Faith Obilor, Roni Peiponen (46' Valtteri Vesiaho), Anthony Annan, Moshtagh Yaghoubi, Sebastian Dahlström, Riku Riski (80' Eetu Vertainen), Evans Mensah, Klauss. Coach: Mika Lehkosuo.
Goals: 9' Sebastian Dahlström 0-1, 29' Atli Gregersen 0-2 (og), 51' Gunnar Vatnhamar 1-2.
Referee: Robert Hennessy (IRL)   Attendance: 300.

(Víkingur Gøta played their home match at Svangaskard instead of their regular stadium, Sarpugerdi).

10.07.18   Telekom Arena, Skopje: KF Shkëndija 79 – The New Saints 5-0 (2-0)
KF Shkëndija 79: Kostadin Zahov, Mevlan Murati, Visar Musliu, Egzon Bejtulai, Mevlan Adili, Armend Alimi, Sciprim Taipi (80' Arbin Zejnulai), Besart Ibraimi (75' Shefit Shefiti), Izair Emini (83' Remzi Selmani), Stênio Júnior, Marjan Radeski. Coach: Qatip Osmani.
The New Saints: Paul Harrison, Simon Spender (73' Kane Lewis), Christopher Marriott, Blaine Hudson, Benjamin Cabango, Jamie Mullan, Jonathan Routledge, Daniel Redmond (67' Aeron Edwards), Ryan Brobbel, Thomas Holland, Dean Ebbe (64' Kurtis Byrne).
Coach: Scott Ruscoe.
Goals: 16' Izair Emini 1-0, 38', 53', 60', 66' Besart Ibraimi 2-0, 3-0, 4-0, 5-0.
Referee: Timotheos Christofi (CYP)   Attendance: 2,700.

(KF Shkëndija 79 played their home match at Telekom Arena instead of their regular stadium, Ecolog Arena, due to renovation).

10.07.18   Stadiumi Olimpik Adem Jashari, Mitrovica: FC Drita – Malmö FF 0-3 (0-2)
FC Drita: Leutrim Rexhepi, Liridon Leci (83' Denis Haliti), Viktor Kuka, Ardian Limani, Arbër Shala, Haxhi Neziraj, Drilon Musaj (76' Leotrim Kryeziu), Bujar Shabani, Xhevdet Shabani, Betim Haxhimusa (54' Përparim Livoreka), Endrit Krasniqi. Coach: Bekim Isufi.
Malmö FF: Johan Dahlin, Behrang Safari (64' Franz Brorsson), Rasmus Bengtsson, Eric Larsson, Lasse Nielsen, Søren Rieks, Fouad Bachirou, Arnór Ingvi Traustason, Oscar Lewicki, Markus Rosenberg (84' Bonke Innocent), Carlos Strandberg (61' Alexander Jeremejeff).
Coach: Uwe Rösler.
Goals: 13' Carlos Strandberg 0-1, 49' Arnór Ingvi Traustason 0-2, 82' Markus Rosenberg 0-3.
Referee: Boris Marhefka (SVK)   Attendance: 9,780.

(FC Drita played their home match at Stadiumi Olimpik Adem Jashari instead of their regular stadium, Gjilan City Stadium).

10.07.18   Turner's Cross, Cork: Cork City – Legia Warszawa 0-1 (0-0)
Cork City: Peter Cherrie, Damien Delaney, Shane Griffin, Conor McCarthy (61' Steven Beattie), Sean McLoughlin, Jimmy Keohane, Conor McCormack, Gearóid Morrissey (52' Graham Cummins), Barry McNamee (82' Kieran Sadlier), Garry Buckley, Karl Sheppard.
Coach: John Caulfield.
Legia Warszawa: Arkadiusz Malarz, Iñaki Astiz, William Rémy, Marko Vesovic, Mateusz Wieteska, Kasper Hämäläinen (82' Sandro Kulenovic), Krzysztof Maczynski, Michal Kucharczyk, Cafú, Sebastian Szymanski (76' Dominik Nagy), José Kanté (76' Adam Hlousek). Coach: Dean Klafuric.
Goal: 79' Michal Kucharczyk 0-1.
Referee: Radu Petrescu (ROM)   Attendance: 5,795.

11.07.18   Astana Arena, Astana: FK Astana – FK Sutjeska Niksic 1-0 (1-0)
FK Astana: Nenad Eric, Antonio Rukavina, Marin Anicic, Dmitriy Shomko, Evgeni Postnikov, Marin Tomasov, Ivan Maevski, Serikzhan Muzhikov (90+2' Baktiyor Zaynutdinov), László Kleinheisler, Djordje Despotovic (73' Aleksey Shchetkin), Roman Murtazaev (86' Marko Stanojevic). Coach: Roman Grygorchuk.
FK Sutjeska Niksic: Vladan Giljen, Darko Bulatovic, Stefan Cicmil, Marko Cetkovic (78' Veljko Vukovic), Stefan Stefanovic, Milos Vucic, Stefan Loncar, Marko Vucic (90+3' Dragan Grivic), Nemanja Nedic, Luka Merdovic, Saleta Kordic (85' Bojan Bozovic).
Coach: Nikola Rakojevic.
Goal: 29' Roman Murtazaev 1-0 (p).
Referee: Ferenc Karakó (HUN)   Attendance: 20,500.

11.07.18   Marijamolés sporto centro stadione, Marijampolé:
            FK Sūduva Marijampolé – APOEL Nicosia 3-1 (3-0)
FK Sūduva Marijampolé: Ivan Kardum, Vaidas Slavickas, Algis Jankauskas, Andro Svrljuga, Aleksandar Zivanovic, Povilas Leimonas, Gerson Acevedo (59' Gui Finkler), Ovidijus Verbickas (83' Bruno Dybal), Giedrius Matulevicius, Mihret Topcagic (30' Robertas Vézevicius), Rigino Cicilia. Coach: Vladimir Cheburin.
APOEL Nicosia: Boy Waterman, Zhivko Milanov (63' Leonardo Natel), Giorgios Merkis, Yohan Tavares, Caju, Nuno Morais, Tomás De Vincenti (46' Mickaël Poté), Lucas Souza, Roland Sallai (46' Efstathios Aloneftis), Dellatorre, Musa Al-Taamari. Coach: Bruno Baltazar.
Goals: 9', 13', 19' Rigino Cicilia 1-0, 2-0, 3-0, 90+4' Caju 3-1.
Referee: Fedayi San (SUI)   Attendance: 3,378.

11.07.18   Stadions Skonto, Riga: FK Spartaks Jūrmala – Crvena Zvezda Beograd 0-0
FK Spartaks Jūrmala: Jevgēnijs Nerugals, Gints Freimanis, Aleksandr Kosoric, Mārcis Oss, Ingus Slampe, Aleksejs Visnakovs, Artemiy Maleev, Oleg Dmitriev (77' Pāvels Mihadjuks), Evgeni Kobzar (60' Denis Davydov), Kaspars Svārups (66' Diego Aguirre), Vitor Faísca. Coach: Aleksandr Grishin.
Crvena Zvezda Beograd: Milan Borjan, Vujadin Savic, Milan Rodic, Filip Stojkovic, Srdjan Babic, Nenad Krsticic, Branko Jovicic, Nemanja Milic (46' Lorenzo Ebecilio), Nikola Stojiljkovic (18' Milan Pavkov), Mohamed Ben Nabouhane, Nemanja Radonjic (82' Milan Jevtovic). Coach: Vladan Milojevic.
Referee: Mykola Balakin (UKR)   Attendance: 2,068.

(FK Spartaks Jūrmala played their home match at Stadions Skonto instead of their regular stadium, Slokas Stadions).

11.07.18   City Arena – Stadión Antona Malatinského, Trnava:
            FC Spartak Trnava – HSK Zrinjski Mostar 1-0 (0-0)
FC Spartak Trnava: Martin Chudy, Matús Conka, Ivan Hladík, Boris Godál, Andrej Kadlec, Erik Grendel (78' Senad Jarovic), Jakub Rada, Lukás Gressák, Vakhtang Chanturishvili, Erik Jirka, Marvin Egho (87' Fabian Miesenböck). Coach: Radoslav Látal.
HSK Zrinjski Mostar: Ivan Brkic, Pero Stojkic, Slobodan Jakovljevic, Ognjen Todorovic (73' Semir Pezer), Milos Filipovic (89' Marko Bencun), Hrvoje Barisic, Frane Cirjak, Edin Rustemovic, Marin Galic, Nemanja Bilbija, Milos Acimovic (68' Toni Jovic). Coach: Ante Mise.
Goal: 79' Erik Jirka 1-0.
Referee: Denis Scherbakov (BLS)
Sent off: 70' Frane Cirjak, 89' Vakhtang Chanturishvili.

Match was played behind closed doors.

11.07.18   Ludogorets Arena, Razgrad: PFC Ludogorets Razgrad – Crusaders FC 7-0 (2-0)
PFC Ludogorets Razgrad: Renan, Cosmin Moti, Cicinho, Rafael Forster, Svetoslav Dyakov, Gustavo Campanharo (64' Lucas Sasha), Wanderson (77' Jody Lukoki), Natanael Pimienta, Claudiu Keserü (68' Jakub Swierczok), Marcelinho, Virgil Misidjan. Coach: Paulo Autuori.
Crusaders FC: Sean O'Neill, Billy Joe Burns, Howard Beverland, Rodney Brown, Declan Caddell (59' Kyle Owens), Philip Lowry, Jordan Forsythe, Paul Heatley (75' Jamie Glackin), Matthew Snoddy, Michael Carvill (76' Ross Clarke), Jordan Owens. Coach: Stephen Baxter.
Goals: 25' Marcelinho 1-0, 40' Rodney Brown 2-0 (og), 53' Claudiu Keserü 3-0, 66' Marcelinho 4-0, 73', 78', 80' Jakub Swierczok 5-0, 6-0, 7-0.
Referee: Dumitri Muntean (MOL)   Attendance: 4,597.

11.07.18 Stadiumi Loro Boriçi, Shkodër: FK Kukësi – Valletta FC 0-0
FK Kukësi: Stivi Frashëri, Ylli Shameti, Willian Cordeiro, Simon Rrumbullaku, Vangjel Zguro (58' Valon Ethemi), Harallamb Qaqi, Irakli Dzaria, Donjet Shkodra (80' Dino Spehar), Arber Çyrbja, Besar Musolli, Sebino Plaku (75' Haris Harba). Coach: Peter Pacult.
Valetta FC: Henry Bonello, Joseph Zerafa, Ryan Camilleri, Steve Borg, Rowen Muscat (70' Juan Gill), Raed Ibrahim Al Mukhaini (90+1' Jean Borg), Enmy Peña, Santiago Malano, Miguel Alba (76' Kyrian Nwoko), Matteo Piciollo, Mario Fontanella. Coach: Gilbert Agius.
Referee: Thóroddur Hjaltalín (ISL)   Attendance: 350.

(FK Kukësi played their home match at Stadiumi Loro Boriçi instead of their regular stadium, Zeqir Yemeri Stadium).

11.07.18 Stadion Stozice, Ljubljana: Olimpija Ljubljana – Qarabag FK 0-1 (0-0)
Olimpija Ljubljana: Aljaz Ivacic, Aris Zarifovic, Dino Stiglec, Macky Bagnack, Marko Gajic, Rok Kronaveter (81' Goran Brkic), Marko Putincanin, Stefan Savic (71' Matic Crnic), Daniel Avramovski (88' Kingsley Boateng), Tomislav Tomic, Issah Abass. Coach: Ilija Stolica.
Qarabag FK: Vagner, Jakub Rzezniczak, Maksim Medvedev, Badavi Hüseynov, Míchel, Gara Garayev, Filip Ozobic (63' Dani Quintana), Wilde Guerrier, Joshgun Diniyev (46' Simeon Slavchev), Abdellah Zoubir (90+3' Rashad Sadygov), Mahir Madatov.
Coach: Gurban Gurbanov.
Goal: 79' Wilde Guerrier 0-1.
Referee: Lawrence Visser (BEL)   Attendance: 5,248.
Sent off: 85' Issah Abass, 90+1' Gara Garayev.

11.07.18 Vodafonevöllurinn, Reykjavík: Valur Reykjavík – Rosenborg BK 1-0 (0-0)
Valur Reykjavík: Anton Ari Einarsson, Birkir Sævarsson, Bjarni Eiríksson, Eidur Sigurbjörnsson, Arnar Geirsson, Haukur Sigurdsson, Kristinn Sigurdsson, Sigurdur Lárusson, Ólafur Finsen (74' Gudjon Lydsson), Patrick Pedersen, Tobias Thomsen (85' Kristinn Halldórsson). Coach: Ólafur Jóhannesson.
Rosenborg BK: André Hansen, Tore Reginiussen, Even Hovland, Vegar Hedenstad (41' Marius Lundemo), Birger Meling, Erlend Reitan, Mike Jensen, Anders Trondsen, Nicklas Bendtner, Erik Botheim (64' Alexander Søderlund), Jonathan Levi. Coach: Kåre Ingebrigtsen.
Goal: 84' Eidur Sigurbjörnsson 1-0.
Referee: Rade Obrenovic (SVN)   Attendance: 1,088.

17.07.18 Telia 5G-areena, Helsinki: HJK Helsinki – Víkingur Gøta 3-1 (3-1)
HJK Helsinki: Maksim Rudakov, Rafinha, Hannu Patronen, Daniel O'Shaughnessy, Faith Obilor, Anthony Annan, Moshtagh Yaghoubi, Sebastian Dahlström (84' Otto Ollikainen), Riku Riski, Evans Mensah (71' Enoch Banza), Klauss (67' Filip Valencic). Coach: Mika Lehkosuo.
Víkingur Gøta: Elias Rasmussen, Atli Gregersen, Hans Djurhuus (59' Karl Løkin), Hanus Jacobsen, Adrian Cascaval (67' Hedin Hansen), Dennis Nieblas, Gunnar Vatnhamar, Elias Jóhannesson Lervig, Sølvi Vatnhamar, Filip Djordjevic, Adeshina Lawal (72' Andreas Olsen). Coach: Sigfrídur Clementsen.
Goals: 1' Klauss 1-0, 10' Evans Mensah 2-0, 19' Moshtagh Yaghoubi 3-0, 21' Gunnar Vatnhamar 3-1.
Referee: Duje Strukan (CRO)   Attendance: 5,125.

Klauss missed a penalty kick (55').

17.07.18 MFA Centenary Stadium, Ta'Qali: Valletta FC – FK Kukësi 1-1 (0-0)
Valetta FC: Henry Bonello, Joseph Zerafa (88' Kyrian Nwoko), Ryan Camilleri, Steve Borg, Rowen Muscat, Raed Ibrahim Al Mukhaini (83' Juan Gill), Enmy Peña, Santiago Malano, Miguel Alba (90' Bogdan Gavrila), Matteo Piciollo, Mario Fontanella. Coach: Gilbert Agius.
FK Kukësi: Stivi Frashëri, Ylli Shameti, Willian Cordeiro, Simon Rrumbullaku, Vangjel Zguro (57' Dino Spehar), Albi Alla, Irakli Dzaria, Donjet Shkodra (57' Haris Harba), Arber Çyrbja (65' Valon Ethemi), Besar Musolli, Sebino Plaku. Coach: Armando Cungu.
Goals: 67' Santiago Malano 1-0, 84' Irakli Dzaria 1-1.
Referee: Igor Pajac (CRO)   Attendance: 1,307.
Sent off: 87' Vangjel Zguro.

FK Kukësi won on away goals.

17.07.18 Neo GSP Stadium, Nicosia: APOEL Nicosia – FK Sūduva Marijampolé 1-0 (1-0)
APOEL Nicosia: Boy Waterman, Zhivko Milanov, Carlão, Yohan Tavares, Nicolas Ioannou (77' Leonardo Natel), Nuno Morais, Giorgos Efrem (77' Efstathios Aloneftis), Lucas Souza, Mickaël Poté, Dellatorre, Musa Al-Taamari (65' Roland Sallai). Coach: Bruno Baltazar.
FK Sūduva Marijampolé: Ivan Kardum, Vaidas Slavickas, Algis Jankauskas, Andro Svrljuga, Aleksandar Zivanovic, Povilas Leimonas, Gerson Acevedo (76' Robertas Vézevicius), Ovidijus Verbickas, Giedrius Matulevicius, Mihret Topcagic (53' Julius Kasparavicius), Rigino Cicilia (90+5' Gui Finkler). Coach: Vladimir Cheburin.
Goal: 20' Mickaël Poté 1-0.
Referee: Glenn Nyberg (SWE)   Attendance: 12,149.

17.07.18 Swedbank Stadion, Malmö: Malmö FF – FC Drita 2-0 (0-0)
Malmö FF: Johan Dahlin, Rasmus Bengtsson (64' Behrang Safari), Eric Larsson, Lasse Nielsen, Franz Brorsson, Søren Rieks (58' Egzon Binaku), Fouad Bachirou (71' Bonke Innocent), Oscar Lewicki, Samuel Adrian, Alexander Jeremejeff, Carlos Strandberg. Coach: Uwe Rösler.
FC Drita: Edvan Bakaj, Liridon Leci, Viktor Kuka, Ardian Limani, Arbër Shala, Haxhi Neziraj, Drilon Musaj (88' Përparim Livoreka), Bujar Shabani, Xhevdet Shabani, Endrit Krasniqi (62' Betim Haxhimusa), Leotrim Kryeziu (72' Zgjim Mustafa). Coach: Bekim Isufi.
Goals: 55' Carlos Strandberg 1-0, 60' Eric Larsson 2-0.
Referee: Laurent Kopriwa (LUX)   Attendance: 10,623.

17.07.18 Yaakov Turner Toto Stadium, Beersheba:
          Hapoel Be'er Sheva – FC Flora Tallinn 3-1 (2-0)
Hapoel Be'er Sheva: Giannis Anestis, Julien Cétout, Ben Bitton, Loai Taha, Shir Tzedek (74' Amit Bitton), Oren Bitton, John Ogu (57' Daniel Einbinder), Hen Ezra, Maor Melikson, Hanan Maman (67' Niv Zrihan), Ben Sahar. Coach: Bachar Bakhar.
FC Flora Tallinn: Mait Toom, Gert Kams, Kevin Aloe, Jürgen Lorenz, Madis Vihmann, Aleksandr Dmitrijev, Mihkel Ainsalu (57' German Slein), Markus Poom, Rauno Alliku, Rauno Sappinen, Frank Liivak (46' Maksim Gussev). Coach: Arno Pijpers.
Goals: 15' Hen Ezra 1-0, 27' Hanan Maman 2-0, 48' Maor Melikson 3-0, 86' Rauno Alliku 3-1.
Referee: Tomasz Musial (POL)   Attendance: 11,850

17.07.18   Park Hall Stadium, Oswestry: The New Saints – KF Shkëndija 79 4-0 (3-0)
The New Saints: Paul Harrison, Christopher Marriott, Blaine Hudson, Kane Lewis, Benjamin Cabango, Jamie Mullan, Aeron Edwards, Jonathan Routledge, Daniel Redmond (83' Adrian Cieslewicz), Thomas Holland (89' Kurtis Byrne), Dean Ebbe (56' Greg Draper).
Coach: Scott Ruscoe.
KF Shkëndija 79: Kostadin Zahov, Visar Musliu, Egzon Bejtulai, Mevlan Adili, Alma Wakili, Armend Alimi, Blagoja Todorovski (46' Marjan Radeski), Shefit Shefiti (46' Besart Ibraimi), Arbin Zejnulai (89' Konstantin Cheshmedzhiev), Izair Emini, Stênio Júnior.
Coach: Qatip Osmani.
Goals: 15' Dean Ebbe 1-0, 30' Daniel Redmond 2-0, 35' Benjamin Cabango 3-0, 90+6' Kurtis Byrne 4-0.
Referee: Pavel Orel (CZE)   Attendance: 756.

17.07.18   Puskás Akadémia Pancho Aréna, Felcsút: MOL Vidi FC – F91 Dudelange 2-1 (1-0)
MOL Vidi FC: Ádám Kovácsik, Roland Juhász, Attila Fiola, Loïc Négo, Paulo Vinícius, Stopira, Szabolcs Huszti (63' Boban Nikolov), Anel Hadzic, Máté Pátkai, Danko Lazovic (84' József Varga), Marko Scepovic (89' István Kovács). Coach: Marko Nikolic.
F91 Dudelange: Jonathan Joubert, Tom Schnell, Jerry Prempeh, Bryan Mélisse, Marc-André Kruska (83' Nicolas Perez), Stélvio, Dominik Stolz (70' Sanel Ibrahimovic), Edisson Jordanov, Clément Couturier, Danel Sinani (76' Jordann Yéyé), David Turpel.
Coach: Dino Toppmöller.
Goals: 18' Danko Lazovic 1-0, 54' Clément Couturier 1-1, 58' Marko Scepovic 2-1.
Referee: Donald Robertson (SCO)   Attendance: 2,514.
Sent off: 90+4' Bryan Mélisse.

(MOL Vidi FC played their home match at Puskás Akadémia Aréna instead of their regular stadium, Sóstói Stadion, due to reconstruction).

17.07.18   Stadion Rajko Mitic, Beograd:
          Crvena Zvezda Beograd – FK Spartaks Jūrmala 2-0 (0-0)
Crvena Zvezda Beograd: Milan Borjan, Vujadin Savic, Milan Rodic, Milos Degenek, Filip Stojkovic, Nenad Krsticic, Branko Jovicic, Nemanja Milic (60' Milan Pavkov), Lorenzo Ebecilio (72' Dejan Meleg), Mohamed Ben Nabouhane, Nemanja Radonjic (85' Dusan Jovancic). Coach: Vladan Milojevic.
FK Spartaks Jūrmala: Jevgēnijs Nerugals, Gints Freimanis, Aleksandar Kosoric, Mārcis Oss, Ingus Slampe, Aleksejs Visnakovs (49' Denis Davydov), Artemiy Maleev, Oleg Dmitriev (83' Ariagner Smith), Evgeni Kobzar, Kaspars Svārups (56' Diego Aguirre), Vitor Faísca.
Coach: Aleksandr Grishin.
Goals: 78' Mohamed Ben Nabouhane 1-0, 81' Nenad Krsticic 2-0.
Referee: Alper Ulusoy (TUR)   Attendance: 23,390.

17.07.18 Stadion Mejjski Legii Warszawa im. Marszalka Józefa Pilsudskiego, Warszawa:
Legia Warszawa – Cork City 3-0 (1-0)
Legia Warszawa: Arkadiusz Malarz, Iñaki Astiz, William Rémy, Dominik Nagy, Mateusz Wieteska (69' Domagoj Antolic), Miroslav Radovic, Krzysztof Maczynski, Marko Vesovic, Michal Kucharczyk (46' Adam Hlousek), Cafú, José Kanté (64' Carlitos López).
Coach: Dean Klafuric.
Cork City: Peter Cherrie, Damien Delaney, Steven Beattie (79' Danny Kane), Shane Griffin, Sean McLoughlin, Jimmy Keohane, Conor McCormack, Barry McNamee, Garry Buckley (79' Kieran Sadlier), Graham Cummins (78' Josh O'Hanlon), Karl Sheppard.
Coach: John Caulfield.
Goals: 27' José Kanté 1-0, 73' Miroslav Radovic 2-0 (p), 89' Carlitos López 3-0.
Referee: Kai Erik Steen (NOR)   Attendance: 14,576.

17.07.18 Seaview, Belfast: Crusaders FC – PFC Ludogorets Razgrad 0-2 (0-1)
Crusaders FC: Sean O'Neill, Billy Joe Burns, Howard Beverland, Kyle Owens, Rodney Brown, Philip Lowry (67' Declan Caddell), Jordan Forsythe, Matthew Snoddy, Ross Clarke (81' Jamie Glackin), Michael Carvill, Jordan Owens (32' David Cushley).
Coach: Stephen Baxter.
PFC Ludogorets Razgrad: Jorge Broun, Cosmin Moti, Cicinho (61' Tsvetomir Panov), Georgi Terziev, Svetoslav Dyakov, Lucas Sasha, Natanael Pimienta (70' Anton Nedyalkov), João Paulo, Marcelinho, Jody Lukoki, Jakub Swierczok (79' Dimo Balakov). Coach: Paulo Autuori.
Goals: 11' Rodney Brown 0-1 (og), 65' Jakub Swierczok 0-2.
Referee: Roomer Tarajev (EST)   Attendance: 1,116.

18.07.18 Bolshaya Sportivnaya Arena, Tiraspol:
FC Sheriff Tiraspol – Torpedo Kutaisi 3-0 (2-0)
FC Sheriff Tiraspol: Zvonimir Mikulic, Ante Kulusic, Mateo Susic, Veaceslav Posmac, Cristiano, Antun Palic, Yuri Kendysh (75' Gheorghe Anton), Rifet Kapic (73' Gerson Rodrigues), Ziguy Badibanga, Joálisson (89' Vladimir Kovacevic), Al-Hadji Kamara.
Coach: Goran Sablic.
Torpedo Kutaisi: Roin Kvaskhvadze, Davit Khurtsilava, Manuka Kobakhidze, Giorgi Kimadze, Levan Gegetchkori (46' Arfang Daffé), Oleksandr Azatskyi, Lazar Marin, Levan Kutalia (68' Tornike Kapanadze), Giorgi Kukhianidze (57' Beka Tugushi), Marek Hlinka, Mate Tsintsadze. Coach: Kakhaber Chkhetiani.
Goals: 9' Ziguy Badibanga 1-0, 40', 55' Joálisson 2-0, 3-0.
Referee: Peter Kjærsgaard-Andersen (DEN)   Attendance: 5,740.

18.07.18 Tofiq Bahramov adina Respublika stadionu, Baku:
Qarabag FK – Olimpija Ljubljana 0-0
Qarabag FK: Vagner, Jakub Rzezniczak, Maksim Medvedev, Badavi Hüseynov, Míchel, Dani Quintana (42' Filip Ozobic), Simeon Slavchev, Wilde Guerrier, Joshgun Diniyev, Abdellah Zoubir, Mahir Madatov (90+4' Ansi Agolli). Coach: Gurban Gurbanov.
Olimpija Ljubljana: Aljaz Ivacic, Aris Zarifovic, Dino Stiglec, Macky Bagnack (74' Branko Ilic), Marko Gajic, Rok Kronaveter (72' Danijel Miskic), Marko Putincanin, Stefan Savic (46' Matic Crnic), Daniel Avramovski, Tomislav Tomic, Kingsley Boateng. Coach: Ilija Stolica.
Referee: Erez Papir (ISR)   Attendance: 21,520.
Sent off: 90+6' Marko Gajic.

(Qarabag FK played their home match at Tofiq Bahramov adina Respublika stadionu instead of their regular stadium, Azersun Arena).

18.07.18   Stadion pod Bijelim Brijegom, Mostar:
   HSK Zrinjski Mostar – FC Spartak Trnava 1-1 (0-1)
HSK Zrinjski Mostar: Ivan Brkic, Pero Stojkic, Slobodan Jakovljevic, Ognjen Todorovic, Milos Filipovic, Hrvoje Barisic, Edin Rustemovic (54' Marko Bencun), Ismar Hairlahovic (81' Semir Pezer), Marin Galic, Nemanja Bilbija, Milos Acimovic (75' Toni Jovic).
Coach: Ante Mise.
FC Spartak Trnava: Martin Chudy, Martin Tóth (17' Fabian Miesenböck), Matús Conka, Ivan Hladík, Boris Godál, Andrej Kadlec, Erik Grendel (79' Matej Oravec), Jakub Rada, Lukás Gressák, Erik Jirka, Marvin Egho (81' Senad Jarovic). Coach: Radoslav Látal.
Goals: 15' Boris Godál 0-1, 58' Ognjen Todorovic 1-1.
Referee: Julian Weinberger (AUT)   Attendance: 5,100.

18.07.18   Lerkendal Stadion, Trondheim: Rosenborg BK – Valur Reykjavík 3-1 (0-0)
Rosenborg BK: André Hansen, Tore Reginiussen, Even Hovland, Vegar Hedenstad, Birger Meling, Mike Jensen, Anders Trondsen, Marius Lundemo (86' Matthías Vilhjálmsson), Nicklas Bendtner, Pål Helland, Jonathan Levi (81' Alexander Søderlund).
Coach: Kåre Ingebrigtsen.
Valur Reykjavík: Anton Ari Einarsson, Birkir Sævarsson, Bjarni Eiríksson, Eidur Sigurbjörnsson, Arnar Geirsson, Haukur Sigurdsson (74' Gudjón Lydsson), Kristinn Sigurdsson, Sigurdur Lárusson, Ólafur Finsen (75' Einar Karl Ingvarsson), Patrick Pedersen (89' Ívar Jónsson), Tobias Thomsen. Coach: Ólafur Jóhannesson.
Goals: 55' Nicklas Bendtner 1-0 (p), 72' Anders Trondsen 2-0, 85' Kristinn Sigurdsson 2-1 (p), 90+4' Nicklas Bendtner 3-1 (p).
Referee: Stefan Apostolov (BUL)   Attendance: 10,604.
Sent off: 90+3' Patrick Pedersen.

18.07.18   Stadion kraj Bistrice, Niksic: FK Sutjeska Niksic – FK Astana 0-2 (0-1)
FK Sutjeska Niksic: Vladan Giljen, Darko Bulatovic, Stefan Cicmil, Marko Cetkovic, Stefan Stefanovic (61' Vladan Bubanja), Milos Vucic, Stefan Loncar, Marko Vucic (54' Stefan Denkovic), Nemanja Nedic, Luka Merdovic, Saleta Kordic (71' Zarko Grbovic).
Coach: Nikola Rakojevic.
FK Astana: Nenad Eric, Antonio Rukavina, Marin Anicic, Dmitriy Shomko, Evgeni Postnikov, Marin Tomasov, Ivan Maevski, Serikzhan Muzhikov, László Kleinheisler (81' Richard Almeyda), Djordje Despotovic (79' Aleksey Shchetkin), Roman Murtazaev (85' Baktiyor Zaynutdinov). Coach: Roman Grygorchuk.
Goals: 38' Djordje Despotovic 0-1, 65' Serikzhan Muzhikov 0-2.
Referee: João Pedro Pinheiro (POR)   Attendance: 3,200.

18.07.18   Celtic Park, Glasgow: Celtic FC – FC Alashkert 3-0 (3-0)
Celtic FC: Craig Gordon, Jozo Simunovic, Kieran Tierney, Kristoffer Ajer, Jack Hendry, Scott Brown, James Forrest (76' Michael Johnson), Callum McGregor, Olivier Ntcham, Moussa Dembélé (66' Ryan Christie), Odsonne Édouard (64' Scott Sinclair). Coach: Brendan Rodgers.
FC Alashkert: Ognjen Cancarevic, Gagik Dagbashyan, Artak Yedigaryan, Oliver Práznovsky, Taron Voskanyan, Artur Yedigaryan, Artak Dashyan, Danilo Sekulic (64' Artem Simonyan), Jefferson (86' César Romero), Artak Grigoryan, Uros Nenadovic (46' Mihran Manasyan).
Coach: Varuzhan Sukiasyan.
Goals: 8', 19' Moussa Dembélé 1-0, 2-0 (p), 35' James Forrest 3-0.
Referee: Horatiu Fesnic (ROM)   Attendance: 59,047.
Sent off: 11' Jozo Simunovic.

SECOND QUALIFYING ROUND

24.07.18   Astana Arena, Astana: FK Astana – FC Midtjylland 2-1 (1-0)
FK Astana: Nenad Eric, Antonio Rukavina, Marin Anicic, Dmitriy Shomko, Evgeni Postnikov, Marin Tomasov, Ivan Maevski, Serikzhan Muzhikov (76' Richard Almeyda), László Kleinheisler, Pedro Henrique (85' Rangelo Janga), Roman Murtazaev (46' Aleksey Shchetkin). Coach: Roman Grygorchuk.
FC Midtjylland: Jesper Hansen, Kian Hansen (77' Zsolt Korcsmár), Erik Sviatchenko, Marc Hende, Bubacarr Sanneh, Alexander Munksgaard, Jakob Poulsen, Tim Sparv, Gustav Wikheim (85' Mayron George), Ayo Simon Okosun (68' Franck Ogochukwu), Ebere Paul Onuachu. Coach: Jess Thorup.
Goals: 31' László Kleinheisler 1-0, 51' Gustav Wikheim 1-1, 90+4' László Kleinheisler 2-1.
Referee: Radu Petrescu (ROM)   Attendance: 23,010.

24.07.18   Stadionul Dr. Constantin Radulescu, Cluj-Napoca: CFR Cluj – Malmö FF 0-1 (0-1)
CFR Cluj: Giedrius Arlauskis, Andrei Muresan, Paulo Vinícius, Camora, Cristian Manea, Emmanuel Culio, Ciprian Deac (79' Alexandru Paun), Ovidiu Hoban (60' Mate Males), Damjan Djokovic (46' Alexandru Ionita (II)), George Tucudean, Billel Omrani. Coach: Eduard Iordanescu.
Malmö FF: Johan Dahlin, Behrang Safari, Rasmus Bengtsson, Eric Larsson (89' Andreas Vindheim), Lasse Nielsen, Søren Rieks, Anders Christiansen, Arnór Ingvi Traustason (89' Samuel Adrian), Oscar Lewicki, Markus Rosenberg, Carlos Strandberg (86' Marcus Antonsson). Coach: Uwe Rösler.
Goal: 45' Carlos Strandberg 0-1.
Referee: Nikoa Dabanovic (MNE)   Attendance: 6,950.

24.07.18   Stadio Toumbas, Thessaloniki: PAOK Saloniki – FC Basel 2-1 (1-0)
PAOK Saloniki: Alexandros Paschalakis, Léo Matos, José Ángel Crespo, Fernando Varela, Vieirinha, Maurício, Cañas, Dimitris Pelkas, Aleksandar Prijovic (83' Amr Warda), Dimitris Limnios (90+3' Yevhen Shakhov), Léo Jabá (72' Omar El Kaddouri). Coach: Razvan Lucescu.
FC Basel: Jonas Omlin, Marek Suchy, Éder Álvarez Balanta, Blas Riveros, Valentin Stocker, Serey Dié, Luca Zuffi, Fabian Frei, Raoul Petretta (44' Yves Kaiser), Albian Ajeti (90+4' Kevin Bua), Dimitri Oberlin (62' Aldo Kalulu). Coach: Raphaël Wicky.
Goals: 32' Cañas 1-0, 80' Aleksandar Prijovic 2-0, 82' Albian Ajeti 2-1.
Referee: Bobby Madley (ENG)   Attendance: 24,670.

24.07.18   Stadion Makdimir, Zagreb: Dinamo Zagreb – Hapoel Be'er Sheva 5-0 (2-0)
Dinamo Zagreb: Daniel Zagorac, Marin Leovac, Kévin Théophile-Catherine, Emir Dilaver, Arijan Ademi, Izet Hajrovic (86' Ivan Fiolic), Petar Stojanovic, Amer Gojak, Daniel Olmo, Mario Budimir (70' Armin Hodzic), Mislav Orsic (74' Mario Situm). Coach: Nenad Bjelica.
Hapoel Be'er Sheva: Giannis Anestis, Julien Cétout (46' Hanan Maman), Ben Bitton, Loai Taha, Shir Tzedek, Oren Bitton, John Ogu, Hen Ezra (54' Anthony Nwakaeme), Maor Melikson, Daniel Einbinder (74' Eden Ben Basat), Ben Sahar. Coach: Bachar Bakhar.
Goals: 22' Izet Hajrovic 1-0, 28' Mislav Orsic 2-0, 51', 62' Arijan Ademi 3-0, 4-0, 82' Armin Hodzic 5-0.
Referee: Ali Palabiyik (TUR)   Attendance: 9,056.

24.07.18   Telekom Arena, Skopje: KF Shkëndija 79 – FC Sheriff Tiraspol 1-0 (1-0)
KF Shkëndija 79: Kostadin Zahov, Mevlan Murati, Visar Musliu, Egzon Bejtulai, Mevlan Adili, Armend Alimi, Ennur Totre (75' Sciprim Taipi), Besart Ibraimi, Izair Emini (86' Konstantin Cheshmedzhiev), Stênio Júnior, Remzi Selmani (66' Shefit Shefiti).
Coach: Qatip Osmani.
FC Sheriff Tiraspol: Zvonimir Mikulic, Ante Kulusic, Mateo Susic, Veaceslav Posmac, Cristiano, Antun Palic, Yuri Kendysh, Rifet Kapic (80' Gerson Rodrigues), Ziguy Badibanga, Joálisson (88' Evgheni Oancea), Al-Hadji Kamara (73' Alexandru Boiciuc).
Coach: Goran Sablic.
Goal: 24' Besart Ibraimi 1-0.
Referee: Mads-Kristoffer Kristoffersen (DEN)   Attendance: 3,696.

(KF Shkëndija 79 played their home match at Telekom Arena instead of their regular stadium, Ecolog Arena, due to renovation).

24.07.18   Stadion Rajko Mitic, Beograd:
Crvena Zvezda Beograd – FK Sūduva Marijampolé 3-0 (2-0)
Crvena Zvezda Beograd: Milan Borjan, Vujadin Savic, Milan Rodic, Milos Degenek, Filip Stojkovic, Nenad Krsticic (37' Dusan Jovancic), Branko Jovicic, Nemanja Milic, Lorenzo Ebecilio (64' Milan Jevtovic), Mohamed Ben Nabouhane, Nemanja Radonjic (78' Marko Gobeljic). Coach: Vladan Milojevic.
FK Sūduva Marijampolé: Ivan Kardum, Vaidas Slavickas, Algis Jankauskas, Andro Svrljuga, Aleksandar Zivanovic, Povilas Leimonas, Gerson Acevedo, Ovidijus Verbickas, Giedrius Matulevicius (80' Vitaly Gayduchik), Mihret Topcagic (8' Robertas Vézevicius), Rigino Cicilia. Coach: Vladimir Cheburin.
Goals: 23' Lorenzo Ebecilio 1-0, 35', 58' Nemanja Radonjic 2-0, 3-0.
Referee: Bastian Dankert (GER)   Attendance: 23,218.

24.07.18   Stadion Miejski Legii Waszawa im. Marszalka Józefa Pilsudskiego, Warszawa:
Legia Warszawa – FC Spartak Trnava 0-2 (0-1)
Legia Warszawa: Arkadiusz Malarz, Iñaki Astiz, Adam Hlousek, Krzysztof Maczynski (17' Mateusz Wieteska), Marko Vesovic, Domagoj Antolic, Chris Philipps (69' Kasper Hämäläinen), Cafú, Sebastian Szymanski (63' Miroslav Radovic), José Kanté, Carlitos López. Coach: Dean Klafuric.
FC Spartak Trnava: Martin Chudy, Martin Tóth, Matús Conka, Boris Godál, Andrej Kadlec, Erik Grendel (64' Fabian Miesenböck), Jakub Rada, Anton Sloboda (86' Ivan Hladík), Lukás Gressák, Erik Jirka, Marvin Egho (90+1' Ján Vlasko). Coach: Radoslav Látal.
Goals: 16' Erik Grendel 0-1, 90+3' Ján Vlasko 0-2.
Referee: Ádám Farkas (HUN)   Attendance: 15,527.

25.07.18   Ludogorets Arena, Razgrad: PFC Ludogorets Razgrad – MOL Vidi FC 0-0
PFC Ludogorets Razgrad: Renan, Cosmin Moti, Cicinho, Rafael Forster, Svetoslav Dyakov, Lucas Sasha (61' Gustavo Campanharo), Wanderson, Natanael Pimienta, Claudiu Keserü (60' Jakub Swierczok), Marcelinho, Virgil Misidjan (84' Jody Lukoki). Coach: Paulo Autuori.
MOL Vidi FC: Ádám Kovácsik, Roland Juhász, Attila Fiola, Loïc Négo, Paulo Vinícius, Stopira, Szabolcs Huszti, József Varga, István Kovács (68' Máté Pátkai), Boban Nikolov (71' Danko Lazovic), Marko Scepovic (80' Stefan Scepovic). Coach: Marko Nikolic.
Referee: Bojan Pandzic (SWE)   Attendance: 5,327.

25.07.18   Stadiumi Loro Boriçi, Shkodër: FK Kukësi – Qarabag FK 0-0
FK Kukësi: Stivi Frashëri, Ylli Shameti, Willian Cordeiro, Simon Rrumbullaku, Edis Maliki, Albi Alla, Harallamb Qaqi, Irakli Dzaria, Arber Çyrbja (90+2' Valon Ethemi), Besar Musolli, Sebino Plaku (76' Haris Harba). Coach: Armando Cungu.
Qarabag FK: Vagner, Rashad Sadygov, Ansi Agolli, Maksim Medvedev, Badavi Hüseynov, Míchel, Gara Garayev, Filip Ozobic, Simeon Slavchev, Wilde Guerrier (89' Abbas Hüseynov), Mahir Madatov. Coach: Gurban Gurbanov.
Referee: Ola Hobber Nilsen (NOR)   Attendance: 700.

(FK Kukësi played their home match at Stadiumi Loro Boriçi instead of their regular stadium, Zeqir Yemeri Stadium).

25.07.18   Borisov Arena, Borisov: BATE Borisov – HJK Helsinki 0-0
BATE Borisov: Denis Scherbitski, Egor Filipenko, Maksim Volodko, Aleksandar Filipovic, Alexei Rios, Igor Stasevich, Dmitri Baga, Stanislav Dragun, Mirko Ivanic, Maksim Skavysh (65' Aliaksandr Hleb), Nikolay Signevich. Coach: Alexey Baga.
HJK Helsinki: Maksim Rudakov, Rafinha, Hannu Patronen, Daniel O'Shaughnessy, Faith Obilor, Anthony Annan, Moshtagh Yaghoubi, Sebastian Dahlström, Riku Riski (70' Nikolai Alho), Evans Mensah (89' Mikko Sumusalo), Klauss (85' Macauley Chrisantus).
Coach: Mika Lehkosuo.
Referee: Marco Di Bello (ITA)   Attendance: 11,567.

25.07.18   Johan Cruijff Arena, Amsterdam: AFC Ajax – SK Sturm Graz 2-0 (1-0)
AFC Ajax: André Onana, Nicolás Tagliafico, Matthijs de Ligt, Lasse Schöne (66' Dusan Tadic), Hakim Ziyech, Donny van de Beek, Carel Eiting (84' Daley Blind), Noussair Mazraoui, Frenkie de Jong, Klaas-Jan Huntelaar (87' Kaj Sierhuis), David Neres.
Coach: Erik ten Hag.
SK Sturm Graz: Jörg Siebenhandl, Fabian Koch, Anastasios Avlonitis, Filipe Ferreira (46' Sandi Lovric), Lukas Spendlhofer, Dario Maresic, Stefan Hierländer, Markus Lackner, Peter Zulj, Lukas Grozurek (76' Philipp Huspek), Emeka Eze (58' Philipp Hosiner).
Coach: Heiko Vogel.
Goals: 15' Hakim Ziyech 1-0, 57' Lasse Schöne 2-0.
Referee: Alejandro Hernández Hernández (ESP)   Attendance: 53,106.

Lasse Schöne missed a penalty kick (57').

25.07.18   Celtic Park, Glasgow: Celtic FC – Rosenborg BK 3-1 (1-1)
Celtic FC: Craig Gordon, Cristian Gamboa, Kieran Tierney, Kristoffer Ajer, Jack Hendry, Scott Brown, Scott Sinclair, James Forrest, Callum McGregor, Olivier Ntcham (76' Tom Rogic), Odsonne Édouard. Coach: Brendan Rodgers.
Rosenborg BK: André Hansen, Tore Reginiussen, Even Hovland, Vegar Hedenstad, Birger Meling, Mike Jensen, Anders Trondsen, Marius Lundemo (61' Alexander Søderlund), Nicklas Bendtner, Pål Helland (72' Alexander Gersbach), Jonathan Levi. Coach: Rini Coolen.
Goals: 16' Birger Meling 0-1, 43' Odsonne Édouard 1-1, 46' Olivier Ntcham 2-1, 75' Odsonne Édouard 3-1.
Referee: Bart Vertenten (BEL)   Attendance: 51,184.

31.07.18   Yaakov Turner Toto Stadium, Beersheva:
Hapoel Be'er Sheva – Dinamo Zagreb 2-2 (2-0)
Hapoel Be'er Sheva: David Goresh, Matan Ohayon, Ben Bitton, Shir Tzedek, Oren Bitton, John Ogu, Maor Melikson (84' Niv Zrihan), Hanan Maman (72' Hen Ezra), Daniel Einbinder, Eden Ben Basat (76' Ben Sahar), Anthony Nwakaeme. Coach: Bachar Bakhar.
Dinamo Zagreb: Daniel Zagorac, Marin Leovac, Kévin Théophile-Catherine, Emir Dilaver, Arijan Ademi, Izet Hajrovic (82' Ivan Fiolic), Petar Stojanovic, Amer Gojak, Daniel Olmo (77' Ivan Sunjic), Mario Budimir (56' Mario Gavranovic), Mislav Orsic.
Coach: Nenad Bjelica.
Goals: 14' John Ogu 1-0, 34' Petar Stojanovic 2-0 (og), 49' Mario Budimir 2-1, 54' Izet Hajrovic 2-2.
Referee: François Letexier (FRA)   Attendance: 10,181.

31.07.18   Bolshaya Sportivnaya Arena, Tiraspol: FC Sheriff Tiraspol – KF Shkëndija 79 0-0
FC Sheriff Tiraspol: Sergei Pascenco, Mateo Susic, Veaceslav Posmac, Vladimir Kovacevic, Cristiano, Antun Palic, Yuri Kendysh, Rifet Kapic (78' Alexandru Boiciuc), Ziguy Badibanga (56' Gerson Rodrigues), Joálisson (69' Wilfred Balima), Al-Hadji Kamara.
Coach: Goran Sablic.
KF Shkëndija 79: Kostadin Zahov, Mevlan Murati, Visar Musliu, Egzon Bejtulai, Mevlan Adili, Armend Alimi, Ennur Totre (84' Sciprim Taipi), Besart Ibraimi, Izair Emini (67' Valmir Nafiu), Stênio Júnior, Remzi Selmani (90+3' Konstantin Cheshmedzhiev).
Coach: Qatip Osmani.
Referee: Ville Nevalainen (FIN)   Attendance: 6,319.

31.07.18   City Arena Trnava, Trnava: FC Spartak Trnava – Legia Warszawa 0-1 (0-0)
FC Spartak Trnava: Martin Chudy, Martin Tóth, Matús Conka, Boris Godál, Andrej Kadlec, Erik Grendel (70' Fabian Miesenböck), Jakub Rada, Anton Sloboda (76' Ján Vlasko), Lukás Gressák, Erik Jirka, Marvin Egho (90+1' Ivan Hladík). Coach: Radoslav Látal.
Legia Warszawa: Arkadiusz Malarz, Michal Pazdan (53' Carlitos López), Iñaki Astiz, Adam Hlousek, Mateusz Wieteska, Miroslav Radovic (46' Cafú), Krzysztof Maczynski (80' Kasper Hämäläinen), Marko Vesovic, Domagoj Antolic, Michal Kucharczyk, José Kanté.
Coach: Dean Klafuric.
Goal: 63' Iñaki Astiz 0-1.
Referee: Roi Reinshreiber (ISR)   Attendance: 17,204.
Sent off: 37' Marko Vesovic, 85' Domagoj Antolic.

01.08.18   Telia 5G-areena, Helsinki: HJK Helsinki – BATE Borisov 1-2 (1-2)
HJK Helsinki: Maksim Rudakov, Rafinha, Hannu Patronen, Mikko Sumusalo, Faith Obilor, Anthony Annan, Moshtagh Yaghoubi, Sebastian Dahlström (74' Eetu Vertainen), Riku Riski (69' Nikolai Alho), Evans Mensah, Klauss. Coach: Mika Lehkosuo.
BATE Borisov: Denis Scherbitski, Egor Filipenko, Maksim Volodko, Aleksandar Filipovic, Alexei Rios, Igor Stasevich (86' Jasse Tuominen), Dmitri Baga (77' Yevgeniy Berezkin), Stanislav Dragun, Mirko Ivanic (67' Maksim Skavysh), Evgeni Yablonski, Nikolay Signevich.
Coach: Alexey Baga.
Goals: 20' Rafinha 0-1 (og), 24' Igor Stasevich 0-2, 28' Moshtagh Yaghoubi 1-2.
Referee: Jonathan Lardot (BEL)   Attendance: 10,210.

01.08.18   MCH Arena, Herning: FC Midtjylland – FK Astana 0-0
FC Midtjylland: Jesper Hansen, Kian Hansen, Erik Sviatchenko (76' Ayo Simon Okosun), Marc Hende, Bubacarr Sanneh, Alexander Munksgaard, Jakob Poulsen, Tim Sparv (59' Awer Mabil), Gustav Wikheim, Franck Ogochukwu (71' Mikkel Duelund), Ebere Paul Onuachu. Coach: Jess Thorup.
FK Astana: Nenad Eric, Antonio Rukavina, Marin Anicic, Dmitriy Shomko, Evgeni Postnikov, Marin Tomasov, Ivan Maevski, Serikzhan Muzhikov, László Kleinheisler (90+2' Yuriy Logvinenko), Pedro Henrique (78' Roman Murtazaev), Junior Kabananga (62' Aleksey Shchetkin). Coach: Roman Grygorchuk.
Referee: Juan Martínez Munuera (ESP)   Attendance: 8,731.

01.08.18   Tofiq Bahramov adina Respublika stadionu, Baku:
Qarabag FK – FK Kukësi 3-0 (1-0)
Qarabag FK: Vagner, Rashad Sadygov (77' Jakup Rzezniczak), Maksim Medvedev, Badavi Hüseynov, Míchel, Dani Quintana (60' Dzon Delarge), Gara Garayev, Simeon Slavchev, Wilde Guerrier, Abdellah Zoubir, Innocent Emeghara (66' Mahir Madatov). Coach: Gurban Gurbanov.
FK Kukësi: Stivi Frashëri, Ylli Shameti, Willian Cordeiro, Simon Rrumbullaku, Edis Maliki, Albi Alla, Harallamb Qaqi, Irakli Dzaria, Arber Çyrbja (46' Dino Spehar), Besar Musolli (84' Donjet Shkodra), Sebino Plaku (46' Reginaldo). Coach: Armando Cungu.
Goals: 24', 57' Dani Quintana 1-0 (p), 2-0 (p), 89' Dzon Delarge 3-0.
Referee: Peter Královic (SVK)   Attendance: 25,030.
Sent off: 52' Albi Alla.

(Qarabag FK played their home match at Tofiq Bahramov adina Respublika stadionu instead of their regular stadium, Azersun Arena).

01.08.18   Swedbank Stadion, Malmö: Malmö FF – CFR Cluj 1-1 (0-1)
Malmö FF: Johan Dahlin, Behrang Safari, Rasmus Bengtsson, Eric Larsson (81' Andreas Vindheim), Lasse Nielsen, Søren Rieks, Anders Christiansen, Fouad Bachirou, Arnór Ingvi Traustason (73' Oscar Lewicki), Markus Rosenberg, Carlos Strandberg (61' Marcus Antonsson). Coach: Uwe Rösler.
CFR Cluj: Giedrius Arlauskis, Andrei Muresan, Paulo Vinícius, Camora, Cristian Manea, Emmanuel Culio, Ciprian Deac (43' Sebastian Mailat), Ovidiu Hoban (64' Giuseppe De Luca), Damjan Djokovic (58' Mihai Bordeianu), George Tucudean, Billel Omrani. Coach: Toni.
Goals: 36' Damjan Djokovic 0-1, 55' Arnór Ingvi Traustason 1-1.
Referee: Andrew Dallas (SCO)   Attendance: 18,153.
Sent off: 77' Emmanuel Culio.

01.08.18   Marijampolés sporto centro stadione, Marijampolé:
FK Sūduva Marijampolé – Crvena Zvezda Beograd 0-2 (0-2)
FK Sūduva Marijampolé: Ivan Kardum, Vaidas Slavickas, Algis Jankauskas, Andro Svrljuga, Aleksandar Zivanovic (68' Vitaly Gayduchik), Guilherme, Povilas Leimonas, Robertas Vézevicius (60' Julius Kasparavicius), Ovidijus Verbickas, Giedrius Matulevicius (77' Gerson Acevedo), Rigino Cicilia. Coach: Vladimir Cheburin.
Crvena Zvezda Beograd: Milan Borjan, Vujadin Savic, Milan Rodic (66' Marko Gobeljic), Milos Degenek, Filip Stojkovic, Nenad Krsticic, Slavoljub Srnic (76' Lorenzo Ebecilio), Branko Jovicic, Nemanja Milic (60' Nikola Stojiljkovic), Mohamed Ben Nabouhane, Nemanja Radonjic. Coach: Vladan Milojevic.
Goals: 8' Mohamed Ben Nabouhane 0-1, 38' Nemanja Radonjic 0-2.
Referee: Tiago Martins (POR)   Attendance: 4,020.

01.08.18   Puskás Akadémia Pancho Aréna, Felcsút:
MOL Vidi FC – PFC Ludogorets Razgrad 1-0 (1-0)
MOL Vidi FC: Ádam Kovácsik, Roland Juhász, Attila Fiola, Loïc Négo, Paulo Vinícius, Stopira, Szabolcs Huszti, Anel Hadzic (89' Boban Nikolov), József Varga, István Kovács (90' Máté Pátkai), Marko Scepovic (75' Stefan Scepovic). Coach: Marko Nikolic.
PFC Ludogorets Razgrad: Renan, Cosmin Moti, Cicinho, Georgi Terziev, Svetoslav Dyakov, Gustavo Campanharo (46' Jacek Góralski), Wanderson (74' João Paulo), Natanael Pimienta, Marcelinho, Virgil Misidjan, Jakub Swierczok (67' Claudiu Keserü). Coach: Paulo Autuori.
Goal: 45' Anel Hadzic 1-0.
Referee: Manuel Schüttengruber (AUT)   Attendance: 2,878.
Sent off: 39' Virgil Misidjan.

(MOL Vidi FC played their home match at Puskás Akadémia Pancho Aréna instead of their regular stadium, Sóstói Stadion, due to reconstruction).

01.08.18   St. Jakob-Park, Basel: FC Basel – PAOK Saloniki 0-3 (0-1)
FC Basel: Jonas Omlin, Marek Suchy, Silvan Widmer, Éder Álvarez Balanta, Eray Cümart, Valentin Stocker (46' Samuele Campo), Serey Dié, Luca Zuffi, Aldo Kalulu (84' Dimitri Oberlin), Kevin Bua, Albian Ajeti (73' Ricky van Wolfswinkel). Coach: Alexander Frei.
PAOK Saloniki: Alexandros Paschalakis, Léo Matos, José Ángel Crespo, Fernando Varela, Evgen Khacheridi, Omar El Kaddouri (74' Léo Jabá), Maurício, Cañas (81' Yevhen Shakhov), Dimitris Pelkas (85' Amr Warda), Aleksandar Prijovic, Dimitris Limnios.
Coach: Razvan Lucescu.
Goals: 7' Fernando Varela 0-1, 52' Aleksandar Prijovic 0-2, 60' Omar El Kaddouri 0-3.
Referee: Paolo Valeri (ITA)   Attendance: 14,328.

01.08.18   Merkur Arena, Graz: Sturm Graz – AFC Ajax 1-3 (0-1)
SK Sturm Graz: Jörg Siebenhandl, Fabian Koch, Filipe Ferreira, Lukas Spendlhofer, Dario Maresic, Stefan Hierländer, Markus Lackner (59' Raphael Obermair), Peter Zulj, Sandi Lovric, Philipp Hosiner (46' Markus Pink), Emeka Eze (66' Philipp Huspek). Coach: Heiko Vogel.
AFC Ajax: André Onana, Nicolás Tagliafico (55' Daley Blind), Matthijs de Ligt, Lasse Schöne, Dusan Tadic (67' Donny van de Beek), Hakim Ziyech, Carel Eiting (75' Maximilian Wöber), Noussair Mazraoui, Frenkie de Jong, Klaas-Jan Huntelaar, David Neres.
Coach: Erik ten Hag.
Goals: 39' Klaas-Jan Huntelaar 0-1, 48' Dusan Tadic 0-2, 77' Klaas-Jan Huntelaar 0-3, 89' André Onana 1-3 (og).
Referee: Bartosz Frankowski (POL)   Attendance: 15,172.

01.08.18   Lerkendal Stadion, Trondheim: Rosenborg BK – Celtic FC 0-0
Rosenborg BK: André Hansen, Tore Reginiussen, Even Hovland, Vegar Hedenstad, Birger Meling, Mike Jensen, Anders Trondsen (75' Matthías Vilhjálmsson), Marius Lundemo (90+2' Erik Botheim), Nicklas Bendtner, Pål Helland (58' Jonathan Levi), Alexander Søderlund.
Coach: Rini Coolen.
Celtic FC: Craig Gordon, Cristian Gamboa, Kieran Tierney (85' Mikael Lustig), Kristoffer Ajer, Jack Hendry, Scott Brown, Scott Sinclair, James Forrest (63' Tom Rogic), Callum McGregor, Olivier Ntcham, Odsonne Édouard (72' Ryan Christie). Coach: Brendan Rodgers.
Referee: Sandro Schärer (SUI)   Attendance: 14,263.

THIRD QUALIFYING ROUND

07.08.18   Astana Arena, Astana: FK Astana – Dinamo Zagreb 0-2 (0-1)
FK Astana: Nenad Eric, Antonio Rukavina, Marin Anicic, Dmitriy Shomko, Evgeni Postnikov, Marin Tomasov (80' Roman Murtazaev), Ivan Maevski, Serikzhan Muzhikov (46' Richard Almeyda), László Kleinheisler, Pedro Henrique, Junior Kabananga (63' Rangelo Janga).
Coach: Roman Grygorchuk.
Dinamo Zagreb: Daniel Zagorac, Marin Leovac, Kévin Théophile-Catherine, Emir Dilaver, Arijan Ademi (63' Ivan Sunjic), Izet Hajrovic (82' Damian Kadzior), Petar Stojanovic, Amer Gojak, Daniel Olmo, Mario Budimir (46' Mario Gavranovic), Mislav Orsic.
Coach: Nenad Bjelica.
Goals: 39' Mario Budimir 0-1, 84' Daniel Olmo 0-2.
Referee: John Beaton (SCO)   Attendance: 26,500.

07.08.18   Tofiq Bahramov adina Respublika stadionu, Baku:
                Qarabag FK – BATE Borisov 0-1 (0-1)
Qarabag FK: Hannes Halldórsson, Rashad Sadygov, Maksim Medvedev, Badavi Hüseynov, Míchel, Gara Garayev, Simeon Slavchev (80' Filip Ozobic), Wilde Guerrier, Abdellah Zoubir, Innocent Emeghara, Dzon Delarge (67' Mahir Madatov). Coach: Gurban Gurbanov.
BATE Borisov: Denis Scherbitski, Egor Filipenko, Maksim Volodko, Aleksandar Filipovic, Alexei Rios, Igor Stasevich (85' Aliaksandr Hleb), Dmitri Baga, Stanislav Dragun (75' Yevgeniy Berezkin), Mirko Ivanic (62' Maksim Skavysh), Evgeni Yablonski, Nikolay Signevich. Coach: Alexey Baga.
Goal: 36' Stanislav Dragun 0-1.
Referee: Andreas Ekberg (SWE)   Attendance: 29,000.

(Qarabag FK played their home match at Tofiq Bahramov adina Respublika stadionu instead of their regular stadium, Azersun Arena).

07.08.18   Swedbank Stadion, Malmö: Malmö FF – MOL Vidi FC 1-1 (0-0)
Malmö FF: Johan Dahlin, Behrang Safari, Rasmus Bengtsson (31' Franz Brorsson), Eric Larsson, Lasse Nielsen, Søren Rieks, Anders Christiansen, Fouad Bachirou, Arnór Ingvi Traustason (46' Oscar Lewicki), Markus Rosenberg, Marcus Antonsson (80' Romain Gall). Coach: Uwe Rösler.
MOL Vidi FC: Ádam Kovácsik, Roland Juhász, Attila Fiola, Loïc Négo, Paulo Vinícius, Stopira, Anel Hadzic, István Kovács (78' Máté Pátkai), Boban Nikolov, Danko Lazovic (89' Stefan Scepovic), Marko Scepovic (82' József Varga). Coach: Marko Nikolic.
Goals: 62' Anders Christiansen 1-0, 71' Loïc Négo 1-1.
Referee: Matej Jug (SVN)   Attendance: 17,209.

07.08.18   Eden Aréna, Praha: SK Slavia Praha – Dynamo Kyiv 1-1 (0-0)
SK Slavia Praha: Ondrej Kolár, Jan Boril, Vladimír Coufal, Simon Deli, Josef Husbauer, Miroslav Stoch, Jan Sykora (Peter Olayinka), Michael Ngadeu-Ngadjui, Jaromír Zmrhal (80' Alexandru Baluta), Tomás Soucek, Milan Skoda (60' Stanislav Teci).
Coach: Jindrich Trpisovsky.
Dynamo Kyiv: Denis Boyko, Mikola Morozyuk, Tamás Kádár, Tomasz Kedziora, Mykyta Burda, Sergiy Sydorchuk, Denys Garmash, Vitaliy Buyalskiy (68' Volodymyr Shepelev), Benjamin Verbic, Viktor Tsygankov (90+1' Oleksandr Andrievsky), Artem Besedin.
Coach: Aleksandr Khatskevich.
Goals: 82' Benjamin Verbic 0-1, 90+5' Josef Husbauer 1-1 (p).
Referee: Craig Pawson (ENG)   Attendance: 19,370.

07.08.18 Stade Maurice Dufrasne, Liège: Standard Liège – AFC Ajax 2-2 (0-2)
Standard Liège: Guillermo Ochoa, Luis Cavanda, Kostas Laifis, Collins Fai, Christian Luyindama Nekadio, Mehdi Carcela-González, Paul M'Poku (85' Moussa Djenepo), Razvan Marin, Uche Agbo, Samuel Bastien (76' Gojko Cimirot), Orlando Sá (66' Renaud Emond). Coach: Michel Preud'homme.
AFC Ajax: André Onana, Daley Blind, Nicolás Tagliafico, Matthijs de Ligt, Lasse Schöne (89' Carel Eiting), Hakim Ziyech (73' Zakaria Labyad), Noussair Mazraoui, Frenkie de Jong (79' Donny van de Beek), Klaas-Jan Huntelaar, Dusan Tadic, David Neres. Coach: Erik ten Hag.
Goals: 19' Klaas-Jan Huntelaar 0-1, 34' Dusan Tadic 0-2, 67' Mehdi Carcela-González 1-2, 90+4' Renaud Emond 2-2 (p).
Referee: Tobias Stieler (GER)   Attendance: 20,355.

07.08.18 Stadion Rajko Mitic, Beograd:
            Crvena Zvezda Beograd – FC Spartak Trnava 1-1 (1-1)
Crvena Zvezda Beograd: Milan Borjan, Vujadin Savic, Milan Rodic, Milos Degenek, Filip Stojkovic, Nenad Krsticic, Branko Jovicic, Nikola Stojiljkovic (53' Nemanja Milic, 73' Slavoljub Srnic), Lorenzo Ebecilio (79' Veljko Simic), Mohamed Ben Nabouhane, Nemanja Radonjic. Coach: Vladan Milojevic.
FC Spartak Trnava: Martin Chudy, Martin Tóth, Matús Conka, Boris Godál, Andrej Kadlec, Erik Grendel (89' Fabian Miesenböck), Jakub Rada (90+5' Ivan Hladík), Anton Sloboda, Lukás Gressák, Erik Jirka, Marek Bakos (75' Marvin Egho). Coach: Radoslav Látal.
Goals: 23' Mohamed Ben Nabouhane 1-0 (p), 25' Erik Grendel 1-1.
Referee: Carlos del Cerro Grande (ESP)   Attendance: 37,112.

07.08.18 Estádio do Sport Lisboa e Benfica, Lisboa: SL Benfica – SK Fenerbahçe 1-0 (0-0)
SL Benfica: Odisseas Vlachodimos, André Almeida, Jardel, Álex Grimaldo, Rúben Dias, Ljubomir Fejsa, Pizzi, Eduardo Salvio (75' Andrija Zivkovic), Franco Cervi, Gedson Fernandes, Facundo Ferreyra (63' Nicolás Castillo). Coach: Rui Vitória.
SK Fenerbahçe: Volkan Demirel, Martin Skrtel, Mauricio Isla, Roman Neustädter, Hasan-Ali Kaldirim, Mathieu Valbuena (61' Mehmet Ekici), Mehmet Topal, Nabil Dirar (87' Baris Alici), Giuliano, Alper Potuk (74' Soldado), Eljif Elmas. Coach: Phillip Cocu.
Goal: 69' Franco Cervi 1-0
Referee: Aleksei Kulbakov (BLS)   Attendance: 57,878.

08.08.18 Red Bull Arena, Wals-Siezenheim: Red Bull Salzburg – KF Shkëndija 79 3-0 (2-0)
Red Bull Salzburg: Cican Stankovic, Andreas Ulmer, Stefan Lainer, André Ramalho, Marin Pongracic, Zlatko Junuzovi, Reinhold Yabo (73' Takumi Minamino), Xaver Schlager (83' Enock Mwepu), Diadié Samassékou, Moanes Dabour (90+1' Patson Daka), Hannes Wolf. Coach: Marco Rose.
KF Shkëndija 79: Kostadin Zahov, Mevlan Murati (75' Gledi Mici), Visar Musliu, Egzon Bejtulai, Mevlan Adili, Armend Alimi, Ennur Totre, Besart Ibraimi, Valmir Nafiu, Stênio Júnior (90+5' Shefit Shefiti), Remzi Selmani (62' Izair Emini). Coach: Qatip Osmani.
Goals: 16', 45+3' Moanes Dabour 1-0 (p), 2-0, 81' Diadié Samassékou 3-0 (p).
Referee: Äliyar Agayev (AZE)   Attendance: 10,050.
Sent off: 83' Zlatko Junuzovi.

08.08.18 Stadio Toumbas, Thessaloniki: PAOK Saloniki – Spartak Moskva 3-2 (3-2)
PAOK Saloniki: Alexandros Paschalakis, Léo Matos, José Ángel Crespo, Fernando Varela, Evgen Khacheridi, Omar El Kaddouri (61' Amr Warda), Maurício (84' Yevhen Shakhov), Cañas, Dimitris Pelkas, Aleksandar Prijovic, Dimitris Limnios (79' Léo Jabá).
Coach: Razvan Lucescu.
Spartak Moskva: Aleksandr Maksimenko, Salvatore Bocchetti (90+4' Nikolai Rasskazov), Andrey Eshchenko, Samuel Gigot, Dmitriy Kombarov, Ivelin Popov (46' Artiom Timofeev), Fernando, Roman Zobnin, Quincy Promes, Aleksandr Lomovitski, Luiz Adriano (77' Zé Luís).
Coach: Massimo Carrera.
Goals: 7' Ivelin Popov 0-1, 17' Quincy Promes 0-2, 29' Aleksandar Prijovic 1-2 (p), 37' Dimitris Limnios 2-2, 44' Dimitris Pelkas 3-2.
Referee: Orel Grinfeld (ISR)   Attendance: 24,463.

Quincy Promis missed a penalty kick (71').

08.08.18 Celtic Park, Glasgow: Celtic FC – AEK Athens 1-1 (1-1)
Celtic FC: Craig Gordon, Mikael Lustig (77' Scott Sinclair), Kieran Tierney, Kristoffer Ajer, Jack Hendry, Scott Brown, James Forrest, Callum McGregor, Tom Rogic (63' Leigh Griffiths), Olivier Ntcham, Odsonne Édouard. Coach: Brendan Rodgers.
AEK Athens: Vassilis Barkas, Niklas Hult, Konstantinos-Vassilios Lambropoulos, Hélder Lopes, Marios Oikonomou, Michalis Bakakis, André Simões, Konstantinos Galanopoulos, Marko Livaja (77' Ezequiel Ponce), Anastasios Bakasetas (66' Alef), Viktor Klonaridis (80' Rodrigo Galo). Coach: Marinos Ouzounidis.
Goals: 17' Callum McGregor 1-0, 44' Viktor Klonaridis 1-1.
Referee: Luca Banti (ITA)   Attendance: 54,370.
Sent off: 57' Konstantinos Galanopoulos.

14.08.18 NSK Olimpijs'kyj, Kyiv: Dynamo Kyiv – SK Slavia Praha 2-0 (1-0)
Dynamo Kyiv: Denis Boyko, Josip Pivaric, Tamás Kádár, Tomasz Kedziora, Mykyta Burda (75' Artem Shabanov), Sergiy Sydorchuk, Denys Garmash, Benjamin Verbic, Viktor Tsygankov (90+2' Mikola Morozyuk), Volodymyr Shepelev (88' Vitaliy Buyalskiy), Artem Besedin. Coach: Aleksandr Khatskevich.
SK Slavia Praha: Ondrej Kolár, Jan Boril, Vladimír Coufal, Simon Deli, Josef Husbauer (85' Michal Frydrych), Miroslav Stoch, Jan Sykora, Michael Ngadeu-Ngadjui, Jaromír Zmrhal (68' Alexandru Baluta), Tomás Soucek, Stanislav Teci (75' Milan Skoda).
Coach: Jindrich Trpisovsky.
Goals: 11' Benjamin Verbic 1-0, 74' Artem Besedin 2-0.
Referee: Daniel Stefanski (POL)   Attendance: 39,318.

14.08.18 Borisov Arena, Borisov: BATE Borisov – Qarabag FK 1-1 (1-0)
BATE Borisov: Denis Scherbitski, Egor Filipenko, Maksim Volodko, Aleksandar Filipovic, Alexei Rios, Igor Stasevich, Dmitri Baga (70' Aliaksandr Hleb), Stanislav Dragun, Mirko Ivanic (78' Maksim Skavysh), Evgeni Yablonski, Nikolay Signevich. Coach: Alexey Baga.
Qarabag FK: Hannes Halldórsson, Rashad Sadygov, Maksim Medvedev (85' Dzon Delarge), Badavi Hüseynov, Míchel, Gara Garayev, Simeon Slavchev (77' Filip Ozobic), Wilde Guerrier, Abdellah Zoubir, Innocent Emeghara, Mahir Madatov. Coach: Gurban Gurbanov.
Goals: 20' Mirko Ivanic 1-0, 54' Míchel 1-1.
Referee: Andris Treimanis (LAT)   Attendance: 12,489.
Sent off: 77' Innocent Emeghara.

14.08.18   Otkrytiye Arena, Moskva: Spartak Moskva – PAOK Saloniki 0-0
Spartak Moskva: Aleksandr Maksimenko, Andrey Eshchenko, Georgi Dzhikiya, Samuel Gigot, Dmitriy Kombarov (76' Lorenzo Melgarejo), Denis Glushakov, Fernando (63' Aleksandr Samedov), Roman Zobnin, Quincy Promes, Aleksandr Tashaev (46' Zé Luís), Luiz Adriano.
Coach: Massimo Carrera.
PAOK Saloniki: Alexandros Paschalakis, Léo Matos, José Ángel Crespo, Fernando Varela, Vieirinha (65' Evgen Khacheridi), Omar El Kaddouri (46' Amr Warda), Maurício, Cañas, Dimitris Pelkas (79' Yevhen Shakhov), Aleksandar Prijovic, Dimitris Limnios.
Coach: Razvan Lucescu.
Referee: Ruddy Buquet (FRA)   Attendance: 40,385.
Sent off: 33' Luiz Adriano.

14.08.18   Olympiako Stadio Spyros Louis, Athens: AEK Athens – Celtic FC 2-1 (1-0)
AEK Athens: Vassilis Barkas, Niklas Hult, Rodrigo Galo (82' Christos Albanis), Konstantinos-Vassilios Lambropoulos, Marios Oikonomou, Michalis Bakakis, André Simões, Alef, Marko Livaja, Anastasios Bakasetas (90+1' Uros Cosic), Viktor Klonaridis (73' Petros Mandalos). Coach: Marinos Ouzounidis.
Celtic FC: Craig Gordon, Mikael Lustig (60' Moussa Dembélé), Jozo Simunovic, Kieran Tierney, Jack Hendry, Scott Brown, James Forrest, Callum McGregor, Tom Rogic (76' Scott Sinclair), Olivier Ntcham, Leigh Griffiths. Coach: Brendan Rodgers.
Goals: 6' Rodrigo Galo 1-0, 50' Marko Livaja 2-0, 78' Scott Sinclair 2-1.
Referee: Vladislav Bezborodov (RUS)   Attendance: 32,300.

14.08.18   Stadion Maksimir, Zagreb: Dinamo Zagreb – FK Astana 1-0 (0-0)
Dinamo Zagreb: Daniel Zagorac, Marin Leovac, Kévin Théophile-Catherine, Emir Dilaver, Arijan Ademi, Izet Hajrovic, Petar Stojanovic, Amer Gojak (70' Ivan Sunjic), Daniel Olmo, Mario Budimir (56' Mario Gavranovic), Mislav Orsic (82' Dino Peric). Coach: Nenad Bjelica.
FK Astana: Nenad Eric, Antonio Rukavina, Dmitriy Shomko, Sergiy Maliy, Evgeni Postnikov, Marin Tomasov, Ivan Maevski, Richard Almeyda (78' Serikzhan Muzhikov), László Kleinheisler (78' Aleksey Shchetkin), Rangelo Janga (78' Junior Kabananga), Pedro Henrique. Coach: Roman Grygorchuk.
Goal: 74' Mario Gavranovic 1-0.
Referee: Gediminas Mazeika (LTU)   Attendance: 11,903.

14.08.18   Puskás Akadémia Pancho Aréna, Felcsút: MOL Vidi FC – Malmö FF 0-0
MOL Vidi FC: Ádám Kovácsik, Roland Juhász, Attila Fiola, Loïc Négo, Paulo Vinícius, Stopira, Anel Hadzic, István Kovács (89' Szabolcs Huszti), Boban Nikolov (85' Máté Pátkai), Danko Lazovic (90+5' Krisztián Tamás), Marko Scepovic. Coach: Marko Nikolic.
Malmö FF: Johan Dahlin, Eric Larsson (75' Andreas Vindheim), Lasse Nielsen, Franz Brorsson, Søren Rieks, Anders Christiansen, Fouad Bachirou, Oscar Lewicki, Bonke Innocent (79' Romain Gall), Markus Rosenberg, Carlos Strandberg (70' Marcus Antonsson).
Coach: Uwe Rösler.
Referee: Xavier Estrada Fernández (ESP)   Attendance: 3,432.

Danko Lazovic missed a penalty kick (67').

MOL Vidi FC won on away goals.

(MOL Vidi FC played their home match at Puskás Akadémia Pancho Aréna instead of their regular stadium, Sóstói Stadion, due to reconstruction).

14.08.18   Ülker Stadyumu Fenerbahçe Sükrü Saracoglu Spor Kompleksi, Istanbul:
SK Fenerbahçe – SL Benfica 1-1 (1-1)
SK Fenerbahçe: Volkan Demirel, Martin Skrtel, Mauricio Isla (80 Sener Özbayrakli), Roman Neustädter, Hasan-Ali Kaldirim, Mathieu Valbuena (65' Soldado), Mehmet Topal (65' Baris Alici), Giuliano, Alper Potuk, Eljif Elmas, André Ayew. Coach: Phillip Cocu.
SL Benfica: Odisseas Vlachodimos, André Almeida, Jardel, Álex Grimaldo, Rúben Dias, Ljubomir Fejsa, Pizzi, Eduardo Salvio (72' Alfa Semedo), Franco Cervi, Gedson Fernandes, Nicolás Castillo (34' Facundo Ferreyra). Coach: Rui Vitória.
Goals: 26' Gedson Fernandes 0-1, 45+1' Alper Potuk 1-1.
Referee: Slavko Vincic (SVN)   Attendance: 42,245.

14.08.18   Telekom Arena, Skopje: KF Shkëndija 79 – Red Bull Salzburg 0-1 (0-0)
KF Shkëndija 79: Kostadin Zahov, Gledi Mici, Visar Musliu, Egzon Bejtulai, Mevlan Adili (71' Remzi Selmani), Armend Alimi, Ennur Totre, Besart Ibraimi, Izair Emini (86' Shefit Shefiti), Valmir Nafiu (46' Besmir Bojku), Stênio Júnior. Coach: Qatip Osmani.
Red Bull Salzburg: Cican Stankovic, Andreas Ulmer, Stefan Lainer, André Ramalho, Marin Pongracic, Reinhold Yabo (68' Takumi Minamino), Xaver Schlager (89' Christoph Leitgeb), Diadié Samassékou, Amadou Haïdara, Moanes Dabour (76' Patson Daka), Hannes Wolf. Coach: Marco Rose.
Goal: 90+2' Takumi Minamino 0-1.
Referee: Tamás Bognár (HUN)   Attendance: 3,213.

(KF Shkëndija 79 played their home match at Telekom Arena instead of their regular stadium, Ecolog Arena, due to renovation).

14.08.18   City Arena Trnava, Trnava:
FC Spartak Trnava – Crvena Zvezda Beograd 1-2 (1-1, 1-1)
FC Spartak Trnava: Martin Chudy, Martin Tóth, Matús Conka (106' Ivan Hladík), Boris Godál, Andrej Kadlec, Erik Grendel, Jakub Rada (100' Filip Dangubic), Anton Sloboda, Lukás Gressák, Erik Jirka, Marek Bakos. Coach: Radoslav Látal.
Crvena Zvezda Beograd: Milan Borjan, Vujadin Savic, Milan Rodic, Milos Degenek, Filip Stojkovic, Nenad Krsticic, Veljko Simic (85' Branko Jovicic), Dusan Jovancic (101' Marko Gobeljic), Nikola Stojiljkovic (75' Milan Pavkov), Mohamed Ben Nabouhane, Nemanja Radonjic (108' Srdan Babic). Coach: Vladan Milojevic.
Goals: 6' Marek Bakos 1-0, 7' Mohamed Ben Nabouhane 1-1, 98' Nemanja Radonjic 1-2.
Referee: Serdar Gözübüyük (HOL)   Attendance: 18,032.

Boris Godál missed a penalty kick (120+2').

Crvena Zvezda Beograd won after extra time.

14.08.18   Johan Cruijff ArenA, Amsterdam: AFC Ajax – Standard Liège 3-0 (2-0)
AFC Ajax: André Onana, Daley Blind, Nicolás Tagliafico, Matthijs de Ligt, Lasse Schöne, Hakim Ziyech (90' Zakaria Labyad), Noussair Mazraoui (76' Rasmus Kristensen), Frenkie de Jong, Klaas-Jan Huntelaar, Dusan Tadic, David Neres (82' Donny van de Beek).
Coach: Erik ten Hag.
Standard Liège: Guillermo Ochoa, Luis Cavanda (Sébastien Pocognoli), Kostas Laifis, Collins Fai, Christian Luyindama Nekadio, Mehdi Carcela-González, Paul M'Poku, Razvan Marin, Uche Agbo, Samuel Bastien (53' Gojko Cimirot), Renaud Emond (78' Orlando Sá).
Coach: Michel Preud'homme.
Goals: 30' Klaas-Jan Huntelaar 1-0, 34' Matthijs de Ligt 2-0, 46' David Neres 3-0.
Referee: Ivan Kruzliak (SVK)   Attendance: 51,841.

PLAY-OFF ROUND

21.08.18 Stadion Rajko Mitic, Beograd: Crvena Zvezda Beograd – Red Bull Salzburg 0-0
Crvena Zvezda Beograd: Milan Borjan, Vujadin Savic (46' Srdan Babic), Milan Rodic, Milos Degenek, Filip Stojkovic, Nenad Krsticic, Branko Jovicic, Nikola Stojiljkovic (79' Dusan Jovancic), Mohamed Ben Nabouhane, Jonathan Cafú (60' Veljko Simic), Nemanja Radonjic. Coach: Vladan Milojevic.
Red Bull Salzburg: Cican Stankovic, Andreas Ulmer, Stefan Lainer, André Ramalho, Marin Pongracic, Zlatko Junuzovic (46' Xaver Schlager), Reinhold Yabo (79' Patson Daka), Diadié Samassékou, Amadou Haïdara, Moanes Dabour, Hannes Wolf (87' Takumi Minamino). Coach: Marco Rose.
Referee: Daniele Orsato (ITA)

Match was played behind closed doors.

21.08.18 Borisov Arena, Borisov: BATE Borisov – PSV Eindhoven 2-3 (1-1)
BATE Borisov: Denis Scherbitski, Egor Filipenko, Nemanja Milunovic, Aleksandar Filipovic, Alexei Rios, Igor Stasevich, Dmitri Baga, Stanislav Dragun (65' Aliaksandr Hleb), Mirko Ivanic (81' Maksim Volodko), Jasse Tuominen (60' Maksim Skavysh), Evgeni Yablonski. Coach: Alexey Baga.
PSV Eindhoven: Jeroen Zoet, Daniel Schwaab, Nick Viergever, José Angeliño, Denzel Dumfries, Jorrit Hendrix, Gastón Pereiro (82' Mauro Júnior), Pablo Rosario (90+4' Nicolas Isimat-Mirin), Luuk de Jong, Steven Bergwijn, Hirving Lozano (87' Donyell Malen). Coach: Mark van Bommel.
Goals: 9' Jasse Tuominen 1-0, 35' Gastón Pereiro 1-1 (p), 61' Hirving Lozano 1-2, 88' Aliaksandr Hleb 2-2, 89' Donyell Malen 2-3.
Referee: Felix Zwayer (GER)   Attendance: 9,284.

21.08.18 Estádio do Sport Lisboa e Benfica, Lisboa: SL Benfica – PAOK Saloniki 1-1 (1-0)
SL Benfica: Odisseas Vlachodimos, André Almeida, Jardel, Álex Grimaldo, Rúben Dias, Ljubomir Fejsa, Pizzi (80' João Félix), Andrija Zickovic (65' Rafa Silva), Franco Cervi (79' Haris Seferovic), Gedson Fernandes, Facundo Ferreyra. Coach: Rui Vitória.
PAOK Saloniki: Alexandros Paschalakis, Léo Matos, José Ángel Crespo, Fernando Varela, Vieirinha, Maurício, Cañas, Dimitris Pelkas, Aleksandar Prijovic (87' Chuba Akpom), Dimitris Limnios (53' Amr Warda), Léo Jabá (81' Yevhen Shakhov). Coach: Razvan Lucescu.
Goals: 45+1' Pizzi 1-0 (p), 76' Amr Warda 1-1.
Referee: Milorad Mazic (SRB)   Attendance: 44,084.

22.08.18 Stade de Suise, Bern: BSC Young Boys – Dinamo Zagreb 1-1 (1-1)
BSC Young Boys: David von Ballmoos, Steve von Bergen, Loris Benito, Kevin Mbabu, Gregory Wüthrich, Miralem Sulejmani, Sékou Junior Sanogo, Nicolas Moumi Ngamaleu (81' Jean Pierre Nsamé), Djibril Sow, Christian Fassnacht (70' Michel Aebischer), Guillaume Hoarau. Coach: Gerardo Seoane.
Dinamo Zagreb: Daniel Zagorac, Marin Leovac, Kévin Théophile-Catherine, Emir Dilaver, Petar Stojanovic, Arijan Ademi, Amer Gojak, Daniel Olmo (86' Ivan Sunjic), Mario Gavranovic (74' Mario Budimir), Mislav Orsic, Izet Hajrovic (83' Damian Kadzior). Coach: Nenad Bjelica.
Goals: 2' Kevin Mbabu 1-0, 40' Mislav Orsic 1-1.
Referee: Alberto Undiano Mallenco (ESP)   Attendance: 21,463.

22.08.18   Groupama Aréna, Budapest: MOL Vidi FC – AEK Athens 1-2 (0-1)
MOL Vidi FC: Ádam Kovácsik, Roland Juhász, Attila Fiola, Loïc Négo, Paulo Vinícius, Stopira, Szabolcs Huszti, Anel Hadzic, István Kovács, Boban Nikolov (54' Marko Scepovic), Danko Lazovic. Coach: Marko Nikolic.
AEK Athens: Vassilis Barkas, Niklas Hult, Konstantinos-Vassilios Lambropoulos, Marios Oikonomou, Petros Mandalos, Michalis Bakakis, André Simões, Konstantinos Galanopoulos (66' Alef), Marko Livaja (86' Ezequiel Ponce), Anastasios Bakasetas, Viktor Klonaridis (82' Hélder Lopes). Coach: Marinos Ouzounidis.
Goals: 34' Viktor Klonaridis 0-1, 49' Anastasios Bakasetas 0-2, 67' Danko Lazovic 1-2.
Referee: Gianluca Rocchi (ITA)   Attendance: 10,681.
Sent off: 22' Szabolcs Huszti, 53' Anastasios Bakasetas.

(MOL Vidi FC played their home match at Groupama Aréna instead of their regular stadium, Sóstói Stadion, due to reconstruction).

22.08.18   Johan Cruijff ArenA, Amsterdam: AFC Ajax – Dynamo Kyiv 3-1 (3-1)
AFC Ajax: André Onana, Daley Blind, Nicolás Tagliafico, Matthijs de Ligt, Lasse Schöne, Hakim Ziyech, Donny van de Beek (87' Dani de Wit), Noussair Mazraoui, Frenkie de Jong, Klaas-Jan Huntelaar, Dusan Tadic. Coach: Erik ten Hag.
Dynamo Kyiv: Denis Boyko, Josip Pivaric, Tamás Kádár, Tomasz Kedziora, Mykyta Burda, Sergiy Sydorchuk (77' Tchê Tchê), Denys Garmash (46' Volodymyr Shepelev), Vitaliy Buyalskiy, Benjamin Verbic, Viktor Tsygankov, Artem Besedin.
Coach: Aleksandr Khatskevich.
Goals: 2' Donny van de Beek 1-0, 16' Tomasz Kedziora 1-1, 35' Hakim Ziyech 2-1, 43' Dusan Tadic 3-1.
Referee: Clément Turpin (FRA)   Attendance: 52,706.

28.08.18   Stadion Maksimir, Zagreb: Dinamo Zagreb – BSC Young Boys 1-2 (1-0)
Dinamo Zagreb: Daniel Zagorac, Marin Leovac (74' Mario Budimir), Kévin Théophile-Catherine, Emir Dilaver, Petar Stojanovic, Arijan Ademi (32' Ivan Sunjic), Amer Gojak, Daniel Olmo, Mario Gavranovic, Mislav Orsic (83' Damian Kadzior), Izet Hajrovic.
Coach: Nenad Bjelica.
BSC Young Boys: David von Ballmoos, Steve von Bergen, Loris Benito, Kevin Mbabu, Gregory Wüthrich, Miralem Sulejmani (55' Roger Assalé), Sékou Junior Sanogo, Nicolas Moumi Ngamaleu (90+3' Michel Aebischer), Djibril Sow, Christian Fassnacht (84' Leonardo Bertone), Guillaume Hoarau. Coach: Gerardo Seoane.
Goals: 7' Izet Hajrovic 1-0, 64', 66' Guillaume Hoarau 1-1 (p), 1-2.
Referee: Björn Kuipers (HOL)   Attendance: 28,137.

28.08.18   Olympiako Stadio Spyros Louis, Athens: AEK Athens – MOL Vidi FC 1-1 (0-0)
AEK Athens: Vassilis Barkas, Niklas Hult, Konstantinos-Vassilios Lambropoulos, Hélder Lopes, Marios Oikonomou, Petros Mandalos (90' Uros Cosic), Michalis Bakakis, André Simões, Konstantinos Galanopoulos, Marko Livaja (84' Alef), Viktor Klonaridis (62' Ezequiel Ponce). Coach: Marinos Ouzounidis.
MOL Vidi FC: Ádam Kovácsik, Roland Juhász, Attila Fiola, Loïc Négo, Paulo Vinícius, Stopira, Anel Hadzic, István Kovács, Boban Nikolov (46' Máté Pátkai), Danko Lazovic, Marko Scepovic. Coach: Marko Nikolic.
Goals: 48' Petros Mandalos 1-0 (p), 57' Loïc Négo 1-1.
Referee: Szymon Marciniak (POL)   Attendance: 29,774.
Sent off: 80' Hélder Lopes, 90+9' Marko Livaja.

28.08.18   NSK Olimpijs'kyj, Kyiv: Dynamo Kyiv – AFC Ajax 0-0
Dynamo Kyiv: Denis Boyko, Josip Pivaric, Tamás Kádár, Tomasz Kedziora, Mykyta Burda, Sergiy Sydorchuk (64' Mykola Shaparenko), Vitaliy Buyalskiy (85' Nazariy Rusyn), Benjamin Verbic, Viktor Tsygankov, Volodymyr Shepelev (46' Denys Garmash), Vladyslav Supriaha. Coach: Aleksandr Khatskevich.
AFC Ajax: André Onana, Daley Blind, Matthijs de Ligt, Maximilian Wöber (79' Carel Eiting), Lasse Schöne, Hakim Ziyech, Donny van de Beek (85' Dani de Wit), Noussair Mazraoui, Frenkie de Jong, Klaas-Jan Huntelaar, Dusan Tadic. Coach: Erik ten Hag.
Referee: Damir Skomina (SVN)   Attendance: 40,131.

Dusan Tadic missed a penalty kick (14').

29.08.18   Red Bull Arena, Wals-Siezenheim:
                Red Bull Salzburg – Crvena Zvezda Beograd 2-2 (1-0)
Red Bull Salzburg: Cican Stankovic, Andreas Ulmer, Stefan Lainer, André Ramalho, Marin Pongracic, Xaver Schlager (83' Smail Prevljak), Diadié Samassékou, Amadou Haïdara, Moanes Dabour, Patson Daka (69' Reinhold Yabo), Hannes Wolf. Coach: Marco Rose.
Crvena Zvezda Beograd: Milan Borjan, Vujadin Savic, Milan Rodic, Milos Degenek, Filip Stojkovic, Nenad Krsticic, Veljko Simic (37' Dusan Jovancic), Branko Jovicic, Nemanja Milic (50' Milan Pavkov), Mohamed Ben Nabouhane, Nemanja Radonjic (82' Marko Gobeljic). Coach: Vladan Milojevic.
Goals: 45', 48' Moanes Dabour 1-0, 2-0 (p), 65', 66' Mohamed Ben Nabouhane 2-1, 2-2.
Referee: Cüneyt Çakir (TUR)   Attendance: 26,500.

Crvena Zvezda Beograd won on away goals.

29.08.18   Philips Stadion, Eindhoven: PSV Eindhoven – BATE Borisov 3-0 (2-0)
PSV Eindhoven: Jeroen Zoet, Daniel Schwaab, Nick Viergever (71' Nicolas Isimat-Mirin), José Angeliño, Denzel Dumfries, Jorrit Hendrix, Gastón Pereiro, Pablo Rosario (74' Bart Ramselaar), Luuk de Jong, Steven Bergwijn (79' Donyell Malen), Hirving Lozano. Coach: Mark van Bommel.
BATE Borisov: Denis Scherbitski, Egor Filipenko, Nemanja Milunovic, Maksim Volodko, Aleksandar Filipovic, Aliaksandr Hleb (30' Mirko Ivanic), Alexei Rios, Igor Stasevich, Dmitri Baga, Stanislav Dragun (76' Yevgeniy Berezkin), Jasse Tuominen (51' Nilolay Signevich). Coach: Alexey Baga.
Goals: 14' Steven Bergwijn 1-0, 36' Luuk de Jong 2-0, 62' Hirving Lozano 3-0
Referee: Anthony Taylor (ENG)   Attendance: 34,200.

29.08.18   Stadio Toumbas, Thessaloniki: PAOK Saloniki – SL Benfica 1-4 (1-3)
PAOK Saloniki: Alexandros Paschalakis, Léo Matos, José Ángel Crespo, Fernando Varela, Vieirinha, Omar El Kaddouri (76' Chuba Akpom), Maurício, Cañas (64' Yevhen Shakhov), Dimitris Pelkas, Aleksandar Prijovic, Dimitris Limnios (46' Amr Warda). Coach: Razvan Lucescu.
SL Benfica: Odisseas Vlachodimos, André Almeida, Jardel, Álex Grimaldo, Rúben Dias, Ljubomir Fejsa, Pizzi (76' Andrija Zickovic), Eduardo Salvio (63' Alfa Semedo), Franco Cervi, Gedson Fernandes, Haris Seferovic (85' João Félix). Coach: Rui Vitória.
Goals: 13' Aleksandar Prijovic 1-0, 20' Jardel 1-1, 26' Eduardo Salvio 1-2 (p), 39' Pizzi 1-3, 50' Eduardo Salvio 1-4 (p).
Referee: Dr. Felix Brych (GER)   Attendance: 26,725.
Sent off: 76' Léo Matos.

GROUP STAGE

GROUP A

Borussia Dortmund	6	4	1	1	10 -	2	13
Atlético Madrid	6	4	1	1	9 -	6	13
Club Brugge KV	6	1	3	2	6 -	5	6
AS Monaco	6	0	1	5	2 -	14	1

GROUP B

FC Barcelona	6	4	2	0	14 -	5	14
Tottenham Hotspur	6	2	2	2	9 -	10	8
Internazionale	6	2	2	2	6 -	7	8
PSV Eindhoven	6	0	2	4	6 -	13	2

GROUP C

Paris Saint-Germain	6	3	2	1	17 -	9	11
Liverpool FC	6	3	0	3	9 -	7	9
SSC Napoli	6	2	3	1	7 -	5	9
Crvena Zvezda Beograd	6	1	1	4	5 -	17	4

GROUP D

FC Porto	6	5	1	0	15 -	6	16
FC Schalke 04	6	3	2	1	6 -	4	11
Galatasaray	6	1	1	4	5 -	8	4
Lokomotiv Moscow	6	1	0	5	4 -	12	3

GROUP E

FC Bayern München	6	4	2	0	15 -	5	14
AFC Ajax	6	3	3	0	11 -	5	12
SL Benfica	6	2	1	3	6 -	11	7
AEK Athens	6	0	0	6	2 -	13	0

GROUP F

Manchester City	6	4	1	1	16 -	6	13
Olympique Lyonnais	6	1	5	0	12 -	11	8
Shakhtar Donetsk	6	1	3	2	8 -	16	6
1899 Hoffenheim	6	0	3	3	11 -	14	3

GROUP G

Real Madrid CF	6	4	0	2	12 -	5	12
AS Roma	6	3	0	3	11 -	8	9
FC Viktoria Plzen	6	2	1	3	7 -	16	7
CSKA Moscow	6	2	1	3	8 -	9	7

GROUP H

Juventus	6	4	0	2	9	-	4	12
Manchester United	6	3	1	2	7	-	4	10
Valencia CF	6	2	2	2	6	-	6	8
BSC Young Boys	6	1	1	4	4	-	12	4

GROUP A

18.09.18   Jan Breydel Stadion, Brugge: Club Brugge KV – Borussia Dortmund 0-1 (0-0)
Club Brugge KV: Karlo Letica, Benoît Poulain, Stefano Denswil, Matej Mitrovic, Thibault Vlietinck (56' Dion Cools), Ruud Vormer, Mats Rits, Hans Vanaken, Jelle Vossen (82' Loïs Openda), Wesley, Arnaut Danjuma Groeneveld (76' Emmanuel Dennis). Coach: Ivan Leko.
Borussia Dortmund: Roman Bürki, Lukasz Piszczek, Marcel Schmelzer, Abdou Diallo, Manuel Akanji, Axel Witsel, Mario Götze (62' Shinji Kagawa), Julian Weigl (84' Mahmoud Dahoud), Jadon Sancho (69' Christian Pulisic), Marco Reus, Marius Wolf.
Coach: Lucien Favre.
Goal: 85' Christian Pulisic 0-1.
Referee: Danny Makkelie (HOL)   Attendance: 25,181.

18.09.18   Stade Louis II, Monaco: AS Monaco – Atlético Madrid 1-2 (1-2)
AS Monaco: Diego Benaglio, Kamil Glik, Djibril Sidibé, Benjamin Henrichs, Jemerson, Nacer Chadli (58' Jordi Mboula), Jean-Eudes Aholou (69' Adama Traoré (II)), Youri Tielemans, Kévin N'Doram, Radamel Falcao, Samuel Grandsir (77' Moussa Sylla).
Coach: Leonardo Jardim.
Atlético Madrid: Jan Oblak, Juanfran, Diego Godín, José Giménez, Lucas Hernández, Saúl, Koke, Rodri Hernández, Diego Costa, Antoine Griezmann, Ángel Correa (70' Thomas Lemar).
Coach: Diego Simeone.
Goals: 18' Samuel Grandsir 1-0, 31' Diego Costa 1-1, 45+1' José Giménez 1-2.
Referee: William Collum (SCO)   Attendance: 10,575.

03.10.18   Estadio Wanda Metropolitano, Madrid:
            Atlético Madrid – Club Brugge KV 3-1 (1-1)
Atlético Madrid: Jan Oblak, Diego Godín, Santiago Arias, José Giménez (46' Filipe Luís), Lucas Hernández, Saúl, Koke, Thomas Lemar, Thomas Partey (63' Ángel Correa), Diego Costa (69' Rodri Hernández), Antoine Griezmann. Coach: Diego Simeone.
Club Brugge KV: Karlo Letica, Benoît Poulain, Stefano Denswil, Brandon Mechele, Thibault Vlietinck (56' Clinton Mata), Ruud Vormer, Mats Rits (75' Loïs Openda), Hans Vanaken, Siebe Schrijvers (56' Marvelous Nakamba), Wesley, Arnaut Danjuma Groeneveld.
Coach: Ivan Leko.
Goals: 28' Antoine Griezmann 1-0, 39' Arnaut Danjuma Groeneveld 1-1,
67' Antoine Griezmann 2-1, 90+4' Koke 3-1.
Referee: Ivan Kruzliak (SVK)   Attendance: 55,742.

03.10.18 Signal-Iduna-Park, Dortmund: Borussia Dortmund – AS Monaco 3-0 (0-0)
Borussia Dortmund: Roman Bürki, Lukasz Piszczek, Abdou Diallo, Manuel Akanji, Dan-Axel Zagadou, Axel Witsel, Thomas Delaney (65' Julian Weigl), Jadon Sancho (84' Maximilian Philipp), Marco Reus, Paco Alcácer, Marius Wolf (46' Jacob Bruun Larsen).
Coach: Lucien Favre.
AS Monaco: Diego Benaglio (45' Danijel Subasic), Andrea Raggi, Kamil Glik, Djibril Sidibé, Benjamin Henrichs, Jemerson, Jean-Eudes Aholou, Aleksandr Golovin (77' Nacer Chadli), Youri Tielemans, Moussa Sylla (70' Samuel Grandsir), Radamel Falcao.
Coach: Leonardo Jardim.
Goals: 51' Jacob Bruun Larsen 1-0, 72' Paco Alcácer 2-0, 90+2' Marco Reus 3-0.
Referee: Aleksei Kulbakov (BLS)   Attendance: 66,099.

Paco Alcácer missed a penalty kick (69').

24.10.18 Jan Breydel Stadion, Brugge: Club Brugge KV – AS Monaco 1-1 (1-1)
Club Brugge KV: Karlo Letica, Benoît Poulain, Stefano Denswil, Brandon Mechele, Thibault Vlietinck (83' Clinton Mata), Ruud Vormer, Hans Vanaken, Marvelous Nakamba, Kaveh Rezaei (79' Loïs Openda), Wesley, Emmanuel Dennis Bonaventure (90' Krépin Diatta).
Coach: Ivan Leko.
AS Monaco: Loïc Badiashile, Andrea Raggi, Kamil Glik, Djibril Sidibé (64' Benjamin Henrichs), Jemerson, Nacer Chadli, Aleksandr Golovin, Youri Tielemans, Youssef Aït Bennasser, Moussa Sylla, Stevan Jovetic (12' Sofiane Diop, 73' Jean-Eudes Aholou).
Coach: Thierry Henry.
Goals: 31' Moussa Sylla 0-1, 39' Wesley 1-1.
Referee: Michael Oliver (ENG)   Attendance: 23,957.

24.10.18 Signal-Iduna-Park, Dortmund: Borussia Dortmund – Atlético Madrid 4-0 (1-0)
Borussia Dortmund: Roman Bürki, Lukasz Piszczek, Abdou Diallo, Achraf Hakimi, Dan-Axel Zagadou, Axel Witsel, Thomas Delaney (35' Mahmoud Dahoud), Mario Götze, Christian Pulisic (79' Jadon Sancho), Marco Reus, Jacob Bruun Larsen (63' Raphaël Guerreiro).
Coach: Lucien Favre.
Atlético Madrid: Jan Oblak, Juanfran, Filipe Luís, Diego Godín, Lucas Hernández, Saúl (70' Ángel Correa), Koke, Thomas Lemar, Thomas Partey (46' Rodri Hernández), Diego Costa, Antoine Griezmann. Coach: Diego Simeone.
Goals: 38' Axel Witsel 1-0, 73' Raphaël Guerreiro 2-0, 83' Jadon Sancho 3-0, 89' Raphaël Guerreiro 4-0.
Referee: Anthony Taylor (ENG)   Attendance: 66,099.

06.11.18 Stade Louis II, Monaco: AS Monaco – Club Brugge KV 0-4 (0-3)
AS Monaco: Diego Benaglio, Kamil Glik (76' Almamy Touré), Djibril Sidibé, Jemerson, Antonio Barreca, Nacer Chadli, Youri Tielemans, Youssef Aït Bennasser (68' Han-Noah Massengo), Moussa Sylla, Sofiane Diop, Radamel Falcao (61' Gobe Gouano). Coach: Thierry Henry.
Club Brugge KV: Ethan Horvath, Benoît Poulain, Stefano Denswil, Clinton Mata (77' Thibault Vlietinck), Brandon Mechele, Ruud Vormer, Mats Rits, Hans Vanaken, Marvelous Nakamba, Wesley (72' Kaveh Rezaei), Krépin Diatta (6' Dion Cools). Coach: Ivan Leko.
Goals: 12', 17' Hans Vanaken 0-1, 0-2 (p), 24' Wesley 0-3, 85' Ruud Vormer 0-4.
Referee: Artur Soares Dias (POR)   Attendance: 8,347.

06.11.18 Estadio Wanda Metropolitano, Madrid:
Atlético Madrid – Borussia Dortmund 2-0 (1-0)
Atlético Madrid: Jan Oblak, Juanfran, Filipe Luís, José Giménez (46' Francisco Montero), Lucas Hernández, Saúl, Thomas Partey, Rodri Hernández, Nikola Kalinic (62' Gelson Martins), Antoine Griezmann, Ángel Correa (81' Vitolo). Coach: Diego Simeone.
Borussia Dortmund: Roman Bürki, Lukasz Piszczek, Ömer Toprak, Manuel Akanji, Achraf Hakimi, Axel Witsel, Thomas Delaney, Christian Pulisic (59' Raphaël Guerreiro), Jadon Sancho (79' Jacob Bruun Larsen), Marco Reus, Paco Alcácer (75' Mario Götze). Coach: Lucien Favre.
Goals: 33' Saúl 1-0, 80' Antoine Griezmann 2-0.
Referee: Daniele Orsato (ITA)   Attendance: 61,023.

28.11.18 Estadio Wanda Metropolitano, Madrid: Atlético Madrid – AS Monaco 2-0 (2-0)
Atlético Madrid: Jan Oblak, Filipe Luís, Santiago Arias, Stefan Savic, Lucas Hernández, Koke (46' Vitolo), Thomas Lemar (63' Nikola Kalinic), Thomas Partey, Rodri Hernández, Antoine Griezmann, Ángel Correa (69' Saúl). Coach: Diego Simeone.
AS Monaco: Diego Benaglio, Andrea Raggi, Jemerson, Benoît Badiashile, Giulian Biancone, Nacer Chadli (63' Sofiane Diop), Aleksandre Golovin (63' Khéphren Thuram-Ulien), Youri Tielemans, Moussa Sylla (55' Radamel Falcao), Han-Noah Massengo, Samuel Grandsir. Coach: Thierry Henry.
Goals: 2' Koke 1-0, 24' Antoine Griezmann 2-0.
Referee: Mattias Gestranius (FIN)   Attendance: 56,314.
Sent off: 82' Stefan Savic.

Radamel Falcao missed a penalty kick (83').

28.11.18 Signal-Iduna-Park, Dortmund: Borussia Dortmund – Club Brugge KV 0-0
Borussia Dortmund: Roman Bürki, Lukasz Piszczek, Raphaël Guerreiro (73' Jadon Sancho), Abdou Diallo (80' Achraf Hakimi), Manuel Akanji, Dan-Axel Zagadou, Axel Witsel (90' Thomas Delaney), Mahmoud Dahoud, Christian Pulisic, Marco Reus, Paco Alcácer. Coach: Lucien Favre.
Club Brugge KV: Ethan Horvath, Benoît Poulain, Stefano Denswil, Clinton Mata, Brandon Mechele, Ruud Vormer (90+3' Saulo Decarli), Hans Vanaken, Marvelous Nakamba, Sofyan Amrabat, Wesley (90+2' Loïs Openda), Emmanuel Dennis (76' Mats Rits). Coach: Ivan Leko.
Referee: Gediminas Mazeika (LTU)   Attendance: 66,099.

11.12.18 Jan Breydel Stadion, Brugge: Club Brugge KV – Atlético Madrid 0-0
Club Brugge KV: Ethan Horvath, Benoît Poulain, Stefano Denswil, Brandon Mechele, Ruud Vormer, Hans Vanaken (90+1' Mats Rits), Marvelous Nakamba, Sofyan Amrabat, Wesley, Loïs Openda (74' Siebe Schrijvers), Cyril Ngonge (69' Luan Peres). Coach: Ivan Leko.
Atlético Madrid: Jan Oblak, Diego Godín, Santiago Arias, Francisco Montero, Saúl, Koke, Thomas Lemar (61' Vitolo), Thomas Partey (68' Nikola Kalinic), Rodri Hernández, Antoine Griezmann, Gelson Martins (60' Ángel Correa). Coach: Diego Simeone.
Referee: Davide Massa (ITA)   Attendance: 25,645.

11.12.18 Stade Louis II, Monaco: AS Monaco – Borussia Dortmund 0-2 (0-1)
AS Monaco: Diego Benaglio, Andrea Raggi, Kamil Glik, Benjamin Henrichs, Benoît Badiashile, Giulian Biancone (78' Julien Serrano), Youri Tielemans, Youssef Aït Bennasser, Han-Noah Massengo (69' Khéphren Thuram-Ulien), Sofiane Diop, Radamel Falcao (64' Moussa Sylla). Coach: Thierry Henry.
Borussia Dortmund: Marwin Hitz, Marcel Schmelzer, Ömer Toprak, Raphaël Guerreiro (90+2' Sergio Gómez), Abdou Diallo, Achraf Hakimi, Mario Götze, Julian Weigl, Mahmoud Dahoud (76' Marius Wolf), Christian Pulisic, Maximilian Philipp (79' Paco Alcácer).
Coach: Lucien Favre.
Goals: 15', 88' Raphaël Guerreiro 0-1, 0-2.
Referee: Craig Pawson (ENG)   Attendance: 8,731.

GROUP B

18.09.18 Camp Nou, Barcelona: FC Barcelona – PSV Eindhoven 4-0 (1-0)
FC Barcelona: Marc-André ter Stegen, Piqué, Jordi Alba, Sergi Roberto, Samuel Umtiti, Ivan Rakitic (85' Arturo Vidal), Sergio Busquets, Philippe Coutinho (81' Clément Lenglet), Lionel Messi, Luis Suárez, Ousmane Dembélé (83' Arthur). Coach: Ernesto Valverde.
PSV Eindhoven: Jeroen Zoet, Daniel Schwaab, Nick Viergever (66' Nicolas Isimat-Mirin), José Angeliño, Denzel Dumfries, Jorrit Hendrix, Gastón Pereiro, Pablo Rosario (82' Érick Gutiérrez), Luuk de Jong, Steven Bergwijn (78' Donyell Malen), Hirving Lozano.
Coach: Mark van Bommel.
Goals: 32' Lionel Messi 1-0, 75' Ousmane Dembélé 2-0, 77', 87' Lionel Messi 3-0, 4-0.
Referee: Anastasios Sidiropoulos (GRE)   Attendance: 73,462.
Sent off: 79' Samuel Umtiti.

18.09.18 Stadio Giuseppe Meazza, Milan: Internazionale – Tottenham Hotspur 2-1 (0-0)
Internazionale: Samir Handanovic, João Miranda, Stefan de Vrij, Milan Skriniar, Ivan Perisic (64' Antonio Candreva), Radja Nainggolan (89' Borja Valero), Kwadwo Asamoah, Matías Vecino, Marcelo Brozovic, Mauro Icardi, Matteo Politano (72' Keita Baldé Diao).
Coach: Luciano Spalletti.
Tottenham Hotspur: Michel Vorm, Jan Vertonghen, Serge Aurier, Benjamin Davies, Davinson Sánchez, Mousa Dembélé, Érik Lamela (72' Harry Winks), Christian Eriksen, Eric Dier, Son Heung-Min (64' Lucas Moura), Harry Kane (90' Danny Rose). Coach: Mauricio Pochettino.
Goals: 53' Christian Eriksen 0-1, 86' Mauro Icardi 1-1, 90+2' Matías Vecino 2-1.
Referee: Clément Turpin (FRA)   Attendance: 64,123.

03.10.18   Wembley Stadium, London: Tottenham Hotspur – FC Barcelona 2-4 (0-2)
Tottenham Hotspur: Hugo Lloris, Toby Alderweireld, Kieran Trippier, Benjamin Davies, Davinson Sánchez, Victor Wanyama (57' Eric Dier), Érik Lamela (79' Llorente), Lucas Moura, Harry Winks, Son Heung-Min (66' Moussa Sissoko), Harry Kane.
Coach: Mauricio Pochettino.
FC Barcelona: Marc-André ter Stegen, Piqué, Jordi Alba, Clément Lenglet, Nélson Semedo, Ivan Rakitic, Sergio Busquets (90+1' Thomas Vermaelen), Philippe Coutinho (83' Rafinha), Arthur (87' Arturo Vidal), Lionel Messi, Luis Suárez. Coach: Ernesto Valverde.
Goals: 2' Philippe Coutinho 0-1, 28' Ivan Rakitic 0-2, 52' Harry Kane 1-2, 56' Lionel Messi 1-3, 66' Érik Lamela 2-3, 90' Lionel Messi 2-4.
Referee: Felix Zwayer (GER)   Attendance: 82,137.

(Tottenham Hotspur played their three home matches at Wembley Stadium instead of their regular stadium, Tottenham Hotspur Stadium, due to delays with the construction of their new stadium).

03.10.18   Philips Stadion, Eindhoven: PSV Eindhoven – Internazionale 1-2 (1-1)
PSV Eindhoven: Jeroen Zoet, Daniel Schwaab, Nick Viergever, José Angeliño, Denzel Dumfries, Jorrit Hendrix, Gastón Pereiro (75' Donyell Malen), Pablo Rosario, Luuk de Jong, Steven Bergwijn, Hirving Lozano. Coach: Mark van Bommel.
Internazionale: Samir Handanovic, Stefan de Vrij, Danilo D'Ambrosio, Milan Skriniar, Ivan Perisic, Radja Nainggolan (86' Borja Valero), Kwadwo Asamoah, Matías Vecino, Marcelo Brozovic, Mauro Icardi, Matteo Politano (90+1' Antonio Candreva). Coach: Luciano Spalletti.
Goals: 27' Pablo Rosario 1-0, 44' Radja Nainggolan 1-1, 60' Mauro Icardi 1-2.
Referee: Milorad Mazic (SRB)   Attendance: 34,750.

24.10.18   Philips Stadion, Eindhoven: PSV Eindhoven – Tottenham Hotspur 2-2 (1-1)
PSV Eindhoven: Jeroen Zoet, Daniel Schwaab, Nick Viergever, José Angeliño, Denzel Dumfries, Jorrit Hendrix, Gastón Pereiro (83' Cody Gakpo), Pablo Rosario, Luuk de Jong, Hirving Lozano, Donyell Malen. Coach: Mark van Bommel.
Tottenham Hotspur: Hugo Lloris, Toby Alderweireld, Kieran Trippier, Benjamin Davies, Davinson Sánchez, Moussa Dembélé (74' Harry Winks), Christian Eriksen, Lucas Moura (64' Érik Lamela), Eric Dier, Son Heung-Min (81' Michel Vorm *goalkeeper*), Harry Kane.
Coach: Mauricio Pochettino.
Goals: 30' Hirving Lozano 1-0, 39' Lucas Moura 1-1, 55' Harry Kane 1-2, 87' Luuk de Jong 2-2.
Referee: Slavko Vincic (SVN)   Attendance: 35,000.
Sent off: 79' Hugo Lloris.

24.10.18   Camp Nou, Barcelona: FC Barcelona – Internazionale 2-0 (1-0)
FC Barcelona: Marc-André ter Stegen, Piqué, Jordi Alba, Sergi Roberto, Clément Lenglet, Ivan Rakitic, Sergio Busquets, Philippe Coutinho (88' Munir), Rafinha (72' Nélson Semedo), Arthur (78' Arturo Vidal), Luis Suárez. Coach: Ernesto Valverde.
Internazionale: Samir Handanovic, João Miranda, Kwadwo Asamoah, Danilo D'Ambrosio, Milan Skriniar, Ivan Perisic (77' Keita Baldé), Antonio Candreva (46' Matteo Politano), Borja Valero (63' Lautaro Martínez), Matías Vecino, Marcelo Brozovic, Mauro Icardi.
Coach: Luciano Spalletti.
Goals: 32' Rafinha 1-0, 83' Jordi Alba 2-0.
Referee: Ovidiu Hategan (ROM)   Attendance: 86,290.

06.11.18   Wembley Stadium, London: Tottenham Hotspur – PSV Eindhoven 2-1 (0-1)
Tottenham Hotspur: Paulo Gazzaniga, Toby Alderweireld, Serge Aurier (75' Kieran Trippier), Benjamin Davies, Davinson Sánchez, Christian Eriksen, Lucas Moura (62' Érik Lamela), Dele Alli, Harry Winks, Son Heung-Min (75' Llorente), Harry Kane. Coach: Mauricio Pochettino.
PSV Eindhoven: Jeroen Zoet, Daniel Schwaab, Nick Viergever, José Angeliño, Denzel Dumfries, Jorrit Hendrix, Gastón Pereiro (73' Donyell Malen), Pablo Rosario, Luuk de Jong (81' Trent Sainsbury), Steven Bergwijn (86' Érick Gutiérrez), Hirving Lozano.
Coach: Mark van Bommel.
Goals: 2' Luuk de Jong 0-1, 78', 89' Harry Kane 1-1, 2-1.
Referee: Ivan Kruzliak (SVK)   Attendance: 46,588.

06.11.18   Stadio Giuseppe Meazza, Milan: Internazionale – FC Barcelona 1-1 (0-0)
Internazionale: Samir Handanovic, Kwadwo Asamoah, Sime Vrsaljko, Stefan de Vrij, Milan Skriniar, Ivan Perisic, Radja Nainggolan (63' Borja Valero), Matías Vecino, Marcelo Brozovic (85' Lautaro Martínez), Mauro Icardi, Matteo Politano (81' Antonio Candreva).
Coach: Luciano Spalletti.
FC Barcelona: Marc-André ter Stegen, Piqué, Jordi Alba, Sergi Roberto, Clément Lenglet, Ivan Rakitic, Sergio Busquets, Philippe Coutinho, Arthur (74' Arturo Vidal), Luis Suárez, Ousmane Dembélé (81' Malcom). Coach: Ernesto Valverde.
Goals: 83' Malcom 0-1, 87' Mauro Icardi 1-1.
Referee: Szymon Marciniak (POL)   Attendance: 70,915.

28.11.18   Philips Stadion, Eindhoven: PSV Eindhoven – FC Barcelona 1-2 (0-0)
PSV Eindhoven: Jeroen Zoet, Daniel Schwaab, Nick Viergever, José Angeliño, Denzel Dumfries, Jorrit Hendrix (71' Érick Gutiérrez), Gastón Pereiro (71' Donyell Malen), Pablo Rosario, Luuk de Jong, Steven Bergwijn (79' Maximiliano Romero), Hirving Lozano.
Coach: Mark van Bommel.
FC Barcelona: Marc-André ter Stegen, Piqué, Jordi Alba, Clément Lenglet, Nélson Semedo, Ivan Rakitic, Arturo Vidal, Sergio Busquets, Philippe Coutinho (69' Malcom), Lionel Messi, Ousmane Dembélé (80' Denis Suárez). Coach: Ernesto Valverde.
Goals: 61' Lionel Messi 0-1, 70' Piqué 0-2, 83' Luuk de Jong 1-2.
Referee: Pavel Královec (CZE)   Attendance: 34,600.

28.11.18   Wembley Stadium, London: Tottenham Hotspur – Internazionale 1-0 (0-0)
Tottenham Hotspur: Hugo Lloris, Jan Vertonghen, Toby Alderweireld, Serge Aurier, Benjamin Davies, Moussa Sissoko, Érik Lamela (70' Christian Eriksen), Lucas Moura (62' Son Heung-Min), Dele Alli, Harry Winks (87' Eric Dier), Harry Kane. Coach: Mauricio Pochettino.
Internazionale: Samir Handanovic, Kwadwo Asamoah, Stefan de Vrij (82' João Miranda), Danilo D'Ambrosio, Milan Skriniar, Ivan Perisic, Radja Nainggolan (44' Borja Valero), Matías Vecino, Marcelo Brozovic, Mauro Icardi, Matteo Politano (83' Keita Baldé).
Coach: Luciano Spalletti.
Goal: 80' Christian Eriksen 1-0.
Referee: Cüneyt Çakir (TUR)   Attendance: 57,132.

11.12.18   Camp Nou, Barcelona: FC Barcelona – Tottenham Hotspur 1-1 (1-0)
FC Barcelona: Jasper Cillessen, Thomas Vermaelen, Clément Lenglet, Nélson Semedo, Juan Miranda, Ivan Rakitic (46' Sergio Busquets), Philippe Coutinho, Arthur, Carles Aleñá, Munir (63' Lionel Messi), Ousmane Dembélé (76' Denis Suárez). Coach: Ernesto Valverde.
Tottenham Hotspur: Hugo Lloris, Jan Vertonghen, Danny Ross, Toby Alderweireld, Kyle Walker-Peters (61' Érik Lamela), Moussa Sissoko, Christian Eriksen, Dele Alli, Harry Winks (83' Llorente), Son Heung-Min (71' Lucas Moura), Harry Kane. Coach: Mauricio Pochettino.
Goals: 7' Ousmane Dembélé 1-0, 85' Lucas Moura 1-1.
Referee: Milorad Mazic (SRB)   Attendance: 69,961.

11.12.18   Stadio Giuseppe Meazza, Milan: Internazionale – PSV Eindhoven 1-1 (0-1)
Internazionale: Samir Handanovic, Kwadwo Asamoah (69' Lautaro Martínez), Stefan de Vrij, Danilo D'Ambrosio, Milan Skriniar, Ivan Perisic, Antonio Candreva (56' Keita Baldé), Borja Valero, Marcelo Brozovic, Mauro Icardi, Matteo Politano (83' Sime Vrsaljko).
Coach: Luciano Spalletti.
PSV Eindhoven: Jeroen Zoet, Nick Viergever, Trent Sainsbury, José Angeliño, Denzel Dumfries, Jorrit Hendrix, Érick Gutiérrez (65' Michal Sadílek), Pablo Rosario, Luuk de Jong, Steven Bergwijn (71' Donyell Malen), Hirving Lozano (90+5' Gastón Pereiro).
Coach: Mark van Bommel.
Goals: 13' Hirving Lozano 0-1, 73' Mauro Icardi 1-1.
Referee: Felix Zwayer (GER)   Attendance: 62,533.

GROUP C

18.09.18   Anfield, Liverpool: Liverpool FC – Paris Saint-Germain 3-2 (2-1)
Liverpool FC: Alisson, Virgil van Dijk, Andrew Robertson, Joseph Gomez, Trent Alexander-Arnold, James Milner, Georginio Wijnaldum, Jordan Henderson, Daniel Sturridge (72' Roberto Firmino), Mohamed Salah (85' Xherdan Shaqiri), Sadio Mané (90+3' Fabinho).
Coach: Jürgen Klopp.
Paris Saint-Germain: Alphonse Aréola, Thiago Silva, Thomas Meunier, Marquinhos, Juan Bernat, Presnel Kimpembe, Ángel Di María (80' Eric Maxim Choupo-Moting), Adrien Rabiot, Edinson Cavani (80' Julian Draxler), Neymar, Kylian Mbappé. Coach: Thomas Tuchel.
Goals: 30' Daniel Sturridge 1-0, 36' James Milner 2-0 (p), 40' Thomas Meunier 2-1, 83' Kylian Mbappé 2-2, 90+2' Roberto Firmino 3-2.
Referee: Cüneyt Çakir (TUR)   Attendance: 52,478.

18.09.18   Stadion Rajko Mitic, Beograd: Crvena Zvezda Beograd – SSC Napoli 0-0
Crvena Zvezda Beograd: Milan Borjan, Vujadin Savic, Milan Rodic, Milos Degenek, Filip Stojkovic, Marko Marin (87' Veljko Simic), Nenad Krsticic, Goran Causic, Branko Jovicic (56' Dusan Jovancic), Richmond Boakye (81' Milan Pavkov), Mohamed Ben Nabouhane.
Coach: Vladan Milojevic.
SSC Napoli: David Ospina, Raúl Albiol, Mário Rui, Kalidou Koulibaly, Elseid Hysaj, Allan (61' Dries Mertens), Piotr Zielinski (75' Marek Hamsík), Fabián Ruiz, José Callejón (75' Adam Ounas), Lorenzo Insigne, Arkadiusz Milik. Coach: Carlo Ancelotti.
Referee: Szymon Marciniak (POL)   Attendance: 49,112.

03.10.18   Parc des Princes, Paris: Paris Saint-Germain – Crvena Zvezda Beograd 6-1 (4-0)
Paris Saint-Germain: Alphonse Aréola, Thiago Silva (76' Thilo Kehrer), Thomas Meunier, Juan Bernat, Presnel Kimpembe, Ángel Di María, Marco Verratti, Adrien Rabiot, Edinson Cavani, Neymar (82' Julian Draxler), Kylian Mbappé (76' Eric Maxim Choupo-Moting). Coach: Thomas Tuchel.
Crvena Zvezda Beograd: Milan Borjan, Vujadin Savic (46' Srdjan Babic), Milan Rodic, Milos Degenek, Filip Stojkovic, Marko Marin, Nenad Krsticic, Goran Causic, Veljko Simic (46' Milan Pavkov), Branko Jovicic, Mohamed Ben Nabouhane (73' Lorenzo Ebecilio). Coach: Vladan Milojevic.
Goals: 20', 22' Neymar 1-0, 2-0, 37' Edinson Cavani 3-0, 42' Ángel Di María 4-0, 70' Kylian Mbappé 5-0, 74' Marko Marin 5-1, 81' Neymar 6-1.
Referee: Artur Soares Dias (POR)   Attendance: 39,979.

03.10.18   Stadio San Paolo, Napoli: SSC Napoli – Liverpool FC 1-0 (0-0)
SSC Napoli: David Ospina, Raúl Albiol, Nikola Maksimovic, Mário Rui, Kalidou Koulibaly, Marek Hamsík (81' Piotr Zielinski), Allan, Fabián Ruiz (68' Simone Verdi), José Callejón, Lorenzo Insigne, Arkadiusz Milik (68' Dries Mertens). Coach: Carlo Ancelotti.
Liverpool FC: Alisson, Virgil van Dijk, Andrew Robertson, Joseph Gomez, Trent Alexander-Arnold, James Milner (76' Fabinho), Georginio Wijnaldum, Naby Keïta (19' Jordan Henderson), Roberto Firmino, Mohamed Salah, Sadio Mané (89' Daniel Sturridge). Coach: Jürgen Klopp.
Goal: 90' Lorenzo Insigne 1-0.
Referee: Viktor Kassai (HUN)   Attendance: 37,057.

24.10.18   Parc des Princes, Paris: Paris Saint-Germain – SSC Napoli 2-2 (0-1)
Paris Saint-Germain: Alphonse Aréola, Thomas Meunier, Marquinhos, Juan Bernat (46' Thilo Kehrer), Presnel Kimpembe, Ángel Di María, Marco Verratti (83' Moussa Diaby), Adrien Rabiot, Edinson Cavani (76' Julian Draxler), Neymar, Kylian Mbappé. Coach: Thomas Tuchel.
SSC Napoli: David Ospina, Raúl Albiol, Nikola Maksimovic, Mário Rui, Kalidou Koulibaly, Marek Hamsík, Allan, Fabián Ruiz, Dries Mertens (84' Arkadiusz Milik), José Callejón (88' Marko Rog), Lorenzo Insigne (53' Piotr Zielinski). Coach: Carlo Ancelotti.
Goals: 29' Lorenzo Insigne 0-1, 61' Mário Rui 1-1 (og), 77' Dries Mertens 1-2, 90+3' Ángel Di María 2-2.
Referee: Felix Zwayer (GER)   Attendance: 46,274.

24.10.18   Anfield, Liverpool: Liverpool FC – Crvena Zvezda Beograd 4-0 (2-0)
Liverpool FC: Alisson, Virgil van Dijk, Andrew Robertson (82' Alberto Moreno), Joseph Gomez, Trent Alexander-Arnold, Georginio Wijnaldum, Fabinho, Xherdan Shaqiri (68' Adam Lallana), Roberto Firmino, Mohamed Salah (73' Daniel Sturridge), Sadio Mané. Coach: Jürgen Klopp.
Crvena Zvezda Beograd: Milan Borjan, Milos Degenek, Filip Stojkovic, Marko Gobeljic, Srdjan Babic, Nenad Krsticic, Lorenzo Ebecilio (65' Dusan Jovancic), Slavoljub Srnic, Branko Jovicic (75' Goran Causic), Richmond Boakye, Mohamed Ben Nabouhane (81' Veljko Simic). Coach: Vladan Milojevic.
Goals: 20' Roberto Firmino 1-0, 45', 51' Mohamed Salah 2-0, 3-0 (p), 80' Sadio Mané 4-0.
Referee: Daniel Siebert (GER)   Attendance: 53,024.

Sadio Mané missed a penalty kick (76').

06.11.18   Stadion Rajko Mitic, Beograd: Crvena Zvezda Beograd – Liverpool FC 2-0 (2-0)
Crvena Zvezda Beograd: Milan Borjan, Vujadin Savic, Milan Rodic, Milos Degenek, Filip Stojkovic (59' Marko Gobeljic), Marko Marin (64' Goran Causic), Nenad Krsticic (73' Branko Jovicic), Slavoljub Srnic, Dusan Jovancic, Mohamed Ben Nabouhane, Milan Pavkov.
Coach: Vladan Milojevic.
Liverpool FC: Alisson, Joel Matip, Virgil van Dijk, Andrew Robertson, Trent Alexander-Arnold (46' Joseph Gomez), James Milner, Georginio Wijnaldum, Adam Lallana (79' Divock Origi), Daniel Sturridge (46' Roberto Firmino), Mohamed Salah, Sadio Mané.
Coach: Jürgen Klopp.
Goals: 22', 29' Milan Pavkov 1-0, 2-0.
Referee: Antonio Mateu Lahoz (ESP)   Attendance: 51,318.

06.11.18   Stadio San Paolo, Napoli: SSC Napoli – Paris Saint-Germain 1-1 (0-1)
SSC Napoli: David Ospina, Raúl Albiol, Nikola Maksimovic (76' Elseid Hysaj), Mário Rui, Kalidou Koulibaly, Marek Hamsík, Allan, Fabián Ruiz (71' Piotr Zielinski), Dries Mertens (83' Adam Ounas), José Callejón, Lorenzo Insigne. Coach: Carlo Ancelotti.
Paris Saint-Germain: Gianluigi Buffon, Thiago Silva, Thomas Meunier (73' Presnel Kimpembe), Marquinhos, Juan Bernat, Thilo Kehrer (90+2' Eric Maxim Choupo-Moting), Ángel Di María (77' Edinson Cavani), Marco Verratti, Julian Draxler, Neymar, Kylian Mbappé. Coach: Thomas Tuchel.
Goals: 45+2' Juan Bernat 0-1, 63' Lorenzo Insigne 1-1 (p).
Referee: Björn Kuipers (HOL)   Attendance: 55,489.

28.11.18   Parc des Princes, Paris: Paris Saint-Germain – Liverpool FC 2-1 (2-1)
Paris Saint-Germain: Gianluigi Buffon, Thiago Silva, Marquinhos, Juan Bernat, Presnel Kimpembe, Thilo Kehrer, Ángel Di María (65' Dani Alves), Marco Verratti, Edinson Cavani (65' Eric Maxim Choupo-Moting), Neymar, Kylian Mbappé (85' Adrien Rabiot).
Coach: Thomas Tuchel.
Liverpool FC: Alisson, Dejan Lovren, Virgil van Dijk, Andrew Robertson, Joseph Gomez, James Milner (77' Xherdan Shaqiri), Georginio Wijnaldum (66' Naby Keïta), Jordan Henderson, Roberto Firmino (71' Daniel Sturridge), Mohamed Salah, Sadio Mané.
Coach: Jürgen Klopp.
Goals: 13' Juan Bernat 1-0, 37' Neymar 2-0, 45+1' James Milner 2-1 (p).
Referee: Szymon Marciniak (POL)   Attendance: 46,880.

28.11.18   Stadio San Paolo, Napoli: SSC Napoli – Crvena Zvezda Beograd 3-1 (2-0)
SSC Napoli: David Ospina, Raúl Albiol (46' Elseid Hysaj), Nikola Maksimovic, Mário Rui, Kalidou Koulibaly, Marek Hamsík, Allan, Fabián Ruiz, Dries Mertens, José Callejón (86' Marko Rog), Lorenzo Insigne (77' Piotr Zielinski). Coach: Carlo Ancelotti.
Crvena Zvezda Beograd: Milan Borjan, Milan Rodic, Milos Degenek, Marko Gobeljic, Srdjan Babic, Marko Marin, Nenad Krsticic, Slavoljub Srnic (64' Dusan Jovancic), Veljko Simic (77' Lorenzo Ebecilio), Nikola Stojiljkovic (46' Dejan Joveljic), Mohamed Ben Nabouhane.
Coach: Vladan Milojevic.
Goals: 11' Marek Hamsík 1-0, 33', 52' Dries Mertens 2-0, 3-0,
57' Mohamed Ben Nabouhane 3-1.
Referee: Jesús Gil Manzano (ESP)   Attendance: 44,470.

11.12.18 Anfield, Liverpool: Liverpool FC – SSC Napoli 1-0 (1-0)
Liverpool FC: Alisson, Joel Matip, Virgil van Dijk, Andrew Robertson, Trent Alexander-Arnold (90' Dejan Lovren), James Milner (85' Fabinho), Georginio Wijnaldum, Jordan Henderson, Roberto Firmino (79' Naby Keïta), Mohamed Salah, Sadio Mané.
Coach: Jürgen Klopp.
SSC Napoli: David Ospina, Raúl Albiol, Nikola Maksimovic, Mário Rui (70' Faouzi Ghoulam), Kalidou Koulibaly, Marek Hamsík, Allan, Fabián Ruiz (62' Piotr Zielinski), Dries Mertens (67' Arkadiusz Milik), José Callejón, Lorenzo Insigne. Coach: Carlo Ancelotti.
Goal: 34' Mohamed Salah 1-0.
Referee: Damir Skomina (SVN)   Attendance: 52,015.

11.12.18 Stadion Rajko Mitic, Beograd:
              Crvena Zvezda Beograd – Paris Saint-Germain 1-4 (0-2)
Crvena Zvezda Beograd: Milan Borjan, Milan Rodic, Milos Degenek, Filip Stojkovic, Marko Gobeljic, Marko Marin (86' Dejan Joveljic), Goran Causic, Veljko Simic (72' Lorenzo Ebecilio), Dusan Jovancic, Mohamed Ben Nabouhane, Milan Pavkov (72' Richmond Boakye). Coach: Vladan Milojevic.
Paris Saint-Germain: Gianluigi Buffon, Thiago Silva, Marquinhos, Juan Bernat, Presnel Kimpembe, Thilo Kehrer, Ángel Di María (88' Julian Draxler), Marco Verratti (83' Adrien Rabiot), Edinson Cavani, Neymar, Kylian Mbappé. Coach: Thomas Tuchel.
Goals: 10' Edinson Cavani 0-1, 40' Neymar 0-2, 56' Marko Gobeljic 1-2, 74' Marquinhos 1-3, 90+2' Kylian Mbappé 1-4.
Referee: William Collum (SCO)   Attendance: 48,357.

GROUP D

18.09.18 Türk Telekom Stadyumu, Istanbul: Galatasaray – Lokomotiv Moscow 3-0 (1-0)
Galatasaray: Fernando Muslera, Serdar Aziz, Yuto Nagatomo, Martin Linnes, Ryan Donk, Fernando, Younès Belhanda (73' Maicon), Papa Alioune "Badou" N'Diaye, Garry Rodrigues (90+1' Selçuk Inan), Emre Akbaba, Eren Derdiyok (82' Henry Onyekuru).
Coach: Fatih Terim.
Lokomotiv Moscow: Guilherme, Vedran Corluka, Benedikt Höwedes, Solomon Kverkvelia, Brian Idowu, Jefferson Farfán, Manuel Fernandes, Igor Denisov, Vladislav Ignatyev (69' Éder), Grzegorz Krychowiak, Aleksey Miranchuk (86' Anton Miranchuk).
Coach: Yuriy Semin.
Goals: 9' Garry Rodrigues 1-0, 67' Eren Derdiyok 2-0, 90+4' Selçuk Inan 3-0 (p).
Referee: Gianluca Rocchi (ITA)   Attendance: 43,542.
Sent off: 87' Papa Alioune "Badou" N'Diaye.

18.09.18 VELTINS-Arena, Gelsenkirchen: FC Schalke 04 – FC Porto 1-1 (0-0)
FC Schalke 04: Ralf Fährmann, Naldo, Matija Nastasic, Salif Sané, Daniel Caligiuri, Nabil Bentaleb, Alessandro Schöpf, Suat Serdar (84' Amine Harit), Weston McKennie, Mark Uth (65' Yevhen Konoplyanka), Breel Embolo (72' Guido Burgstaller).
Coach: Domenico Tedesco.
FC Porto: Iker Casillas, Maxi Pereira, Alex Telles, Felipe Monteiro, Éder Militão, Héctor Herrera, Danilo Pereira, Otavinho (90' Hernâni), Yacine Brahimi (82' Sérgio Oliveira), Vincent Aboubakar (60' Jesús Corona), Moussa Marega. Coach: Sérgio Conceição.
Goals: 64' Breel Embolo 1-0, 75' Otavinho 1-1 (p).
Referee: Jesús Gil Manzano (ESP)   Attendance: 45,755.

Alex Telles missed a penalty kick (13').

03.10.18   RZD Arena, Moscow: Lokomotiv Moscow – FC Schalke 04 0-1 (0-0)
Lokomotiv Moscow: Guilherme, Benedikt Höwedes, Solomon Kverkvelia, Brian Idowu, Manuel Fernandes, Vladislav Ignatyev, Grzegorz Krychowiak, Dmitry Barinov, Aleksey Miranchuk (83' Rifat Zhemaletdinov), Anton Miranchuk (72' Igor Denisov), Éder.
Coach: Yuriy Semin.
FC Schalke 04: Ralf Fährmann, Naldo, Salif Sané, Hamza Mendyl, Sebastian Rudy (55' Nabil Bentaleb), Daniel Caligiuri, Yevhen Konoplyanka, Omar Mascarell (46' Suat Serdar), Weston McKennie, Mark Uth, Breel Embolo (72' Guido Burgstaller). Coach: Domenico Tedesco.
Goal: 88' Weston McKennie 0-1.
Referee: Anthony Taylor (ENG)   Attendance: 21,471.

03.10.18   Estádio do Dragão, Porto: FC Porto – Galatasaray 1-0 (0-0)
FC Porto: Iker Casillas, Maxi Pereira, Alex Telles, Felipe Monteiro, Éder Militão, Héctor Herrera (89' Sérgio Oliveira), Danilo Pereira, Otavinho (80' André Pereira), Yacine Brahimi, Jesús Corona (69' Óliver Torres), Moussa Marega. Coach: Sérgio Conceição.
Galatasaray: Fernando Muslera, Serdar Aziz, Yuto Nagatomo, Maicon, Martin Linnes, Ryan Donk (68' Selçuk Inan), Fernando (86' Yunus Akgün), Younès Belhanda (74' Sofiane Féghouli), Garry Rodrigues, Sinan Gümüs, Henry Onyekuru. Coach: Fatih Terim.
Goal: 49' Moussa Marega 1-0.
Referee: Michael Oliver (ENG)   Attendance: 42,711.

24.10.18   RZD Arena, Moscow: Lokomotiv Moscow – FC Porto 1-3 (1-2)
Lokomotiv Moscow: Guilherme, Benedikt Höwedes, Solomon Kverkvelia, Manuel Fernandes (66' Rifat Zhemaletdinov), Igor Denisov, Vladislav Ignatyev, Grzegorz Krychowiak, Dmitry Barinov, Aleksey Miranchuk, Anton Miranchuk, Éder (81' Mikhail Lysov).
Coach: Yuriy Semin.
FC Porto: Iker Casillas, Maxi Pereira, Alex Telles, Felipe Monteiro, Éder Militão, Héctor Herrera, Danilo Pereira, Óliver Torres (83' Riechedly Bazoer), Yacine Brahimi (82' Adrián), Jesús Corona (69' André Pereira), Moussa Marega. Coach: Sérgio Conceição.
Goals: 26' Moussa Marega 0-1 (p), 35' Héctor Herrera 0-2, 38' Anton Miranchuk 1-2, 47' Jesús Corona 1-3.
Referee: Bobby Madden (SCO)   Attendance: 16,034.
Sent off: 76' Solomon Kverkvelia.

Manuel Fernandes missed a penalty kick (10').

24.10.18   Türk Telekom Stadyumu, Istanbul: Galatasaray – FC Schalke 04 0-0
Galatasaray: Fernando Muslera, Yuto Nagatomo (81' Ömer Bayram), Maicon, Martin Linnes, Ozan Kabak, Ryan Donk, Younès Belhanda, Papa Alioune "Badou" N'Diaye, Garry Rodrigues, Eren Derdiyok (70' Mugdat Çelik), Sinan Gümüs (61' Selçuk Inan).
Coach: Fatih Terim.
FC Schalke 04: Alexander Nübel, Matija Nastasic, Benjamin Stambouli, Salif Sané, Hamza Mendyl, Sebastian Rudy, Daniel Caligiuri, Yevhen Konoplyanka (77' Steven Skrzybski), Suat Serdar, Mark Uth (90' Guido Burgstaller), Breel Embolo (82' Weston McKennie).
Coach: Domenico Tedesco.
Referee: Benoît Bastien (FRA)   Attendance: 46,667.

06.11.18 Estádio do Dragão, Porto: FC Porto – Lokomotiv Moscow 4-1 (2-0)
FC Porto: Iker Casillas, Maxi Pereira, Alex Telles, Felipe Monteiro, Éder Militão, Héctor Herrera, Danilo Pereira, Óliver Torres (85' Sérgio Oliveira), Yacine Brahimi (68' Otavinho), Jesús Corona (77' Hernâni), Moussa Marega. Coach: Sérgio Conceição.
Lokomotiv Moscow: Guilherme, Verdan Corluka, Benedikt Höwedes, Brian Idowu, Manuel Fernandes (46' Jefferson Farfán), Igor Denisov, Vladislav Ignatyev, Grzegorz Krychowiak, Aleksey Miranchuk, Anton Miranchuk, Éder (71' Fyodor Smolov). Coach: Yuriy Semin.
Goals: 2' Héctor Herrera 1-0, 42' Moussa Marega 2-0, 59' Jefferson Farfán 2-1, 67' Jesús Corona 3-1, 90+3' Otavinho 4-1.
Referee: Davide Massa (ITA)   Attendance: 34,616.

06.11.18 VELTINS-Arena, Gelsenkirchen: FC Schalke 04 – Galatasaray 2-0 (1-0)
FC Schalke 04: Alexander Nübel, Matija Nastasic, Benjamin Stambouli, Salif Sané, Sebastian Rudy (76' Suat Serdar), Daniel Caligiuri, Alessandro Schöpf, Amine Harit (56' Weston McKennie), Guido Burgstaller, Mark Uth (63' Nabil Bentaleb), Breel Embolo.
Coach: Domenico Tedesco.
Galatasaray: Fernando Muslera, Serdar Aziz, Mariano, Martin Linnes (46' Ömer Bayram), Ozan Kabak, Ryan Donk, Younès Belhanda, Papa Alioune "Badou" N'Diaye, Garry Rodrigues (63' Selçuk Inan), Sinan Gümüs (72' Mugdat Çelik), Henry Onyekuru. Coach: Fatih Terim.
Goals: 4' Guido Burgstaller 1-0, 57' Mark Uth 2-0.
Referee: William Collum (SCO)   Attendance: 54,740.

28.11.18 RZD Arena, Moscow: Lokomotiv Moscow – Galatasaray 2-0 (1-0)
Lokomotiv Moscow: Guilherme, Verdan Corluka, Solomon Kverkvelia, Jefferson Farfán (90' Boris Rotenberg), Igor Denisov, Maciej Rybus, Vladislav Ignatyev, Grzegorz Krychowiak, Aleksey Miranchuk (77' Dmitry Barinov), Anton Miranchuk, Fyodor Smolov (88' Éder). Coach: Yuriy Semin.
Galatasaray: Fernando Muslera, Serdar Aziz, Yuto Nagatomo, Martin Linnes (89' Mariano), Ozan Kabak, Ryan Donk, Fernando (59' Sofiane Féghouli), Papa Alioune "Badou" N'Diaye (68' Selçuk Inan), Garry Rodrigues, Eren Derdiyok, Henry Onyekuru. Coach: Fatih Terim.
Goals: 43' Ryan Donk 1-0 (og), 54' Vladislav Ignatyev 2-0.
Referee: Antonio Mateu Lahoz (ESP)   Attendance: 14,037.

28.11.18 Estádio do Dragão, Porto: FC Porto – FC Schalke 04 3-1 (0-0)
FC Porto: Iker Casillas, Maxi Pereira, Alex Telles, Felipe Monteiro, Éder Militão, Héctor Herrera (85' Hernâni), Danilo Pereira, Óliver Torres, Yacine Brahimi (74' Adrián), Jesús Corona (79' Otavinho), Moussa Marega. Coach: Sérgio Conceição.
FC Schalke 04: Ralf Fährmann, Naldo, Matija Nastasic, Benjamin Stambouli (71' Sebastian Rudy), Hamza Mendyl, Daniel Caligiuri (62' Alessandro Schöpf), Yevhen Konoplyanka, Omar Mascarell, Nabil Bentaleb, Franco Di Santo, Steven Skrzybski (46' Amine Harit). Coach: Domenico Tedesco.
Goals: 52' Éder Militão 1-0, 55' Jesús Corona 2-0, 89' Nabil Bentaleb 2-1 (p), 90+4' Moussa Marega 3-1.
Referee: Ovidiu Hategan (ROM)   Attendance: 41,603.

11.12.18 Türk Telekom Stadyumu, Istanbul: Galatasaray – FC Porto 2-3 (1-2)
Galatasaray: Fernando Muslera, Mariano, Yuto Nagatomo, Maicon, Ozan Kabak, Ryan Donk (46' Henry Onyekuru), Sofiane Féghouli (89' Mugdat Çelik), Fernando, Papa Alioune "Badou" N'Diaye, Garry Rodrigues, Eren Derdiyok. Coach: Fatih Terim.
FC Porto: Iker Casillas, Maxi Pereira, Alex Telles, Felipe Monteiro, Diogo Leite, Héctor Herrera, Sérgio Oliveira (82' Chidozie Awaziem), Danilo Pereira, Adrián (73' André Pereira), Hernâni (73' Jorge), Moussa Marega. Coach: Sérgio Conceição.
Goals: 17' Felipe Monteiro 0-1, 42' Moussa Marega 0-2 (p), 45+1' Sofiane Féghouli 1-2 (p), 57' Sérgio Oliveira 1-3, 65' Eren Derdiyok 2-3.
Referee: Aleksei Kulbakov (BLS)   Attendance: 33,972.

Sofiane Féghouli missed a penalty kick (67').

11.12.18   VELTINS-Arena, Gelsenkirchen: FC Schalke 04 – Lokomotiv Moscow 1-0 (0-0)
FC Schalke 04: Ralf Fährmann, Naldo, Matija Nastasic, Benjamin Stambouli, Hamza Mendyl (16' Abdul Rahman Baba), Yevhen Konoplyanka, Omar Mascarell, Alessandro Schöpf, Suat Serdar, Benjamin Goller (59' Amine Harit), Cedric Teuchert (72' Ahmed Kutucu). Coach: Domenico Tedesco.
Lokomotiv Moscow: Guilherme, Benedikt Höwedes, Solomon Kverkvelia, Jefferson Farfán (80' Fyodor Smolov), Igor Denisov, Maciej Rybus, Vladislav Ignatyev, Grzegorz Krychowiak, Dmitry Barinov, Aleksey Miranchuk, Éder (46' Anton Miranchuk). Coach: Yuriy Semin.
Goal: 90+1' Alessandro Schöpf 1-0.
Referee: Anastasios Sidiropoulos (GRE)   Attendance: 48,883.

GROUP E

19.09.18   Johan Cruijff ArenA, Amsterdam: AFC Ajax – AEK Athens 3-0 (0-0)
AFC Ajax: André Onana, Daley Blind, Nicolás Tagliafico, Lasse Schöne, Hakim Ziyech, Carel Eiting, Noussair Mazraoui, Frenkie de Jong, Klaas Jan Huntelaar (62' Donny van de Beek), Dusan Tadic, David Neres (78' Kasper Dolberg). Coach: Erik ten Hag.
AEK Athens: Vassilis Barkas, Niklas Hult, Konstantinos-Vassilios Lambropoulos, Uros Cosic, Marios Oikonomou, Petros Mandalos, Michalis Bakakis (70' Giannis Gianniotas), André Simões, Konstantinos Galanopoulos (61' Alef), Viktor Klonaridis, Ezequiel Ponce (81' Georgios Giakoumakis). Coach: Marinos Ouzounidis.
Goals: 46' Nicolás Tagliafico 1-0, 77' Donny van de Beek 2-0, 90' Nicolás Tagliafico 3-0.
Referee: Carlos del Cerro Grande (ESP)   Attendance: 52,285.

19.09.18   Estádio do Sport Lisboa e Benfica, Lisboa:
              SL Benfica – FC Bayern München 0-2 (0-1)
SL Benfica: Odisseas Vlachodimos, André Almeida, Jardel, Álex Grimaldo, Rúben Dias, Ljubomir Fejsa, Pizzi (62' Rafa Silva), Eduardo Salvio (62' Gabriel), Franco Cervi, Gedson Fernandes (76' Andrija Zivkovic), Haris Seferovic. Coach: Rui Vitória.
FC Bayern München: Manuel Neuer, Jérôme Boateng, Mats Hummels, David Alaba, Joshua Kimmich, Arjen Robben, Franck Ribéry (62' Serge Gnabry), Javi Martínez (88' Thomas Müller), James Rodríguez (79' Leon Goretzka), Renato Sanches, Robert Lewandowski. Coach: Niko Kovac.
Goals: 10' Robert Lewandowski 0-1, 54' Renato Sanches 0-2.
Referee: Antonio Mateu Lahoz (ESP)   Attendance: 60,274.

02.10.18   Allianz Arena, München: FC Bayern München – AFC Ajax 1-1 (1-1)
FC Bayern München: Manuel Neuer, Jérôme Boateng, Mats Hummels (90+3' Niklas Süle), David Alaba, Joshua Kimmich, Arjen Robben (62' James Rodríguez), Franck Ribéry (74' Serge Gnabry), Javi Martínez, Thiago Alcântara, Thomas Müller, Robert Lewandowski. Coach: Niko Kovac.
AFC Ajax: André Onana, Daley Blind, Nicolás Tagliafico, Matthijs de Ligt, Max Wöber, Lasse Schöne, Hakim Ziyech, Donny van de Beek (75' Dani de Wit), Noussair Mazraoui, Dusan Tadic, David Neres (85' Kasper Dolberg). Coach: Erik ten Hag.
Goals: 4' Mats Hummels 1-0, 22' Noussair Mazraoui 1-1.
Referee: Pavel Královec (CZE)   Attendance: 70,000.

02.10.18   Olympiako Stadio Spyros Louis, Athens: AEK Athens – SL Benfica 2-3 (0-2)
AEK Athens: Vassilis Barkas, Dmitro Chigrinskiy, Niklas Hult, Marios Oikonomou (68' Uros Cosic), Petros Mandalos, Michalis Bakakis, André Simões (79' Rodrigo Galo), Konstantinos Galanopoulos, Anastasios Bakasetas, Viktor Klonaridis, Ezequiel Ponce (60' Georgios Giakoumakis). Coach: Marinos Ouzounidis.
SL Benfica: Odisseas Vlachodimos, André Almeida, Álex Grimaldo, Rúben Dias, Germán Conti, Ljubomir Fejsa, Pizzi (62' Alfa Semedo), Eduardo Salvio (46' Christian Lema), Rafa Silva (84' Franco Cervi), Gedson Fernandes, Haris Seferovic. Coach: Rui Vitória.
Goals: 6' Haris Seferovic 0-1, 15' Álex Grimaldo 0-2, 53', 63' Viktor Klonaridis 1-2, 2-2, 74' Alfa Semedo 2-3.
Referee: Orel Grinfeld (ISR)   Attendance: 31,154.
Sent off: 45+4' Rúben Dias.

23.10.18   Olympiako Stadio Spyros Louis, Athens:
         AEK Athens – FC Bayern München 0-2 (0-0)
AEK Athens: Vassilis Barkas, Dmitro Chigrinskiy, Niklas Hult, Konstantinos-Vassilios Lambropoulos, Petros Mandalos (76' Alef), Michalis Bakakis, André Simões, Konstantinos Galanopoulos (84' Rodrigo Galo), Anastasios Bakasetas, Viktor Klonaridis (64' Lucas Boyé), Ezequiel Ponce. Coach: Marinos Ouzounidis.
FC Bayern München: Manuel Neuer, Rafinha, Mats Hummels, Niklas Süle, Joshua Kimmich, Arjen Robben, Javi Martínez, James Rodríguez (62' Leon Goretzka), Thiago Alcântara, Serge Gnabry (75' Thomas Müller), Robert Lewandowski (84' Sandro Wagner). Coach: Niko Kovac.
Goals: 61' Javi Martínez 0-1, 63' Robert Lewandowski 0-2.
Referee: Aleksei Kulbakov (BLS)   Attendance: 61,221.

23.10.18   Johan Cruijff ArenA, Amsterdam: AFC Ajax – SL Benfica 1-0 (0-0)
AFC Ajax: André Onana, Daley Blind, Nicolás Tagliafico, Matthijs de Ligt, Lasse Schöne, Hakim Ziyech, Donny van de Beek (88' David Neres), Noussair Mazraoui, Frenkie de Jong, Dusan Tadic, Kasper Dolberg. Coach: Erik ten Hag.
SL Benfica: Odisseas Vlachodimos, André Almeida, Jardel, Álex Grimaldo, Germán Conti, Ljubomir Fejsa, Pizzi (79' Gabriel), Eduardo Salvio, Rafa Silva (90' Franco Cervi), Gedson Fernandes, Haris Seferovic. Coach: Rui Vitória.
Goal: 90+2' Noussair Mazraoui 1-0.
Referee: Ruddy Buquet (FRA)   Attendance: 52,489.

07.11.18 Allianz Arena, München: FC Bayern München – AEK Athens 2-0 (1-0)
FC Bayern München: Manuel Neuer, Jérôme Boateng, Mats Hummels, David Alaba, Joshua Kimmich, Franck Ribéry (84' Rafinha), Javi Martínez, Leon Goretzka, Serge Gnabry (87' Renato Sanches), Thomas Müller, Robert Lewandowski (90+1' Sandro Wagner).
Coach: Niko Kovac.
AEK Athens: Vassilis Barkas, Dmitro Chigrinskiy, Niklas Hult, Konstantinos-Vassilios Lambropoulos, Uros Cosic, Petros Mandalos (80' Lucas Boyé), Michalis Bakakis, André Simões, Alef (67' Erik Morán), Konstantinos Galanopoulos (78' Rodrigo Galo), Ezequiel Ponce. Coach: Marinos Ouzounidis.
Goals: 31', 71' Robert Lewandowski 1-0 (p), 2-0.
Referee: Matej Jug (SVN)   Attendance: 70,000.

07.11.18 Estádio do Sport Lisboa e Benfica, Lisboa: SL Benfica – AFC Ajax 1-1 (1-0)
SL Benfica: Odisseas Vlachodimos, André Almeida, Jardel, Álex Grimaldo, Rúben Dias, Ljubomir Fejsa, Eduardo Salvio (48' Rafa Silva), Gabriel, Franco Cervi, Gedson Fernandes (75' Pizzi), Jonas (55' Haris Seferovic). Coach: Rui Vitória.
AFC Ajax: André Onana, Daley Blind, Nicolás Tagliafico, Matthijs de Ligt, Lasse Schöne, Hakim Ziyech, Donny van de Beek, Noussair Mazraoui, Frenkie de Jong (86' Max Wöber), Dusan Tadic, David Neres (74' Kasper Dolberg). Coach: Erik ten Hag.
Goals: 29' Jonas 1-0, 61' Dusan Tadic 1-1.
Referee: Gianluca Rocchi (ITA)   Attendance: 51,328.

27.11.18 Olympiako Stadio Spyros Louis, Athens: AEK Athens – AFC Ajax 0-2 (0-0)
AEK Athens: Vassilis Barkas, Dmitro Chigrinskiy, Niklas Hult, Rodrigo Galo (73' Lucas Boyé), Marios Oikonomou, Petros Mandalos (78' Viktor Klonaridis), Michalis Bakakis, Alef, Konstantinos Galanopoulos, Marko Livaja, Ezequiel Ponce (82' Georgios Giakoumakis).
Coach: Marinos Ouzounidis.
AFC Ajax: André Onana, Daley Blind, Matthijs de Ligt, Max Wöber, Lasse Schöne, Donny van de Beek (86' Zakaria Labyad), Noussair Mazraoui (82' Rasmus Kristensen), Frenkie de Jong, Dusan Tadic, Kasper Dolberg (62' Klaas Jan Huntelaar), David Neres.
Coach: Erik ten Hag.
Goals: 68', 72' Dusan Tadic 0-1 (p), 0-2.
Referee: Michael Oliver (ENG)   Attendance: 25,756.
Sent off: 67' Marko Livaja.

27.11.18 Allianz Arena, München: FC Bayern München – SL Benfica 5-1 (3-0)
FC Bayern München: Manuel Neuer, Rafinha, Jérôme Boateng, David Alaba, Niklas Süle, Joshua Kimmich, Arjen Robben (72' Renato Sanches), Franck Ribéry (78' Sandro Wagner), Leon Goretzka, Thomas Müller (81' Jeong Woo-Yeong), Robert Lewandowski.
Coach: Niko Kovac.
SL Benfica: Odisseas Vlachodimos, André Almeida, Álex Grimaldo, Rúben Dias, Germán Conti, Ljubomir Fejsa (76' Alfa Semedo), Pizzi (46' Gedson Fernandes), Gabriel, Rafa Silva, Franco Cervi, Jonas (59' Haris Seferovic). Coach: Rui Vitória.
Goals: 13', 30' Arjen Robben 1-0, 2-0, 36' Robert Lewandowski 3-0,
46' Gedson Fernandes 3-1, 51' Robert Lewandowski 4-1, 76' Franck Ribéry 5-1.
Referee: Daniele Orsato (ITA)   Attendance: 70,000.

12.12.18 Johan Cruijff ArenA, Amsterdam: AFC Ajax – FC Bayern München 3-3 (0-1)
AFC Ajax: André Onana, Daley Blind, Nicolás Tagliafico, Matthijs de Ligt, Max Wöber, Hakim Ziyech, Donny van de Beek (78' Kasper Dolberg), Noussair Mazraoui, Frenkie de Jong, Dusan Tadic, David Neres (89' Klaas Jan Huntelaar). Coach: Erik ten Hag.
FC Bayern München: Manuel Neuer, Rafinha, Jérôme Boateng, David Alaba, Niklas Süle, Joshua Kimmich, Franck Ribéry (71' Kingsley Coman), Leon Goretzka (89' Renato Sanches), Serge Gnabry (62' Thiago Alcântara), Thomas Müller, Robert Lewandowski.
Coach: Niko Kovac.
Goals: 13' Robert Lewandowski 0-1, 61', 82' Dusan Tadic 1-1, 2-1 (p),
87' Robert Lewandowski 2-2 (p), 90' Kingsley Coman 2-3, 90+5' Nicolás Tagliafico 3-3.
Referee: Clément Turpin (FRA)   Attendance: 52,244.
Sent off: 67' Max Wöber, 75' Thomas Müller.

12.12.18 Estádio do Sport Lisboa e Benfica, Lisboa: SL Benfica – AEK Athens 1-0 (0-0)
SL Benfica: Odisseas Vlachodimos, André Almeida, Jardel, Álex Grimaldo, Rúben Dias, Pizzi (59' Franco Cervi), Rafa Silva (35' Andrija Zivkovic), Gedson Fernandes, Alfa Semedo, Haris Seferovic, João Félix (77' Nicolás Castillo). Coach: Rui Vitória.
AEK Athens: Vassilis Barkas, Dmitro Chigrinskiy, Niklas Hult, Uros Cosic, Marios Oikonomou, Erik Morán (77' Rodrigo Galo), Michalis Bakakis, Konstantinos Galanopoulos, Viktor Klonaridis (61' Giannis Gianniotas), Ezequiel Ponce, Lucas Boyé (68' Petros Mandalos). Coach: Marinos Ouzounidis.
Goal: 88' Álex Grimaldo 1-0.
Referee: Bobby Madden (SCO)   Attendance: 33,633.
Sent off: 87' Konstantinos Galanopoulos.

GROUP F

19.09.18 Oblasny SportKomplex Metalist, Kharkiv:
Shakhtar Donetsk – 1899 Hoffenheim 2-2 (1-2)
Shakhtar Donetsk: Andriy Pyatov, Yaroslav Rakitskiy, Ismaily, Bogdan Butko, Davit Khotcholava, Marlos, Taras Stepanenko, Taison, Alan Patrick (76' Maycon), Sergiy Bolbat (57' Viktor Kovalenko), Júnior Moraes. Coach: Paulo Fonseca.
1899 Hoffenheim: Oliver Baumann, Håvard Nordtveit, Kevin Vogt, Pavel Kaderábek, Stefan Posch, Nico Schulz, Leonardo Bittencourt (64' Kerem Demirbay), Florian Grillitsch, Ádám Szalai (75' Steven Zuber), Andrej Kramaric (85' Reiss Nelson), Joelinton.
Coach: Julian Nagelsmann.
Goals: 6' Florian Grillitsch 0-1, 27' Ismaily 1-1, 38' Håvard Nordtveit 1-2, 81' Maycon 2-2.
Referee: Jakob Kehlet (DEN)   Attendance: 28,336.

(Shakhtar Donetsk played their home match at Oblasny SportKomplex Metalist, Kharkiv, instead of their regular stadium Donbass Arena, Donetsk, due to the war conditions in Eastern Ukraine)

19.09.18 Etihad Stadium, Manchester: Manchester City – Olympique Lyonnais 1-2 (0-2)
Manchester City: Ederson Moraes, Kyle Walker, Aymeric Laporte, John Stones, David Silva, Fernandinho, Fabian Delph, Ilkay Gündogan (55' Leroy Sané), Bernardo Silva, Raheem Sterling (76' Riyad Mahrez), Gabriel Jesus (63' Sergio "Kun" Agüero). Coach: Pep Guardiola.
Olympique Lyonnais: Anthony Lopes, Marcelo, Rafael (76' Léo Dubois), Ferland Mendy, Jason Denayer, Tanguy Ndombélé, Pape Diop, Houssem Aouar, Memphis Depay, Nabil Fekir (79' Lucas Tousart), Maxwel Cornet (90+2' Bertrand Traoré). Coach: Bruno Génésio.
Goals: 26' Maxwel Cornet 0-1, 43' Nabil Fekir 0-2, 67' Bernardo Silva 1-2.
Referee: Daniele Orsato (ITA)   Attendance: 40,111.

02.10.18 WIRSOL Rhein-Neckar-Arena, Sinsheim:
        1899 Hoffenheim – Manchester City 1-2 (1-1)
1899 Hoffenheim: Oliver Baumann, Pavel Kaderábek, Kevin Akpoguma, Joshua Brenet, Stefan Posch, Justin Hoogma, Florian Grillitsch (82' Leonardo Bittencourt), Kerem Demirbay (89' Robin Hack), Ádám Szalai (54' Andrej Kramaric), Ishak Belfodil, Joelinton.
Coach: Julian Nagelsmann.
Manchester City: Ederson Moraes, Vincent Kompany, Nicolás Otamendi (64' John Stones), Kyle Walker, Aymeric Laporte, David Silva, Fernandinho, Ilkay Gündogan (68' Bernardo Silva), Sergio "Kun" Agüero, Raheem Sterling (75' Riyad Mahrez), Leroy Sané.
Coach: Pep Guardiola.
Goals: 1' Ishak Belfodil 1-0, 8' Sergio "Kun" Agüero 1-1, 87' David Silva 1-2.
Referee: Damir Skomina (SVN)   Attendance: 24,851.

02.10.18 Groupama Stadium, Décines-Charpieu:
        Olympique Lyonnais – Shakhtar Donetsk 2-2 (0-1)
Olympique Lyonnais: Anthony Lopes, Marcelo, Léo Dubois, Ferland Mendy, Jason Denayer, Tanguy Ndombélé (87' Pape Diop), Lucas Tousart, Houssem Aouar, Bertrand Traoré (63' Memphis Depay), Nabil Fekir, Moussa Dembélé (81' Maxwel Cornet). Coach: Bruno Génésio.
Shakhtar Donetsk: Andriy Pyatov, Sergiy Krivtsov, Yaroslav Rakitskiy, Ismaily, Mykola Matvienko, Marlos (90+1' Fernando), Taras Stepanenko, Taison, Alan Patrick (75' Viktor Kovalenko), Maycon, Júnior Moraes (83' Olarenwaju Kayode). Coach: Paulo Fonseca.
Goals: 44', 55' Júnior Moraes 0-1, 0-2, 70' Moussa Dembélé 1-2, 72' Léo Dubois 2-2.
Referee: Andris Treimanis (LAT)

Match was played behind closed doors.

23.10.18 WIRSOL Rhein-Neckar-Arena, Sinsheim:
        1899 Hoffenheim – Olympique Lyonnais 3-3 (1-1)
1899 Hoffenheim: Oliver Baumann, Kevin Vogt, Ermin Bicakcic (73' Reiss Nelson), Pavel Kaderábek, Kevin Akpoguma, Nico Schultz, Florian Grillitsch, Kerem Demirbay, Ádám Szalai (60' Joelinton), Andrej Kramaric, Ishak Belfodil (81' Steven Zuber).
Coach: Julian Nagelsmann.
Olympique Lyonnais: Anthony Lopes, Marcelo, Kenny Tete, Ferland Mendy, Jason Denayer, Tanguy Ndombélé, Lucas Tousart, Martin Terrier (82' Jordan Ferri), Houssem Aouar, Bertrand Traoré (90+1' Pape Diop), Memphis Depay (81' Moussa Dembélé). Coach: Bruno Génésio.
Goals: 27' Bertrand Traoré 0-1, 33', 47' Andrej Kramaric 1-1, 2-1, 59' Tanguy Ndombélé 2-2, 67' Memphis Depay 2-3, 90+2' Joelinton 3-3.
Referee: Alberto Undiano Mallenco (ESP)   Attendance: 24,144.

23.10.18   Oblasny SportKomplex Metalist, Kharkiv:
Shakhtar Donetsk – Manchester City 0-3 (0-2)
Shakhtar Donetsk: Andriy Pyatov, Sergiy Krivtsov, Yaroslav Rakitskiy, Ismaily, Mykola Matvienko, Taras Stepanenko, Viktor Kovalenko (62' Alan Patrick), Maycon, Júnior Moraes, Wellington Nem (69' Sergiy Bolbat), Fernando (84' Dentinho). Coach: Paulo Fonseca.
Manchester City: Ederson Moraes, Nicolás Otamendi, Benjamin Mendy, Aymeric Laporte, John Stones (80' Kyle Walker), David Silva, Fernandinho, Kevin De Bruyne (69' Bernardo Silva), Riyad Mahrez, Raheem Sterling, Gabriel Jesus (87' Phil Foden). Coach: Pep Guardiola.
Goals: 30' David Silva 0-1, 35' Aymeric Laporte 0-2, 71' Bernardo Silva 0-3.
Referee: Carlos del Cerro Grande (ESP)   Attendance: 37,106.

(Shakhtar Donetsk played their home match at Oblasny SportKomplex Metalist, Kharkiv, instead of their regular stadium Donbass Arena, Donetsk, due to the war conditions in Eastern Ukraine)

07.11.18   Groupama Stadium, Décines-Charpieu:
Olympique Lyonnais – 1899 Hoffenheim 2-2 (2-0)
Olympique Lyonnais: Anthony Lopes, Jérémy Morel, Marcelo, Rafael, Ferland Mendy, Jason Denayer, Tanguy Ndombélé (88' Pape Diop), Lucas Tousart, Houssem Aouar, Memphis Depay (87' Bertrand Traoré), Nabil Fekir (74' Moussa Dembélé). Coach: Bruno Génésio.
1899 Hoffenheim: Oliver Baumann, Kevin Vogt, Ermin Bicakcic, Pavel Kaderábek, Kasim Nuhu, Nico Schultz, Florian Grillitsch (57' Reiss Nelson), Kerem Demirbay (79' Håvard Nordtveit), Andrej Kramaric, Ishak Belfodil (67' Ádám Szalai), Joelinton.
Coach: Julian Nagelsmann.
Goals: 19' Nabil Fekir 1-0, 28' Tanguy Ndombélé 2-0, 65' Andrej Kramaric 2-1, 90+2' Pavel Kaderábek 2-2.
Referee: Danny Makkelie (HOL)   Attendance: 53,850.
Sent off: 51' Kasim Nuhu.

07.11.18   Etihad Stadium, Manchester: Manchester City – Shakhtar Donetsk 6-0 (2-0)
Manchester City: Ederson Moraes, Kyle Walker (61' Danilo), Aymeric Laporte, John Stones, David Silva (73' Ilkay Gündogan), Fernandinho (76' Fabian Delph), Riyad Mahrez, Oleksandr Zinchenko, Bernardo Silva, Raheem Sterling, Gabriel Jesus. Coach: Pep Guardiola.
Shakhtar Donetsk: Andriy Pyatov, Sergiy Krivtsov, Yaroslav Rakitskiy, Ismaily, Mykola Matvienko, Taras Stepanenko, Taison (77' Wellington Nem), Sergiy Bolbat, Viktor Kovalenko, Maycon (77' Alan Patrick), Júnior Moraes (63' Olarenwaju Kayode).
Coach: Paulo Fonseca.
Goals: 13' David Silva 1-0, 24' Gabriel Jesus 2-0 (p), 49' Raheem Sterling 3-0, 72' Gabriel Jesus 4-0 (p), 84' Riyad Mahrez 5-0, 90+2' Gabriel Jesus 6-0.
Referee: Viktor Kassai (HUN)   Attendance: 52,286.

27.11.18 WIRSOL Rhein-Neckar-Arena, Sinsheim:
　　　　　1899 Hoffenheim – Shakhtar Donetsk 2-3 (2-2)
1899 Hoffenheim: Oliver Baumann, Håvard Nordtveit (84' Florian Grillitsch), Kevin Vogt, Ermin Bicakcic, Pavel Kaderábek, Steven Zuber (77' Reiss Nelson), Nico Schultz (84' Vincenzo Grifo), Kerem Demirbay, Ádám Szalai, Andrej Kramaric, Ishak Belfodil.
Coach: Julian Nagelsmann.
Shakhtar Donetsk: Andriy Pyatov, Sergiy Krivtsov, Ismaily, Davit Khotcholava, Mykola Matvienko, Taras Stepanenko (77' Alan Patrick), Taison, Viktor Kovalenko (85' Dentinho), Oleg Danchenko (90+4' Bogdan Butko), Maycon, Júnior Moraes. Coach: Paulo Fonseca.
Goals: 14' Ismaily 0-1, 15' Taison 0-2, 17' Andrej Kramaric 1-2, 40' Steven Zuber 2-2, 90+2' Taison 2-3.
Referee: Ivan Kruzliak (SVK)　　Attendance: 22,920.
Sent off: 59' Ádám Szalai.

27.11.18 Groupama Stadium, Décines-Charpieu:
　　　　　Olympique Lyonnais – Manchester City 2-2 (0-0)
Olympique Lyonnais: Anthony Lopes, Marcelo, Rafael (74' Kenny Tete), Fernando Marçal, Ferland Mendy, Jason Denayer, Tanguy Ndombélé, Houssem Aouar, Memphis Depay, Nabil Fekir (84' Bertrand Traoré), Maxwel Cornet (89' Martin Terrier). Coach: Bruno Génésio.
Manchester City: Ederson Moraes, Kyle Walker, Aymeric Laporte, John Stones, David Silva, Fernandinho, Riyad Mahrez, Oleksandr Zinchenko, Sergio "Kun" Agüero (90+1' Phil Foden), Raheem Sterling, Leroy Sané (71' Fabian Delph). Coach: Pep Guardiola.
Goals: 55' Maxwel Cornet 1-0, 62' Aymeric Laporte 1-1, 81' Maxwel Cornet 2-1, 83' Sergio "Kun" Agüero 2-2.
Referee: Gianluca Rocchi (ITA)　　Attendance: 56,039.

12.12.18 NSC Olimpiyskiy Stadium, Kiev:
　　　　　Shakhtar Donetsk – Olympique Lyonnais 1-1 (1-0)
Shakhtar Donetsk: Andriy Pyatov, Sergiy Krivtsov, Ismaily, Davit Khotcholava (46' Bogdan Butko), Mykola Matvienko, Marlos (87' Sergiy Bolbat), Taras Stepanenko, Taison, Viktor Kovalenko (83' Olarenwaju Kayode), Maycon, Júnior Moraes. Coach: Paulo Fonseca.
Olympique Lyonnais: Anthony Lopes, Marcelo, Fernando Marçal, Kenny Tete, Ferland Mendy, Jason Denayer, Lucas Tousart, Houssem Aouar, Bertrand Traoré (72' Tanguy Ndombélé), Memphis Depay (80' Moussa Dembélé), Nabil Fekir (89' Léo Dubois).
Coach: Bruno Génésio.
Goals: 22' Júnior Moraes 1-0, 65' Nabil Fekir 1-1.
Referee: Björn Kuipers (HOL)　　Attendance: 38,916.

(Shakhtar Donetsk played their home match at NSC Olimpiyskiy Stadium, Kiev, instead of their regular stadium Donbass Arena, Donetsk, due to the war conditions in Eastern Ukraine)

12.12.18 Etihad Stadium, Manchester: Manchester City – 1899 Hoffenheim 2-1 (1-1)
Manchester City: Ederson Moraes, Nicolás Otamendi, Aymeric Laporte, John Stones (46' Kyle Walker), Ilkay Gündogan, Oleksandr Zinchenko (64' Fabian Delph), Bernardo Silva (85' Vincent Kompany), Phil Foden, Raheem Sterling, Leroy Sané, Gabriel Jesus.
Coach: Pep Guardiola.
1899 Hoffenheim: Oliver Baumann, Benjamin Hübner, Pavel Kaderábek, Joshua Brenet (46' Reiss Nelson), Kasim Nuhu, Nico Schultz, Leonardo Bittencourt (70' Ishak Belfodil), Florian Grillitsch, Dennis Geiger (63' Nadiem Amiri), Andrej Kramaric, Joelinton.
Coach: Julian Nagelsmann.
Goals: 16' Andrej Kramaric 0-1, 45+1', 61' Leroy Sané 1-1, 2-1.
Referee: Andreas Ekberg (SWE)　　Attendance: 50,411.

GROUP G

19.09.18 Estadio Santiago Bernabéu, Madrid: Real Madrid CF – AS Roma 3-0 (1-0)
Real Madrid CF: Keylor Navas, Sergio Ramos, Marcelo, Daniel Carvajal, Raphaël Varane, Luka Modric (85' Dani Ceballos), Toni Kroos, Casemiro, Isco, Karim Benzema (62' Marco Asensio), Gareth Bale (73' Mariano Díaz). Coach: Lopetegui.
AS Roma: Robin Olsen, Aleksandar Kolarov, Federico Fazio, Kostas Manolas, Alessandro Florenzi, Daniele De Rossi, Steven N'Zonzi (69' Patrik Schick), Cengiz Ünder, Nicolò Zaniolo (54' Lorenzo Pellegrini), Edin Dzeko, Stephan El Shaarawy (62' Diego Perotti).
Coach: Eusebio Di Francesco.
Goals: 45' Isco 1-0, 58' Gareth Bale 2-0, 90+1' Mariano Díaz 3-0.
Referee: Björn Kuipers (HOL)   Attendance: 69,251.

19.09.18 Doosan Aréna, Plzen: FC Viktoria Plzen – CSKA Moscow 2-2 (2-0)
FC Viktoria Plzen: Matús Kozácik, Roman Hubník, Radim Reznik, David Limbersky, Ludek Pernica, Daniel Kolár (64' Ales Cermák), Tomás Horava (89' Lukás Hejda), Jan Kovarík, Jan Kopic, Patrik Hrosovsky, Michal Krmencík (74' Jakub Reznícek). Coach: Pavel Vrba.
CSKA Moscow: Igor Akinfeev, Kirill Nababkin, Mário Fernandes, Nikita Chernov, Rodrigo Becão, Alan Dzagoev (74' Timur Zhamaletdinov), Dmitri Efremov (46' Ilzat Akhmetov), Nikola Vlasic, Ivan Oblyakov, Jaka Bijol, Fedor Chalov (81' Arnór Sigurdsson).
Coach: Goncharenko.
Goals: 29', 41' Michal Krmencík 1-0, 2-0, 49' Fedor Chalov 2-1, 90+5' Nikola Vlasic 2-2 (p).
Referee: Benoît Bastien (FRA)   Attendance: 11,312.

02.10.18 Stadion Luzhniki, Moscow: CSKA Moscow – Real Madrid CF 1-0 (1-0)
CSKA Moscow: Igor Akinfeev, Kirill Nababkin, Mário Fernandes, Nikita Chernov, Rodrigo Becão, Alan Dzagoev (65' Dmitri Efremov), Nikola Vlasic, Ilzat Akhmetov, Ivan Oblyakov (90+8' Georgy Kyrnats), Jaka Bijol, Fedor Chalov (78' Arnór Sigurdsson).
Coach: Viktor Goncharenko.
Real Madrid CF: Keylor Navas, Nacho, Daniel Carvajal (43' Álvaro Odriozola), Raphaël Varane, Reguilón, Toni Kroos, Casemiro (58' Luka Modric), Lucas Vázquez (58' Mariano Díaz), Marco Asensio, Dani Ceballos, Karim Benzema. Coach: Lopetegui.
Goal: 2' Nikola Vlasic 1-0.
Referee: Ovidiu Hategan (ROM)   Attendance: 71,811.
Sent off: 90+5' Igor Akinfeev.

(CSKA Moscow played their three home match at Stadion Luzhniki, Moscow, instead of their regular stadium VEB Arena, Moscow)

02.10.18 Stadio Olimpico, Roma: AS Roma – FC Viktoria Plzen 5-0 (2-0)
AS Roma: Robin Olsen, Aleksandar Kolarov (74' Luca Pellegrini), Federico Fazio, Juan Jesus, Alessandro Florenzi, Steven N'Zonzi, Bryan Cristante, Lorenzo Pellegrini (74' Patrik Schick), Cengiz Ünder (74' Nicolò Zaniolo), Edin Dzeko, Justin Kluivert.
Coach: Eusebio Di Francesco.
FC Viktoria Plzen: Matús Kozácik, Roman Hubník, Radim Reznik, David Limbersky, Lukás Hejda, Martin Zeman (71' Ubong Moses Ekpai), Tomás Horava (64' Daniel Kolár), Roman Procházka, Jan Kovarík, Patrik Hrosovsky, Michal Krmencík (78' Jakub Reznícek).
Coach: Pavel Vrba.
Goals: 3', 40' Edin Dzeko 1-0, 2-0, 64' Cengiz Ünder 3-0, 73' Justin Kluivert 4-0, 90+2' Edin Dzeko 5-0.
Referee: Pawel Raczkowski (POL)   Attendance: 41,243.

23.10.18   Stadio Olimpico, Roma: AS Roma – CSKA Moscow 3-0 (2-0)
AS Roma: Robin Olsen, Federico Fazio, Davide Santon, Kostas Manolas, Alessandro Florenzi, Daniele De Rossi (81' Patrik Schick), Steven N'Zonzi, Lorenzo Pellegrini (68' Bryan Cristante), Cengiz Ünder (73' Aleksandar Kolarov), Edin Dzeko, Stephan El Shaarawy.
Coach: Eusebio Di Francesco.
CSKA Moscow: Ilya Pomazun, Kirill Nababkin, Mário Fernandes, Hördur Magnússon, Nikita Chernov (57' Khetag Khosonov), Rodrigo Becão, Nikola Vlasic, Ilzat Akhmetov, Arnór Sigurdsson, Ivan Oblyakov (57' Alan Dzagoev), Fedor Chalov (89' Takuma Nishimura).
Coach: Viktor Goncharenko.
Goals: 30', 43' Edin Dzeko 1-0, 2-0, 50' Cengiz Ünder 3-0.
Referee: Anastasios Sidiropoulos (GRE)   Attendance: 46,005.

23.10.18   Estadio Santiago Bernabéu, Madrid: Real Madrid CF – FC Viktoria Plzen 2-1 (1-0)
Real Madrid CF: Keylor Navas, Sergio Ramos, Marcelo, Nacho, Luka Modric, Toni Kroos, Casemiro, Isco (54' Federico Valverde), Lucas Vázquez, Karim Benzema (88' Mariano Díaz), Gareth Bale (75' Marco Asensio). Coach: Lopetegui.
FC Viktoria Plzen: Ales Hruska, Roman Hubník, Radim Reznik, David Limbersky, Lukás Hejda, Milan Havel (76' Ubong Moses Ekpai), Milan Petrzela (86' Jakub Reznícek), Roman Procházka (65' Tomás Horava), Ales Cermák, Patrik Hrosovsky, Michal Krmencík.
Coach: Pavel Vrba.
Goals: 11' Karim Benzema 1-0, 55' Marcelo 2-0, 79' Patrik Hrosovsky 2-1.
Referee: Orel Grinfeld (ISR)   Attendance: 67,356.

07.11.18   Stadion Luzhniki, Moscow: CSKA Moscow – AS Roma 1-2 (0-1)
CSKA Moscow: Igor Akinfeev, Kirill Nababkin, Mário Fernandes (12' Georgiy Shchennikov), Hördur Magnússon, Rodrigo Becão, Nikola Vlasic, Ilzat Akhmetov (76' Khetag Khosonov), Arnór Sigurdsson (64' Nikita Chernov), Ivan Oblyakov, Jaka Bijol, Fedor Chalov.
Coach: Viktor Goncharenko.
AS Roma: Robin Olsen, Aleksandar Kolarov, Federico Fazio, Davide Santon, Kostas Manolas, Alessandro Florenzi (88' Juan Jesus), Steven N'Zonzi, Bryan Cristante, Lorenzo Pellegrini (82' Nicolò Zaniolo), Edin Dzeko, Justin Kluivert (70' Cengiz Ünder).
Coach: Eusebio Di Francesco.
Goals: 4' Kostas Manolas 0-1, 50' Arnór Sigurdsson 1-1, 59' Lorenzo Pellegrini 1-2.
Referee: Cüneyt Çakir (TUR)   Attendance: 64,454.
Sent off: 56' Hördur Magnússon.

07.11.18   Doosan Aréna, Plzen: FC Viktoria Plzen – Real Madrid CF 0-5 (0-4)
FC Viktoria Plzen: Ales Hruska, Roman Hubník, Radim Reznik, David Limbersky, Lukás Hejda, Milan Havel (38' Milan Petrzela), Roman Procházka, Jan Kopic, Ales Cermák (61' Tomás Horava), Patrik Hrosovsky, Tomás Chory (80' Jakub Reznícek). Coach: Pavel Vrba.
Real Madrid CF: Thibaut Courtois, Sergio Ramos (59' Javier Sánchez), Nacho, Álvaro Odriozola, Reguilón, Toni Kroos (73' Isco), Casemiro, Lucas Vázquez, Dani Ceballos, Karim Benzema (62' Vinícius Júnior), Gareth Bale. Coach: Santiago Solari.
Goals: 21' Karim Benzema 0-1, 23' Casemiro 0-2, 37' Karim Benzema 0-3, 40' Gareth Bale 0-4, 67' Toni Kroos 0-5.
Referee: Deniz Aytekin (GER)   Attendance: 11,483.

27.11.18 Stadion Luzhniki, Moscow: CSKA Moscow – FC Viktoria Plzen 1-2 (1-0)
CSKA Moscow: Igor Akinfeev, Kirill Nababkin, Georgiy Shchennikov (46' Dmitri Efremov), Mário Fernandes, Nikita Chernov, Rodrigo Becão, Nikola Vlasic, Kristijan Bistrovic, Arnór Sigurdsson, Ivan Oblyakov (72' Konstantin Kuchaev), Fedor Chalov (80' Timur Zhamaletdinov). Coach: Viktor Goncharenko.
FC Viktoria Plzen: Ales Hruska, Roman Hubník, Radim Rezník, David Limbersky (46' Jan Kopic), Lukás Hejda, Milan Petrzela (70' Milan Havel), Roman Procházka, Jan Kovarík, Ales Cermák, Patrik Hrosovsky, Tomás Chory (80' Jakub Reznícek). Coach: Pavel Vrba.
Goals: 10' Nikola Vlasic 1-0 (p), 56' Roman Procházka 1-1, 81' Lukás Hejda 1-2.
Referee: Danny Makkelie (HOL)   Attendance: 52,892.

Roman Procházka missed a penalty kick (44').

27.11.18 Stadio Olimpico, Roma: AS Roma – Real Madrid CF 0-2 (0-0)
AS Roma: Robin Olsen, Aleksandar Kolarov, Federico Fazio, Kostas Manolas, Alessandro Florenzi, Steven N'Zonzi (64' Ante Coric), Bryan Cristante, Cengiz Ünder, Nicolò Zaniolo (69' Rick Karsdorp), Stephan El Shaarawy (22' Justin Kluivert), Patrik Schick. Coach: Eusebio Di Francesco.
Real Madrid CF: Thibaut Courtois, Sergio Ramos, Marcelo, Daniel Carvajal, Raphaël Varane, Luka Modric (80' Federico Valverde), Toni Kroos, Lucas Vázquez, Marcos Llorente, Karim Benzema (77' Mariano Díaz), Gareth Bale (84' Marco Asensio). Coach: Santiago Solari.
Goals: 47' Gareth Bale 0-1, 59' Lucas Vázquez 0-2.
Referee: Clément Turpin (FRA)   Attendance: 59,124.

12.12.18 Estadio Santiago Bernabéu, Madrid: Real Madrid CF – CSKA Moscow 0-3 (0-2)
Real Madrid CF: Thibaut Courtois, Marcelo (74' Daniel Carvajal), Álvaro Odriozola, Jesús Vallejo, Javier Sánchez, Isco, Marcos Llorente (58' Toni Kroos), Marco Asensio, Federico Valverde, Karim Benzema (46' Gareth Bale), Vinícius Júnior. Coach: Santiago Solari.
CSKA Moscow: Igor Akinfeev, Kirill Nababkin, Georgiy Shchennikov, Mário Fernandes, Hördur Magnússon, Rodrigo Becão, Nikola Vlasic, Kristijan Bistrovic, Arnór Sigurdsson (90+4' Takuma Nishimura), Ivan Oblyakov (89' Konstantin Kuchaev), Fedor Chalov (84' Abel Hernández). Coach: Viktor Goncharenko.
Goals: 37' Fedor Chalov 0-1, 43' Georgiy Shchennikov 0-2, 73' Arnór Sigurdsson 0-3.
Referee: Artur Soares Dias (POR)   Attendance: 51,636.

12.12.18 Doosan Aréna, Plzen: FC Viktoria Plzen – AS Roma 2-1 (0-0)
FC Viktoria Plzen: Ales Hruska, Roman Hubník, David Limbersky, Lukás Hejda, Milan Havel, Roman Procházka, Jan Kovarík, Jan Kopic (71' Milan Petrzela), Ales Cermák (82' Tomás Horava), Patrik Hrosovsky, Tomás Chory (87' Jakub Reznícek). Coach: Pavel Vrba.
AS Roma: Antonio Mirante, Aleksandar Kolarov, Ivan Marcano, Davide Santon (75' Alessandro Florenzi), Kostas Manolas, Javier Pastore (59' Nicolò Zaniolo), Steven N'Zonzi (80' Luca Pellegrini), Bryan Cristante, Cengiz Ünder, Patrik Schick, Justin Kluivert. Coach: Eusebio Di Francesco.
Goals: 62' Jan Kovarík 1-0, 68' Cengiz Ünder 1-1, 72' Tomás Chory 2-1.
Referee: Anthony Taylor (ENG)   Attendance: 11,217.
Sent off: 90+2' Luca Pellegrini.

GROUP H

19.09.18   STADE DE SUISSE Wankdorf, Bern:
BSC Young Boys – Manchester United 0-3 (0-2)
BSC Young Boys: David von Ballmoos, Steve von Bergen, Loris Benito, Kevin Mbabu, Mohamed Aly Camara, Miralem Sulejmani, Sékou Junior Sanogo, Djibril Sow (59' Michel Aebischer), Christian Fassnacht (65' Nicolas Moumi Ngamaleu), Guillaume Hoarau (75' Jean Pierre Nsamé), Roger Assalé. Coach: Gerardo Seoane.
Manchester United: David de Gea, Chris Smalling, Victor Lindelöf, Luke Shaw, Diogo Dalot, Nemanja Matic, Paul Pogba (75' Andreas Pereira), Fred (69' Marouane Fellaini), Romelu Lukaku, Anthony Martial, Marcus Rashford (69' Mata). Coach: José Mourinho.
Goals: 35', 44' Paul Pogba 0-1, 0-2 (p), 66' Anthony Martial 0-3.
Referee: Deniz Aytekin (GER)   Attendance: 31,120.

19.09.18   Estadio de Mestalla, Valencia: Valencia CF – Juventus 0-2 (0-1)
Valencia CF: Neto, Jeison Murillo, Gabriel Paulista, José Gayà, Rúben Vezo (57' Denis Cheryshev), Daniel Wass, Dani Parejo, Gonçalo Guedes (70' Santi Mina), Carlos Soler, Rodrigo, Michy Batshuayi (70' Kevin Gameiro). Coach: Marcelino.
Juventus: Wojciech Szczesny, Leonardo Bonucci, Giorgio Chiellini, Alex Sandro, João Cancelo, Blaise Matuidi, Sami Khedira (23' Emre Can), Miralem Pjanic (67' Douglas Costa, 89' Daniele Rugani), Cristiano Ronaldo, Mario Mandzukic, Federico Bernardeschi.
Coach: Massimiliano Allegri.
Goals: 45', 51' Miralem Pjanic 0-1 (p), 0-2 (p).
Referee: Dr. Felix Brych (GER)   Attendance: 46,067.
Sent off: 29' Cristiano Ronaldo.

Dani Parejo missed a penalty kick (90+6').

02.10.18   Allianz Stadium, Torino: Juventus – BSC Young Boys 3-0 (2-0)
Juventus: Wojciech Szczesny, Andrea Barzagli, Leonardo Bonucci, Medhi Benatia, Alex Sandro, Blaise Matuidi (46' Emre Can), Miralem Pjanic (70' Sami Khedira), Juan Cuadrado, Mario Mandzukic (78' Moise Kean), Paulo Dybala, Federico Bernardeschi.
Coach: Massimiliano Allegri.
BSC Young Boys: David von Ballmoos, Steve von Bergen, Loris Benito, Mohamed Aly Camara, Miralem Sulejmani (70' Nicolas Moumi Ngamaleu), Thorsten Schick, Sékou Junior Sanogo (46' Sandro Lauper), Leonardo Bertone, Djibril Sow, Christian Fassnacht (71' Roger Assalé), Guillaume Hoarau. Coach: Gerardo Seoane.
Goals: 5', 33', 69' Paulo Dybala 1-0, 2-0, 3-0.
Referee: Sergei Karasev (RUS)   Attendance: 40,961.
Sent off: 78' Mohamed Aly Camara.

02.10.18   Old Trafford, Manchester: Manchester United – Valencia 0-0
Manchester United: David de Gea, Antonio Valencia, Chris Smalling, Luke Shaw, Eric Bailly, Marouane Fellaini, Nemanja Matic, Paul Pogba, Alexis Sánchez (76' Anthony Martial), Romelu Lukaku, Marcus Rashford. Coach: José Mourinho.
Valencia CF: Neto, Ezequiel Garay, Gabriel Paulista, Cristiano Piccini, José Gayà, Dani Parejo, Francis Coquelin (78' Carlos Soler), Geoffrey Kondogbia, Gonçalo Guedes (83' Denis Cheryshev), Rodrigo, Michy Batshuayi (73' Kevin Gameiro). Coach: Marcelino.
Referee: Slavko Vincic (SVN)   Attendance: 73,569.

23.10.18   STADE DE SUISSE Wankdorf, Bern: BSC Young Boys – Valencia 1-1 (0-1)
BSC Young Boys: Marco Wölfli, Steve von Bergen, Loris Benito, Kevin Mbabu, Miralem Sulejmani (74' Nicolas Moumi Ngamaleu), Sékou Junior Sanogo, Djibril Sow, Christian Fassnacht (85' Leonardo Bertone), Sandro Lauper, Guillaume Hoarau (79' Jean Pierre Nsamé), Roger Assalé. Coach: Gerardo Seoane.
Valencia CF: Neto, Gabriel Paulista, Cristiano Piccini, José Gayà, Mouctar Daikhaby, Dani Parejo, Geoffrey Kondogbia (70' Francis Coquelin), Carlos Soler, Ferrán Torres (67' Kevin Gameiro), Rodrigo, Michy Batshuayi. Coach: Marcelino.
Goals: 26' Michy Batshuayi 0-1, 55' Guillaume Hoarau 1-1 (p).
Referee: Andris Treimanis (LAT)   Attendance: 31,120.

23.10.18   Old Trafford, Manchester: Manchester United – Juventus 0-1 (0-1)
Manchester United: David de Gea, Ashley Young, Chris Smalling, Victor Lindelöf, Luke Shaw, Mata, Nemanja Matic, Paul Pogba, Romelu Lukaku, Anthony Martial, Marcus Rashford. Coach: José Mourinho.
Juventus: Wojciech Szczesny, Leonardo Bonucci, Giorgio Chiellini, Alex Sandro, João Cancelo (87' Douglas Costa), Blaise Matuidi, Miralem Pjanic, Juan Cuadrado (81' Andrea Barzagli), Rodrigo Bentancur, Cristiano Ronaldo, Paulo Dybala (78' Federico Bernardeschi). Coach: Massimiliano Allegri.
Goal: 17' Paulo Dybala 0-1.
Referee: Milorad Mazic (SRB)   Attendance: 73,946.

07.11.18   Estadio de Mestalla, Valencia: Valencia CF – BSC Young Boys 3-1 (2-1)
Valencia CF: Neto, Ezequiel Garay, Gabriel Paulista, José Gayà, Daniel Wass, Francis Coquelin, Geoffrey Kondogbia (87' Rúben Vezo), Gonçalo Guedes (75' Ferrán Torres), Carlos Soler, Rodrigo, Santi Mina (68' Kevin Gameiro). Coach: Marcelino.
BSC Young Boys: David von Ballmoos, Steve von Bergen, Loris Benito, Kevin Mbabu, Sékou Junior Sanogo, Nicolas Moumi Ngamaleu (46' Miralem Sulejmani), Djibril Sow, Christian Fassnacht (61' Jean Pierre Nsamé), Sandro Lauper, Guillaume Hoarau (75' Michel Aebischer), Roger Assalé. Coach: Gerardo Seoane.
Goals: 14' Santi Mina 1-0, 37' Roger Assalé 1-1, 42' Santi Mina 2-1, 56' Carlos Soler 3-1.
Referee: István Kovács (ROM)   Attendance: 36,480.
Sent off: 77' Sékou Junior Sanogo.

07.11.18   Allianz Stadium, Torino: Juventus – Manchester United 1-2 (0-0)
Juventus: Wojciech Szczesny, Leonardo Bonucci, Giorgio Chiellini, Alex Sandro, Mattia De Sciglio (83' Andrea Barzagli), Sami Khedira (61' Blaise Matuidi), Miralem Pjanic, Juan Cuadrado (90+2' Mario Mandzukic), Rodrigo Bentancur, Cristiano Ronaldo, Paulo Dybala. Coach: Massimiliano Allegri.
Manchester United: David de Gea, Ashley Young, Chris Smalling, Victor Lindelöf, Luke Shaw, Nemanja Matic, Ander Herrera (79' Mata), Paul Pogba, Jesse Lingard (70' Marcus Rashford), Alexis Sánchez (79' Marouane Fellaini), Anthony Martial. Coach: José Mourinho.
Goals: 65' Cristiano Ronaldo 1-0, 86' Mata 1-1, 90' Leonardo Bonucci 1-2 (og).
Referee: Ovidiu Hategan (ROM)   Attendance: 41,470.

27.11.18   Old Trafford, Manchester: Manchester United – BSC Young Boys 1-0 (0-0)
Manchester United: David de Gea, Antonio Valencia (72' Mata), Chris Smalling, Phil Jones, Luke Shaw, Marouane Fellaini, Nemanja Matic, Fred (64' Paul Pogba), Jesse Lingard (64' Romelu Lukaku), Anthony Martial, Marcus Rashford. Coach: José Mourinho.
BSC Young Boys: David von Ballmoos, Steve von Bergen (46' Ulisses Garcia), Loris Benito, Kevin Mbabu, Mohamed Aly Camara, Miralem Sulejmani (66' Christian Fassnacht), Djibril Sow, Sandro Lauper, Michel Aebischer, Jean Pierre Nsamé (83' Nicolas Moumi Ngamaleu), Roger Assalé. Coach: Gerardo Seoane.
Goal: 90+1' Marouane Fellaini 1-0.
Referee: Dr. Felix Brych (GER)   Attendance: 72,876.

27.11.18   Allianz Stadium, Torino: Juventus – Valencia CF 1-0 (0-0)
Juventus: Wojciech Szczesny, Leonardo Bonucci, Giorgio Chiellini, Alex Sandro (46' Juan Cuadrado), João Cancelo, Blaise Matuidi, Miralem Pjanic, Rodrigo Bentancur, Cristiano Ronaldo, Mario Mandzukic, Paulo Dybala (79' Douglas Costa). Coach: Massimiliano Allegri.
Valencia CF: Neto, Gabriel Paulista, José Gayà, Mouctar Daikhaby, Daniel Wass, Dani Parejo, Francis Coquelin, Geoffrey Kondogbia (72' Carlos Soler), Gonçalo Guedes, Rodrigo (46' Kevin Gameiro), Santi Mina (67' Michy Batshuayi). Coach: Marcelino.
Goal: 59' Mario Mandzukic 1-0.
Referee: William Collum (SCO)   Attendance: 39,070.

12.12.18   STADE DE SUISSE Wankdorf, Bern: BSC Young Boys – Juventus 2-1 (1-0)
BSC Young Boys: Marco Wölfli, Loris Benito, Kevin Mbabu, Ulisses Garcia, Mohamed Aly Camara, Nicolas Moumi Ngamaleu (85' Thorsten Schick), Djibril Sow (90+1' Gregory Wüthrich), Christian Fassnacht (80' Leonardo Bertone), Sandro Lauper, Michel Aebischer, Guillaume Hoarau. Coach: Gerardo Seoane.
Juventus: Wojciech Szczesny, Leonardo Bonucci, Mattia De Sciglio (72' Paulo Dybala), Daniele Rugani, Miralem Pjanic (65' Emre Can), Juan Cuadrado (23' Alex Sandro), Douglas Costa, Rodrigo Bentancur, Cristiano Ronaldo, Mario Mandzukic, Federico Bernardeschi. Coach: Massimiliano Allegri.
Goals: 30', 68' Guillaume Hoarau 1-0 (p), 2-0, 80' Paulo Dybala 2-1.
Referee: Tobias Stieler (GER)   Attendance: 30,114.

12.12.18   Estadio de Mestalla, Valencia: Valencia CF – Manchester United 2-1 (1-0)
Valencia CF: Jaume Doménech, Cristiano Piccini, Rúben Vezo, Mouctar Daikhaby, Toni Lato (51' Ezequiel Garay), Dani Parejo, Denis Cheryshev (66' Ferrán Torres), Geoffrey Kondogbia, Carlos Soler, Michy Batshuayi, Santi Mina (68' Rodrigo). Coach: Marcelino.
Manchester United: Sergio Romero, Antonio Valencia, Marcos Rojo (46' Ashley Young), Phil Jones, Eric Bailly, Marouane Fellaini, Mata, Paul Pogba, Fred (57' Marcus Rashford), Andreas Pereira, Romelu Lukaku (69' Jesse Lingard). Coach: José Mourinho.
Goals: 17' Carlos Soler 1-0, 47' Phil Jones 2-0 (og), 87' Marcus Rashford 2-1.
Referee: Georgi Kabakov (BUL)   Attendance: 36,544.

KNOCKOUT PHASE
ROUND OF 16

12.02.19   Old Trafford, Manchester: Manchester United – Paris Saint-Germain 0-2 (0-0)
Manchester United: David de Gea, Ashley Young, Victor Lindelöf, Luke Shaw, Eric Bailly, Nemanja Matic, Ander Herrera, Paul Pogba, Jesse Lingard (45+4' Alexis Sánchez), Anthony Martial (46' Mata), Marcus Rashford (84' Romelu Lukaku). Coach: Ole Gunnar Solskjær.
Paris Saint-Germain: Gianluigi Buffon, Dani Alves, Thiago Silva, Marquinhos, Juan Bernat, Presnel Kimpembe, Thilo Kehrer, Ángel Di María (81' Colin Dagba), Marco Verratti (75' Leandro Paredes), Julian Draxler, Kylian Mbappé. Coach: Thomas Tuchel.
Goals: 53' Presnel Kimpembe 0-1, 60' Kylian Mbappé 0-2.
Referee: Daniele Orsato (ITA)   Attendance: 74,054.
Sent off: 89' Paul Pogba.

12.02.19   Stadio Olimpico, Roma: AS Roma – FC Porto 2-1 (0-0)
AS Roma: Antonio Mirante, Aleksandar Kolarov, Federico Fazio, Kostas Manolas, Alessandro Florenzi, Daniele De Rossi, Bryan Cristante, Lorenzo Pellegrini (83' Steven N'Zonzi), Nicolò Zaniolo (87' Davide Santon), Edin Dzeko, Stephan El Shaarawy (90' Justin Kluivert). Coach: Eusebio Di Francesco.
FC Porto: Iker Casillas, Pepe, Alex Telles, Felipe Monteiro, Éder Militão, Héctor Herrera, Danilo Pereira, Otávio (84' Hernâni), Yacine Brahimi (68' Adrián), Tiquinho Soares, Fernando Andrade (76' André Pereira). Coach: Sérgio Conceição.
Goals: 70', 76' Nicolò Zaniolo 1-0, 2-0, 79' Adrián 2-1.
Referee: Danny Makkelie (HOL)   Attendance: 51,727.

13.02.19   Wembley Stadium, London: Tottenham Hotspur – Borussia Dortmund 3-0 (0-0)
Tottenham Hotspur: Hugo Lloris, Jan Vertonghen, Toby Alderweireld, Serge Aurier, Davinson Sánchez, Juan Foyth, Moussa Sissoko (90+1' Victor Wanyama), Christian Eriksen, Lucas Moura (84' Llorente), Harry Winks, Son Heung-Min (90' Érik Lamela).
Coach: Mauricio Pochettino.
Borussia Dortmund: Roman Bürki, Ömer Toprak, Abdou Diallo, Achraf Hakimi, Dan-Axel Zagadou (77' Marcel Schmelzer), Axel Witsel, Thomas Delaney, Mario Götze, Mahmoud Dahoud, Christian Pulisic (88' Jacob Bruun Larsen), Jadon Sancho (88' Raphaël Guerreiro).
Coach: Lucien Favre.
Goals: 47' Son Heung-Min 1-0, 83' Jan Vertonghen 2-0, 86' Llorente 3-0.
Referee: Antonio Mateu Lahoz (ESP)   Attendance: 71,214.

13.02.19   Johan Cruijff ArenA, Amsterdam: AFC Ajax – Real Madrid CF 1-2 (0-0)
AFC Ajax: André Onana, Daley Blind, Nicolás Tagliafico, Matthijs de Ligt, Lasse Schöne (73' Kasper Dolberg), Hakim Ziyech, Donny van de Beek, Noussair Mazraoui, Frenkie de Jong, Dusan Tadic, David Neres. Coach: Erik ten Hag.
Real Madrid CF: Thibaut Courtois, Sergio Ramos, Nacho, Daniel Carvajal, Reguilón, Luka Modric, Toni Kroos, Casemiro, Karim Benzema (73' Marco Asensio), Gareth Bale (61' Lucas Vázquez), Vinícius Júnior (81' Mariano). Coach: Santiago Solari.
Goals: 60' Karim Benzema 0-1, 75' Hakim Ziyech 1-1, 87' Marco Asensio 1-2.
Referee: Damir Skomina (SVN)   Attendance: 52,286.

19.02.19 Groupama Stadium, Décines-Charpieu: Olympique Lyonnais – FC Barcelona 0-0
Olympique Lyonnais: Anthony Lopes, Marcelo, Léo Dubois, Ferland Mendy, Jason Denayer, Tanguy Ndombélé (84' Pape Diop), Martin Terrier (76' Maxwel Cornet), Houssem Aouar, Bertrand Traoré (69' Lucas Tousart), Memphis Depay, Moussa Dembélé.
Coach: Bruno Génésio.
FC Barcelona: Marc-André ter Stegen, Piqué, Jordi Alba, Sergi Roberto (81' Arturo Vidal), Clément Lenglet, Nélson Semedo, Ivan Rakitic, Sergio Busquets, Lionel Messi, Luis Suárez, Ousmane Dembélé (67' Philippe Coutinho). Coach: Ernesto Valverde.
Referee: Cüneyt Çakir (TUR)   Attendance: 57,889.

19.02.19 Anfield, Liverpool: Liverpool FC – FC Bayern München 0-0
Liverpool FC: Alisson, Joel Matip, Andrew Robertson, Trent Alexander-Arnold, Georginio Wijnaldum, Jordan Henderson, Fabinho, Naby Keïta (76' James Milner), Roberto Firmino (76' Divock Origi), Mohamed Salah, Sadio Mané. Coach: Jürgen Klopp.
FC Bayern München: Manuel Neuer, Mats Hummels, David Alaba, Niklas Süle, Joshua Kimmich, Javi Martínez, James Rodríguez (88' Renato Sanches), Thiago Alcântara, Serge Gnabry (90+1' Rafinha), Kingsley Coman (81' Franck Ribéry), Robert Lewandowski.
Coach: Niko Kovac.
Referee: Gianluca Rocchi (ITA)   Attendance: 52,250.

20.02.19   VELTINS-Arena, Gelsenkirchen: FC Schalke 04 – Manchester City 2-3 (2-1)
FC Schalke 04: Ralf Fährmann, Bastian Oczipka, Jeffrey Bruma, Matija Nastasic, Salif Sané, Hamza Mendyl (65' Guido Burgstaller), Daniel Caligiuri, Nabil Bentaleb, Suat Serdar, Weston McKennie (78' Steven Skrzybski), Mark Uth (87' Amine Harit). Coach: Domenico Tedesco.
Manchester City: Ederson Moraes, Nicolás Otamendi, Kyle Walker, Aymeric Laporte, David Silva (70' Vincent Kompany), Fernandinho, Ilkay Gündogan, Kevin De Bruyne (87' Oleksandr Zinchenko), Bernardo Silva, Sergio "Kun" Agüero (78' Leroy Sané), Raheem Sterling. Coach: Pep Guardiola.
Goals: 18' Sergio "Kun" Agüero 0-1, 38', 45' Nabil Bentaleb 1-1 (p), 2-1 (p),
85' Leroy Sané 2-2, 90' Raheem Sterling 2-3.
Referee: Carlos del Cerro Grande (ESP)   Attendance: 54,417.
Sent off: 68' Nicolás Otamendi.

20.02.19   Estadio Wanda Metropolitano, Madrid: Atlético Madrid – Juventus 2-0 (0-0)
Atlético Madrid: Jan Oblak, Juanfran, Filipe Luís, Diego Godín, José Giménez, Saúl, Koke (67' Ángel Correa), Thomas Partey (61' Thomas Lemar), Rodri Hernández, Diego Costa (58' Álvaro Morata), Antoine Griezmann. Coach: Diego Simeone.
Juventus: Wojciech Szczesny, Leonardo Bonucci, Giorgio Chiellini, Alex Sandro, Mattia De Sciglio, Blaise Matuidi (84' João Cancelo), Miralem Pjanic (73' Emre Can), Rodrigo Bentancur, Cristiano Ronaldo, Mario Mandzukic, Paulo Dybala (80' Federico Bernardeschi).
Coach: Massimiliano Allegri.
Goals: 78' José Giménez 1-0, 83' Diego Godín (83').
Referee: Felix Zwayer (GER)   Attendance: 67,193.

04.03.19 Signal-Iduna-Park, Dortmund: Borussia Dortmund – Tottenham Hotspur 0-1 (0-0)
Borussia Dortmund: Roman Bürki, Raphaël Guerreiro (62' Christian Pulisic), Abdou Diallo, Manuel Akanji, Axel Witsel, Mario Götze, Julian Weigl, Jadon Sancho, Marco Reus (74' Thomas Delaney), Paco Alcácer, Marius Wolf (62' Jacob Bruun Larsen). Coach: Lucien Favre.
Tottenham Hotspur: Hugo Lloris, Jan Vertonghen, Toby Alderweireld, Serge Aurier, Ben Davies, Davinson Sánchez, Moussa Sissoko, Christian Eriksen (83' Danny Rose), Harry Winks (55' Eric Dier), Son Heung-Min (71' Érik Lamela), Harry Kane. Coach: Mauricio Pochettino.
Goal: 49' Harry Kane 0-1.
Referee: Danny Makkelie (HOL)   Attendance: 66,099.

05.03.19 Estadio Santiago Bernabéu, Madrid: Real Madrid CF – AFC Ajax 1-4 (0-2)
Real Madrid CF: Thibaut Courtois, Nacho, Daniel Carvajal, Raphaël Varane, Reguilón, Luka Modric, Toni Kroos, Casemiro (87' Federico Valverde), Lucas Vázquez (29' Gareth Bale), Karim Benzema, Vinícius Júnior (35' Marco Asensio). Coach: Santiago Solari.
AFC Ajax: André Onana, Daley Blind, Nicolás Tagliafico, Matthijs de Ligt, Lasse Schöne (73' Dani de Wit), Hakim Ziyech, Donny van de Beek, Noussair Mazraoui (81' Joël Veltman), Frenkie de Jong, Dusan Tadic, David Neres (74' Kasper Dolberg). Coach: Erik ten Hag.
Goals: 7' Hakim Ziyech 0-1, 18' David Neres 0-2, 62' Dusan Tadic 0-3,
70' Marco Asensio 1-3, 72' Lasse Schöne 1-4.
Referee: Dr.Felix Brych (GER)   Attendance: 77,013.
Sent off: 90+3' Nacho.

06.03.19 Parc des Princes, Paris: Paris Saint-Germain – Manchester United 1-3 (1-2)
Paris Saint-Germain: Gianluigi Buffon, Dani Alves (90+5' Edinson Cavani), Thiago Silva, Marquinhos, Juan Bernat, Presnel Kimpembe, Thilo Kehrer (70' Leandro Paredes), Ángel Di María, Marco Verratti, Julian Draxler (70' Thomas Meunier), Kylian Mbappé.
Coach: Thomas Tuchel.
Manchester United: David de Gea, Ashley Young (87' Mason Greenwood), Chris Smalling, Victor Lindelöf, Luke Shaw, Eric Bailly (36' Diogo Dalot), Fred, Andreas Pereira (80' Tahith Chong), Scott McTominay, Romelu Lukaku, Marcus Rashford. Coach: Ole Gunnar Solskjær.
Goals: 2' Romelu Lukaku 0-1, 12' Juan Bernat 1-1, 30' Romelu Lukaku 1-2,
90+4' Marcus Rashford 1-3 (p).
Referee: Damir Skomina (SVN)   Attendance: 47,441.

Manchester United won on away goals.

06.03.19 Estádio do Dragão, Porto: FC Porto – AS Roma 3-1 (1-1, 2-1)
FC Porto: Iker Casillas, Pepe, Alex Telles, Felipe Monteiro, Éder Militão (103' Maxi Pereira), Héctor Herrera, Danilo Pereira, Otávio (94' Hernâni), Tiquinho Soares (78' Fernando Andrade), Jesús Corona (69' Yacine Brahimi), Moussa Marega. Coach: Sérgio Conceição.
AS Roma: Robin Olsen, Aleksandar Kolarov, Ivan Marcano (76' Bryan Cristante), Kostas Manolas, Juan Jesus, Rick Karsdorp (55' Alessandro Florenzi), Daniele De Rossi (45+4' Lorenzo Pellegrini, 96' Patrik Schick), Steven N'Zonzi, Nicolò Zaniolo, Edin Dzeko, Diego Perotti. Coach: Eusebio Di Francesco.
Goals: 26' Tiquinho Soares 1-0, 37' Daniele De Rossi 1-1 (p), 52' Moussa Marega 2-1,
117' Alex Telles 3-1 (p).
Referee: Cüneyt Çakir (TUR)   Attendance: 49,029.

FC Porto won after extra time.

12.03.19   Etihad Stadium, Manchester: Manchester City – FC Schalke 04 7-0 (3-0)
Manchester City: Ederson Moraes, Kyle Walker, Danilo, Aymeric Laporte (72' Fabian Delph), David Silva (64' Phil Foden), Ilkay Gündogan, Oleksandr Zinchenko, Bernardo Silva, Sergio "Kun" Agüero (64' Gabriel Jesus), Raheem Sterling, Leroy Sané. Coach: Pep Guardiola.
FC Schalke 04: Ralf Fährmann, Bastian Oczipka, Jeffrey Bruma, Benjamin Stambouli, Salif Sané, Yevhen Konoplyanka, Nabil Bentaleb, Suat Serdar, Weston McKennie (74' Hamza Mendyl), Guido Burgstaller (79' Cedric Teuchert), Breel Embolo (69' Steven Skrzybski). Coach: Domenico Tedesco.
Goals: 35', 38' Sergio "Kun" Agüero 1-0 (p), 2-0, 42' Leroy Sané 3-0, 56' Raheem Sterling 4-0, 71' Bernardo Silva 5-0, 78' Phil Foden 6-0, 84' Gabriel Jesus 7-0.
Referee: Clément Turpin (FRA)   Attendance: 51,518.

12.03.19   Allianz Stadium, Torino: Juventus – Atlético Madrid 3-0 (1-0)
Juventus: Wojciech Szczesny, Leonardo Bonucci, Giorgio Chiellini, João Cancelo, Leonardo Spinazzola (67' Paulo Dybala), Blaise Matuidi, Miralem Pjanic, Emre Can, Cristiano Ronaldo, Mario Mandzukic (80' Moise Kean), Federico Bernardeschi. Coach: Massimiliano Allegri.
Atlético Madrid: Jan Oblak, Juanfran, Diego Godín, Santiago Arias (77' Vitolo), José Giménez, Saúl, Koke, Thomas Lemar (57' Ángel Correa), Rodri Hernández, Antoine Griezmann, Álvaro Morata. Coach: Diego Simeone.
Goals: 27', 48' 86' Cristiano Ronaldo 1-0, 2-0, 3-0 (p).
Referee: Björn Kuipers (HOL)   Attendance: 40,884.

13.03.19   Camp Nou, Barcelona: FC Barcelona – Olympique Lyonnais 5-1 (2-0)
FC Barcelona: Marc-André ter Stegen, Piqué, Jordi Alba, Sergi Roberto (83' Nélson Semedo), Clément Lenglet, Ivan Rakitic, Sergio Busquets, Philippe Coutinho (70' Ousmane Dembélé), Arthur (74' Arturo Vidal), Lionel Messi, Luis Suárez. Coach: Ernesto Valverde.
Olympique Lyonnais: Anthony Lopes (34' Mathieu Gorgelin), Marcelo, Fernando Marçal, Léo Dubois, Ferland Mendy (77' Maxwel Cornet), Jason Denayer, Tanguy Ndombélé, Lucas Tousart, Memphis Depay (73' Bertrand Traoré), Nabil Fekir, Moussa Dembélé. Coach: Bruno Génésio.
Goals: 18' Lionel Messi 1-0 (p), 31' Philippe Coutinho 2-0, 58' Lucas Tousart 2-1, 78' Lionel Messi 3-1, 81' Piqué 4-1, 86' Ousmane Dembélé 5-1.
Referee: Szymon Marciniak (POL)   Attendance: 92,346.

13.03.19   Allianz Arena, München: FC Bayern München – Liverpool FC 1-3 (1-1)
FC Bayern München: Manuel Neuer, Rafinha, Mats Hummels, David Alaba, Niklas Süle, Franck Ribéry (61' Kingsley Coman), Javi Martínez (72' Leon Goretzka), James Rodríguez (79' Renato Sanches), Thiago Alcântara, Serge Gnabry, Robert Lewandowski. Coach: Niko Kovac.
Liverpool FC: Alisson, Joel Matip, Virgil van Dijk, Andrew Robertson, Trent Alexander-Arnold, James Milner (87' Adam Lallana), Georginio Wijnaldum, Jordan Henderson (13' Fabinho), Roberto Firmino (83' Divock Origi), Mohamed Salah, Sadio Mané. Coach: Jürgen Klopp.
Goals: 26' Sadio Mané 0-1, 39' Joel Matip 1-1 (og), 69' Virgil van Dijk 1-2, 84' Sadio Mané 1-3.
Referee: Daniele Orsato (ITA)   Attendance: 68,145.

QUARTER FINALS

09.04.19 Anfield, Liverpool: Liverpool FC – FC Porto 2-0 (2-0)
Liverpool FC: Alisson, Dejan Lovren, Virgil van Dijk, Trent Alexander-Arnold, James Milner, Jordan Henderson, Fabinho, Naby Keïta, Roberto Firmino (82' Daniel Sturridge), Mohamed Salah, Sadio Mané (73' Divock Origi). Coach: Jürgen Klopp.
FC Porto: Iker Casillas, Maxi Pereira (77' Fernando Andrade), Alex Telles, Felipe Monteiro, Éder Militão, Danilo Pereira, Óliver Torres (73' Bruno Costa), Otávio, Tiquinho Soares (62' Yacine Brahimi), Jesús Corona, Moussa Marega. Coach: Sérgio Conceição.
Goals: 5' Naby Keïta 1-0, 26' Roberto Firmino 2-0.
Referee: Antonio Mateu Lahoz (ESP)   Attendance: 52,465.

09.04.19 Tottenham Hotspur Stadium, London:
           Tottenham Hotspur – Manchester City 1-0 (0-0)
Tottenham Hotspur: Hugo Lloris, Jan Vertonghen, Danny Rose, Toby Alderweireld, Kieran Trippier, Moussa Sissoko, Christian Eriksen, Dele Alli (87' Llorente), Harry Winks (81' Victor Wanyama), Son Heung-Min, Harry Kane (58' Lucas Moura). Coach: Mauricio Pochettino.
Manchester City: Ederson Moraes, Nicolás Otamendi, Kyle Walker, Aymeric Laporte, David Silva (89' Kevin De Bruyne), Fernandinho, Fabian Delph, Ilkay Gündogan, Riyad Mahrez (89' Leroy Sané), Sergio "Kun" Agüero (71' Gabriel Jesus), Raheem Sterling.
Coach: Pep Guardiola.
Goal: 78' Son Heung-Min 1-0.
Referee: Björn Kuipers (HOL)   Attendance: 60.044.

Sergio "Kun" Agüero missed a penalty kick (13').

10.04.19 Johan Cruijff ArenA, Amsterdam: AFC Ajax – Juventus 1-1 (0-1)
AFC Ajax: André Onana, Daley Blind, Nicolás Tagliafico, Joël Veltman, Matthijs de Ligt, Lasse Schöne (75' Jurgen Ekkelenkamp), Hakim Ziyech, Donny van de Beek, Frenkie de Jong, Dusan Tadic, David Neres. Coach: Erik ten Hag.
Juventus: Wojciech Szczesny, Leonardo Bonucci, Alex Sandro, João Cancelo, Daniele Rugani, Blaise Matuidi (75' Paulo Dybala), Miralem Pjanic, Rodrigo Bentancur, Cristiano Ronaldo, Mario Mandzukic (60' Douglas Costa), Federico Bernardeschi (90+3' Sami Khedira).
Coach: Massimiliano Allegri.
Goals: 45' Cristiano Ronaldo 0-1, 46' David Neres 1-1.
Referee: Carlos del Cerro Grande (ESP)   Attendance: 50.390.

10.04.19 Old Trafford, Manchester: Manchester United – FC Barcelona 0-1 (0-1)
Manchester United: David de Gea, Ashley Young, Chris Smalling, Victor Lindelöf, Luke Shaw, Diogo Dalot (74' Jesse Lingard), Paul Pogba, Fred, Scott McTominay, Romelu Lukaku (68' Anthony Martial), Marcus Rashford (85' Andreas Pereira). Coach: Ole Gunnar Solskjær.
FC Barcelona: Marc-André ter Stegen, Piqué, Jordi Alba, Clément Lenglet, Nélson Semedo, Ivan Rakitic, Sergio Busquets (90+3' Carles Aleñà), Philippe Coutinho (65' Arturo Vidal), Arthur (66' Sergi Roberto), Lionel Messi, Luis Suárez. Coach: Ernesto Valverde.
Goal: 12' Luke Shaw 0-1 (og).
Referee: Gianluca Rocchi (ITA)   Attendance: 74.093.

16.04.19 Allianz Stadium, Torino: Juventus – AFC Ajax 1-2 (1-1)
Juventus: Wojciech Szczesny, Leonardo Bonucci, Alex Sandro, Mattia De Sciglio (64' João Cancelo), Daniele Rugani, Blaise Matuidi, Miralem Pjanic, Emre Can, Cristiano Ronaldo, Paulo Dybala (46' Moise Kean), Federico Bernardeschi (80' Rodrigo Bentancur).
Coach: Massimiliano Allegri.
AFC Ajax: André Onana, Daley Blind, Joël Veltman, Matthijs de Ligt, Lasse Schöne, Hakim Ziyech (88' Klaas-Jan Huntelaar), Donny van de Beek, Noussair Mazraoui (11' Daley Sinkgraven, 82' Lisandro Magallán), Frenkie de Jong, Dusan Tadic, David Neres.
Coach: Erik ten Hag.
Goals: 28' Cristiano Ronaldo 1-0, 34' Donny van de Beek 1-1, 67' Matthijs de Ligt 1-2.
Referee: Clément Turpin (FRA)   Attendance: 41.445

16.04.19   Camp Nou, Barcelona: FC Barcelona – Manchester United 3-0 (2-0)
FC Barcelona: Marc-André ter Stegen, Piqué, Jordi Alba, Sergi Roberto (71' Nélson Semedo), Clément Lenglet, Ivan Rakitic, Sergio Busquets, Philippe Coutinho (81' Ousmane Dembélé), Arthur (75' Arturo Vidal), Lionel Messi, Luis Suárez. Coach: Ernesto Valverde.
Manchester United: David de Gea, Ashley Young, Chris Smalling, Phil Jones, Victor Lindelöf, Paul Pogba, Fred, Jesse Lingard (80' Alexis Sánchez), Scott McTominay, Anthony Martial (65' Diogo Dalot), Marcus Rashford (73' Romelu Lukaku). Coach: Ole Gunnar Solskjær.
Goals: 16', 20' Lionel Messi 1-0, 2-0, 61' Philippe Coutinho 3-0.
Referee: Dr.Felix Brych (GER)   Attendance: 96.708.

17.04.19   Estádio do Dragão, Porto: FC Porto – Liverpool FC 1-4 (0-1)
FC Porto: Iker Casillas, Pepe, Alex Telles, Felipe Monteiro, Éder Militão, Héctor Herrera, Danilo Pereira, Otávio (46' Tiquinho Soares), Yacine Brahimi (81' Bruno Costa), Jesús Corona (78' Fernando Andrade), Moussa Marega. Coach: Sérgio Conceição.
Liverpool FC: Alisson, Joel Matip, Virgil van Dijk, Andrew Robertson (71' Jordan Henderson), Trent Alexander-Arnold (66' Joseph Gomez), James Milner, Georginio Wijnaldum, Fabinho, Mohamed Salah, Sadio Mané, Divock Origi (46' Roberto Firmino).
Coach: Jürgen Klopp.
Goals: 26' Sadio Mané 0-1, 65' Mohamed Salah 0-2, 69' Éder Militão 1-2, 77' Roberto Firmino 1-3, 84' Virgil van Dijk 1-4.
Referee: Danny Makkelie (HOL)   Attendance: 49,117.

17.04.19   Etihad Stadium, Manchester: Manchester City – Tottenham Hotspur 4-3 (3-2)
Manchester City: Ederson Moraes, Vincent Kompany, Kyle Walker, Benjamin Mendy (84' Leroy Sané), Aymeric Laporte, David Silva (63' Fernandinho), Ilkay Gündogan, Kevin De Bruyne, Bernardo Silva, Sergio "Kun" Agüero, Raheem Sterling. Coach: Pep Guardiola.
Tottenham Hotspur: Hugo Lloris, Jan Vertonghen, Danny Rose (90+1' Davinson Sánchez), Toby Alderweireld, Kieran Trippier, Moussa Sissoko (41' Llorente), Victor Wanyama, Christian Eriksen, Lucas Moura (82' Benjamin Davies), Dele Alli, Son Heung-Min.
Coach: Mauricio Pochettino.
Goals: 4' Raheem Sterling 1-0, 7', 10' Son Heung-Min 1-1, 1-2, 11' Bernardo Silva 2-2, 21' Raheem Sterling 3-2, 59' Sergio "Kun" Agüero 4-2, 73' Llorente 4-3.
Referee: Cüneyt Çakir (TUR)   Attendance: 53.348.

SEMI-FINALS

30.04.19 <u>Tottenham Hotspur Stadium, London:</u> Tottenham Hotspur – AFC Ajax 0-1 (0-1)
<u>Tottenham Hotspur:</u> Hugo Lloris, Jan Vertonghen (39' Moussa Sissoko), Danny Rose (79' Benjamin Davies), Toby Alderweireld, Kieran Trippier (80' Juan Foyth), Davinson Sánchez, Victor Wanyama, Christian Eriksen, Lucas Moura, Dele Alli, Llorente.
Coach: Mauricio Pochettino.
<u>AFC Ajax:</u> André Onana, Daley Blind, Nicolás Tagliafico <u>(YC30)</u>, Joël Veltman <u>(YC63)</u>, Matthijs de Ligt, Lasse Schöne (65' Noussair Mazraoui), Hakim Ziyech (87' Klaas-Jan Huntelaar), Donny van de Beek, Frenkie de Jong, Dusan Tadic, David Neres.
Coach: Erik ten Hag.
<u>Goal:</u> 15' Donny van de Beek 0-1.
<u>Referee:</u> Antonio Mateu Lahoz (ESP)   Attendance: 60,243.

01.05.19 <u>Camp Nou, Barcelona:</u> FC Barcelona – Liverpool FC 3-0 (1-0)
<u>FC Barcelona:</u> Marc-André ter Stegen, Piqué, Jordi Alba <u>(YC86)</u>, Sergi Roberto (90+3' Carles Aleñá), Clément Lenglet <u>(YC39)</u>, Ivan Rakitic, Arturo Vidal, Sergio Busquets, Philippe Coutinho (60' Nélson Semedo), Lionel Messi, Luis Suárez <u>(YC81)</u> (90+3' Ousmane Dembélé). Coach: Ernesto Valverde.
<u>Liverpool FC:</u> Alisson, Joel Matip, Virgil van Dijk, Andrew Robertson, Joseph Gomez, James Milner (85' Divock Origi), Georginio Wijnaldum (79' Roberto Firmino), Fabinho <u>(YC81)</u>, Naby Keïta (24' Jordan Henderson), Mohamed Salah, Sadio Mané. Coach: Jürgen Klopp.
<u>Goals:</u> 26' Luis Suárez 1-0, 75', 82' Lionel Messi 2-0, 3-0.
<u>Referee:</u> Björn Kuipers (HOL)   Attendance: 98,299.

07.05.19 <u>Anfield, Liverpool:</u> Liverpool FC – FC Barcelona 4-0 (1-0)
<u>Liverpool FC:</u> Alisson, Joel Matip <u>(YC66)</u>, Virgil van Dijk, Andrew Robertson (46' Georginio Wijnaldum), Trent Alexander-Arnold, James Milner, Jordan Henderson, Fabinho <u>(YC11)</u>, Xherdan Shaqiri (90' Daniel Sturridge), Sadio Mané, Divock Origi (85' Joseph Gomez).
Coach: Jürgen Klopp.
<u>FC Barcelona:</u> Marc-André ter Stegen, Piqué, Jordi Alba, Sergi Roberto, Clément Lenglet, Ivan Rakitic <u>(YC53)</u> (80' Malcom), Arturo Vidal (75' Arthur), Sergio Busquets <u>(YC45+1)</u>, Philippe Coutinho (60' Nélson Semedo <u>(YC75)</u>), Lionel Messi, Luis Suárez.
Coach: Ernesto Valverde.
<u>Goals:</u> 7' Divock Origi 1-0, 54', 56' Georginio Wijnaldum 2-0, 3-0, 79' Divock Origi 4-0.
<u>Referee:</u> Cüneyt Çakir (TUR)   Attendance: 55,212.

08.05.19 <u>Johan Cruijff ArenA, Amsterdam:</u> AFC Ajax – Tottenham Hotspur 2-3 (2-0)
<u>AFC Ajax:</u> André Onana (YC90+5), Daley Blind, Nicolás Tagliafico, Matthijs de Ligt, Lasse Schöne (60' Joël Veltman), Hakim Ziyech <u>(YC77)</u>, Donny van de Beek (90' Lisandro Magallán), Noussair Mazraoui, Frenkie de Jong, Dusan Tadic, Kasper Dolberg <u>(YC50)</u> (67' Daley Sinkgraven). Coach: Erik ten Hag.
<u>Tottenham Hotspur:</u> Hugo Lloris, Jan Vertonghen, Danny Rose <u>(YC76)</u> (82' Benjamin Davies), Toby Alderweireld, Kieran Trippier (81' Érik Lamela), Moussa Sissoko <u>(YC16)</u>, Victor Wanyama (46' Llorente), Christian Eriksen, Lucas Moura, Dele Alli, Son Heung-Min.
Coach: Mauricio Pochettino.
<u>Goals:</u> 5' Matthijs de Ligt 1-0, 35' Hakim Ziyech 2-0,
55', 59', 90+6' Lucas Moura 2-1, 2-2, 2-3.
<u>Referee:</u> Dr.Felix Brych (GER)   Attendance: 52,641.

FINAL

01.06.19 Estadio Wanda Metropolitano, Madrid (ESP):
Tottenham Hotspur – Liverpool FC 0-2 (0-1)
Tottenham Hotspur: Hugo Lloris, Jan Vertonghen, Danny Rose, Toby Alderweireld, Kieran Trippier, Moussa Sissoko (74' Eric Dier), Christian Eriksen, Son Heung-Min, Dele Alli (82' Llorente), Harry Winks (66' Lucas Moura), Harry Kane. Coach: Mauricio Pochettino.
Liverpool FC: Alisson, Joel Matip, Virgil van Dijk, Andrew Robertson, Trent Alexander-Arnold, Georginio Wijnaldum (62' James Milner), Jordan Henderson, Fabinho, Robert Firmino (58' Divock Origi), Mohamed Salah, Sadio Mané (90' Joseph Gomez).
Coach: Jürgen Klopp.
Goals: 2' Mohamed Salah 0-1 (p), 87' Divock Origi 0-2.
Referee: Damir Skomina (SVN)   Attendance: 63,272.

UEFA CHAMPIONS LEAGUE 2019-2020

PRELIMINARY ROUND
SEMI-FINAL ROUND

25.06.19   Stadiumi Fadil Vokrri, Pristina: SP Tre Penne – FC Santa Coloma 0-1 (0-0)
SP Tre Penne: Mattia Migani, Mirko Palazzi, Davide Cesarini (46' Matteo Semprini), Alex Colonna, Nicola Chiaruzzi, Nicola Gai, Enrico Cibelli, Matteo Derjai (79' Aron Giacomoni), Federico Innocenti (58' Riccardo Innocenti), Luca Ceccaroli, Michael Angelini. Coach: Stefano Ceci.
FC Santa Coloma: Eloy Casals, Moisés San Nicolás, Marc Rebés, Andreu Ramos, Juanma Miranda, Pedro Santos (87' Nicolás Medina), Jordi Aláez (81' Enric Pi), Loren Burón, Aleix Cistero, Javi Camochu, André Azevedo (68' Chus Sosa). Coach: Marc Rodríguez Rebull.
Goal: 76' Javi Camochu 0-1.
Referee: Ian McNabb (NIR)   Attendance: 35.

25.06.19   Stadiumi Fadil Vokrri, Pristina: KF Feronikeli – Lincoln Red Imps FC 1-0 (1-0)
KF Feronikeli: Deniz Troshupa, Lapidar Lladrovci, Arber Prekazi, Perparim Islami, Jean Carioca, Yll Hoxha, Albert Dabiqaj, Kastriot Rexha, Besmir Bojku (82' Astrit Thaqi), Astrit Fazliu (87' Argjend Malaj), Mendurim Hoti (74' Mevlan Zeka). Coach: Zekirija Ramadani.
Lincoln Red Imps FC: Lolo Soler, Marcos Pérez (56' Jesús Toscano), Joseph Chipolina, Bernardo Lopes, Roy Chipolina, Borja Gil, Monti Montesinos, Gato (79' Falu Aranda), Sergio Molina, Iván Aguilar (74' Anthony Hernandez), Héctor Figueroa. Coach: Víctor Afonso.
Goal: 3' Mendurim Hoti 1-0.
Referee: Fedayi San (SUI)   Attendance: 3,000.

Both losers SP Tre Penne and Lincoln Red Imps FC enter the 2019-2020 UEFA Europa League Second Qualifying Round.

PRELIMINARY ROUND
FINAL ROUND

28.06.19   Stadiumi Fadil Vokrri, Pristina: KF Feronikeli – FC Santa Coloma 2-1 (0-0)
KF Feronikeli: Deniz Troshupa, Lapidar Lladrovci, Arber Prekazi, Perparim Islami, Jean Carioca (67' Jetmir Topalli), Yll Hoxha, Albert Dabiqaj, Kastriot Rexha, Besmir Bojku (90+1' Arbër Potoku), Astrit Fazliu, Mevlan Zeka (79' Argjend Malaj). Coach: Zekirija Ramadani.
FC Santa Coloma: Eloy Casals, Moisés San Nicolás, Marc Rebés (59' Enric Pi), Andreu Ramos, Juanma Miranda, Chus Sosa (82' André Azevedo), Pedro Santos, Loren Burón, Aleix Cistero, Nicolás Medina, Javi Camochu (64' Jordi Aláez). Coach: Marc Rodríguez Rebull.
Goals: 52' Chus Sosa 0-1, 58' Mevlan Zeka 1-1, 87' Kastriot Rexha 2-1.
Referee: Emmanouil Skoulas (GRE)   Attendance: 1,900.
Sent off: 49' Yll Hoxha.

Loser FC Santa Coloma enter the 2019-2020 UEFA Europa League Second Qualifying Round.

FIRST QUALIFYING ROUND

09.07.19   Astana Arena, Nur-Sultan: FK Astana – CFR Cluj 1-0 (0-0)
FK Astana: Nenad Eric, Antonio Rukavina, Yuriy Logvinenko, Abzal Beysebekov, Evgeni Postnikov, Luka Simunovic, Rúnar Sigurjónsson, Marin Tomasov (58' Rangelo Janga), Ivan Maevski, Roman Murtazaev (84' Ndombe Mubele), Dorin Rotariu.
Coach: Roman Grygorchuk.
CFR Cluj: Giedrius Arlauskis, Paulo Vinícius, Mateo Susic, Camora, Andrei Burca, Emmanuel Culio, Ciprian Deac, Ovidiu Hoban (75' Mário Rondón), Mihai Bordeianu (90' Luís Aurélio), Alexandru Paun (65' Sebastian Mailat), Billel Omrani. Coach: Dan Petrescu.
Goal: 68' Evgeni Postnikov 1-0.
Referee: Lawrence Visser (BEL)   Attendance: 18,587.

09.07.19   Yerevan Football Academy Stadium, Yerevan:
            FC Ararat-Armenia – AIK Solna 2-1 (2-1)
FC Ararat-Armenia: Dmitriy Abakumov, Rochdi Achenteh, Dmitri Guzj, Ângelo Meneses, Georgi Pashov, Gor Malakyan (46' Ilja Antonov), Kódjo Alphonse, Petros Avetisyan (71' Armen Ambartsumyan), Anton Kobyalko (70' Louis Ogana), Furdjel Narsingh, Zakaria Sanogo. Coach: Vardan Minasyan.
AIK Solna: Oscar Linnér, Robert Lundström, Karol Mets, Daniel Granli, Panajotis Dimitriadis, Enoch Adu, Anton Salétros (84' Rasmus Lindkvist), Bilal Hussein (46' Sebastian Larsson), Tarik Elyounoussi, Henok Goitom, Chinedu Obasi (65' Kolbeinn Sigthórsson).
Coach: Rikard Norling.
Goals: 3' Petros Avetisyan 1-0 (p), 39' Chinedu Obasi 1-1, 45' Petros Avetisyan 2-1.
Referee: Duje Strukan (CRO)   Attendance: 1,497.
Sent off: 13' Robert Lundström.

09.07.19   Kadrioru staadion, Tallinn: JK Nõmme Kalju – KF Shkëndija 79 0-1 (0-0)
JK Nõmme Kalju: Pavel Londak, Aleksandr Kulinits, Maximiliano Uggè, Vladimir Avilov, Andriy Markovych, Nikolaj Mashichev (76' Peeter Klein), Igor Subbotin, Réginald Mbu-Alidor, Kaspar Paur, Liliu, Robert Kirss (57' Aleksandr Volkov).
Coach: Roman Kozhukhovskyi.
KF Shkëndija 79: Kostadin Zahov, Gledi Mici, Mevlan Murati, Visar Musliu, Egzon Bejtulai, Armend Alimi, Zeni Husmani, Ennur Totre (85' Arbin Zejnullai), Besart Ibraimi (77' Valjmir Nafiu), Agim Ibraimi (90+1' Omar Imeri), Marjan Radeski. (Coach: Qatip Osmani).
Goal: 81' Agim Ibraimi 0-1 (p).
Referee: Donald Robertson (SCO)   Attendance: 1,640.

JK Nõmme Kalju played their home match at Kadrioru staadion, Tallinn, instead of their regular stadium Hiiu Stadium, Tallinn which does not meet UEFA requirements.

09.07.19   Telia 5G -areena, Helsinki: HJK Helsinki – HB Tórshavn 3-0 (2-0)
HJK Helsinki: Maksim Rudakov, Rafinha, Nikolai Alho, Daniel O'Shaughnessy, Faith Obilor, Riku Riski, Kaan Kairinen, Sebastian Dahlström, Lassi Lappalainen (89' Akseli Pelvas), Evans Mensah (78' Eetu Vertainen), Santeri Väänänen (33' Henri Toivomäki). Coach: Toni Koskela.
HB Tórshav: Teitur Gestsson, Jógvan Davidsen, Bartal Wardum (82' Daniel Johansen), Lasse Andersen, Símun Samuelsen, Magnus Egilsson, Hørdur Askham, Tróndur Jensen, Dan í Soylu (81' Brynjar Hlödversson), Adrian Justinussen, Ari Olsen (46' Sebastian Pingel). Coach: Heimir Gudjonsson.
Goals: 21' Lassi Lappalainen 1-0, 42' Daniel O'Shaughnessy 2-0, 66' Lassi Lappalainen 3-0.
Referee: Giorgi Kruashvili (GEO)   Attendance: 4,719.
Sent off: 31' Faith Obilor.

09.07.19   Olimpijski Stadion Asim Ferhatovic Hase, Sarajevo:
           FK Sarajevo – Celtic FC 1-3 (1-1)
FK Sarajevo: Vladan Kovacevic, Darko Lazic, Dusan Hodzic (87' Andrej Djokanovic), Besim Serbecic, Halid Sabanovic (66' Benjamin Tatar), Mirko Oremus, Amar Rahmanovic (78' Aladin Sisic), Anel Hebibovic, Mersudin Ahmetovic, Krste Velkoski, Slobodan Milanovic. Coach: Husref Musemic.
Celtic FC: Scott Bain, Jozo Simunovic, Boli Bolingoli-Mbombo (57' Jonny Hayes), Kristoffer Ajer, Scott Brown, Nir Bitton, James Forrest (78' Scott Sinclair), Callum McGregor, Ryan Christie, Odsonne Édouard, Michael Johnston (65' Lewis Morgan). Coach: Neil Lennon.
Goals: 29' Mirko Oremus 1-0, 35' Michael Johnston 1-1, 51' Odsonne Édouard 1-2, 85' Scott Sinclair 1-3.
Referee: Glenn Nyberg (SWE)   Attendance: 24,723.

09.07.19   Marijampolès sporto centro stadione, Marijampolè:
           FK Sūduva Marijampolè – Crvena Zvezda Beograd 0-0
FK Sūduva Marijampolè: Ivan Kardum, Vaidas Slavickas, Algis Jankauskas, Andro Svrljuga, Aleksandar Zivanovic, Semir Kerla, Jovan Cadenovic, Ovidijus Verbickas (90+1' Eligijus Jankauskas), Giedrius Matulevicius (58' Paulius Golubickas), Josip Tadic (46' Sandro Gotal), Mihret Topcagic. Coach: Vladimir Cheburin.
Crvena Zvezda Beograd: Milan Borjan, Nemanja Milunovic, Milan Rodic, Marko Gobeljic, Srdjan Babic, Marko Marin, Branko Jovicic (69' Cañas), Dusan Jovancic, Mirko Ivanic, Richmond Boakye (71' Milan Pavkov), Mohamed Ben Nabouhane (86' Aleksa Vukanovic). Coach: Vladan Milojevic.
Referee: Jørgen Daugbjerg Burchardt (DEN)   Attendance: 3,200.

09.07.19   Stade Josy Barthel, Luxembourg: F91 Dudelange – Valletta FC 2-2 (2-0)
F91 Dudelange: Tim Kips, Tom Schnell, Ricardo Delgado, Chris Stumpf, Mohamed Bouchouari, Mario Pokar, Dominik Stolz, Mickaël Garos (76' Charles Morren), Sabir Bougrine (65' Danel Sinani), Bertino Cabral Barbosa, Adel Bettaieb (84' Laurent Pomponi). Coach: Henri Bossi.
Valletta FC: Henry Bonello, Joseph Zerafa, Steve Borg, Douglas Packer (83' Antonio Monticelli), Rowen Muscat, Kyrian Nwoko, Jean Borg, Enmy Peña, Santiago Malano (53' Nicholas Pulis), Kevin Tulimieri (62' Shaun Dimech), Mario Fontanella. Coach: Darren Abdilla.
Goals: 26' Adel Bettaieb 1-0, 45+2' Dominik Stolz 2-0, 64' Douglas Parker 2-1, 70' Jean Borg 2-2.
Referee: Arnold Hunter (NIR)   Attendance: 1,152.
Sent off: 89' Rowen Muscat.

F91 Dudelange played their home match at Stade Josy Barthel, Luxembourg, instead of their regular Stadium Stade Jos Nosbaum, Dudelange.

09.07.19   Park Hall Stadium, Oswestry: The New Saints – KF Feronikeli 2-2 (0-0)
The New Saints: Paul Harrison, Simon Spender, Chris Marriott (57' Ryan Harrington), Keston Davies, Aeron Edwards, Jon Routledge, Daniel Redmond, Ryan Brobbel (66' Joash Nembhard), Greg Draper (76' Kurtis Byrne), Jamie Mullan, Adrian Cieslewicz. Coach: Scott Ruscoe.
KF Feronikeli: Deniz Troshupa, Lapidar Lladrovci, Arber Prekazi, Perparim Islami, Arbër Potoku, Jean Carioca (68' Jetmir Topalli), Albert Dabiqaj, Kastriot Rexha, Besmir Bojku (68' Argjend Malaj), Astrit Fazliu (90+4' Astrit Thaçi), Mevlan Zeka. Coach: Zekirija Ramadani.
Goals: 49' Greg Draper 1-0 (p), 77' Aeron Edwards 2-0, 89' Mevlan Zeka 2-1, 90+3' Astrit Fazliu 2-2 (p).
Referee: Trustin Farrugia Cann (MLT)   Attendance: 1,140.

10.07.19   Stadiumi Selman Stërmasi, Tiranë: FK Partizani – Qarabag FK 0-0
FK Partizani: Alban Hoxha, Egzon Belica, Enea Bitri, Labinot Ibrahimi, Esin Hakaj (80' Lorenc Trashi), Bruno Telushi, William Cordeiro (68' Ron Broja), Esat Mala, Emmanuel Mensah (58' Brian Brown), Jasir Asani, Eraldo Çinari. Coach: Franco Lerda.
Qarabag FK: Vagner, Rashad Sadigov, Maksim Medvedev, Abbas Hüseynov, Rahil Mammadov, Míchel, Dani Quintana (62' Jaime Romero), Richard Almeyda, Filip Ozobic (85' Gara Garayev), Abdellah Zoubir, Mahir Emreli (73' Araz Abdullayev). Coach: Gurban Gurbanov.
Referee: Thorvaldur Árnason (ISL)   Attendance: 2,210.

10.07.19   Bolshaya Sportivnaya Arena, Tiraspol:
            FC Sheriff Tiraspol – FC Saburtalo Tbilisi 0-3 (0-1)
FC Sheriff Tiraspol: Zvonimir Mikulic, Veaceslav Posmac, Artem Gordienko, Matej Palcic (69' Robert Tambe), Cristiano, Jaroslaw Jach, Antun Palic (46' Wilfried Balima), Jury Kendysh, José Ángel Jurado (46' Gheorghe Anton), Liridon Latifi, Gabrijel Boban. Coach: Zoran Zekic.
FC Saburtalo Tbilisi: Omar Migineishvili, Giorgi Rekhviashvili, Gagi Margvelashvili, Luka Lakvekheliani, Tornike Gorgiashvili (60' Levan Kakubava), Giorgi Diasamidze, Sandro Altunashvili, Nikoloz Mali, Ognjen Rolovic, Vagner Gonçalves (70' Lasha Shindagoridze), Giorgi Kokhreidze (77' Giorgi Gabedava). Coach: Giorgi Chiabrishvili.
Goals: 30' Ognjen Rolovic 0-1, 67' Giorgi Kokhreidze 0-2, 71' Levan Kakubava 0-3.
Referee: Iwan Arwel Griffith (WAL)   Attendance: 5,706.

10.07.19 Borisov Arena, Borisov: BATE Borisov – Piast Gliwice 1-1 (0-1)
BATE Borisov: Anton Chichkan, Egor Filipenko (10' Slobodan Simovic), Aleksandar Filipovic, Aleksey Rios, Igor Stasevich, Dmitriy Baga, Stanislav Dragun, Hervaine Moukam (66' Nemanja Milic), Evgeni Yablonski, Zakhar Volkov, Bojan Dubajic (56' Maksim Skavysh). Coach: Aleksei Baga.
Piast Gliwice: Frantisek Plach, Uros Korun, Mikkel Kirkeskov, Jakub Czerwinski, Martin Konczkowski, Marcin Pietrowski, Tom Hateley, Patryk Dziczek (61' Patryk Sokolowski), Joel Valencia (90' Gerard Badía), Piotr Parzyszek (85' Dani Aquino), Jorge Félix.
Coach: Waldemar Fornalik.
Goals: 36' Piotr Parzyszek 0-1, 64' Stanislav Dragun 1-1.
Referee: Mete Kalkavan (TUR)   Attendance: 11,529.
Sent off: 89' Stanislav Dragun.

10.07.19 Groupama Aréna, Budapest: Ferencvárosi TC – PFC Ludogorets Razgrad 2-1 (1-1)
Ferencvárosi TC: Dénes Dibusz, Marcel Heister, Miha Blazic, Lasha Dvali, Michal Skvarka, Gergö Lovrencsics, Igor Kharatin (77' Dávid Sigér), Oleksandr Zubkov, Danylo Ignatenko, Tamás Priskin (66' Davide Lanzafame), Tokmac Nguen (83' Roland Varga).
Coach: Serhiy Rebrov.
PFC Ludogorets Razgrad: Plamen Iliev, Cosmin Moti, Georgi Terziev, Jordan Ikoko, Anton Nedyalkov, Svetoslav Dyakov, Jacek Góralski (78' Stéphane Badji), Dan Biton (66' Marcelinho), Jody Lukoki (83' Jorginho), Mavis Tchibota, Jakub Swierczok.
Coach: Stoicho Stoev.
Goals: 6' Tokmac Nguen 1-0, 31' Jakub Swierczok 1-1, 65' Oleksandr Zubkov 2-1.
Referee: Eitan Shemeulevitch (ISR)   Attendance: 18,115.

10.07.19 Národny Futbalovy Stadión, Bratislava:
          Slovan Bratislava – FK Sutjeska Niksic 1-1 (0-0)
Slovan Bratislava: Dominik Greif, Mitch Apau, Vasil Bozhikov, Artem Sukhotsky, Marin Ljubicic, Kenan Bajric, "Moha" Mohammed Rharsalla (77' Erik Daniel), Aleksandar Cavric (64' Joeri de Kamps), Andraz Sporar, Rafael Ratão (64' Dávid Holman), Dejan Drazic.
Coach: Martin Sevela.
FK Sutjeska Niksic: Vladan Giljen, Darko Bulatovic, Aleksandar Sofranac, Bojan Ciger, Marko Cetkovic, Damir Kojasevic, Branislav Jankovic, Marko Vucic (81' Milutin Osmajic), Nemanja Nedic, Novica Erakovic, Bozo Markovic (88' Bojan Bozovic).
Coach: Nikola Rakojevic.
Goals: 82' Andraz Sporar 1-0, 90+5' Damir Kojasevic 1-1.
Referee: Vitali Meshkov (RUS)   Attendance: 11,250.

10.07.19 Windsor Park, Belfast: Linfield FC – Rosenborg BK 0-2 (0-1)
Linfield FC: Gareth Deane, Chris Casement, Matthew Clarke, Mark Stafford, Niall Quinn, Jamie Mulgrew, Jimmy Callacher, Kirk Millar (68' Shayne Lavery), Bastien Héry, Andrew Waterworth, Jordan Stewart (89' Stephen Fallon). Coach: David Healy.
Rosenborg BK: André Hansen, Tore Reginiussen, Even Hovland, Vegar Hedenstad, Birger Meling, Mike Jensen, Anders Konradsen (72' Anders Trondsen), Gjermund Åsen (70' Pål Helland), Marius Lundemo, Alexander Søderlund, Babajide Akintola (61' Yann-Erik De Lanlay). Coach: Eirik Horneland.
Goals: 22' Mike Jensen 0-1, 69' Alexander Søderlund 0-2.
Referee: Ivaylo Stoyanov (BUL)   Attendance: 2,710.

10.07.19   Oriel Park, Dundalk: Dundalk FC – Riga FC 0-0
Dundalk FC: Gary Rogers, Dean Jarvis, Sean Gannon, Sean Hoare, Daniel Cleary, Chris Shields (46' Andy Boyle), Patrick McEleney, John Mountney (58' Robbie Benson), Jamie McGrath (80' Daniel Kelly), Patrick Hoban, Michael Duffy. Coach: Vinny Perth.
Riga FC: Roberts Ozols, Herdi Prenga, Antonijs Cernomordijs, Aleksejs Visnakovs, Olegs Laizāns, Ritvars Rugins, Tomislav Saric, Joël Bopesu, Roger Rodrigues Figueira (79' Deniss Rakels), Armands Pētersons, Roman Debelko. Coach: Mihails Konevs.
Referee: Peter Královic (SVK)   Attendance: 3,100.

10.07.19   Vodafonevöllurinn, Reykjavík: Valur Reykjavík – NK Maribor 0-3 (0-1)
Valur Reykjavík: Hannes Halldórsson, Bjarni Eiríksson, Eidur Sigurbjörnsson, Sebastian Hedlund, Haukur Sigurdsson, Kristinn Sigurdsson, Sigurdur Lárusson (76' Kaj Leo í Bartalsstovu), Andri Adolphsson (84' Birnir Snær Ingason), Lasse Petry (78' Einar Karl Ingvarsson), Ólafur Finsen, Patrick Pedersen. Coach: Ólafur Jóhannesson.
NK Maribor: Kenan Piric, Mitja Viler, Martin Milec, Sasa Ivkovic, Spiro Pericic, Rok Kronaveter (89' Jasmin Mesanovic), Blaz Vrhovec, Alexandru Cretu, Dino Hotic (83' Martin Kramaric), Andrej Kotnik, Marcos Tavares (75' Rudi Pozeg Vancas). Coach: Darko Milanic.
Goals: 43' Spiro Pericic 0-1, 60' Dino Hotic 0-2, 86' Rok Kronaveter 0-3 (p).
Referee: Krzysztof Jakubik (POL)   Attendance: 1,201.

16.07.19   Tose Proeski Arena, Skopje: KF Shkëndija 79 – JK Nõmme Kalju 1-2 (0-1)
KF Shkëndija 79: Kostadin Zahov, Gledi Mici, Mevlan Murati, Visar Musliu, Egzon Bejtulai, Armend Alimi, Zeni Husmani (46' Valjmir Nafiu), Ennur Totre, Besart Ibraimi (63' Stênio Júnior), Agim Ibraimi, Marjan Radeski. Coach: Qatip Osmani.
JK Nõmme Kalju: Pavel Londak, Aleksandr Kulinits, Maximiliano Uggè, Vladimir Avilov, Andriy Markovych, Nikolaj Mashichev (60' Aleksandr Volkov), Igor Subbotin, Réginald Mbu-Alidor, Kaspar Paur (87' Deniss Tjapkin), Liliu, Peeter Klein.
Coach: Roman Kozhukhovskyi.
Goals: 5' Maximiliano Uggè 0-1, 62' Agim Ibraimi 1-1 (p), 90+1' Liliu 1-2.
Referee: Alain Bieri (SUI)   Attendance: 2,546.

JK Nõmme Kalju won on away goals.

FK Shkëndija 79 played their home match at Tose Proeski Arena, Skopje, instead of their regular stadium Ecolog Arena, Tetovo which was undergoing renovation.

16.07.19   Mikheil Meskhis sakhelobis Stadioni, Tbilisi:
          FC Saburtalo Tbilisi – FC Sheriff Tiraspol 1-3 (0-3)
FC Saburtalo Tbilisi: Omar Migineishvili, Giorgi Rekhviashvili, Gagi Margvelashvili, Luka Lakvekheliani, Tornike Gorgiashvili, Giorgi Diasamidze, Sandro Altunashvili (70' Alwyn Tera), Nikoloz Mali, Ognjen Rolovic (77' Giorgi Gabedava), Vagner Gonçalves (81' Lasha Shindagoridze), Giorgi Kokhreidze. Coach: Giorgi Chiabrishvili.
FC Sheriff Tiraspol: Zvonimir Mikulic, Artem Gordienko (69' Antun Palic), Ousmane N'Diaye, Matej Palcic, Mateo Muzek, Cristiano, Jury Kendysh, Gheorghe Anton (82' Jaroslaw Jach), Liridon Latifi, Gabrijel Boban (69' Leandro Ribeiro), Robert Tambe.
Coach: Zoran Zekic.
Goals: 3' Liridon Latifi 0-1, 8' Gagi Margvelashvili 0-2 (og), 11' Robert Tambe 0-3, 59' Ognjen Rolovic 1-3.
Referee: Pavel Orel (CZE)   Attendance: 7,560.
Sent off: 72' Matej Palcic.

16.07.19   MFA Centenary Stadium, Ta'Qali: Valletta FC – F91 Dudelange 1-1 (1-0)
Valletta FC: Henry Bonello, Joseph Zerafa, Ryan Camilleri, Steve Borg (90+3' Juan Gill), Douglas Packer, Kyrian Nwoko (69' Shaun Dimech), Jean Borg, Enmy Peña, Kevin Tulimieri (78' Antonio Monticelli), Nicholas Pulis, Mario Fontanella. Coach: Darren Abdilla.
F91 Dudelange: Tim Kips, Tom Schnell, Ricardo Delgado, Mehdi Kirch, Mohamed Bouchouari, Mario Pokar, Dominik Stolz, Mickaël Garos, Corenthyn Lavie (76' Bertino Cabral Barbosa), Sabir Bougrine (86' Omar Natami), Danel Sinani. Coach: Henri Bossi.
Goals: 35' Mario Fontanella 1-0, 59' Mario Pokar 1-1.
Referee: Juri Frischer (EST)   Attendance: 1,512.

Valletta FC won on away goals.

16.07.19   Gundadalur, Tórshavn: HB Tórshavn – HJK Helsinki 2-2 (1-0)
HB Tórshav: Teitur Gestsson, Jógvan Davidsen, Lasse Andersen, Símun Samuelsen, Magnus Egilsson, Hørdur Askham, Tróndur Jensen, Dan í Soylu (78' Brynjar Hlödversson), Pætur Petersen, Daniel Johansen, Sebastian Pingel. Coach: Heimir Gudjonsson.
HJK Helsinki: Maksim Rudakov, Rafinha, Henri Toivomäki, Nikolai Alho, Daniel O'Shaughnessy, Kevin Kouassivi-Benissan (46' Riku Riski), Erfan Zeneli (46' Lassi Lappalainen), Kaan Kairinen (81' Sebastian Dahlström), Evans Mensah, Santeri Väänänen, Eetu Vertainen. Coach: Toni Koskela.
Goals: 17' Sebastian Pingel 1-0, 56' Lasse Andersen 2-0, 60', 77' Riku Riski 2-1, 2-2.
Referee: Goergios Kominis (GRE)   Attendance: 620.

16.07.19   Stadion Rajko Mitic, Beograd:
            Crvena Zvezda Beograd – FK Sūduva Marijampolè 2-1 (2-0)
Crvena Zvezda Beograd: Milan Borjan, Nemanja Milunovic, Milan Rodic, Marko Gobeljic, Srdjan Babic, Marko Marin (88' Milan Pavkov), Branko Jovicic, Dusan Jovancic, Mirko Ivanic (82' Aleksa Vukanovic), Richmond Boakye (62' Filip Stojkovic), Mohamed Ben Nabouhane. Coach: Vladan Milojevic.
FK Sūduva Marijampolè: Ivan Kardum, Vaidas Slavickas (63' Ivan Hladík), Algis Jankauskas, Andro Svrljuga, Aleksandr Zivanovic, Semir Kerla, Jovan Cadenovic, Ovidijus Verbickas (76' Tosaint Ricketts), Mihret Topcagic, Sandro Gotal (51' Josip Tadic), Paulius Golubickas. Coach: Vladimir Cheburin.
Goals: 4' Richmond Boakye 1-0, 29' Marko Marin 2-0, 90+6' Mihret Topcagic 2-1.
Referee: Ádám Farkas (HUN)   Attendance: 23,751.
Sent off: 60' Marko Gobeljic.

16.07.19   Stadiumu Fadil Vokrri, Pristina: KF Feronikeli – The New Saints 0-1 (0-0)
KF Feronikeli: Florian Smakiqi, Lapidar Lladrovci, Arber Prekazi, Perparim Islami, Yll Hoxha, Albert Dabiqaj, Kastriot Rexha, Besmir Bojku (82' Argjend Malaj), Astrit Fazliu, Mendurim Hoti (72' Jean Carioca), Mevlan Zeka (64' Jetmir Topalli). Coach: Zekirija Ramadani.
The New Saints: Paul Harrison, Simon Spender, Keston Davies, Aeron Edwards, Jon Routledge, Daniel Redmond, Ryan Brobbel, Ryan Harrington, Greg Draper (80' Joash Nembhard), Jamie Mullan, Adrian Cieslewicz (65' Dean Ebbe). Coach: Scott Ruscoe.
Goal: 67' Dean Ebbe 0-1.
Referee: Espen Eskås (NOR)   Attendance: 7,800.

KF Feronikeli played their home match at Stadiumi Fadil Vokrri, Pristina, instead of their regular stadium Rexhepi Stadium, Drenas wgich did not meet UEFA requirements.

17.07.19   Stadions Skonto, Riga: Riga FC – Dundalk FC 0-0 (a.e.t.)
Riga FC: Roberts Ozols, Herdi Prenga, Antonijs Cernomordijs, Aleksejs Visnakovs (106' Vladislavs Gabovs), Olegs Laizāns (81' Stefan Panic), Ritvars Rugins, Tomislav Saric, Joël Bopesu (52' Deniss Rakels), Roger Rodrigues Figueira (51' Felipe Brisola), Armands Pētersons, Roman Debelko. Coach: Mihails Konevs.
Dundalk FC: Gary Rogers, Dane Massey, Andy Boyle, Sean Gannon, Sean Hoare, Chris Shields (99' Dean Jarvis), Robbie Benson (81' Daniel Kelly), Patrick McEleney (112' Georgie Kelly), John Mountney (65' Sean Murray), Jamie McGrath, Patrick Hoban.
Coach: Vinny Perth.
Referee: Dimitar Meckarovski (MCD)   Attendance: 6,050.
Sent off: 111' Herdi Prenga.

Dundalk FC won 5-4 on penalties after extra time.

Penalties: Debelko 1-0, Hoban 1-1, Saric 2-1, Murray 2-2, Gabovs 3-2, Jarvis 3-3, Felipe Brisola missed, Massey missed, Panic missed, Kelly missed, Rakels 4-3, McGrath 4-4, Pētersons missed, Hoare 4-5.

17.07.19   Friends Arena, Solna: AIK Solna – FC Ararat-Armenia 3-1 (0-0)
AIK Solna: Oscar Linnér, Per Karlsson (46' Rasmus Lindkvist), Karol Mets, Daniel Granli, Sebastian Larsson, Enoch Adu, Anton Salétros, Heradi Rashidi, Tarik Elyounoussi, Henok Goitom (90+3' Panajotis Dimitriadis), Chinedu Obasi (72' Kolbeinn Sigthórsson). Coach: Rikard Norling.
FC Ararat-Armenia: Dmitriy Abakumov, Dmitri Guzj, Ângelo Meneses, Alex Júnior Christian, Georgi Pashov, Ilja Antonov (86' Rochdi Achenteh), Kódjo Alphonse, Petros Avetisyan (68' Armen Ambartsumyan), Anton Kobyalko, Furdjel Narsingh, Zakaria Sanogo (60' Mailson). Coach: Vardan Minasyan.
Goals: 47', 52' Henok Goitom 1-0, 2-0, 62' Sebastian Larsson 3-0 (p), 77' Anton Kobyalko 3-1.
Referee: Robert Hennessy (IRL)   Attendance: 11,382.

17.07.19   Lerkendal Stadion, Trondheim: Rosenborg BK – Linfield FC 4-0 (1-0)
Rosenborg BK: André Hansen, Tore Reginiussen, Even Hovland, Vegar Hedenstad (46' Anders Trondsen), Birger Meling, Anders Konradsen (71' Emil Ceide), Gjermund Åsen, Marius Lundemo, Pål Helland, Alexander Søderlund (58' Babajide Akintola), Yann-Erik De Lanlay. Coach: Eirik Horneland.
Linfield FC: Gareth Deane, Chris Casement, Matthew Clarke, Niall Quinn, Jamie Mulgrew (59' Stephen Fallon), Jimmy Callacher, Daniel Kearns, Bastien Héry, Shayne Lavery (58' Andrew Waterworth), Jordan Stewart (74' Kirk Millar), Ross Larkin. Coach: David Healy.
Goals: 20', 51' Anders Konradsen 1-0, 2-0, 69' Babajide Akintola 3-0, 85' Pål Helland 4-0.
Referee: Enea Jorgji (ALB)   Attendance: 11,904.

17.07.19   Dalga Arena, Baku: Qarabag FK – FK Partizani 2-0 (0-0)
Qarabag FK: Vagner, Rashad Sadigov, Maksim Medvedev, Ailton, Rahil Mammadov, Míchel, Jaime Romero (90+4' Dani Quintana), Araz Abdullayev (78' Mahir Emreli), Richard Almeyda, Filip Ozobic (73' Simeon Slavchev), Abdellah Zoubir. Coach: Gurban Gurbanov.
FK Partizani: Alban Hoxha, Egzon Belica, Enea Bitri, Labinot Ibrahimi, Esin Hakaj (83' Brian Brown), Bruno Telushi, William Cordeiro, Esat Mala, Jasir Asani, Eraldo Çinari (61' Lorenc Trashi), Theophilus Solomon (75' Joseph Ekuban). Coach: Franco Lerda.
Goals: 51' Filip Ozobic 1-0, 90+4' Dani Quintana 2-0.
Referee: Dumitru Muntean (MOL)   Attendance: 5,932.

Qarabag FK played their home match at Dalga Arena, Baku, instead of their regular stadium Azersun Arena, Baku.

17.07.19   Ludogorets Arena, Razgrad: PFC Ludogorest Razgrad – Ferencvárosi TC 2-3 (1-2)
PFC Ludogorets Razgrad: Renan, Cosmin Moti, Georgi Terziev, Jordan Ikoko (64' Cicinho), Anton Nedyalkov, Svetoslav Dyakov, Jacek Góralski, Marcelinho (64' Dan Biton), Mavis Tchibota, Jakub Swierczok (46' Claudiu Keserü), Jorginho. Coach: Stoicho Stoev.
Ferencvárosi TC: Dénes Dibusz, Marcel Heister, Miha Blazic, Lasha Dvali, Michal Skvarka, Gergö Lovrencsics, Igor Kharatin, Oleksandr Zubkov, Danylo Ignatenko (57' Dávid Sigér), Tamás Priskin (73' Davide Lanzafame), Tokmac Nguen (61' Roland Varga).
Coach: Serhiy Rebrov.
Goals: 17' Igor Kharatin 0-1, 21' Michal Skvarka 0-2, 24' Georgi Terziev 1-2, 48' Tokmac Nguen 1-3, 69' Marcel Heister 2-3 (og).
Referee: Donatas Rumsas (LTU)   Attendance: 7,365.
Sent off: 82' Cosmin Moti.

17.07.19   Stadionul Dr. Constantin Radulescu, Cluj-Napoca: CFR Cluj – FK Astana 3-1 (2-1)
CFR Cluj: Giedrius Arlauskis, Paulo Vinícius, Mateo Susic, Camora, Andrei Burca, Emmanuel Culio, Ciprian Deac (86' Ovidiu Hoban), Damjan Djokovic, Mihai Bordeianu, Mário Rondón (66' Valentin Costache), Billel Omrani (84' Mickaël Pereira). Coach: Dan Petrescu.
FK Astana: Nenad Eric, Antonio Rukavina, Yuriy Logvinenko, Abzal Beysebekov (81' Marin Anicic), Evgeni Postnikov, Luka Simunovic, Rúnar Sigurjónsson (82' Rangelo Janga), Marin Tomasov (62' Ndombe Mubele), Ivan Maevski, Roman Murtazaev, Dorin Rotariu.
Coach: Roman Grygorchuk.
Goals: 4' Roman Murtazaev 0-1, 10', 26', 73' Billel Omrani 1-1, 2-1, 3-1.
Referee: Alexander Harkam (AUT)   Attendance: 8,092.

17.07.19   Stadion Miejski, Gliwice: Piast Gliwice – BATE Borisov 1-2 (1-0)
Piast Gliwice: Frantisek Plach, Uros Korun, Mikkel Kirkeskov, Jakub Czerwinski, Martin Konczkowski (83' Gerard Badía), Marcin Pietrowski, Tom Hateley, Patryk Dziczek, Joel Valencia, Piotr Parzyszek, Jorge Félix (87' Dani Aquino). Coach: Waldemar Fornalik.
BATE Borisov: Anton Chichkan, Aleksandar Filipovic, Aleksey Rios, Igor Stasevich, Dmitriy Baga, Slobodan Simovic, Jasse Tuominen (57' Nemanja Milic), Evgeni Yablonski, Evgeniy Berezkin (75' Hervaine Moukam), Zakhar Volkov, Maksim Skavysh. Coach: Aleksei Baga.
Goals: 21' Jakub Czerwinski 1-0, 82' Hervaine Moukam 1-1 (p), 87' Zakhar Volkov 1-2.
Referee: Antti Munukka (FIN)   Attendance: 9,312.

17.07.19   Stadion Kraj Bistrice, Niksic:
FK Sutjeska Niksic – Slovan Bratislava 1-1 (0-0, 1-1) (a.e.t.)
FK Sutjeska Niksic: Vladan Giljen, Darko Bulatovic, Aleksandar Sofranac, Bojan Ciger, Marko Cetkovic (74' Stefan Nikolic), Damir Kojasevic, Branislav Jankovic (115' Vladan Bubanja), Marko Vucic (69' Miljan Vlaisavljevic), Nemanja Nedic, Novica Erakovic, Bozo Markovic (86' Milutin Osmajic). Coach: Nikola Rakojevic.
Slovan Bratislava: Dominik Greif, Vasil Bozhikov, Artem Sukhotsky, Jurij Medvedev, Marin Ljubicic (106' Rafael Ratão), Dávid Holman (71' Myenty Abena), Joeri de Kamps (86' Dejan Drazic), Erik Daniel (46' Aleksandar Cavric), Kenan Bajric, "Moha" Mohammed Rharsalla, Andraz Sporar. Coach: Martin Sevela.
Goals: 49' Nemanja Nedic 0-1 (og), 90+3' Aleksandar Sofranac 1-1.
Referee: Horatiu Fesnic (ROM)   Attendance: 4,764.

FK Sutjeska Niksic won 3-2 penalties after extra time.
Penalties: Nikolic 1-0, Drazic missed, Kojasevic missed, Bozhikov missed, Vlaisavljevic 2-0, Rafael Ratão 2-1, Bubanja 3-1, Abena 3-2, Bulatovic missed, Sporar missed.

17.07.19   Ljudski vrt, Maribor: NK Maribor – Valur Reykjavík 2-0 (2-0)
NK Maribor: Kenan Piric, Mitja Viler, Martin Milec, Sasa Ivkovic, Spiro Pericic, Rok Kronaveter (58' Rudi Pozeg Vancas), Blaz Vrhovec (73' Martin Kramaric), Alexandru Cretu, Dino Hotic, Andrej Kotnik (57' Jasmin Mesanovic), Marcos Tavares. Coach: Darko Milanic.
Valur Reykjavík: Hannes Halldórsson, Birkir Sævarsson, Eidur Sigurbjörnsson, Orri Ómarsson, Haukur Sigurdsson (19' Lasse Petry), Kristinn Sigurdsson (77' Sebastian Hedlund), Andri Adolphsson (62' Birnir Snær Ingason), Kaj Leo í Bartalsstovu, Einar Karl Ingvarsson, Ívar Jónsson, Patrick Pedersen. Coach: Ólafur Jóhannesson.
Goals: 11' Rok Kronaveter 1-0, 32' Marcos Tavares 2-0.
Referee: João Pedro Pinheiro (POR)   Attendance: 6,716.

17.07.19   Celtic Park, Glasgow: Celtic FC – FK Sarajevo 2-1 (1-0)
Celtic FC: Scott Bain, Jozo Simunovic, Boli Bolingoli-Mbombo, Kristoffer Ajer, Scott Brown, Nir Bitton, James Forrest, Callum McGregor, Ryan Christie (89' Ewan Henderson), Lewis Morgan (87' Scott Sinclair), Odsonne Édouard (78' Leigh Griffiths). Coach: Neil Lennon.
FK Sarajevo: Vladan Kovacevic, Darko Lazic, Dusan Hodzic, Besim Serbecic, Mirko Oremus, Amar Rahmanovic (83' Gedeon Guzina), Anel Hebibovic, Mersudin Ahmetovic, Krste Velkoski, Slobodan Milanovic (60' Aladin Sisic), Benjamin Tatar (72' Andrej Djokanovic). Coach: Husref Musemic.
Goals: 26' Ryan Christie 1-0, 62' Benjamin Tatar 1-1, 75' Callum McGregor 2-1.
Referee: Alain Durieux (LUX)   Attendance: 58,662.

The following losers enter the 2019-2020 UEFA Europa League Second Qualifying Round:
KF Shkëndija 79, FK Sūduva Marijampolé, FC Ararat-Armenia, FK Astana, PFC Ludogorets Razgrad, FK Partizani, Slovan Bratislava, FC Sheriff Tiraspol, F91 Dudelange, Linfield FC, Valur Reykjavík, Riga FC, KF Feronikeli, HB Tórshavn, Piast Gliwice.

The loser FK Sarajevo were drawn to receive a bye to the 2019-2020 UEFA Europa League Third Qualifying Round.

SECOND QUALIFYING ROUND

23.07.19   Doosan Aréna, Plzen: FC Viktoria Plzen – Olympiacos Piraeus FC 0-0
FC Viktoria Plzen: Ales Hruska, Adam Hlousek, Jakub Brabec (72' Lukás Hejda), Ludek Pernica, Milan Havel, Jan Kopic, Ales Cermák (83' Ondrej Mihálik), Patrik Hrosovsky, Lukás Kalvach, Joel Kayamba, Michal Krmencík (69' Tomás Chory). Coach: Pavel Vrba.
Olympiacos Piraeus FC: José Sá, Avram Papadopoulos (22' Ousseynou Ba), Omar Elabdellaoui, Rúben Semedo, Kostas Tsimikas, Mathieu Valbuena (57' Mady Camara), Guilherme, Andreas Bouchalakis, Daniel Podence, Georgios Masouras (81' Lazar Randjelovic), Guerrero. Coach: Pedro Martins.
Referee: Marco Guida (ITA)   Attendance: 10,632.

23.07.19   Mikheil Meskhis sakhelobis Stadioni, Tbilisi:
            FC Saburtalo Tbilisi – Dinamo Zagreb 0-2 (0-0)
FC Saburtalo Tbilisi: Omar Migineishvili, Giorgi Rekhviashvili, Gagi Margvelashvili, Luka Lakvekheliani, Giorgi Diasamidze (82' Dachi Tsnobiladze), Sandro Altunashvili (70' Giorgi Gabedava), Nikoloz Mali, Alwyn Tera (57' Levan Kakubava), Ognjen Rolovic, Vagner Gonçalves, Giorgi Kokhreidze. Coach: Giorgi Chiabrishvili.
Dinamo Zagreb: Dominik Livakovic, Marin Leovac, Ivo Pinto (50' Mario Situm), Marko Leskovic, Dino Peric, Arijan Ademi, Amer Gojak (86' Ivan Sunjic), Mario Gavranovic (68' Bruno Petkovic), Mislav Orsic, Izet Hajrovic, Damian Kadzior. Coach: Nenad Bjelica.
Goals: 67' Mislav Orsic 0-1, 78' Bruno Petkovic 0-2 (p).
Referee: Petr Ardeleánu (CZE)   Attendance: 15,165.

23.07.19   Park Hall Stadium, Oswestry: The New Saints – FC København 0-2 (0-1)
The New Saints: Paul Harrison, Simon Spender, Keston Davies, Ryan Harrington, Aeron Edwards, Jon Routledge, Daniel Redmond, Ryan Brobbel, Jamie Mullan, Adrian Cieslewicz (75' Joash Nembhard), Dean Ebbe (56' Greg Draper). Coach: Scott Ruscoe.
FC København: Sten Grytebust, Pierre Bengtsson, Sotirios Papagiannopoulos, Karlo Bartolec, Victor Nelsson, Rasmus Falk (35' Zeca), Robert Skov, Jens Stage, Dame N'Doye (46' Jonas Wind), Pieros Sotiriou (62' Viktor Fischer), Carlo Holse. Coach: Ståle Solbakken.
Goals: 18' Pieros Sotiriou 0-1, 61' Robert Skov 0-2 (p).
Referee: Alexander Harkam (AUT)   Attendance: 1,230.

23.07.19   Philips Stadion, Eindhoven: PSV Eindhoven – FC Basel 3-2 (1-1)
PSV Eindhoven: Jeroen Zoet, Nick Viergever, Derrick Luckassen, Denzel Dumfries, Bruma (78' Cody Gakpo), Érick Gutiérrez, Michal Sadílek, Pablo Rosario, Steven Bergwijn, Hirving Lozano (82' Sam Lammers), Donyell Malen. Coach: Mark van Bommel.
FC Basel: Jonas Omlin, Silvan Widmer, Éder Álvarez Balanta (90' Afimico Pululu), Omar Alderete, Eray Cömert, Valentin Stocker (65' Noah Okafor), Luca Zuffi, Fabian Frei, Taulant Xhaka, Ricky van Wolfswinkel, Albian Ajeti (87' Kemal Ademi). Coach: Marcelo Koller.
Goals: 14' Bruma 1-0, 45+1' Albian Ajeti 1-1, 79' Omar Alderete 1-2, 89' Sam Lammers 2-2, 90+2' Donyell Malen 3-2.
Referee: Andris Treimanis (LAT)   Attendance: 31,638.

23.07.19   Stadion Kraj Bistrice, Niksic: FK Sutjeska Niksic – APOEL Nicosia 0-1 (0-1)
FK Sutjeska Niksic: Vladan Giljen, Darko Bulatovic, Aleksandar Sofranac, Bojan Ciger, Marko Cetkovic (40' Milutin Osmajic), Damir Kojasevic, Branislav Jankovic, Marko Vucic (79' Miljan Vlaisavljevic), Nemanja Nedic, Novica Erakovic, Bozo Markovic (66' Stefan Nikolic). Coach: Nikola Rakojevic.
APOEL Nicosia: Vid Belec, Kevin Lafrance, Praxitelis Vouros, Nicholas Ioannou, Dragan Mihajlovic, Savvas Gentsoglou, Antonio Jakolis (59' Vujadin Savic), Tomás De Vincenti (90+3' Uros Matic), Lucas Souza, Musa Al-Taamari, Linus Hallenius (60' Andrija Pavlovic). Coach: Paolo Tramezzani.
Goal: 42' Tomás De Vincenti 0-1 (p).
Referee: István Vad (HUN)   Attendance: 5,500.

24.07.19   Borisov Arena, Borisov: BATE Borisov – Rosenborg BK 2-1 (1-1)
BATE Borisov: Anton Chichkan, Aleksandar Filipovic, Aleksey Rios, Igor Stasevich, Dmitriy Baga, Stanislav Dragun, Slobodan Simovic, Evgeni Yablonski, Zakhar Volkov, Nemanja Milic (78' Hervaine Moukam), Maksim Skavysh (85' Jasse Tuominen). Coach: Aleksei Baga.
Rosenborg BK: André Hansen, Tore Reginiussen, Even Hovland, Vegar Hedenstad, Birger Meling, Mike Jensen, Anders Konradsen, Marius Lundemo, Alexander Søderlund, Yann-Erik De Lanlay (77' Pål Helland), Babajide Akintola (64' Samuel Adegbenro). Coach: Eirik Horneland.
Goals: 5' Igor Stasevich 1-0 (p), 25' Anders Konradsen 1-1, 51' Maksim Skavysh 2-1.
Referee: Sandro Schärer (SUI)   Attendance: 12,696.

24.07.19   Stadionul Dr. Constantin Radulescu, Cluj-Napoca:
CFR Cluj – Maccabi Tel Aviv FC 1-0 (1-0)
CFR Cluj: Giedrius Arlauskis, Paulo Vinícius, Mateo Susic, Camora, Andrei Burca, Emmanuel Culio, Ciprian Deac (90+1' Mickaël Pereira), Damjan Djokovic (79' Yacouba Sylla), Mihai Bordeianu, Mário Rondón (73' Adrian Paun), Billel Omrani. Coach: Dan Petrescu.
Maccabi Tel Aviv FC: Andreas Gianniotis, Ofir Davidzada, Shahar Piven-Bachtiar, Jair Amador, Maor Kandil, Avi Rikan, Dor Peretz, Dan Glazer, Itay Shechter (83' Eliran Atar), Chikeluba Ofoedu (67' Nick Blackman), Yonatan Cohen (55' Dor Micha). Coach: Vladimir Ivic.
Goal: 22' Billel Omrani 1-0.
Referee: José María Sánchez Martínez (ESP)   Attendance: 11,150.

24.07.19   Groupama Aréna, Budapest: Ferencvárosi TC – Valletta FC 3-1 (2-0)
Ferencvárosi TC: Dénes Dibusz, Miha Blazic, Lasha Dvali, Eldar Civic, Michal Skvarka (82' Dávid Sigér), Gergö Lovrencsics, Igor Kharatin, Oleksandr Zubkov, Danylo Ignatenko, Davide Lanzafame (66' Nikolay Signevich), Tokmac Nguen (65' Lukács Böle). Coach: Serhiy Rebrov.
Valletta FC: Henry Bonello, Joseph Zerafa, Steve Borg, Douglas Packer (70' Yuri Messias), Rowen Muscat, Kyrian Nwoko (83' Matteo Piciollo), Jean Borg, Enmy Peña, Kevin Tulimieri, Nicholas Pulis (57' Shaun Dimech), Mario Fontanella. Coach: Darren Abdilla.
Goals: 19' Henry Bonello 1-0 (og), 36', 59' Davide Lanzafame 2-0 (p), 3-0, 85' Yuri Messias 3-1.
Referee: Radu Petrescu (ROM)   Attendance: 18,603.
Sent off: 90+4' Steve Borg.

24.07.19   Ljudski vrt, Maribor: NK Maribor – AIK Solna 2-1 (2-1)
NK Maribor: Kenan Piric, Mitja Viler, Martin Milec, Sasa Ivkovic, Spiro Pericic, Rok Kronaveter, Blaz Vrhovec, Alexandru Cretu, Dino Hotic, Andrej Kotnik (80' Rudi Pozeg Vancas), Marcos Tavares (87' Jasmin Mesanovic). Coach: Darko Milanic.
AIK Solna: Oscar Linnér, Per Karlsson, Karol Mets, Daniel Granli, Sebastian Larsson, Enoch Adu, Anton Salétros (79' Rasmus Lindkvist), Heradi Rashidi, Tarik Elyounoussi, Kolbeinn Sigthórsson (62' Chinedu Obasi), Henok Goitom. Coach: Rikard Norling.
Goals: 6' Rok Kronaveter 1-0, 28' Henok Goitom 1-1, 38' Sasa Ivkovic 2-1.
Referee: Sascha Stegemann (GER)   Attendance: 7,816.

24.07.19   Oriel Park, Dundalk: Dundalk FC – Qarabag FK 1-1 (0-1)
Dundalk FC: Gary Rogers, Dane Massey, Andy Boyle, Sean Gannon, Sean Hoare, Chris Shields, Robbie Benson (27' Sean Murray), Patrick McEleney (69' John Mountney), Jamie McGrath, Patrick Hoban (83' Georgie Kelly), Michael Duffy. Coach: Vinny Perth.
Qarabag FK: Vagner, Rashad Sadigov, Maksim Medvedev (53' Abbas Hüseynov), Ailton, Rahil Mammadov, Jaime Romero (87' Araz Abdullayev), Gara Garayev, Richard Almeyda, Simeon Slavchev, Abdellah Zoubir, Mahir Emreli. Coach: Gurban Gurbanov.
Goals: 4' Mahir Emreli 0-1, 78' Patrick Hoban 1-1.
Referee: Bartosz Frankowski (POL)   Attendance: 3,100.

24.07.19   Stadion Rajko Mitic, Beograd: Crvena Zvezda Beograd – HJK Helsinki 2-0 (1-0)
Crvena Zvezda Beograd: Milan Borjan, Nemanja Milunovic, Milan Rodic, Filip Stojkovic, Srdjan Babic, Marko Marin, Branko Jovicic, Dusan Jovancic, Mirko Ivanic (63' Milan Jevtovic), Richmond Boakye (72' Milan Pavkov), Mohamed Ben Nabouhane (85' Aleksa Vukanovic). Coach: Vladan Milojevic.
HJK Helsinki: Maksim Rudakov, Rafinha, Henri Toivomäki, Nikolai Alho, Faith Obilor, William Parra, Riku Riski, Kaan Kairinen, Sebastian Dahlström, Evans Mensah (90+1' Tim Väyrynen), Ivan Tarasov (81' Kevin Kouassivi-Benissan). Coach: Toni Koskela.
Goals: 27' Richmond Boakye 1-0, 90' Milan Pavkov 2-0.
Referee: Pawel Gil (POL)   Attendance: 36,289.

24.07.19   Celtic Park, Glasgow: Celtic FC – JK Nõmme Kalju 5-0 (3-0)
Celtic FC: Scott Bain, Jozo Simunovic, Boli Bolingoli-Mbombo (37' Michael Johnston), Kristoffer Ajer, Scott Brown, Nir Bitton, James Forrest, Callum McGregor, Ryan Christie (71' Jules Olivier Ntcham), Leigh Griffiths (59' Lewis Morgan), Odsonne Édouard.
Coach: Neil Lennon.
JK Nõmme Kalju: Pavel Londak, Aleksandr Kulinits, Maximiliano Uggè, Vladimir Avilov, Andriy Markovych, Sander Puri, Igor Subbotin, Réginald Mbu-Alidor, Kaspar Paur (75' Aleksandr Volkov), Liliu (84' Nikolaj Mashichev), Peeter Klein (46' Max Mata).
Coach: Roman Kozhukhovskyi.
Goals: 36' Kristoffer Ajer 1-0, 44' Ryan Christie 2-0 (p), 45+3' Leigh Griffiths 3-0, 65' Ryan Christie 4-0, 77' Callum McGregor 5-0.
Referee: Jakob Kehlet (DEN)   Attendance: 41,872.

30.07.19   Winner Stadium, Netanya: Maccabi Tel Aviv FC – CFR Cluj 2-2 (1-2)
Maccabi Tel Aviv FC: Andreas Gianniotis, Ofir Davidzada, Shahar Piven-Bachtiar, Jair Amador, Maor Kandil (59' Geraldes), Avi Rikan (46' Yonatan Cohen), Dor Micha, Dor Peretz, Dan Glazer, Nick Blackman (72' Eliran Atar), Itay Shechter. Coach: Vladimir Ivic.
CFR Cluj: Giedrius Arlauskis, Paulo Vinícius, Mateo Susic, Camora, Andrei Burca, Emmanuel Culio, Ciprian Deac (52' Adrian Paun), Damjan Djokovic, Mihai Bordeianu, Mário Rondón (82' George Tucudean), Billel Omrani (86' Andrei Muresan). Coach: Dan Petrescu.
Goals: 15' Nick Blackman 1-0, 19' Emmanuel Culio 1-1 (p), 42' Mário Rondón 1-2, 48' Yonatan Cohen 2-2.
Referee: Marco Fritz (GER)   Attendance:

Maccabi Tel Aviv FC played their home match at Netanya Stadium, Netanya, instead of their regular stadium Bloomfield Stadium, Tel Aviv which is undergoing renovation.

30.07.19   Neo GSP Stadium, Nicosia: APOEL Nicosia – FK Sutjeska Niksic 3-0 (2-0)
APOEL Nicosia: Vid Belec, Vujadin Savic (76' Giorgios Merkis), Praxitelis Vouros, Nicholas Ioannou, Dragan Mihajlovic, Savvas Gentsoglou (78' Alef), Antonio Jakolis, Uros Matic, Tomás De Vincenti, Musa Al-Taamari, Andrija Pavlovic (71' Roman Bezjak). Coach: Paolo Tramezzani.
FK Sutjeska Niksic: Vladan Giljen, Darko Bulatovic, Aleksandar Sofranac, Bojan Ciger, Damir Kojasevic, Branislav Jankovic, Aleksa Marusic (60' Marko Cetkovic), Nemanja Nedic, Vladan Bubanja, Milutin Osmajic (72' Miljan Vlaisavljevic), Bojan Bozovic (67' Stefan Nikolic). Coach: Nikola Rakojevic.
Goals: 13', 25', 66' Andrija Pavlovic 1-0, 2-0, 3-0.
Referee: Roi Reinshreiber (ISR)   Attendance:

30.07.19   A. Le Coq Arena, Tallinn: JK Nõmme Kalju – Celtic FC 0-2 (0-1)
JK Nõmme Kalju: Pavel Londak, Aleksandr Kulinits, Maximiliano Uggè, Vladimir Avilov, Deniss Tjapkin, Andriy Markovych, Sander Puri, Igor Subbotin (79' Nikolaj Mashichev), Kaspar Paur (83' Aleksandr Ivanjusin), Liliu (38' Max Mata), Peeter Klein.
Coach: Roman Kozhukhovskyi.
Celtic FC: Craig Gordon, Jozo Simunovic, Christopher Jullien, Boli Bolingoli-Mbombo, Tony Ralston, Scott Brown, Nir Bitton (70' Marian Shved), Jules Olivier Ntcham (84' Ryan Christie), Lewis Morgan, Leigh Griffiths, Michael Johnston (61' Scott Sinclair).
Coach: Neil Lennon.
Goals: 10' Aleksandr Kulinits 0-1 (og), 90+3' Marian Shved 0-2.
Referee: Benoît Millot (FRA)   Attendance:

JK Nõmme Kalju played their home match at A. Le Coq Arena, Tallinn, instead of their regular stadium Hiiu Stadium, Tallinn which did not meet UEFA requirements,

30.07.19   St. Jakob-Park, Basel: FC Basel – PSV Eindhoven 2-1 (1-1)
FC Basel: Jonas Omlin, Silvan Widmer, Éder Álvarez Balanta, Omar Alderete, Eray Cömert, Valentin Stocker, Luca Zuffi, Fabian Frei, Taulant Xhaka (81' Raoul Petretta), Ricky van Wolfswinkel, Albian Ajeti. Coach: Marcelo Koller.
PSV Eindhoven: Jeroen Zoet, Nick Viergever, Derrick Luckassen, Denzel Dumfries, Bruma, Érick Gutiérrez, Michal Sadílek, Pablo Rosario, Steven Bergwijn, Hirving Lozano (76' Cody Gakpo), Donyell Malen. Coach: Mark van Bommel.
Goals: 8' Eray Cömert 1-0, 23' Bruma 1-1, 68' Ricky van Wolfswinkel 2-1.
Referee: Fábio Veríssimo (POR)   Attendance: 29,216.

FC Basel won on away goals.

30.07.19   Stadion Maksimir, Zagreb: Dinamo Zagreb – FC Saburtalo Tbilisi 3-0 (0-0)
Dinamo Zagreb: Dominik Livakovic, Marin Leovac, Ivo Pinto, Marko Leskovic, Dino Peric, Arijan Ademi, Amer Gojak, Mario Gavranovic (63' Bruno Petkovic), Mislav Orsic, Izet Hajrovic (84' Lovro Majer), Damian Kadzior (75' Daniel Olmo). Coach: Nenad Bjelica.
FC Saburtalo Tbilisi: Lazare Kupatadze, Giorgi Rekhviashvili, Dachi Tsnobiladze, Gagi Margvelashvili, Grigol Chabradze (69' Jemali-Giorgi Jinjolava), Tornike Gorgiashvili (61' Giorgi Diasamidze), Levan Kakubava, Sandro Altunashvili, Nikoloz Mali (59' Iuri Tabatadze), Giorgi Gabedava, Ognjen Rolovic. Coach: Giorgi Chiabrishvili.
Goals: 77' Mislav Orsic 1-0, 88' Bruno Petkovic 2-0, 90+4' Daniel Olmo 3-0.
Referee: Daniele Doveri (ITA)   Attendance:

30.07.19   MFA Centenary Stadium, Ta'Qali: Valletta FC – Ferencvarósi TC 1-1 (1-0)
Valletta FC: Henry Bonello, Joseph Zerafa, Ryan Camilleri, Rowen Muscat (80' Antonio Monticelli), Jean Borg, Enmy Peña, Shaun Dimech (75' Kyrian Nwoko), Matteo Piciollo (90' Ryan Tonna), Kevin Tulimieri, Yuri Messias, Mario Fontanella. Coach: Darren Abdilla.
Ferencvárosi TC: Dénes Dibusz, Miha Blazic, Lasha Dvali, Eldar Civic, Michal Skvarka, Gergö Lovrencsics, Igor Kharatin, Oleksandr Zubkov, Danylo Ignatenko (33' Dávid Sigér), Davide Lanzafame (75' Nikolay Signevich), Tokmac Nguen (85' Roland Varga).
Coach: Serhiy Rebrov.
Goals: 27' Mario Fontanella 1-0 (p), 60' Tokmac Nguen 1-1.
Referee: Jonathan Lardot (BEL)   Attendance:

30.07.19   Stadio Georgios Karaiskáki, Piraeus:
            Olympiacos Piraeus FC – FC Viktoria Plzen 4-0 (0-0)
Olympiacos Piraeus FC: José Sá, Omar Elabdellaoui, Rúben Semedo, Yassine Meriah, Kostas Tsimikas, Mathieu Valbuena (66' Mady Camara), Guilherme, Andreas Bouchalakis, Daniel Podence (85' Lazar Randjelovic), Georgios Masouras, Guerrero (80' Youssef El-Arabi). Coach: Pedro Martins.
FC Viktoria Plzen: Ales Hruska, Adam Hlousek, Radim Reznik, Jakub Brabec, Ludek Pernica, Jan Kopic, Patrik Hrosovsky, Lukás Kalvach (79' Dominik Janosek), Joel Kayamba (56' Jan Kovarík), Michal Krmencík, Ondrej Mihálik (74' Tomás Chory). Coach: Pavel Vrba.
Goals: 51' Guilherme 1-0, 70' Guerrero 2-0, 73' Guilherme 3-0, 82' Rúben Semedo 4-0.
Referee: Juan Martínez Munuera (ESP)   Attendance:

31.07.19   Telia 5G -areena, Helsinki: HJK Helsinki – Crvena Zvezda Beograd 2-1 (0-0)
HJK Helsinki: Maksim Rudakov, Rafinha (66' Victor Luiz Prestes Filho), Nikolai Alho, Daniel O'Shaughnessy, Faith Obilor, William Parra (77' Santeri Väänänen), Riku Riski, Kaan Kairinen, Sebastian Dahlström, Evans Mensah, Ivan Tarasov (46' Tim Väyrynen).
Coach: Toni Koskela.
Crvena Zvezda Beograd: Milan Borjan, Nemanja Milunovic, Milan Rodic, Filip Stojkovic, Srdjan Babic, Marko Marin, Cañas (88' Milos Degenek), Dusan Jovancic, Milan Jevtovic (74' Mirko Ivanic), Richmond Boakye (55' Milan Pavkov), Mohamed Ben Nabouhane.
Coach: Vladan Milojevic.
Goals: 46' Sebastian Dahlström 1-0, 56' Dusan Jovancic 1-1, 90+2' Riku Riski 2-1.
Referee: Alain Bieri (SUI)   Attendance:

31.07.19   Lerkendal Stadion, Trondheim: Rosenborg BK – BATE Borisov 2-0 (0-0)
Rosenborg BK: André Hansen, Tore Reginiussen, Even Hovland, Vegar Hedenstad, Birger Meling, Mike Jensen, Anders Konradsen, Anders Trondsen, Alexander Søderlund, Samuel Adegbenro (78' Yann-Erik De Lanlay), Babajide Akintola (70' Pål Helland).
Coach: Eirik Horneland.
BATE Borisov: Anton Chichkan, Aleksandar Filipovic, Aleksey Rios (62' Emil Jonassen), Igor Stasevich, Dmitriy Baga, Stanislav Dragun (87' Bojan Dubajic), Slobodan Simovic, Jasse Tuominen (76' Hervaine Moukam), Evgeni Yablonski, Zakhar Volkov, Maksim Skavysh.
Coach: Aleksei Baga.
Goals: 73' Pål Helland 1-0 (p), 85' Alexander Søderlund 2-0.
Referee: Marco Di Bello (ITA)   Attendance: 14,875.

31.07.19   Dalga Arena, Baku: Qarabag FK – Dundalk FC 3-0 (1-0)
Qarabag FK: Vagner, Rashad Sadigov, Maksim Medvedev (82' Abbas Hüseynov), Ailton, Rahil Mammadov, Míchel (73' Simeon Slavchev), Jaime Romero, Richard Almeyda, Filip Ozobic (25' Dani Quintana), Abdellah Zoubir, Mahir Emreli. Coach: Gurban Gurbanov.
Dundalk FC: Gary Rogers, Dane Massey, Andy Boyle, Sean Gannon, Sean Hoare (56' Sean Murray), Daniel Cleary, Chris Shields, Patrick McEleney (65' John Mountney), Jamie McGrath, Patrick Hoban, Michael Duffy (79' Daniel Kelly). Coach: Vinny Perth.
Goals: 12' Jaime Romero 1-0, 76' Ailton 2-0, 87' Jaime Romero 3-0.
Referee: Svein Oddvar Moen (NOR)   Attendance:

Qarabag FK played their home match at Dalga Arena, Baku, instead ot their regular stadium Azersun Arena, Baku.

31.07.19   Friends Arena, Solna: AIK Solna – NK Maribor 3-2 (1-0, 2-1) (a.e.t.)
AIK Solna: Oscar Linnér, Per Karlsson, Robert Lundström (77' Heradi Rashidi), Karol Mets, Daniel Granli (105' Panajotis Dimitriadis), Sebastian Larsson (102' Bilal Hussein), Enoch Adu, Anton Salétros, Tarik Elyounoussi, Henok Goitom, Chinedu Obasi (32' Kolbeinn Sigthórsson). Coach: Rikard Norling.
NK Maribor: Kenan Piric, Mitja Viler, Martin Milec, Sasa Ivkovic, Spiro Pericic, Rok Kronaveter (118' Aleks Pihler), Blaz Vrhovec (105' Martin Kramaric), Alexandru Cretu, Dino Hotic, Andrej Kotnik (90' Rudi Pozeg Vancas), Marcos Tavares (86' Jasmin Mesanovic).
Coach: Darko Milanic.
Goals: 4' Per Karlsson 1-0, 48' Andrej Kotnik 1-1, 61' Sebastian Larsson 2-1, 93' Tarik Elyounoussi 3-1, 117' Alexandru Cretu 3-2.
Referee: Adrien Jaccottet (SUI)   Attendance: 19,179.

NK Maribor won on away goals.

31.07.19   Telia Parken, København: FC København – The New Saints 1-0 (0-0)
FC København: Karl-Johan Johnsson, Pierre Bengtsson (79' Guillermo Varela), Sotirios Papagiannopoulos, Karlo Bartolec, Victor Nelsson, Zeca (60' Ahmed Daghim), Nikolaj Thomsen, Jens Stage, Pieros Sotiriou, Jonas Wind (60' Carlo Holse), Mohammed Daramy.
Coach: Ståle Solbakken.
The New Saints: Paul Harrison, Simon Spender, Chris Marriott (78' Blaine Hudson), Ryan Harrington, Aeron Edwards, Jon Routledge, Daniel Redmond, Ryan Brobbel, Jamie Mullan, Adrian Cieslewicz (59' Kane Lewis), Dean Ebbe (66' Greg Draper). Coach: Scott Ruscoe.
Goal: 52' Zeca 1-0.
Referee: Karim Abed (FRA)   Attendance:

The following losers enter the 2019-2020 UEFA Europa League Third Qualifying Round: FC Viktoria Plzen, FC Saburtalo Tbilisi, PSV Eindhoven, The New Saints, FK Sutjeska Niksic, BATE Borisov, Maccabi Tel Aviv FC, Valletta FC, AIK Solna, JK Nõmme Kalju, HJK Helsinki, Dundalk FC.

THIRD QUALIFYING ROUND

06.08.19   Neo GSP Stadium, Nicosia: APOEL Nicosia – Qarabag FK 1-2 (0-0)
APOEL Nicosia: Vid Belec, Giorgios Merkis, Praxitelis Vouros, Nicholas Ioannou, Dragan Mihajlovic, Savvas Gentsoglou (86' Linus Hallenius), Antonio Jakolis (64' André Vidigal), Uros Matic (65' Alef), Tomás De Vincenti, Musa Al-Taamari, Andrija Pavlovic.
Coach: Paolo Tramezzani.
Qarabag FK: Vagner, Rashad Sadigov, Maksim Medvedev, Ailton, Rahil Mammadov, Míchel, Jaime Romero (85' Araz Abdullayev), Richard Almeyda (86' Gara Garayev), Simeon Slavchev, Abdellah Zoubir, Mahir Emreli (68' Magaye Gueye). Coach: Gurban Gurbanov.
Goals: 54' Mahir Emreli 0-1, 69' Magaye Gueye 0-2, 90+5' Giorgios Merkis 1-2.
Referee: Davide Massa (ITA)   Attendance: 9,481.

06.08.19   Stadio Toumbas, Thessaloniki: PAOK Saloniki – AFC Ajax 2-2 (2-1)
PAOK Saloniki: Alexandros Paschalakis, Léo Matos, José Ángel Crespo, Fernando Varela, Dimitris Giannoulis, Diego Biseswar (73' Douglas Augusto), Omar El Kaddouri, Dimitris Pelkas (65' Dimitris Limnios), Anderson Esiti, Chuba Akpom, Léo Jabá (79' Miroslav Stoch).
Coach: Abel Ferreira.
AFC Ajax: André Onana, Daley Blind, Nicolás Tagliafico, Joël Veltman, Noussair Mazraoui (82' Razvan Marin), Perr Schuurs, Lisandro Martínez, Hakim Ziyech (82' David Neres), Donny van de Beek, Dusan Tadic, Kasper Dolberg (33' Klaas Jan Huntelaar).
Coach: Erik ten Hag.
Goals: 10' Hakim Ziyech 0-1, 32' Chuba Akpom 1-1, 39' Léo Matos 2-1, 57' Klaas Jan Huntelaar 2-2.
Referee: Slavko Vincic (SVN)   Attendance: 23,418.

06.08.19   Stadion Maksimir, Zagreb: Dinamo Zagreb – Ferencvárosi TC 1-1 (1-0)
Dinamo Zagreb: Dominik Livakovic, Marin Leovac, Marko Leskovic, Petar Stojanovic, Dino Peric, Arijan Ademi, Amer Gojak (69' Nikola Moro), Daniel Olmo, Mislav Orsic, Izet Hajrovic (69' Lovro Majer), Bruno Petkovic (76' Mario Gavranovic). Coach: Nenad Bjelica.
Ferencvárosi TC: Dénes Dibusz, Marcel Heister, Miha Blazic, Lasha Dvali, Michal Skvarka (89' Danylo Ignatenko), Gergö Lovrencsics, Dávid Sigér, Igor Kharatin, Oleksandr Zubkov, Nikolay Signevich (78' Davide Lanzafame), Tokmac Nguen (83' Eldar Civic).
Coach: Serhiy Rebrov.
Goals: 7' Daniel Olmo 1-0, 59' Dávid Sigér (1-1)
Referee: Pawel Raczkowski (POL)   Attendance: 14,283.

06.08.19   Jan Breydel Stadium, Brugge: Club Brugge – Dynamo Kyiv 1-0 (1-0)
Club Brugge KV: Simon Mignolet, Eduard Sobol, Clinton Mata, Matej Mitrovic, Simon Deli, Ruud Vormer, Mats Rits, Hans Vanaken, Percy Tau, David Okereke, Emmanuel Dennis Bonaventure (63' Siebe Schrijvers). Coach: Philippe Clement.
Dynamo Kyiv: Denis Boyko, Tamás Kádár, Tomasz Kedziora, Mykyta Burda, Vitali Mykolenko, Sergiy Sydorchuk, Denys Garmash, Vitaliy Buyalskiy, Benjamin Verbic (64' Carlos de Pena), Oleksandr Karavayev (46' Viktor Tsygankov), Artem Besedin (46' Gerson Rodrigues). Coach: Aleksandr Khatskevich.
Goal: 37' Hans Vanaken 1-0 (p).
Referee: Xavier Estrada Fernández (ESP)   Attendance: 27,018.

06.08.19   Stadion Rajko Mitic, Beograd: Crvena Zvezda Beograd – FC København 1-1 (1-0)
Crvena Zvezda Beograd: Milan Borjan, Nemanja Milunovic, Milan Rodic (65' Jander), Milos Degenek, Marko Gobeljic, Marko Marin, Cañas, Dusan Jovancic, Mirko Ivanic, Milan Pavkov (46' Richmond Boakye), Aleksa Vukanovic (76' Mohamed Ben Nabouhane).
Coach: Vladan Milojevic.
FC København: Sten Grytebust, Bryan Oviedo (72' Pierre Bengtsson), Sotirios Papagiannopoulos, Guillermo Varela, Victor Nelsson, Zeca, Viktor Fischer (64' Pep Biel Mas), Jens Stage, Dame N'Doye, Jonas Wind, Carlo Holse (88' Karlo Bartolec).
Coach: Ståle Solbakken.
Goals: 44' Milan Pavkov 1-0, 84' Jonas Wind 1-1 (p).
Referee: Tiago Martins (POR)   Attendance: 40,812.

07.08.19   Stadion FK Krasnodar, Krasnodar: FK Krasnodar – FC Porto 0-1 (0-0)
FK Krasnodar: Matvei Safonov, Aleksandr Martynovich, Sergej Petrov, Uros Spajic, Cristian Ramírez, Ruslan Kambolov (72' Jón Fjóluson), Rémy Cabella, Tonny Vilhena, Wamberto, Younes Namli (66' Magomed Suleymanov), Marcus Berg (62' Ari). Coach: Sergei Matveev.
FC Porto: Agustín Marchesín, Pepe, Ivan Marcano, Alex Telles, Wilson Manafá, Sérgio Oliveira, Danilo Pereira, Romário Baró (55' Luis Díaz), Tiquinho Soares (74' Zé Luís), Jesús Corona (85' Otavinho), Moussa Marega. Coach: Sérgio Conceição.
Goal: 89' Sérgio Oliveira 0-1.
Referee: Tobias Stieler (GER)   Attendance: 38,874.

07.08.19   Basaksehir Fatih Terim Stadyumu, Istanbul:
Istanbul Basaksehir FK – Olympiacos Piraeus FC 0-1 (0-0)
Istanbul Basaksehir FK: Mert Günok, Gaël Clichy, Aurélien Chedjou, Júnior Caiçara, Miguel Vieira, Mahmut Tekdemir (62' Azubuike Okechukwu), Edin Visca, Irfan Kahveci, Robinho, Fredrik Gulbrandsen (69' Eljero Elia), Enzo Crivelli (81' Demba Ba). Coach: Okan Buruk.
Olympiacos Piraeus FC: José Sá, Omar Elabdellaoui, Rúben Semedo, Yassine Meriah, Kostas Tsimikas, Mathieu Valbuena (73' Mady Camara), Guilherme, Andreas Bouchalakis, Daniel Podence, Georgios Masouras (83' Bruno Souza), Guerrero (89' Youssef El-Arabi).
Coach: Pedro Martins.
Goal: 53' Georgios Masouras 0-1.
Referee: Orel Grinfeld (ISR)   Attendance: 4,301.
Sent off: 80' Irfan Kahveci.

Edin Visca missed a penalty kick (90+2').

07.08.19   Stadionul Dr. Constantin Radulescu, Cluj-Napoca: CFR Cluj – Celtic FC 1-1 (1-1)
CFR Cluj: Giedrius Arlauskis, Paulo Vinícius, Mateo Susic, Camora, Andrei Burca, Ciprian Deac, Damjan Djokovic, Mihai Bordeianu, Luís Aurélio, Mário Rondón (75' George Tucudean), Billel Omrani (66' Adrian Paun). Coach: Dan Petrescu.
Celtic FC: Scott Bain, Hatem Abd Elhamed (87' Nir Bitton), Jozo Simunovic (74' Christopher Jullien), Boli Bolingoli-Mbombo, Kristoffer Ajer, Scott Brown, James Forrest, Callum McGregor, Ryan Christie, Lewis Morgan (67' Jules Olivier Ntcham), Odsonne Édouard.
Coach: Neil Lennon.
Goals: 28' Mário Rondón 1-0, 37' James Forrest 1-1.
Referee: Srdjan Jovanovic (SRB)   Attendance: 13,055.

07.08.19   St. Jakob-Park, Basel: FC Basel – LASK Linz 1-2 (0-0)
FC Basel: Jonas Omlin, Silvan Widmer, Éder Álvarez Balanta (76' Kevin Bua), Omar Alderete, Eray Cömert, Blas Riveros, Valentin Stocker (65' Kemal Ademi), Luca Zuffi, Fabian Frei, Ricky van Wolfswinkel, Afimico Pululu (76' Noah Okafor). Coach: Marcelo Koller.
LASK Linz: Alexander Schlager, Christian Ramsebner (17' Emanuel Pogatetz), Gernot Trauner, Reinhold Ranftl, Philipp Wiesinger, James Holland, Thomas Goiginger (63' Dominik Frieser), Peter Michorl, René Renner, Samuel Tetteh, Klauss (83' Marko Raguz).
Coach: Valérien Ismaël.
Goals: 51' Gernot Trauner 0-1, 82' Klauss 0-2, 87' Luca Zuffi 1-2.
Referee: Andreas Ekberg (SWE)   Attendance: 20,470

07.08.19   Ljudski vrt, Maribor: NK Maribor – Rosenborg BK 1-3 (0-0)
NK Maribor: Kenan Piric, Mitja Viler, Martin Milec, Sasa Ivkovic, Spiro Pericic, Rok Kronaveter, Blaz Vrhovec, Aleks Pihler, Dino Hotic (64' Rudi Pozeg Vancas), Andrej Kotnik (85' Martin Kramaric), Marcos Tavares. Coach: Darko Milanic.
Rosenborg BK: André Hansen, Tore Reginiussen (14' Gustav Valsvik), Even Hovland, Vegar Hedenstad, Birger Meling, Mike Jensen, Gjermund Åsen (79' Anders Trondsen), Marius Lundemo, Alexander Søderlund (68' Pål Helland), Samuel Adegbenro, Babajide Akintola.
Coach: Eirik Horneland.
Goals: 50', 64' Alexander Søderlund 0-1, 0-2, 70' Marcos Tavares 1-2, 71' Mike Jensen 1-3.
Referee: François Letexier (FRA)   Attendance: 10,316.

13.08.19   Tofiq Bahramov adina Respublika stadionu, Baku:
Qarabag FK – APOEL Nicosia 0-2 (0-1)
Qarabag FK: Vagner, Rashad Sadigov, Maksim Medvedev, Ailton (87' Araz Abdullayev), Rahil Mammadov, Míchel, Jaime Romero, Richard Almeyda, Simeon Slavchev (73' Dani Quintana), Abdellah Zoubir (80' Magaye Gueye), Mahir Emreli. Coach: Gurban Gurbanov.
APOEL Nicosia: Vid Belec, Giorgios Merkis, Kevin Lafrance, Nicholas Ioannou, Dragan Mihajlovic, Savvas Gentsoglou, Uros Matic, Tomás De Vincenti (61' Linus Hallenius), Musa Al-Taamari, Roman Bezjak (82' Antonio Jakolis), Andrija Pavlovic (73' Lucas Souza). Coach: Thomas Doll.
Goals: 34' Tomás De Vincenti 0-1 (p), 68' Uros Matic 0-2.
Referee: Daniel Siebert (GER)   Attendance: 31,531.
Sent off: 90+3' Richard Almeyda.

Qarabag FK played their home match at Tofiq Bahramov adina Respublika stadionu instead of their regular stadium, Azersun Arena.

13.08.19   Lerkendal Stadion, Trondheim: Rosenborg BK – NK Maribor 3-1 (0-1)
Rosenborg BK: André Hansen, Tore Reginiussen, Even Hovland, Vegar Hedenstad, Birger Meling, Mike Jensen (87' Anders Trondsen), Anders Konradsen (90' Emil Ceide), Marius Lundemo, Alexander Søderlund, Samuel Adegbenro (78' Gjermund Åsen), Babajide Akintola. Coach: Eirik Horneland.
NK Maribor: Kenan Piric, Mitja Viler, Martin Milec, Sasa Ivkovic, Spiro Pericic, Rok Kronaveter (69' Andrej Kotnik), Blaz Vrhovec, Alexandru Cretu, Rudi Pozeg Vancas, Dino Hotic (82' Martin Kramaric), Marcos Tavares (69' Luka Zahovic). Coach: Darko Milanic.
Goals: 45+2' Rudi Pozeg Vancas 0-1, 53' Alexander Søderlund 1-1, 61', 81' Anders Konradsen 2-1, 3-1.
Referee: Serdar Gözübüyük (HOL)   Attendance: 18,564.

13.08.19   NSK Olimpijs'kyj, Kyiv: Dynamo Kyiv – Club Brugge KV 3-3 (1-1)
Dynamo Kyiv: Denis Boyko, Tamás Kádár, Tomasz Kedziora, Mykyta Burda, Vitali Mykolenko, Vitaliy Buyalskiy, Benjamin Verbic (69' Artem Besedin), Oleksandr Andrievsky (46' Carlos de Pena), Viktor Tsygankov, Volodymyr Shepelev (83' Fran Sol), Gerson Rodrigues. Coach: Aleksandr Khatskevich.
Club Brugge KV: Simon Mignolet, Eduard Sobol, Clinton Mata, Simon Deli, Brandon Mechele, Ruud Vormer, Mats Rits, Hans Vanaken, Percy Tau, David Okereke (81' Loïs Openda), Emmanuel Dennis Bonaventure (52' Krépin Diatta). Coach: Philippe Clement.
Goals: 6' Vitaliy Buyalskiy 1-0, 38' Simon Deli 1-1, 50' Volodymyr Shepelev 2-1, 88' Ruud Vormer 2-2, 90+3' Brandon Mechele 3-2 (og), 90+5' Loïs Openda 3-3.
Referee: Ivan Bebek (CRO)   Attendance: 42,152.
Sent off: 82' Mykyta Burda, 84' Percy Tau.

13.08.19   Groupama Aréna, Budapest: Ferencvárosi TC – Dinamo Zagreb 0-4 (0-1)
Ferencvárosi TC: Dénes Dibusz, Miha Blazic, Lasha Dvali, Eldar Civic, Michal Skvarka (71' Marcel Heister), Gergö Lovrencsics, Dávid Sigér, Igor Kharatin, Oleksandr Zubkov, Nikolay Signevich (84' Franck Boli), Tokmac Nguen (65' Roland Varga). Coach: Serhiy Rebrov.
Dinamo Zagreb: Dominik Livakovic, Marin Leovac, Emir Dilaver, Petar Stojanovic, Dino Peric, Arijan Ademi (70' Amer Gojak), Nikola Moro, Daniel Olmo (84' Mario Situm), Mislav Orsic, Izet Hajrovic (77' Lovro Majer), Bruno Petkovic. Coach: Nenad Bjelica.
Goals: 16' Arijan Ademi 0-1, 47' Bruno Petkovic 0-2, 55' Daniel Olmo 0-3, 79' Amer Gojak 0-4.
Referee: Ruddy Buquet (FRA)   Attendance: 20,321.
Sent off: 68' Eldar Civic.

Bruno Petkovic missed a penalty kick (89').

13.08.19   Telia Parken, København:
           FC København – Crvena Zvezda Beograd 1-1 (1-1, 1-1) (a.e.t.)
FC København: Sten Grytebust, Pierre Bengtsson, Sotirios Papagiannopoulos, Guillermo Varela (81' Karlo Bartolec), Victor Nelsson, Zeca, Viktor Fischer, Jens Stage (60' Rasmus Falk, 120' Pieros Soteriou), Dame N'Doye, Jonas Wind, Carlo Holse (74' Pep Biel Mas). Coach: Ståle Solbakken.
Crvena Zvezda Beograd: Milan Borjan, Nemanja Milunovic, Milan Rodic (46' Jander), Milos Degenek, Marko Gobeljic, Marko Marin, Cañas (58' Radovan Pankov), Dusan Jovancic, Mirko Ivanic, Richmond Boakye (81' Veljko Simic), Aleksa Vukanovic (90' Milan Jevtovic). Coach: Vladan Milojevic.
Goals: 17' Richmond Boakye 0-1, 45' Dame N'Doye 1-1.
Referee: Gediminas Mazeika (LTU)   Attendance: 29,872
Sent off: 54' Nemanja Milunovic, 112' Pep Biel Mas.

Crvena Zvezda Beograd won 7-6 on penalties after extra-time.
Penalties: Marin missed, Wind 1-0, Ivanic 1-1, Fischer missed, Jevtovic missed, Soteriou 1-2, Jander 2-2, Bengtsson missed, Pankov 3-2, Zeca 3-3, Jovancic missed, N'Doye missed, Simic missed, Bartolec missed, Degenek 4-3, Nelsson 4-4, Gobeljic 5-4, Papagiannopoulos 5-5, Borjan 6-5, Grytebust 6-6, Pankov 7-6, Wind missed.

13.08.19   Johan Cruyff ArenA, Amsterdam: AFC Ajax – PAOK Saloniki 3-2 (1-1)
AFC Ajax: André Onana, Daley Blind, Nicolás Tagliafico, Joël Veltman, Noussair Mazraoui, Lisandro Martínez, Hakim Ziyech, Razvan Marin (46' Sergiño Dest), Donny van de Beek (89' Dani de Wit), Dusan Tadic, David Neres (78' Klaas Jan Huntelaar). Coach: Erik ten Hag.
PAOK Saloniki: Alexandros Paschalakis, Léo Matos, José Ángel Crespo, Fernando Varela, Dimitris Giannoulis, Diego Biseswar, Omar El Kaddouri, Dimitris Pelkas (63' Karol Swiderski), Anderson Esiti (82' Josip Misic), Chuba Akpom, Léo Jabá (71' Dimitris Limnios). Coach: Abel Ferreira.
Goals: 23' Diego Biseswar 0-1, 43' Dusan Tadic 1-1 (p), 79' Nicolás Tagliafico 2-1, 85' Dusan Tadic 3-1 (p), 90+4' Diego Biseswar 3-2.
Referee: Craig Pawson (ENG)   Attendance: 53,942.

Dusan Tadic missed a penalty kick (32').

13.08.19   Stadio Georgios Karaiskáki, Piraeus:
Olympiacos Piraeus FC – Istanbul Basaksehir FK 2-0 (0-0)
Olympiacos Piraeus FC: José Sá, Omar Elabdellaoui, Rúben Semedo, Yassine Meriah, Kostas Tsimikas, Mathieu Valbuena (82' Mady Camara), Guilherme (89' Leonardo Koutris), Andreas Bouchalakis, Daniel Podence (68' Lazar Randjelovic), Georgios Masouras, Guerrero.
Coach: Pedro Martins.
Istanbul Basaksehir FK: Mert Günok, Gaël Clichy, Júnior Caiçara, Miguel Vieira, Carlos Ponck, Eljero Elia, Edin Visca, Joseph Attamah (59' Demba Ba), Azubuike Okechukwu, Robinho (46' Arda Turan), Enzo Crivelli (75' Fredrik Gulbrandsen). Coach: Okan Buruk.
Goals: 55' Rúben Semedo 1-0, 78' Mathieu Valbuena 2-0 (p).
Referee: Bobby Madden (SCO)   Attendance: 28,521.

13.08.19   Linzer Stadion, Linz: LASK Linz – FC Basel 3-1 (0-0)
LASK Linz: Alexander Schlager, Emanuel Pogatetz, Gernot Trauner, Reinhold Ranftl, Philipp Wiesinger, James Holland, Thomas Goiginger (90+4' Thomas Sabitzer), Peter Michorl, René Renner, Samuel Tetteh (77' Dominik Frieser), Klauss (87' Marko Raguz).
Coach: Valérien Ismaël.
FC Basel: Jonas Omlin, Silvan Widmer, Éder Álvarez Balanta (86' Afimico Pululu), Omar Alderete, Raoul Petretta, Eray Cömert, Valentin Stocker, Luca Zuffi (55' Kevin Bua), Fabian Frei, Kemal Ademi, Noah Okafor (64' Samuele Campo). Coach: Marcelo Koller.
Goals: 59' Reinhold Ranftl 1-0, 80' Kemal Ademi 1-1, 89' Thomas Goiginger 2-1, 90+4' Marko Raguz 3-1.
Referee: Aliyar Agayev (AZE)   Attendance: 12,966.

13.08.19   Celtic Park, Glasgow: Celtic FC – CFR Cluj 3-4 (0-1)
Celtic FC: Scott Bain, Hatem Abd Elhamed, Jozo Simunovic, Kristoffer Ajer, Scott Brown (88' Vakoun Bayo), James Forrest, Callum McGregor, Jules Olivier Ntcham (83' Leigh Griffiths), Ryan Christie, Odsonne Édouard, Michael Johnston (75' Lewis Morgan).
Coach: Neil Lennon.
CFR Cluj: Giedrius Arlauskis, Paulo Vinícius, Mateo Susic, Camora, Andrei Burca, Ciprian Deac, Damjan Djokovic, Mihai Bordeianu, Luís Aurélio (78' Adrian Paun), Mário Rondón (46' George Tucudean), Billel Omrani (84' Andrei Muresan). Coach: Dan Petrescu.
Goals: 27' Ciprian Deac 0-1, 51' James Forrest 1-1, 61' Odsonne Édouard 2-1, 74' Billel Omrani 2-2 (p), 76' Ryan Christie 3-2, 80' Billel Omrani 3-3, 90+7' George Tucudean 3-4.
Referee: Andris Treimanis (LAT)   Attendance: 50,964.

13.08.19   Estádio do Dragão, Porto: FC Porto – FK Krasnodar 2-3 (0-3)
FC Porto: Agustín Marchesín, Pepe, Ivan Marcano, Alex Telles, Renzo Saravia (38' Zé Luís), Sérgio Oliveira (49' Mateus Uribe), Danilo Pereira, Shoya Nakajima, Luis Díaz, Jesús Corona (86' Vincent Aboubakar), Moussa Marega. Coach: Sérgio Conceição.
FK Krasnodar: Matvei Safonov, Aleksandr Martynovich, Sergej Petrov, Uros Spajic, Cristian Ramírez, Ruslan Kambolov, Rémy Cabella (80' Dmitriy Stotskiy), Tonny Vilhena, Wamberto, Marcus Berg (73' Ivan Ignatyev), Magomed Suleymanov (65' Jón Fjóluson).
Coach: Sergei Matveev.
Goals: 3' Tonny Vilhena 0-1, 13', 34' Magomed Suleymanov 0-2, 0-3, 57' Zé Luís 1-3, 76' Luis Díaz 2-3.
Referee: Marco Guida (ITA)   Attendance: 48,520.

FK Krasnodar won on away goals.

PLAY-OFF ROUND

20.08.19   Stadionul Dr. Constantin Radulescu, Cluj-Napoca:
            CFR Cluj – SK Slavia Praha 0-1 (0-1)
CFR Cluj: Giedrius Arlauskis, Mateo Susic, Camora, Mike Cestor, Andrei Burca, Ciprian Deac, Damjan Djokovic, Mihai Bordeianu (87' Ovidiu Hoban), Luís Aurélio (72' Adrian Paun), George Tucudean (46' Mário Rondón), Billel Omrani. Coach: Dan Petrescu.
SK Slavia Praha: Ondrej Kolár, Ondrej Kúdela, Jan Boril, Vladimír Coufal, David Hovorka, Nicolae Stanciu, Lukás Masopust (84' Tomás Holes), Peter Olayinka, Tomás Soucek, Ibrahim Traoré (64' Alex Král), Mick van Buren (68' Milan Skoda). Coach: Jindrich Trpisovsky.
Goal: 28' Lukás Masopust 0-1.
Referee: Cüneyt Çakir (TUR)   Attendance: 15,196.

Billel Omrani missed a penalty kick (79').

20.08.19   Neo GSP Stadium, Nicosia: APOEL Nicosia – AFC Ajax 0-0
APOEL Nicosia: Vid Belec, Giorgios Merkis, Joãozinho (82' André Vidigal), Nicholas Ioannou, Dragan Mihajlovic, Savvas Gentsoglou, Uros Matic, Lucas Souza, Musa Al-Taamari, Roman Bezjak (68' Antonio Jakolis), Andrija Pavlovic (68' Linus Hallenius).
Coach: Thomas Doll.
AFC Ajax: André Onana, Daley Blind, Nicolás Tagliafico, Joël Veltman, Noussair Mazraoui, Lisandro Martínez, Hakim Ziyech, Razvan Marin (62' Sergiño Dest), Donny van de Beek, Dusan Tadic, David Neres (72' Klaas Jan Huntelaar). Coach: Erik ten Hag.
Referee: Antonio Mateu Lahoz (ESP)   Attendance: 14,549.
Sent off: 80' Noussair Mazraoui.

20.08.19   Linzer Stadion, Linz: LASK Linz – Club Brugge KV 0-1 (0-1)
LASK Linz: Alexander Schlager, Emanuel Pogatetz, Gernot Trauner, Reinhold Ranftl, Philipp Wiesinger, James Holland, Thomas Goiginger (83' Yusuf Otubanjo), Peter Michorl, René Renner (67' Marko Raguz), Samuel Tetteh (53' Dominik Frieser), Klauss.
Coach: Valérien Ismaël.
Club Brugge KV: Simon Mignolet, Eduard Sobol (66' Federico Ricca), Clinton Mata, Matej Mitrovic, Simon Deli, Ruud Vormer, Mats Rits, Hans Vanaken, Loïs Openda (74' Kaveh Rezaei), David Okereke (89' Krépin Diatta), Emmanuel Dennis Bonaventure.
Coach: Philippe Clement.
Goal: 10' Hans Vanaken 0-1 (p).
Referee: Szymon Marciniak (POL)   Attendance: 12,637.

21.08.19   Stadion Maksimir, Zagreb: Dinamo Zagreb – Rosenborg BK 2-0 (2-0)
Dinamo Zagreb: Dominik Livakovic, Marin Leovac, Emir Dilaver, Petar Stojanovic, Dino Peric, Arijan Ademi, Nikola Moro, Daniel Olmo, Mislav Orsic (84' Iyayi Atiemwven), Izet Hajrovic (64' Amer Gojak), Bruno Petkovic (87' Mario Gavranovic). Coach: Nenad Bjelica.
Rosenborg BK: André Hansen, Tore Reginiussen, Even Hovland, Vegar Hedenstad, Birger Meling, Mike Jensen, Anders Konradsen, Marius Lundemo, Alexander Søderlund, Samuel Adegbenro, Babajide Akintola (84' Pål Helland). Coach: Eirik Horneland.
Goals: 8' Bruno Petkovic 1-0 (p), 28' Mislav Orsic 2-0.
Referee: Daniele Orsato (ITA)   Attendance: 23,859.

21.08.19   STADE DE SUISSE Wankdorf, Bern:
BSC Young Boys – Crvena Zvezda Beograd 2-2 (1-1)
BSC Young Boys: David von Ballmoos, Fabian Lustenberger, Ulisses Garcia (67' Saidy Janko), Jordan Lotomba, Cedric Zesiger, Christopher Martins Pereira, Nicolas Moumi Ngamaleu, Vincent Sierro (57' Christian Fassnacht), Michel Aebischer (73' Guillaume Hoarau), Jean Pierre Nsamé, Roger Assalé. Coach: Gerardo Seoane.
Crvena Zvezda Beograd: Milan Borjan, Milan Rodic, Milos Degenek, Marko Gobeljic, Radovan Pankov, Marko Marin, Cañas, Mirko Ivanic, Mateo García (55' Jander), Richmond Boakye (77' Tómané), Aleksa Vukanovic (85' Njego Petrovic). Coach: Vladan Milojevic.
Goals: 7' Roger Assalé 1-0, 18' Milos Degenek 1-1, 46' Mateo García 1-2, 76' Guillaume Hoarau 2-2 (p).
Referee: Danny Makkelie (HOL)   Attendance: 26,375.

21.08.19   Stadio Georgios Karaiskáki, Piraeus:
Olympiacos Piraeus FC – FK Krasnodar 4-0 (1-0)
Olympiacos Piraeus FC: José Sá, Omar Elabdellaoui, Rúben Semedo, Yassine Meriah, Kostas Tsimikas, Mathieu Valbuena (87' Mady Camara), Guilherme, Andreas Bouchalakis, Daniel Podence (90+2' Vasilis Torosidis), Georgios Masouras (76' Lazar Randjelovic), Guerrero. Coach: Pedro Martins.
FK Krasnodar: Matvei Safonov, Jón Fjóluson, Sergej Petrov, Uros Spajic, Cristian Ramírez, Ruslan Kambolov, Rémy Cabella (26' Kristoffer Olsson), Tonny Vilhena, Wamberto, Younes Namli (59' Magomed Suleymanov), Marcus Berg (69' Ivan Ignatyev). Coach: Sergei Matveev.
Goals: 30' Geurrero 1-0, 78', 85' Lazar Randjelovic 2-0, 3-0, 89' Daniel Podence 4-0.
Referee: Carlos del Cerro Grande (ESP)   Attendance: 29,132.

27.08.19   Lerkendal Stadion, Trondheim: Rosenborg BK – Dinamo Zagreb 1-1 (1-0)
Rosenborg BK: André Hansen, Tore Reginiussen, Even Hovland, Vegar Hedenstad (84' Emil Ceide), Birger Meling, Mike Jensen, Anders Konradsen, Marius Lundemo (74' Anders Trondsen), Alexander Søderlund, Samuel Adegbenro, Babajide Akintola (74' Yann-Erik De Lanlay). Coach: Eirik Horneland.
Dinamo Zagreb: Dominik Livakovic, Marin Leovac, Emir Dilaver, Petar Stojanovic, Dino Peric, Arijan Ademi, Nikola Moro, Daniel Olmo (90+2' Mario Gavranovic), Mislav Orsic (81' Iyayi Atiemwen), Izet Hajrovic (66' Amer Gojak), Bruno Petkovic. Coach: Nenad Bjelica.
Goals: 11' Babajide Akintola 1-0, 71' Amer Gojak 1-1.
Referee: Ovidiu Hategan (ROM)   Attendance: 18,173.

27.08.19   Stadion Rajko Mitic, Beograd:
Crvena Zvezda Beograd – BSC Young Boys 1-1 (0-0)
Crvena Zvezda Beograd: Milan Borjan, Nemanja Milunovic, Milan Rodic, Milos Degenek, Marko Gobeljic, Marko Marin, Cañas, Dusan Jovancic, Mateo García (69' Mohamed Ben Nabouhane), Richmond Boakye (62' Tó Mané), Aleksa Vukanovic (83' Mirko Ivanic). Coach: Vladan Milojevic.
BSC Young Boys: David von Ballmoos, Fabian Lustenberger, Frederik Sørensen, Saidy Janko, Jordan Lotomba, Cédric Zesiger (52' Christian Fassnacht), Nicolas Moumi Ngamaleu, Vincent Sierro (65' Miralem Sulejmani), Michel Aebischer, Jean-Pierre Nsamé, Roger Assalé (65' Guillaume Hoarau). Coach: Gerardo Seoane.
Goals: 59' Aleksa Vukanovic 1-0, 82' Mohamed Ben Nabouhane 1-1 (og).
Referee: Anthony Taylor (ENG)   Attendance: 47,487.
Sent off: 90+6' Tó Mané.

Crvena Zvezda Beograd won on away goals.

27.08.19   Stadion FK Krasnodar, Krasnodar:
           FK Krasnodar – Olympiacos Piraeus FC 1-2 (1-1)
FK Krasnodar: Stanislav Kritsyuk, Jón Fjóluson, Sergej Petrov (56' Dmitriy Skopintsev), Uros Spajic, Dmitriy Stotskiy, Tonny Vilhena, Kristoffer Olsson, Wamberto, Daniil Utkin (67' Ivan Ignatyev), Marcus Berg, Magomed Suleymanov (32' Younes Namli). Coach: Sergei Matveev.
Olympiacos Piraeus FC: José Sá, Omar Elabdellaoui, Rúben Semedo (65' Pape Cissé), Yassine Meriah, Kostas Tsimikas, Mathieu Valbuena, Guilherme, Andreas Bouchalakis, Daniel Podence (84' Mady Camara), Georgios Masouras, Youssef El-Arabi (73' El Arbi Soudani). Coach: Pedro Martins.
Goals: 10' Daniil Utkin 1-0, 11', 48' Youssef El-Arabi 1-1, 1-2.
Referee: Damir Skomina (SVN)   Attendance: 34,627.

28.08.19   Sinobo Stadium, Praha: SK Slavia Praha – CFR Cluj 1-0 (0-0)
SK Slavia Praha: Ondrej Kolár, Ondrej Kúdela, Jan Boril, Vladimír Coufal, David Hovorka, Nicolae Stanciu (90' Michal Frydrych), Lukás Masopust (84' Ibrahim Traoré), Peter Olayinka, Tomás Soucek, Alex Král, Milan Skoda (79' Abdulla Yusuf Helal).
Coach: Jindrich Trpisovsky.
CFR Cluj: Giedrius Arlauskis, Andrei Muresan, Mateo Susic, Camora, Andrei Burca, Ciprian Deac (70' Ovidiu Hoban), Damjan Djokovic, Mihai Bordeianu, Luís Aurélio (64' Adrian Paun), Mário Rondón (69' George Tucudean), Billel Omrani. Coach: Dan Petrescu.
Goal: 66' Jan Boril 1-0.
Referee: Gianluca Rocchi (ITA)   Attendance: 18,562.

28.08.19   Johan Cruyff ArenA, Amsterdam: AFC Ajax – APOEL Nicosia 2-0 (1-0)
AFC Ajax: André Onana, Daley Blind, Nicolás Tagliafico, Joël Veltman, Edson Álvarez (89' Razvan Marin), Lisandro Martínez, Sergiño Dest, Hakim Ziyech (87' Dani de Wit), Klaas Jan Huntelaar, Dusan Tadic, David Neres. Coach: Erik ten Hag.
APOEL Nicosia: Vid Belec, Giorgios Merkis, Joãozinho, Nicholas Ioannou, Dragan Mihajlovic, Antonio Jakolis (64' Tomás De Vincenti), Uros Matic (78' Linus Hallenius), Lucas Souza, Musa Al-Taamari (72' André Vidigal), Roman Bezjak, Andrija Pavlovic. Coach: Thomas Doll.
Goals: 43' Edson Álvarez 1-0, 80' Dusan Tadic 2-0.
Referee: Felix Zwayer (GER)   Attendance: 51,645.

28.08.19   Jan Breydel Stadium, Brugge: Club Brugge KV – LASK Linz 2-1 (0-0)
Club Brugge KV: Simon Mignolet, Clinton Mata, Matej Mitrovic, Simon Deli, Federico Ricca, Ruud Vormer, Mats Rits, Hans Vanaken, Loïs Openda (46' Percy Tau), David Okereke (88' Emmanuel Dennis Bonaventure), Krépin Diatta. Coach: Philippe Clement.
LASK Linz: Alexander Schlager, Emanuel Pogatetz, Gernot Trauner, Reinhold Ranftl, Philipp Wiesinger, James Holland (90' Yusuf Otubanjo), Thomas Goiginger (72' Marko Raguz), Peter Michorl, René Renner, Dominik Frieser (62' Samuel Tetteh), Klauss. Coach: Valérien Ismaël.
Goals: 70' Hans Vanaken 1-0, 74' Klauss 1-1 (p), 89' Emmanuel Dennis Bonaventure 2-1.
Referee: Dr.Felix Brych (GER)   Attendance: 25,319.
Sent off: 81' Gernot Trauner.

GROUP STAGE

GROUP A

Paris Saint-Germain	6	5	1	0	17 -	2	16
Real Madrid CF	6	3	2	1	14 -	8	11
Club Brugge KV	6	0	3	3	4 -	12	3
Galatasaray	6	0	2	4	1 -	14	2

GROUP B

FC Bayern München	6	6	0	0	24 -	5	18
Tottenham Hotspur	6	3	1	2	18 -	14	10
Olympiacos Piraeus FC	6	1	1	4	8 -	14	4
Crvena Zvezda Beograd	6	1	0	5	3 -	20	3

GROUP C

Manchester City	6	4	2	0	16 -	4	14
Atalanta Bergamo	6	2	1	3	8 -	12	7
Shakhtar Donetsk	6	1	3	2	8 -	13	6
Dinamo Zagreb	6	1	2	3	10 -	13	5

GROUP D

Juventus	6	5	1	0	12 -	4	16
Atlético Madrid	6	3	1	2	8 -	5	10
Bayer Leverkusen	6	2	0	4	5 -	9	6
Lokomotiv Moscow	6	1	0	5	4 -	11	3

GROUP E

Liverpool FC	6	4	1	1	13 -	8	13
SSC Napoli	6	3	3	0	11 -	4	12
Red Bull Salzburg	6	2	1	3	16 -	13	7
KRC Genk	6	0	1	5	5 -	20	1

GROUP F

FC Barcelona	6	4	2	0	9 -	4	14
Borussia Dortmund	6	3	1	2	8 -	8	10
Internazionale	6	2	1	3	10 -	9	7
SK Slavia Praha	6	0	2	4	4 -	10	2

GROUP G

RB Leipzig	6	3	2	1	10 -	8	11
Olympique Lyonnais	6	2	2	2	9 -	8	8
SL Benfica	6	2	1	3	10 -	11	7
Zenit Saint Petersburg	6	2	1	3	7 -	9	7

GROUP H

Valencia CF	6	3	2	1	9 - 7	11
Chelsea FC	6	3	2	1	11 - 9	11
AFC Ajax	6	3	1	2	12 - 6	10
Lille OSC	6	0	1	5	4 - 14	1

GROUP A

18.09.19   Jan Breydelstadio, Brugge: Club Brugge KV – Galatasaray 0-0
Club Brugge KV: Simon Mignolet, Clinton Mata, Matej Mitrovic, Simon Deli, Federico Ricca, Ruud Vormer, Mats Rits (86' Éder Balanta), Hans Vanaken, David Okereke (60' Loïs Openda), Emmanuel Dennis Bonaventure (73' Mbaye Diagne), Krépin Diatta.
Coach: Philippe Clement.
Galatasaray: Fernando Muslera, Mariano (90' Sener Özbayrakli), Yuto Nagatomo, Marcâo Teixeira, Christian Luyindama, Sofiane Féghouli, Steven N'Zonzi, Mario Lemina (60' Emre Mor), Jean Michaël Seri (90+3' Ryan Donk), Ryan Babel, Radamel Falcao.
Coach: Fatih Terim.
Referee: Slavko Vincic (SVN)   Attendance: 26,616.

18.09.19   Parc des Princes, Paris: Paris Saint-Germain – Real Madrid CF 3-0 (2-0)
Paris Saint-Germain: Keylor Navas, Thiago Silva, Thomas Meunier, Marquinhos (70' Ander Herrera), Juan Bernat, Presnel Kimpembe, Ángel Di María, Marco Verratti, Idrissa Gueye, Pablo Sarabia (89' Abdou Diallo), Mauro Icardi (60' Eric Maxim Choupo-Moting).
Coach: Thomas Tuchel.
Real Madrid CF: Thibaut Courtois, Dani Carvajal, Raphaël Varane, Ferland Mendy, Éder Militão, Toni Kroos, James Rodríguez (70' Luka Jovic), Casemiro, Karim Benzema, Gareth Bale (79' Vinícius Júnior), Eden Hazard (70' Lucas Vázquez). Coach: Zinédine Zidane.
Goals: 14' Ángel Di María 1-0, 33' Ángel Di María 2-0, 90+1' Thomas Meunier 3-0.
Referee: Anthony Taylor (ENG)   Attendance: 46,361.

01.10.19   Estadio Santiago Bernabéu, Madrid: Real Madrid CF – Club Brugge KV 2-2 (0-2)
Real Madrid CF: Thibaut Courtois (46' Alphonse Aréola), Sergio Ramos, Nacho (46' Marcelo), Dani Carvajal, Raphaël Varane, Luka Modric, Toni Kroos, Casemiro, Lucas Vázquez (67' Vinícius Júnior), Karim Benzema, Eden Hazard. Coach: Zinédine Zidane.
Club Brugge KV: Simon Mignolet, Eduard Sobol, Clinton Mata, Simon Deli, Brandon Mechele, Ruud Vormer, Mats Rits, Hans Vanaken, Percy Tau (90+2' Siebe Schrijvers), Emmanuel Dennis Bonaventure (71' Loïs Openda, 87' Dion Cools), Krépin Diatta.
Coach: Philippe Clement.
Goals: 9', 39' Emmanuel Dennis Bonaventure 0-1, 0-2, 55' Sergio Ramos 1-2, 85' Casemiro 2-2.
Referee: Georgi Kabakov (BUL)   Attendance: 65,112.
Sent off: 84' Ruud Vormer.

01.10.19   Türk Telekom Stadyumu, Istanbul: Galatasaray – Paris Saint-Germain 0-1 (0-0)
Galatasaray: Fernando Muslera, Mariano, Yuto Nagatomo (77' Ömer Bayram), Marcâo Teixeira, Christian Luyindama, Ryan Donk, Steven N'Zonzi, Younès Belhanda (62' Sofiane Féghouli), Jean Michaël Seri, Ryan Babel (64' Florin Andone), Radamel Falcao.
Coach: Fatih Terim.
Paris Saint-Germain: Keylor Navas, Thiago Silva, Thomas Meunier, Marquinhos, Juan Bernat, Presnel Kimpembe, Ángel Di María (83' Ander Herrera), Marco Verratti, Idrissa Gueye, Pablo Sarabia (71' Eric Maxim Choupo-Moting), Mauro Icardi (61' Kylian Mbappé).
Coach: Thomas Tuchel.
Goal: 52' Mauro Icardi 0-1.
Referee: Szymon Marciniak (POL)   Attendance: 46,532.

22.10.19   Türk Telekom Stadyumu, Istanbul: Galatasaray – Real Madrid CF 0-1 (0-1)
Galatasaray: Fernando Muslera, Mariano, Yuto Nagatomo, Marcâo Teixeira, Christian Luyindama, Ryan Donk (46' Sofiane Féghouli), Steven N'Zonzi, Younès Belhanda (67' Ömer Bayram), Jean Michaël Seri (77' Emre Mor), Ryan Babel, Florin Andone. Coach: Fatih Terim.
Real Madrid CF: Thibaut Courtois, Sergio Ramos, Marcelo, Dani Carvajal, Raphaël Varane, Toni Kroos, Casemiro, Federico Valverde (79' James Rodríguez), Karim Benzema, Eden Hazard (79' Vinícius Júnior), Rodrygo (82' Luka Jovic). Coach: Zinédine Zidane.
Goal: 18' Toni Kroos 0-1.
Referee: Daniele Orsato (ITA)   Attendance: 48,886.

22.10.19   Jan Breydelstadion, Brugge: Club Brugge KV – Paris Saint-Germain 0-5 (0-1)
Club Brugge KV: Simon Mignolet, Eduard Sobol (80' Éder Álvarez Balanta), Clinton Mata, Simon Deli, Brandon Mechele, Mats Rits, Hans Vanaken, Charles De Ketelaere (57' David Okereke), Percy Tau, Emmanuel Dennis Bonaventure (76' Loïs Openda), Krépin Diatta. Coach: Philippe Clement.
Paris Saint-Germain: Keylor Navas, Thiago Silva, Thomas Meunier, Marquinhos, Juan Bernat, Presnel Kimpembe, Ángel Di María, Ander Herrera (72' Abdou Diallo), Marco Verratti, Eric Maxim Choupo-Moting (52' Kylian Mbappé), Mauro Icardi (65' Leandro Paredes).
Coach: Thomas Tuchel.
Goals: 7' Mauro Icardi 0-1, 61' Kylian Mbappé 0-2, 63' Mauro Icardi 0-3,
79', 83' Kylian Mbappé 0-4, 0-5.
Referee: Daniel Siebert (GER)   Attendance: 26,946.

06.11.19   Estadio Santiago Bernabéu, Madrid: Real Madrid CF – Galatasaray 6-0 (4-0)
Real Madrid CF: Thibaut Courtois, Sergio Ramos, Marcelo (42' Ferland Mendy), Dani Carvajal, Raphaël Varane, Toni Kroos, Casemiro (60' Luka Modric), Federico Valverde, Karim Benzema, Eden Hazard (68' Isco), Rodrygo. Coach: Zinédine Zidane.
Galatasaray: Fernando Muslera, Mariano, Yuto Nagatomo (88' Adem Büyük), Marcâo Teixeira, Christian Luyindama, Sofiane Féghouli, Steven N'Zonzi (46' Ömer Bayram), Mario Lemina, Jean Michaël Seri, Ryan Babel, Florin Andone (46' Ryan Donk). Coach: Fatih Terim.
Goals: 4', 7' Rodrygo 1-0, 2-0, 14' Sergio Ramos 3-0 (p), 45', 81' Karim Benzema 4-0, 5-0, 90+2' Rodrygo 6-0.
Referee: Felix Zwayer (GER)   Attendance: 65,492.

06.11.19   Parc des Princes, Paris: Paris Saint-Germain – Club Brugge KV 1-0 (1-0)
Paris Saint-Germain: Keylor Navas, Thiago Silva, Marquinhos, Juan Bernat, Presnel Kimpembe, Colin Dagba, Ángel Di María, Marco Verratti (90' Pablo Sarabia), Idrissa Gueye, Mauro Icardi (72' Edinson Cavani), Kylian Mbappé (83' Julian Draxler).
Coach: Thomas Tuchel.
Club Brugge KV: Simon Mignolet, Éder Álvarez Balanta, Simon Deli, Brandon Mechele, Federico Ricca, Odilon Kossounou, Mats Rits (86' Charles De Ketelaere), Hans Vanaken, David Okereke (67' Mbaye Diagne), Emmanuel Dennis Bonaventure, Krépin Diatta (77' Siebe Schrijvers). Coach: Philippe Clement.
Goal: 22' Mauro Icardi 1-0.
Referee: Bobby Madden (SCO)   Attendance: 47,418.

Mbaye Diagne missed a penalty kick (76').

26.11.19   Türk Telekom Stadyumu, Istanbul: Galatasaray – Club Brugge KV 1-1 (1-0)
Galatasaray: Fernando Muslera, Mariano, Yuto Nagatomo, Ömer Bayram (80' Selçuk Inan), Marcâo Teixeira, Ryan Donk, Sofiane Féghouli, Younès Belhanda (87' Emre Mor), Mario Lemina, Jean Michaël Seri (90+4' Erencan Yardimci), Adem Büyük. Coach: Fatih Terim.
Club Brugge KV: Simon Mignolet, Clinton Mata, Éder Álvarez Balanta, Simon Deli, Brandon Mechele, Federico Ricca, Mats Rits (46' Charles De Ketelaere), Hans Vanaken, Loïs Openda (77' David Okereke), Emmanuel Dennis Bonaventure (58' Siebe Schrijvers), Krépin Diatta. Coach: Philippe Clement.
Goals: 11' Adem Büyük 1-0, 90+2' Krépin Diatta 1-1.
Referee: Ivan Kruzliak (SVK)   Attendance: 34,500.
Sent off: 90+3' Krépin Diatta, Clinton Mata,

26.11.19   Estadio Santiago Bernabéu, Madrid:
            Real Madrid CF – Paris Saint-Germain 2-2 (1-0)
Real Madrid CF: Thibaut Courtois, Sergio Ramos, Marcelo, Dani Carvajal, Raphaël Varane, Toni Kroos, Casemiro, Isco (82' Rodrygo), Federico Valverde (76' Luka Modric), Karim Benzema, Eden Hazard (68' Gareth Bale). Coach: Zinédine Zidane.
Paris Saint-Germain: Keylor Navas, Thiago Silva, Thomas Meunier, Marquinhos, Juan Bernat, Presnel Kimpembe, Ángel Di María (75' Julian Draxler), Marco Verratti, Idrissa Gueye (46' Neymar), Mauro Icardi (75' Pablo Sarabia), Kylian Mbappé. Coach: Thomas Tuchel.
Goals: 17', 79' Karim Benzema 1-0, 2-0, 81' Kylian Mbappé 2-1, 83' Pablo Sarabia 2-2.
Referee: Artur Soares Dias (POR)   Attendance: 75,534.

11.12.19   Jan Breydelstadion, Brugge: Club Brugge KV – Real Madrid CF 1-3 (0-0)
Club Brugge KV: Simon Mignolet, Eduard Sobol, Éder Álvarez Balanta, Simon Deli, Brandon Mechele, Thibault Vlietinck (70' Charles De Ketelaere), Odilon Kossounou, Ruud Vormer, Hans Vanaken, Percy Tau (59' Siebe Schrijvers), Emmanuel Dennis Bonaventure.
Coach: Philippe Clement.
Real Madrid CF: Alphonse Aréola, Raphaël Varane, Odriozola, Ferland Mendy, Éder Militão, Luka Modric, Casemiro, Isco (84' Federico Valverde), Luka Jovic (77' Karim Benzema), Vinicíus Júnior (73' Brahim Díaz), Rodrygo. Coach: Zinédine Zidane.
Goals: 53' Rodrygo 0-1, 55' Hans Vanaken 1-1, 64' Vinicíus Júnior 1-2, 90+1' Luka Modric 1-3.
Referee: Tobias Stieler (GER)   Attendance: 27,308.

11.12.19   Parc des Princes, Paris: Paris Saint-Germain – Galatarasay 5-0 (2-0)
Paris Saint-Germain: Sergio Rico, Layvin Kurzawa, Marquinhos, Juan Bernat (75' Thilo Kehrer), Abdou Diallo, Nianzou Kouassi (75' Marco Verratti), Pablo Sarabia, Leandro Paredes, Neymar, Mauro Icardi (68' Edinson Cavani), Kylian Mbappé. Coach: Thomas Tuchel.
Galatasaray: Fernando Muslera, Mariano, Yuto Nagatomo, Ömer Bayram, Marcâo Teixeira, Ryan Donk, Steven N'Zonzi (72' Sener Özbayrakli), Younès Belhanda, Mario Lemina, Jean Michaël Seri (41' Selçuk Inan), Emre Mor (62' Radamel Falcao). Coach: Fatih Terim.
Goals: 32' Mauro Icardi 1-0, 35' Pablo Sarabia 2-0, 46' Neymar 3-0, 63' Kylian Mbappé 4-0, 84' Edinson Cavani 5-0 (p).
Referee: István Kovács (ROM)   Attendance: 46,509.

GROUP B

18.09.19   Stadio Georgios Karaiskáki, Piraeus:
           Olympiacos Piraeus FC – Tottenham Hotspur 2-2 (1-2)
Olympiacos Piraeus FC: José Sá, Omar Elabdellaoui, Rúben Semedo, Yassine Meriah, Kostas Tsimikas, Mathieu Valbuena (69' Yassine Benzia), Guilherme, Andreas Bouchalakis, Daniel Podence, Georgios Masouras (78' Lazar Randjelovic), Guerrero (89' Youssef El-Arbi).
Coach: Pedro Martins.
Tottenham Hotspur: Hugo Lloris, Jan Vertonghen, Toby Alderweireld, Ben Davies, Davinson Sánchez, Christian Eriksen, Lucas Moura (76' Érik Lamela), Dele Alli (73' Son Heung-Min), Harry Winks, Tanguy NDombèlé (62' Moussa Sissoko), Harry Kane.
Coach: Mauricio Pochettino.
Goals: 26' Harry Kane 0-1 (p), 30' Lucas Moura 0-2, 44' Daniel Podence 1-2, 54' Mathieu Valbuena 2-2 (p).
Referee: Gianluca Rocchi (ITA)   Attendance: 31,001.

18.09.19   Allianz Arena, München: FC Bayern München – Crvena Zvezda Beograd 3-0 (1-0)
FC Bayern München: Manuel Neuer, Niklas Süle, Joshua Kimmich, Lucas Hernández, Benjamin Pavard, Ivan Perisic (66' Serge Gnabry), Thiago Alcântara, Philippe Coutinho (83' Thomas Müller), Corentin Tolisso (65' Javi Martínez), Robert Lewandowski, Kingsley Coman. Coach: Niko Kovac.
Crvena Zvezda Beograd: Milan Borjan, Nemanja Milunovic, Jander, Milos Degenek, Marko Gobeljic, Marko Marin, Rajiv van La Parra, Cañas, Dusan Jovancic (62' Milos Vulic), Mateo García (83' Aleksa Vukanovic), Milan Pavkov (70' Richmond Boakye).
Coach: Vladan Milojevic.
Goals: 34' Kingsley Coman 1-0, 80' Robert Lewandowski 2-0, 90+1' Thomas Müller 3-0.
Referee: Bobby Madden (SCO)   Attendance: 70,000.

01.10.19   Stadion Rajko Mitic, Beograd:
   Crvena Zvezda Beograd – Olympiacos Piraues FC 3-1 (0-1)
Crvena Zvezda Beograd: Milan Borjan, Nemanja Milunovic, Milan Rodic, Milos Degenek, Marko Gobeljic, Marko Marin, Rajiv van La Parra (61' Richmond Boakye), Cañas (73' Njegos Petrovic), Dusan Jovancic (55' Milos Vulic), Mateo García, Tó Mané.
Coach: Vladan Milojevic.
Olympiacos Piraeus FC: José Sá, Vasilios Torosidis, Rúben Semedo, Yassine Meriah, Kostas Tsimikas, Andreas Bouchalakis, Georgios Masouras (79' Omar Elabdellaoui), Mohamed Mady Camara (89' Youssef El-Arbi), Guerrero, Yassine Benzia, Maximiliano Lovera (61' Daniel Podence). Coach: Pedro Martins.
Goals: 37' Rúben Semedo 0-1, 62' Milos Vulic 1-1, 87' Nemanja Milunovic 2-1, 90' Richmond Boakye 3-1.
Referee: Benoît Bastien (FRA)   Attendance: 43,291.
Sent off: 57' Yassine Benzia.

01.10.19   Tottenham Hotspur Stadium, London:
   Tottenham Hotspur – FC Bayern München 2-7 (1-2)
Tottenham Hotspur: Hugo Lloris, Jan Vertonghen, Danny Rose, Toby Alderweireld, Serge Aurier, Moussa Sissoko, Dele Alli (71' Lucas Moura), Harry Winks (81' Érik Lamela), Tanguy NDombèlé (64' Christian Eriksen), Son Heung-Min, Harry Kane.
Coach: Mauricio Pochettino.
FC Bayern München: Manuel Neuer, Jérôme Boateng (72' Javi Martínez), David Alaba (46' Thiago Alcântara), Niklas Süle, Joshua Kimmich, Benjamin Pavard, Philippe Coutinho, Serge Gnabry, Corentin Tolisso, Robert Lewandowski, Kingsley Coman (71' Ivan Perisic).
Coach: Niko Kovac.
Goals: 12' Son Heung-Min 1-0, 15' Joshua Kimmich 1-1, 45' Robert Lewandowski 1-2, 53', 55' Serge Gnabry 1-3, 1-4, 61' Harry Kane 2-4 (p), 83' Serge Gnabry 2-5, 87' Robert Lewandowski 2-6, 88' Serge Gnabry 2-7.
Referee: Clément Turpin (FRA)   Attendance: 60,127.

22.10.19   Tottenham Hotspur Stadium, London:
   Tottenham Hotspur – Crvena Zvezda Beograd 5-0 (3-0)
Tottenham Hotspur: Paulo Gazzaniga, Jan Vertonghen (73' Juan Foyth), Serge Aurier, Ben Davies, Davinson Sánchez, Moussa Sissoko, Érik Lamela, Dele Alli (79' Giovani Lo Celso), Tanguy NDombèlé, Son Heung-Min (68' Eric Dier), Harry Kane. Coach: Mauricio Pochettino.
Crvena Zvezda Beograd: Milan Borjan, Nemanja Milunovic, Milan Rodic, Milos Degenek, Marko Gobeljic, Marko Marin, Rajiv van La Parra (82' Aleksa Vukanovic), Cañas (62' Njegos Petrovic), Milos Vulic, Mateo García, Tó Mané (62' Milan Pavkov). Coach: Vladan Milojevic.
Goals: 9' Harry Kane 1-0, 16', 44' Son Heung-Min 2-0, 3-0, 57' Érik Lamela 4-0, 72' Harry Kane 5-0.
Referee: Marco Guida (ITA)   Attendance: 51,743.

22.10.19   Stadio Georgios Karaiskáki, Piraeus:
Olympiacos Piraeus FC – FC Bayern München 2-3 (1-1)
Olympiacos Piraeus FC: José Sá, Omar Elabdellaoui, Rúben Semedo, Yassine Meriah, Kostas Tsimikas, Guilherme, Andreas Bouchalakis (69' Maximiliano Lovera), Daniel Podence, Georgios Masouras (78' Guerrero), Mohamed Mady Camara (88' Lazar Randjelovic), Youssef El-Arbi. Coach: Pedro Martins.
FC Bayern München: Manuel Neuer, David Alaba, Joshua Kimmich, Lucas Hernández (59' Jérôme Boateng), Benjamin Pavard, Javi Martínez (46' Corentin Tolisso), Thiago Alcântara, Philippe Coutinho, Serge Gnabry, Thomas Müller (86' Ivan Perisic), Robert Lewandowski. Coach: Niko Kovac.
Goals: 23' Youssef El-Arbi 1-0, 34', 62' Robert Lewandowski 1-1, 1-2,
75' Corentin Tolisso 1-3, 79' Guilherme 2-3.
Referee: Danny Makkelie (HOL)   Attendance: 31,670.

06.11.19   Allianz Arena, München: FC Bayern München – Olympiacos Piraeus FC 2-0 (0-0)
FC Bayern München: Manuel Neuer, David Alaba, Joshua Kimmich, Benjamin Pavard, Javi Martínez, Leon Goretzka (82' Corentin Tolisso), Serge Gnabry (88' Ivan Perisic), Alphonso Davies, Thomas Müller, Robert Lewandowski, Kingsley Coman (90+1' Philippe Coutinho). Coach: Hansi Flick.
Olympiacos Piraeus FC: José Sá, Omar Elabdellaoui, Rúben Semedo, Yassine Meriah, Kostas Tsimikas, Guilherme, Andreas Bouchalakis (71' Mathieu Valbuena), Daniel Podence (80' Youssef El-Arbi), Lazar Randjelovic (61' Georgios Masouras), Mohamed Mady Camara, Guerrero. Coach: Pedro Martins.
Goals: 69' Robert Lewandowski 1-0, 89' Ivan Perisic 2-0.
Referee: Pawel Raczkowski (POL)   Attendance: 63,646.

06.11.19   Stadion Rajko Mitic, Beograd:
Crvena Zvezda Beograd – Tottenham Hotspur 0-4 (0-1)
Crvena Zvezda Beograd: Milan Borjan, Nemanja Milunovic, Milan Rodic, Milos Degenek, Marko Gobeljic (46' Jander), Marko Marin, Rajiv van La Parra, Dusan Jovancic (62' Cañas), Mateo García (68' Richmond Boakye), Njegos Petrovic, Milan Pavkov.
Coach: Vladan Milojevic.
Tottenham Hotspur: Paulo Gazzaniga, Danny Rose, Davinson Sánchez, Juan Foyth, Moussa Sissoko, Dele Alli (62' Christian Eriksen), Eric Dier, Tanguy NDombèlé, Giovani Lo Celso (86' Oliver Skipp), Son Heung-Min (75' Ryan Sessegnon), Harry Kane.
Coach: Mauricio Pochettino.
Goals: 34' Giovani Lo Celso 0-1, 57', 61' Son Heung-Min 0-2, 0-3, 85' Christian Eriksen 0-4.
Referee: Carlos del Cerro Grande (ESP)   Attendance: 42,381.

26.11.19   Tottenham Hotspur Stadium, London:
Tottenham Hotspur – Olympiacos Piraeus FC 4-2 (1-2)
Tottenham Hotspur: Paulo Gazzaniga, Danny Rose, Toby Alderweireld, Serge Aurier, Davinson Sánchez, Lucas Moura (61' Moussa Sissoko), Dele Alli (83' Tanguy NDombèlé), Eric Dier (29' Christian Eriksen), Harry Winks, Son Heung-Min, Harry Kane.
Coach: José Mourinho.
Olympiacos Piraeus FC: José Sá, Omar Elabdellaoui, Rúben Semedo, Yassine Meriah, Kostas Tsimikas, Guilherme, Andreas Bouchalakis (74' Mathieu Valbuena), Daniel Podence (79' Lazar Randjelovic), Georgios Masouras, Mohamed Mady Camara, Youssef El-Arbi (85' Guerrero). Coach: Pedro Martins.
Goals: 6' Youssef El-Arbi 0-1, 19' Rúben Semedo 0-2, 45+1' Dele Alli 1-2,
50' Harry Kane 2-2, 73' Serge Aurier 3-2, 77' Harry Kane 4-2.
Referee: Georgi Kabakov (BUL)   Attendance: 57,024.

26.11.19   Stadion Rajko Mitic, Beograd:
           Crvena Zvezda Beograd – FC Bayern München 0-6 (0-1)
Crvena Zvezda Beograd: Milan Borjan, Nemanja Milunovic, Milan Rodic, Milos Degenek, Marko Gobeljic, Marko Marin, Cañas (61' Milos Vulic), Mateo García (69' Radovan Pankov), Njegos Petrovic (76' Mirko Ivanic), Richmond Boakye, Aleksa Vukanovic.
Coach: Vladan Milojevic.
FC Bayern München: Manuel Neuer, Jérôme Boateng, Benjamin Pavard, Javi Martínez (68' Joshua Kimmich), Thiago Alcântara, Philippe Coutinho (60' Ivan Perisic), Leon Goretzka, Corentin Tolisso, Alphonso Davies, Robert Lewandowski (77' Thomas Müller), Kingsley Coman. Coach: Hansi Flick.
Goals: 14' Leon Goretzka 0-1, 53', 60', 64', 68' Robert Lewandowski 0-2 (p), 0-3, 0-4, 0-5, 89' Corentin Tolisso 0-6.
Referee: Björn Kuipers (HOL)   Attendance: 44,118.

11.12.19   Stadio Georgios Karaiskáki, Piraeus:
           Olympiacos Piraeus FC – Crvena Zvezda Beograd 1-0 (0-0)
Olympiacos Piraeus FC: José Sá, Omar Elabdellaoui, Rúben Semedo, Yassine Meriah, Kostas Tsimikas, Guilherme, Andreas Bouchalakis, Daniel Podence, Georgios Masouras (71' Maximiliano Lovera), Mohamed Mady Camara (61' Guerrero), Youssef El-Arbi (90' Yassine Benzia). Coach: Pedro Martins.
Crvena Zvezda Beograd: Milan Borjan, Nemanja Milunovic, Milan Rodic (82' Jander), Milos Degenek, Marko Gobeljic, Marko Marin, Mirko Ivanic, Mateo García, Njegos Petrovic, Tó Mané (58' Rajiv van La Parra), Aleksa Vukanovic (65' Richmond Boakye).
Coach: Vladan Milojevic.
Goal: 87' Youssef El-Arbi 1-0 (p).
Referee: Daniele Orsato (ITA)   Attendance: 31,898.

Tó Mané missed a penalty kick (42').

11.12.19   Allianz Arena, München: FC Bayern München – Tottenham Hotspur 3-1 (2-1)
FC Bayern München: Manuel Neuer, Jérôme Boateng, Joshua Kimmich, Benjamin Pavard, Javi Martínez (87' Leon Goretzka), Ivan Perisic (86' Joshua Zirkzee), Thiago Alcântara, Philippe Coutinho, Serge Gnabry, Alphonso Davies, Kingsley Coman (27' Thomas Müller).
Coach: Hansi Flick.
Tottenham Hotspur: Paulo Gazzaniga, Danny Rose, Toby Alderweireld, Kyle Walker-Peters, Juan Foyth, Moussa Sissoko, Christian Eriksen, Lucas Moura (65' Son Heung-Min), Eric Dier (81' Victor Wanyama), Giovani Lo Celso (65' Oliver Skipp), Ryan Sessegnon.
Coach: José Mourinho.
Goals: 14' Kingsley Coman 1-0, 20' Ryan Sessegnon 1-1, 45' Thomas Müller 2-1, 64' Philippe Coutinho 3-1.
Referee: Gianluca Rocchi (ITA)   Attendance: 66,353.

GROUP C

18.09.19   Oblasny SportKomplex Metalist, Kharkiv:
Shakhtar Donetsk – Manchester City 0-3 (0-2)
Shakhtar Donetsk: Andriy Pyatov, Sergiy Krivtsov, Ismaily, Mykola Matvienko, Marlos, Taras Stepanenko, Taison, Alan Patrick (74' Marcos Antônio), Sergiy Bolbat, Manor Solomon (46' Yevhen Konoplyanka), Júnior Moraes (77' Dentinho). Coach: Luís Castro.
Manchester City: Ederson Moraes, Nicolás Otamendi, Kyle Walker (81' João Cancelo), Oleksandr Zinchenko, Fernandinho, Ilkay Gündogan, Kevin De Bruyne (77' Bernardo Silva), Rodri Hernández (83' Benjamin Mendy), Riyad Mahrez, Raheem Sterling, Gabriel Jesus. Coach: Pep Guardiola.
Goals: Manchester City: 24' Riyad Mahrez 0-1, 38' Ilkay Gündogan 0-2, 76' Gabriel Jesus 0-3.
Referee: Artur Soares Dias (POR)   Attendance: 36,675.

(Shakhtar Donetsk played their home matches at Oblasny SportKomplex Metalist, Kharkiv, instead of their regular stadium Donbass Arena, Donetsk, due to the war conditions in Eastern Ukraine)

18.09.19   Stadion Maksimir, Zagreb: Dinamo Zagreb – Atalanta Bergamo 4-0 (3-0)
Dinamo Zagreb: Dominik Livakovic, Marin Leovac, Kévin Théophile-Catherine, Emir Dilaver, Petar Stojanovic, Dino Peric, Arijan Ademi, Nikola Moro (73' Amer Gojak), Daniel Olmo, Mislav Orsic (76' Luka Ivanusec), Bruno Petkovic (83' Mario Gavranovic). Coach: Nenad Bjelica.
Atalanta Bergamo: Pierluigi Gollini, Andrea Masiello (46' Ruslan Malinovskiy), Rafael Tolói, Berat Djimsiti, Hans Hateboer, Robin Gosens, Papu Gómez, Josip Ilicic (88' Musa Barrow), Marten van Roon, Remo Freuler (46' Mario Pasalic), Duván Zapata.
Coach: Gian Piero Gasperini.
Goals: 10' Marin Leovac 1-0, 31', 42', 68' Mislav Orsic 2-0, 3-0, 4-0.
Referee: Jesús Gil Manzano (ESP)   Attendance: 28,863.

01.10.19   Stadio Giuseppe Meazza, Milan: Atalanta Bergamo – Shakhtar Donetsk 1-2 (1-1)
Atalanta Bergamo: Pierluigi Gollini, Andrea Masiello (68' Luis Muriel), Rafael Tolói, José Palomino, Timothy Castagne, Hans Hateboer (57' Robin Gosens), Papu Gómez, Josip Ilicic (57' Ruslan Malinovskiy), Marten van Roon, Mario Pasalic, Duván Zapata.
Coach: Gian Piero Gasperini.
Shakhtar Donetsk: Andriy Pyatov, Sergiy Krivtsov, Ismaily, Mykola Matvienko, Marlos (86' Yevhen Konoplyanka), Taras Stepanenko, Taison, Alan Patrick (69' Manor Solomon), Sergiy Bolbat (90+3' Dodô), Viktor Kovalenko, Júnior Moraes. Coach: Luís Castro.
Goals: 28' Duván Zapata 1-0, 41' Júnior Moraes 1-1, 90+5' Manor Solomon 1-2.
Referee: Tobias Stieler (GER)   Attendance: 26,022.

Josip Ilicic missed a penalty kick (16').

(Atalanta Bergamo played their home matches at Stadio Giuseppe Meazza, Milan, instead of their regular stadium Stadio Atleti Azzurri d'Italia, Bergamo, which is undergoing renovation)

01.10.19   Etihad Stadium, Manchester: Manchester City – Dinamo Zagreb 2-0 (0-0)
Manchester City: Ederson Moraes, Nicolás Otamendi, João Cancelo, Benjamin Mendy, David Silva (90+1' Phil Foden), Fernandinho, Ilkay Gündogan, Bernardo Silva (56' Raheem Sterling), Rodri Hernández, Kun Agüero (89' Gabriel Jesus), Riyad Mahrez.
Coach: Pep Guardiola.
Dinamo Zagreb: Dominik Livakovic, Marin Leovac, Kévin Théophile-Catherine (76' Mario Gavranovic), Emir Dilaver, Petar Stojanovic, Dino Peric, Arijan Ademi, Nikola Moro, Daniel Olmo, Mislav Orsic (62' Amer Gojak), Bruno Petkovic (84' Iyayi Atiemwen).
Coach: Nenad Bjelica.
Goals: 66' Raheem Sterling 1-0, 90+5' Phil Foden 2-0.
Referee: Serdar Gözübüyük (HOL)   Attendance: 49,046.

22.10.19   Oblasny SportKomplex Metalist, Kharkiv:
            Shakhtar Donetsk – Dinamo Zagreb 2-2 (1-1)
Shakhtar Donetsk: Andriy Pyatov, Sergiy Krivtsov, Ismaily, Mykola Matvienko, Marlos (84' Viktor Kovalenko), Taras Stepanenko, Taison, Yevhen Konoplyanka (66' Manor Solomon), Alan Patrick, Sergiy Bolbat (66' Dodô), Júnior Moraes. Coach: Luís Castro.
Dinamo Zagreb: Dominik Livakovic, Marin Leovac, Kévin Théophile-Catherine, Emir Dilaver, Petar Stojanovic, Dino Peric, Arijan Ademi (68' Amer Gojak), Nikola Moro, Daniel Olmo, Mario Gavranovic (62' Bruno Petkovic), Mislav Orsic (90' Luka Ivanusec).
Coach: Nenad Bjelica.
Goals: 16' Yevhen Konoplyanka 1-0, 25' Daniel Olmo 1-1, 60' Mislav Orsic 1-2 (p), 75' Dodô (75').
Referee: Antonio Mateu Lahoz (ESP)   Attendance: 21,526.

22.10.19   Etihad Stadium, Manchester: Manchester City – Atalanta Bergamo 5-1 (2-1)
Manchester City: Ederson Moraes, Kyle Walker, Benjamin Mendy (71' João Cancelo), Fernandinho, Ilkay Gündogan, Kevin De Bruyne (67' Nicolás Otamendi), Rodri Hernández (41' John Stones), Phil Foden, Kun Agüero, Riyad Mahrez, Raheem Sterling.
Coach: Pep Guardiola.
Atalanta Bergamo: Pierluigi Gollini, Andrea Masiello (46' Mario Pasalic), Rafael Tolói, Berat Djimsiti, Timothy Castagne, Robin Gosens, Papu Gómez (46' Luis Muriel), Josip Ilicic (72' Hans Hateboer), Marten van Roon, Remo Freuler, Ruslan Malinovskiy.
Coach: Gian Piero Gasperini.
Goals: 28' Ruslan Malinovskiy 0-1 (p), 34', 38' Kun Agüero 1-1, 2-1 (p),
58', 64', 69' Raheem Sterling 3-1, 4-1, 5-1.
Referee: Orel Grinfeld (ISR)   Attendance: 49,308.
Sent off: 82' Phil Foden.

06.11.19   Stadio Giuseppe Meazza, Milan: Atalanta Bergamo – Manchester City 1-1 (0-1)
Atalanta Bergamo: Pierluigi Gollini, Rafael Tolói, José Palomino, Berat Djimsiti, Timothy Castagne (90+2' Luis Muriel), Hans Hateboer, Papu Gómez, Josip Ilicic, Marten van Roon, Remo Freuler (84' Ruslan Malinovskiy), Mario Pasalic. Coach: Gian Piero Gasperini.
Manchester City: Ederson Moraes (46' Claudio Bravo), Nicolás Otamendi, João Cancelo, Benjamin Mendy, Fernandinho, Ilkay Gündogan, Kevin De Bruyne, Bernardo Silva, Riyad Mahrez (88' Kyle Walker), Raheem Sterling, Gabriel Jesus (73' Kun Agüero).
Coach: Pep Guardiola.
Goals: 7' Raheem Sterling 0-1, 49' Mario Pasalic 1-1.
Referee: Aleksei Kulbakov (BLS)   Attendance: 34,326.
Sent off: 81' Claudio Bravo.

Gabriel Jesus missed a penalty kick (43').

06.11.19 Stadion Maksimir, Zagreb: Dinamo Zagreb – Shakhtar Donetsk 3-3 (1-1)
Dinamo Zagreb: Dominik Livakovic, Marin Leovac, Kévin Théophile-Catherine, Emir Dilaver, Petar Stojanovic (72' Luka Ivanusec), Dino Peric, Arijan Ademi, Nikola Moro, Daniel Olmo, Mislav Orsic (77' Marko Djira), Bruno Petkovic (90+1' Damian Kadzior).
Coach: Nenad Bjelica.
Shakhtar Donetsk: Andriy Pyatov, Sergiy Krivtsov, Ismaily, Mykola Matvienko (86' Dentinho), Dodô, Marlos, Taras Stepanenko (90+1' Marcos Antônio), Taison, Alan Patrick (84' Mateus Martins Tetê), Viktor Kovalenko, Júnior Moraes. Coach: Luís Castro.
Goals: 13' Alan Patrick 0-1, 25' Bruno Petkovic 1-1, 83' Luka Ivanusec 2-1, 89' Arijan Ademi 3-1, 90+3' Júnior Moraes 3-2, 90+8' Mateus Martins Tetê 3-3 (p).
Referee: Felix Brych (GER)   Attendance: 28,316.
Sent off: 74' Nikola Moro, 79' Marlos.

26.11.19 Etihad Stadium, Manchester: Manchester City – Shakhtar Donetsk 1-1 (0-0)
Manchester City: Ederson Moraes, Nicolás Otamendi, João Cancelo, José Angeliño, Fernandinho, Ilkay Gündogan, Kevin De Bruyne (70' David Silva), Bernardo Silva, Rodri Hernández (76' Phil Foden), Raheem Sterling, Gabriel Jesus. Coach: Pep Guardiola.
Shakhtar Donetsk: Andriy Pyatov, Sergiy Krivtsov, Ismaily, Mykola Matvienko, Dodô, Taras Stepanenko, Yevhen Konoplyanka (65' Manor Solomon), Alan Patrick, Viktor Kovalenko (81' Marcos Antônio), Mateus Martins Tetê, Júnior Moraes (90' Danylo Sikan).
Coach: Luís Castro.
Goals: 56' Ilkay Gündogan 1-0, 69' Manor Solomon 1-1.
Referee: Slavko Vincic (SVN)   Attendance: 52,020.

26.11.19   Stadio Giuseppe Meazza, Milan: Atalanta Bergamo – Dinamo Zagreb 2-0 (1-0)
Atalanta Bergamo: Pierluigi Gollini, Simon Kjær, Rafael Tolói, José Palomino, Hans Hateboer (65' Timothy Castagne), Robin Gosens, Papu Gómez (90' Ruslan Malinovskiy), Marten van Roon, Remo Freuler, Mario Pasalic, Luis Muriel (61' Josip Ilicic).
Coach: Gian Piero Gasperini.
Dinamo Zagreb: Dominik Livakovic, Marin Leovac, Kévin Théophile-Catherine, Emir Dilaver, Petar Stojanovic (75' Marko Djira), Dino Peric, Arijan Ademi, Daniel Olmo (90+2' Mario Situm), Luka Ivanusec (67' Amer Gojak), Mislav Orsic, Bruno Petkovic.
Coach: Nenad Bjelica.
Goals: 27' Luis Muriel 1-0 (p), 47' Papu Gómez 2-0.
Referee: Sergei Karasev (RUS)   Attendance: 28,365.

11.12.19   Oblasny SportKomplex Metalist, Kharkiv:
             Shakhtar Donetsk – Atalanta Bergamo 0-3 (0-0)
Shakhtar Donetsk: Andriy Pyatov, Sergiy Krivtsov, Ismaily, Mykola Matvienko, Dodô, Taras Stepanenko, Taison, Alan Patrick, Viktor Kovalenko (71' Manor Solomon), Mateus Martins Tetê (59' Marlos), Júnior Moraes. Coach: Luís Castro.
Atalanta Bergamo: Pierluigi Gollini, Andrea Masiello (61' Ruslan Malinovskiy), José Palomino, Berat Djimsiti, Timothy Castagne, Robin Gosens, Papu Gómez (90' Hans Hateboer), Marten van Roon, Remo Freuler, Mario Pasalic, Luis Muriel (71' Ibañez).
Coach: Gian Piero Gasperini.
Goals: 66' Timothy Castagne 0-1, 80' Mario Pasalic 0-2, 90+4' Robin Gosens 0-3.
Referee: Felix Zwayer (GER)   Attendance: 26,536.
Sent off: 77' Dodô.

11.12.19 Stadion Maksimir, Zagreb: Dinamo Zagreb – Manchester City 1-4 (1-1)
Dinamo Zagreb: Dominik Livakovic, Emir Dilaver, François Moubandje, Petar Stojanovic, Arijan Ademi, Amer Gojak (81' Lovro Majer), Nikola Moro, Daniel Olmo, Mislav Orsic (81' Izet Hajrovic), Damian Kadzior (59' Marko Djira), Bruno Petkovic. Coach: Nenad Bjelica.
Manchester City: Claudio Bravo, Nicolás Otamendi (82' Taylor Harwood-Bellis), João Cancelo, Benjamin Mendy, Eric García, Ilkay Gündogan, Bernardo Silva, Rodri Hernández (73' Raheem Sterling), Phil Foden, Riyad Mahrez, Gabriel Jesus (66' Oleksandr Zinchenko). Coach: Pep Guardiola.
Goals: 10' Daniel Olmo 1-0, 34', 50', 54' Gabriel Jesus 1-1, 1-2, 1-3, 84' Phil Foden 1-4.
Referee: Carlos del Cerro Grande (ESP)   Attendance: 29,385.

GROUP D

18.09.19 Estadio Wanda Metropolitano, Madrid: Atlético Madrid – Juventus 2-2 (0-0)
Atlético Madrid: Jan Oblak, Stefan Savic, Kieran Trippier, José Giménez, Renan Lodi (76' Vitolo), Saúl, Koke, Thomas Lemar (60' Ángel Correa), Thomas Partey (76' Héctor Herrera), Diego Costa, João Félix. Coach: Diego Simeone.
Juventus: Wojciech Szczesny, Leonardo Bonucci, Danilo, Alex Sandro, Matthijs de Ligt, Blaise Matuidi, Sami Khedira (69' Rodrigo Bentancur), Miralem Pjanic (87' Aaron Ramsey), Juan Cuadrado, Cristiano Ronaldo, Gonzalo Higuaín (80' Paulo Dybala).
Coach: Maurizio Sarri.
Goals: 48' Juan Cuadrado 0-1, 65' Blaise Matuidi 0-2, 70' Stefan Savic 1-2, 90' Héctor Herrera 2-2.
Referee: Danny Makkelie (HOL)   Attendance: 66,283.

18.09.19 BayArena, Leverkusen: Bayer Leverkusen – Lokomotiv Moscow 1-2 (1-2)
Bayer Leverkusen: Lukás Hrádecky, Sven Bender, Wendell, Jonathan Tah, Lars Bender, Charles Aránguiz, Julian Baumgartlinger (71' Nadiem Amiri), Karim Bellarabi, Kai Havertz, Kevin Volland, Leon Bailey (46' Lucas Alario). Coach: Peter Bosz.
Lokomotiv Moscow: Guilherme, Vedran Corluka, Benedikt Höwedes, Murilo Cerqueira, Maciej Rybus, Vladislav Ignatyev, Grzegorz Krychowiak, João Mário (90+3' Brian Idowu), Dmitry Barinov, Fyodor Smolov, Rifat Zhemaletdinov. Coach: Yuriy Semin.
Goals: 16' Grzegorz Krychowiak 0-1, 25' Benedikt Höwedes 1-1 (og), 37' Dmitry Barinov 1-2.
Referee: Pawel Raczkowski (POL)   Attendance: 26,592.

01.10.19 RZD Arena, Moscow: Lokomotiv Moscow – Atlético Madrid 0-2 (0-0)
Lokomotiv Moscow: Guilherme, Vedran Corluka, Benedikt Höwedes, Murilo Cerqueira, Maciej Rybus, Vladislav Ignatyev (80' Éder), Grzegorz Krychowiak, João Mário, Dmitry Barinov, Fyodor Smolov (83' Aleksandr Kolomeytsev), Rifat Zhemaletdinov (33' Brian Idowu). Coach: Yuriy Semin.
Atlético Madrid: Jan Oblak, Santiago Arias, Felipe Monteiro, José Giménez, Renan Lodi, Saúl, Koke (87' Ángel Correa), Thomas Partey, Diego Costa (77' Thomas Lemar), Álvaro Morata, João Félix (84' Mario Hermoso). Coach: Diego Simeone.
Goals: 48' João Félix 0-1, 58' Thomas Partey 0-2.
Referee: Orel Grinfeld (ISR)   Attendance: 27,051.

01.10.19   Allianz Stadium, Torino: Juventus – Bayer Leverkusen 3-0 (1-0)
Juventus: Wojciech Szczesny, Leonardo Bonucci, Alex Sandro, Matthijs de Ligt, Blaise Matuidi, Sami Khedira (74' Rodrigo Bentancur), Miralem Pjanic, Juan Cuadrado, Cristiano Ronaldo, Gonzalo Higuaín (83' Paulo Dybala), Federico Bernardeschi (78' Aaron Ramsey). Coach: Maurizio Sarri.
Bayer Leverkusen: Lukáš Hrádecky, Sven Bender, Mitchell Weiser, Wendell, Jonathan Tah, Charles Aránguiz (80' Daley Sinkgraven), Julian Baumgartlinger, Kerem Demirbay (46' Nadiem Amiri), Kai Havertz, Kevin Volland, Lucas Alario (68' Paulinho). Coach: Peter Bosz.
Goals: 17' Gonzalo Higuaín 1-0, 62' Federico Bernardeschi 2-0, 89' Cristiano Ronaldo 3-0.
Referee: William Collum (SCO)   Attendance: 34,525.

22.10.19   Estadio Wanda Metropolitano, Madrid:
         Atlético Madrid – Bayer Leverkusen 1-0 (0-0)
Atlético Madrid: Jan Oblak, Kieran Trippier, Felipe Monteiro, José Giménez (15' Mario Hermoso), Renan Lodi, Héctor Herrera, Saúl, Koke (70' Álvaro Morata), Thomas Partey, Diego Costa, Ángel Correa (62' Thomas Lemar). Coach: Diego Simeone.
Bayer Leverkusen: Lukáš Hrádecky, Sven Bender (90+2' Aleksandar Dragovic), Mitchell Weiser, Jonathan Tah, Lars Bender, Julian Baumgartlinger, Karim Bellarabi, Kerem Demirbay (84' Lucas Alario), Nadiem Amiri, Kai Havertz (76' Paulinho), Kevin Volland. Coach: Peter Bosz.
Goal: 78' Álvaro Morata 1-0.
Referee: Artur Soares Dias (POR)   Attendance: 56,776.

22.10.19   Allianz Stadium, Torino: Juventus – Lokomotiv Moscow 2-1 (0-1)
Juventus: Wojciech Szczesny, Leonardo Bonucci, Alex Sandro, Matthijs de Ligt, Blaise Matuidi (65' Adrien Rabiot), Sami Khedira (48' Gonzalo Higuaín), Miralem Pjanic, Juan Cuadrado, Rodrigo Bentancur, Cristiano Ronaldo, Paulo Dybala (81' Federico Bernardeschi). Coach: Maurizio Sarri.
Lokomotiv Moscow: Guilherme, Vedran Corluka, Benedikt Höwedes, Brian Idowu, Murilo Cerqueira, Vladislav Ignatyev, Grzegorz Krychowiak (83' Aleksandr Kolomeytsev), João Mário, Dmitry Barinov, Aleksey Miranchuk, Éder. Coach: Yuriy Semin.
Goals: 30' Aleksey Miranchuk 0-1, 77', 79' Paulo Dybala 1-1, 2-1.
Referee: Anastasios Sidiropoulos (GRE)   Attendance: 38,547.

06.11.19   RZD Arena, Moscow: Lokomotiv Moscow – Juventus 1-2 (1-1)
Lokomotiv Moscow: Guilherme, Vedran Corluka, Benedikt Höwedes, Maciej Rybus, Vladislav Ignatyev, Grzegorz Krychowiak, João Mário (85' Aleksandr Kolomeytsev), Dmitry Barinov, Aleksey Miranchuk, Éder, Rifat Zhemaletdinov (81' Murilo Cerqueira). Coach: Yuriy Semin.
Juventus: Wojciech Szczesny, Leonardo Bonucci, Danilo, Alex Sandro, Daniele Rugani, Sami Khedira (70' Douglas Costa), Miralem Pjanic, Aaron Ramsey (64' Rodrigo Bentancur), Adrien Rabiot, Cristiano Ronaldo (82' Paulo Dybala), Gonzalo Higuaín. Coach: Maurizio Sarri.
Goals: 4' Aaron Ramsey 0-1, 12' Aleksey Miranchuk 1-1, 90+3' Douglas Costa 1-2.
Referee: Ruddy Buquet (FRA)   Attendance: 26,861.

06.11.19 BayArena, Leverkusen: Bayer Leverkusen – Atlético Madrid 2-1 (1-0)
Bayer Leverkusen: Lukás Hrádecky, Sven Bender, Mitchell Weiser, Wendell (81' Panagiotis Retsos), Jonathan Tah, Charles Aránguiz (65' Julian Baumgartlinger), Karim Bellarabi, Kerem Demirbay, Nadiem Amiri, Kai Havertz (88' Aleksandar Dragovic), Kevin Volland.
Coach: Peter Bosz.
Atlético Madrid: Jan Oblak, Santiago Arias, Felipe Monteiro, Mario Hermoso, Renan Lodi (52' Thomas Lemar), Saúl, Koke, Thomas Partey, Diego Costa (61' Vitolo), Álvaro Morata, Ángel Correa (70' Héctor Herrera). Coach: Diego Simeone.
Goals: 41' Thomas Partey 1-0 (og), 55' Kevin Volland 2-0, 90+4' Álvaro Morata 2-1.
Referee: Damir Skomina (SVN)   Attendance: 28,160.
Sent off: 84' Nadiem Amiri.

26.11.19   RZD Arena, Moscow: Lokomotiv Moscow – Bayer Leverkusen 0-2 (0-1)
Lokomotiv Moscow: Guilherme, Vedran Corluka, Benedikt Höwedes, Maciej Rybus, Vladislav Ignatyev, Grzegorz Krychowiak, Dmitry Barinov, Aleksey Miranchuk, Anton Miranchuk, Éder (77' Fedor Smolov), Rifat Zhemaletdinov (65' Daniil Kulikov).
Coach: Yuriy Semin.
Bayer Leverkusen: Lukás Hrádecky, Sven Bender, Wendell, Jonathan Tah, Panagiotis Retsos, Charles Aránguiz, Karim Bellarabi (77' Lucas Alario), Kerem Demirbay (90' Lars Bender), Kevin Volland, Leon Bailey (46' Julian Baumgartlinger), Moussa Diaby. Coach: Peter Bosz.
Goals: 11' Rifat Zhemaletdinov 0-1 (og), 54' Sven Bender 0-2.
Referee: Michael Oliver (ENG)   Attendance: 25,757.

26.11.19   Allianz Stadium, Torino: Juventus – Atlético Madrid 1-0 (1-0)
Juventus: Wojciech Szczesny, Leonardo Bonucci, Danilo, Mattia De Sciglio, Matthijs de Ligt, Blaise Matuidi, Miralem Pjanic, Aaron Ramsey (63' Federico Bernardeschi), Rodrigo Bentancur (86' Sami Khedira), Cristiano Ronaldo, Paulo Dybala (76' Gonzalo Higuaín).
Coach: Maurizio Sarri.
Atlético Madrid: Jan Oblak, Kieran Trippier, Felipe Monteiro, Mario Hermoso, Renan Lodi (64' Thomas Lemar), Héctor Herrera (60' Ángel Correa), Vitolo (54' João Félix), Saúl, Koke, Thomas Partey, Álvaro Morata. Coach: Diego Simeone.
Goal: 45+2' Paulo Dybala 1-0.
Referee: Anthony Taylor (ENG)   Attendance: 40,486.

11.12.19   Estadio Wanda Metropolitano, Madrid:
            Atlético Madrid – Lokomotiv Moscow 2-0 (1-0)
Atlético Madrid: Jan Oblak, Kieran Trippier, Felipe Monteiro, Mario Hermoso, Renan Lodi, Saúl, Koke (73' Thomas Lemar), Thomas Partey, Álvaro Morata, Ángel Correa (68' Héctor Herrera), João Félix (81' Marcos Llorente). Coach: Diego Simeone.
Lokomotiv Moscow: Anton Kochenkov, Vedran Corluka (69' Stanislav Magkeev), Benedikt Höwedes, Solomon Kverkvelia, Brian Idowu, Murilo Cerqueira, Maciej Rybus, Grzegorz Krychowiak, Aleksey Miranchuk, Éder (75' Fedor Smolov), Rifat Zhemaletdinov.
Coach: Yuriy Semin.
Goals: 17' João Félix 1-0 (p), 54' Felipe Monteiro 2-0.
Referee: Viktor Kassai (HUN)   Attendance: 58,426.

Kieran Trippier missed a penalty kick (2').

11.12.19 BayArena, Leverkusen: Bayer Leverkusen – Juventus 0-2 (0-0)
Bayer Leverkusen: Lukás Hrádecky, Sven Bender, Aleksandar Dragovic, Daley Sinkgraven, Lars Bender, Charles Aránguiz, Karim Bellarabi (66' Leon Bailey), Kerem Demirbay (66' Julian Baumgartlinger), Kai Havertz, Lucas Alario (82' Kevin Volland), Moussa Diaby.
Coach: Peter Bosz.
Juventus: Gianluigi Buffon, Danilo, Mattia De Sciglio, Daniele Rugani, Merih Demiral, Miralem Pjanic, Juan Cuadrado (90+3' Simone Muratore), Adrien Rabiot (85' Blaise Matuidi), Cristiano Ronaldo, Gonzalo Higuaín, Federico Bernardeschi (66' Paulo Dybala).
Coach: Maurizio Sarri.
Goals: 75' Cristiano Ronaldo 0-1, 90+2' Gonzalo Higuaín 0-2.
Referee: Benoît Bastien (FRA)   Attendance: 29,542.

GROUP E

17.09.19   Red Bull Arena, Wals-Siezenheim: Red Bull Salzburg – KRC Genk 6-2 (5-1)
Red Bull Salzburg: Cican Stankovic, Andreas Ulmer, André Ramalho, Max Wöber, Rasmus Kristensen (83' Patrick Farkas), Zlatko Junuzovic, Antoine Bernède, Dominik Szoboszlai (62' Masaya Okugawa), Takumi Minamino, Hwang Hee-Chan, Erling Håland (72' Patson Daka).
Coach: Jesse Marsch.
KRC Genk: Gaëtan Coucke, Sebastien Dewaest, Jere Uronen, Jhon Lucumí, Joakim Mæhle, Patrik Hrosovsky, Sander Berge, Bryan Heynen (85' Paul Onuachu), Mbwana Samatta, Dieumerci Ndongala (72' Ianis Hagi), Junya Ito (46' Théo Bongonda). Coach: Felice Mazzù.
Goals: 2', 34' Erling Håland 1-0, 2-0, 36' Hwang Hee-Chan 3-0, 40' Jhon Lucumí 3-1, 45' Erling Håland 4-1, 45+2' Dominik Szoboszlai 5-1, 52' Mbwana Samatta 5-2, 66' Andreas Ulmer 6-2.
Referee: Felix Zwayer (GER)   Attendance: 29,520.

17.09.19   Stadio San Paolo, Napoli: SSC Napoli – Liverpool FC 2-0 (0-0)
SSC Napoli: Alex Meret, Kostas Manolas, Mário Rui, Kalidou Koulibaly, Giovanni Di Lorenzo, Allan (75' Eljif Elmas), Fabián Ruiz, Dries Mertens, José Callejón, Lorenzo Insigne (66' Piotr Zielinski), Hirving Lozano (69' Llorente). Coach: Carlo Ancelotti.
Liverpool FC: Adrián, Joel Matip, Virgil van Dijk, Andrew Robertson, Trent Alexander-Arnold, James Milner (66' Georginio Wijnaldum), Jordan Henderson (87' Xherdan Shaqiri), Fabinho, Roberto Firmino, Mohamed Salah, Sadio Mané. Coach: Jürgen Klopp.
Goals: 82' Dries Mertens 1-0 (p), 90+2' Llorente 2-0.
Referee: Felix Brych (GER)   Attendance: 38,878.

02.10.19   Luminus Arena, Genk: KRC Genk – SSC Napoli 0-0
KRC Genk: Gaëtan Coucke, Jere Uronen, Jhon Lucumí, Carlos Cuesta, Joakim Mæhle, Patrik Hrosovsky, Ianis Hagi (90+2' Bryan Heynen), Sander Berge, Mbwana Samatta, Théo Bongonda (89' Joseph Paintsil), Junya Ito. Coach: Felice Mazzù.
SSC Napoli: Alex Meret, Kostas Manolas, Mário Rui (33' Kévin Malcuit), Kalidou Koulibaly, Giovanni Di Lorenzo, Allan, Fabián Ruiz, Eljif Elmas (58' Dries Mertens), José Callejón, Arkadiusz Milik (72' Llorente), Hirving Lozano. Coach: Carlo Ancelotti.
Referee: István Kovács (ROM)   Attendance: 19,962.

02.10.19   Anfield, Liverpool: Liverpool FC – Red Bull Salzburg 4-3 (3-1)
Liverpool FC: Adrián, Virgil van Dijk, Andrew Robertson, Joe Gomez, Trent Alexander-Arnold, Georginio Wijnaldum (64' Divock Origi), Jordan Henderson (62' James Milner), Fabinho, Roberto Firmino, Mohamed Salah (90+1' Naby Keïta), Sadio Mané.
Coach: Jürgen Klopp.
Red Bull Salzburg: Cican Stankovic, Andreas Ulmer, Jérôme Onguéné, Max Wöber, Rasmus Kristensen, Zlatko Junuzovic (78' Majeed Ashimeru), Dominik Szoboszlai (71' Masaya Okugawa), Enock Mwepu, Takumi Minamino, Hwang Hee-Chan, Patson Daka (56' Erling Håland). Coach: Jesse Marsch.
Goals: 9' Sadio Mané 1-0, 25' Andrew Robertson 2-0, 36' Mohamed Salah 3-0, 39' Hwang Hee-Chan 3-1, 56' Takumi Minamino 3-2, 60' Erling Håland 3-3, 69' Mohamed Salah 4-3.
Referee: Andreas Ekberg (SWE)   Attendance: 52,243.

23.10.19   Luminus Arena, Genk: KRC Genk – Liverpool FC 1-4 (0-1)
KRC Genk: Gaëtan Coucke, Jere Uronen, Jhon Lucumí, Carlos Cuesta, Joakim Mæhle, Sander Berge, Bryan Heynen, Mbwana Samatta, Paul Onuachu (81' Stephen Odey), Théo Bongonda (66' Dieumerci Ndongala), Junya Ito (87' Ianis Hagi). Coach: Felice Mazzù.
Liverpool FC: Alisson, Dejan Lovren, Virgil van Dijk, Andrew Robertson (63' Joe Gomez), James Milner, Alex Oxlade-Chamberlain (74' Georginio Wijnaldum), Fabinho, Naby Keïta, Roberto Firmino (80' Divock Origi), Mohamed Salah, Sadio Mané. Coach: Jürgen Klopp.
Goals: 2', 57' Alex Oxlade-Chamberlain 0-1, 0-2, 77' Sadio Mané 0-3,
87' Mohamed Salah 0-4, 88' Stephen Odey 1-4.
Referee: Slavko Vincic (SVN)   Attendance: 19,626.

23.10.19   Red Bull Arena, Wals-Siezenheim: Red Bull Salzburg – SSC Napoli 2-3 (1-1)
Red Bull Salzburg: Cican Stankovic (33' Carlos Coronel), Andreas Ulmer, André Ramalho, Max Wöber, Rasmus Kristensen, Zlatko Junuzovic, Enock Mwepu (89' Sékou Koïta), Takumi Minamino, Hwang Hee-Chan, Patson Daka (68' Majeed Ashimeru), Erling Håland.
Coach: Jesse Marsch.
SSC Napoli: Alex Meret, Kalidou Koulibaly, Kévin Malcuit, Giovanni Di Lorenzo, Sebastiano Luperto, Allan, Piotr Zielinski, Fabián Ruiz, Dries Mertens (76' Llorente), José Callejón (80' Eljif Elmas), Hirving Lozano (65' Lorenzo Insigne). Coach: Carlo Ancelotti.
Goals: 17' Dries Mertens 0-1, 40' Erling Håland 1-1 (p), 64' Dries Mertens 1-2,
72' Erling Håland 2-2, 73' Lorenzo Insigne 2-3.
Referee: Clément Turpin (FRA)   Attendance: 29,520.

05.11.19   Anfield, Liverpool: Liverpool FC – KRC Genk 2-1 (1-1)
Liverpool FC: Alisson, Virgil van Dijk, Joe Gomez, Trent Alexander-Arnold, James Milner, Georginio Wijnaldum, Alex Oxlade-Chamberlain (75' Sadio Mané), Fabinho, Naby Keïta (74' Andrew Robertson), Mohamed Salah, Divock Origi (89' Roberto Firmino).
Coach: Jürgen Klopp.
KRC Genk: Gaëtan Coucke, Sebastien Dewaest, Casper De Norre (85' Paul Onuachu), Jhon Lucumí, Carlos Cuesta, Joakim Mæhle, Patrik Hrosovsky (85' Théo Bongonda), Sander Berge, Bryan Heynen, Mbwana Samatta, Junya Ito (68' Dieumerci Ndongala). Coach: Felice Mazzù.
Goals: 14' Georginio Wijnaldum 1-0, 41' Mbwana Samatta 1-1,
53' Alex Oxlade-Chamberlain 2-1.
Referee: Ivan Kruzliak (SVK)   Attendance: 52,611.

05.11.19   Stadio San Paolo, Napoli: SSC Napoli – Red Bull Salzburg 1-1 (1-1)
SSC Napoli: Alex Meret, Nikola Maksimovic, Mário Rui (46' Sebastiano Luperto), Kalidou Koulibaly, Giovanni Di Lorenzo, Piotr Zielinski, Fabián Ruiz, Dries Mertens (73' Arkadiusz Milik), José Callejón, Lorenzo Insigne, Hirving Lozano (86' Llorente). Coach: Carlo Ancelotti.
Red Bull Salzburg: Carlos Coronel, Andreas Ulmer, Jérôme Onguéné, Max Wöber, Marin Pongracic (46' Enock Mwepu), Rasmus Kristensen, Zlatko Junuzovic, Dominik Szoboszlai, Takumi Minamino (61' Majeed Ashimeru), Hwang Hee-Chan, Erling Håland (75' Patson Daka). Coach: Jesse Marsch.
Goals: 11' Erling Håland 0-1 (p), 44' Hirving Lozano 1-1.
Referee: Szymon Marciniak (POL)   Attendance: 32,862.

27.11.19   Luminus Arena, Genk: KRC Genk – Red Bull Salzburg 1-4 (0-2)
KRC Genk: Gaëtan Coucke, Sebastien Dewaest, Casper De Norre, Jhon Lucumí, Carlos Cuesta, Joakim Mæhle, Patrik Hrosovsky (59' Paul Onuachu), Sander Berge, Mbwana Samatta, Junya Ito (79' Ianis Hagi), Joseph Paintsil (65' Théo Bongonda). Coach: Hannes Wolf.
Red Bull Salzburg: Carlos Coronel, Andreas Ulmer, Jérôme Onguéné, Max Wöber, Rasmus Kristensen, Zlatko Junuzovic, Dominik Szoboszlai (80' Masaya Okugawa), Enock Mwepu, Takumi Minamino (89' Albert Vallci), Hwang Hee-Chan, Patson Daka (62' Erling Håland). Coach: Jesse Marsch.
Goals: 43' Patson Daka 0-1, 45' Takumi Minamino 0-2, 69' Hwang Hee-Chan 0-3, 85' Mbwana Samatta 1-3, 87' Erling Håland 1-4.
Referee: Mattias Gestranius (FIN)   Attendance: 17,284.

27.11.19   Anfield, Liverpool: Liverpool FC – SSC Napoli 1-1 (0-1)
Liverpool FC: Alisson, Dejan Lovren, Virgil van Dijk, Andrew Robertson, Joe Gomez (57' Alex Oxlade-Chamberlain), James Milner (78' Trent Alexander-Arnold), Jordan Henderson, Fabinho (19' Georginio Wijnaldum), Roberto Firmino, Mohamed Salah, Sadio Mané. Coach: Jürgen Klopp.
SSC Napoli: Alex Meret, Kostas Manolas, Nikola Maksimovic, Mário Rui, Kalidou Koulibaly, Giovanni Di Lorenzo, Allan, Piotr Zielinski (85' Amin Younes), Fabián Ruiz, Dries Mertens (81' Eljif Elmas), Hirving Lozano (72' Llorente). Coach: Carlo Ancelotti.
Goals: 21' Dries Mertens 0-1, 65' Dejan Lovren 1-1.
Referee: Carlos del Cerro Grande (ESP)   Attendance: 52,128.

10.12.19   Red Bull Arena, Wals-Siezenheim: Red Bull Salzburg – Liverpool FC 0-2 (0-0)
Red Bull Salzburg: Cican Stankovic, Andreas Ulmer, Jérôme Onguéné, Max Wöber, Rasmus Kristensen, Zlatko Junuzovic (68' Patson Daka), Dominik Szoboszlai (90' Majeed Ashimeru), Enock Mwepu, Takumi Minamino, Hwang Hee-Chan, Erling Håland (75' Masaya Okugawa). Coach: Jesse Marsch.
Liverpool FC: Alisson, Dejan Lovren (53' Joe Gomez), Virgil van Dijk, Andrew Robertson, Trent Alexander-Arnold, Georginio Wijnaldum, Jordan Henderson, Naby Keïta (87' Divock Origi), Roberto Firmino (75' James Milner), Mohamed Salah, Sadio Mané. Coach: Jürgen Klopp.
Goals: 57' Naby Keïta 0-1, 58' Mohamed Salah 0-2.
Referee: Danny Makkelie (HOL)   Attendance: 29,520.

10.12.19   Stadio San Paolo, Napoli: SSC Napoli – KRC Genk 4-0 (3-0)
SSC Napoli: Alex Meret, Kostas Manolas, Mário Rui, Kalidou Koulibaly, Giovanni Di Lorenzo, Allan, Piotr Zielinski (72' Gianluca Gaetano), Fabián Ruiz, Dries Mertens, José Callejón (79' Llorente), Arkadiusz Milik (78' Hirving Lozano). Coach: Carlo Ancelotti.
KRC Genk: Maarten Vandevoordt, Sebastien Dewaest, Casper De Norre (82' Neto Borges), Jhon Lucumí, Joakim Mæhle, Patrik Hrosovsky, Sander Berge, Mbwana Samatta (63' Théo Bongonda), Paul Onuachu, Junya Ito (72' Ianis Hagi), Joseph Paintsil. Coach: Hannes Wolf.
Goals: 3', 26', 38' Arkadiusz Milik 1-0, 2-0, 3-0 (p), 74' Dries Mertens 4-0 (p).
Referee: Cüneyt Çakir (TUR)   Attendance: 22,265.

GROUP F

17.09.19   Stadio Giuseppe Meazza, Milano: Internazionale – SK Slavia Praha 1-1 (0-0)
Internazionale: Samir Handanovic, Kwadwo Asamoah, Stefan de Vrij, Danilo D'Ambrosio, Milan Skriniar, Antonio Candreva (49' Valentino Lazaro), Marcelo Brozovic (71' Nicolò Barella), Roberto Gagliardini, Stefano Sensi, Romelu Lukaku, Lautaro Martínez (72' Matteo Politano). Coach: Antonio Conte.
SK Slavia Praha: Ondrej Kolár, Ondrej Kúdela, Jan Boril, Vladimír Coufal, David Hovorka, Josef Husbauer, Nicolae Stanciu, Lukás Masopust (79' Abdulla Yusuf Helal), Peter Olayinka (85' Lukás Provod), Tomás Soucek, Ibrahim Traoré (60' Jaroslav Zeleny).
Coach: Jindrich Trpisovsky.
Goals: 63' Peter Olayinka 0-1, 90+2' Nicolò Barella 1-1.
Referee: Ruddy Buquet (FRA)   Attendance: 50,128.

17.09.19   Signal-Iduna-Park, Dortmund: Borussia Dortmund – FC Barcelona 0-0
Borussia Dortmund: Roman Bürki, Mats Hummels, Raphaël Guerreiro, Manuel Akanji, Achraf Hakimi, Axel Witsel, Thomas Delaney, Jadon Sancho, Marco Reus, Thorgan Hazard (73' Julian Brandt), Paco Alcácer (87' Jacob Bruun Larsen). Coach: Lucien Favre.
FC Barcelona: Marc-André ter Stegen, Piqué, Jordi Alba (40' Sergi Roberto), Clément Lenglet, Nélson Semedo, Sergio Busquets (60' Ivan Rakitic), Arthur, Frenkie de Jong, Luis Suárez, Antoine Griezmann, Ansu Fati (59' Lionel Messi). Coach: Ernesto Valverde.
Referee: Ovidiu Hategan (ROM)   Attendance: 66,099.

Marco Reus missed a penalty kick (57').

02.10.19   Sinobo Stadium, Praha: SK Slavia Praha – Borussia Dortmund 0-2 (0-1)
SK Slavia Praha: Ondrej Kolár, Ondrej Kúdela, Jan Boril, Vladimír Coufal, David Hovorka, Nicolae Stanciu (83' Milan Skoda), Lukás Masopust (76' Jaroslav Zeleny), Petr Sevcík, Peter Olayinka, Tomás Soucek, Stanislav Tecl (59' Mick van Buren). Coach: Jindrich Trpisovsky.
Borussia Dortmund: Roman Bürki, Mats Hummels, Lukasz Piszczek, Raphaël Guerreiro, Manuel Akanji, Achraf Hakimi (90' Dan-Axel Zagadou), Axel Witsel, Thomas Delaney, Jadon Sancho (74' Thorgan Hazard), Marco Reus, Julian Brandt (90+2' Mario Götze).
Coach: Lucien Favre.
Goals: 35', 89' Achraf Hakimi 0-1, 0-2.
Referee: Björn Kuipers (HOL)   Attendance: 19,370.

02.10.19   Camp Nou, Barcelona: FC Barcelona – Internazionale 2-1 (0-1)
FC Barcelona: Marc-André ter Stegen, Piqué, Sergi Roberto, Clément Lenglet, Nélson Semedo, Sergio Busquets (53' Arturo Vidal), Arthur, Frenkie de Jong, Lionel Messi, Luis Suárez, Antoine Griezmann (66' Ousmane Dembélé). Coach: Ernesto Valverde.
Internazionale: Samir Handanovic, Diego Godín, Kwadwo Asamoah, Stefan de Vrij, Milan Skriniar, Antonio Candreva (71' Danilo D'Ambrosio), Marcelo Brozovic, Stefano Sensi (79' Matteo Politano), Nicolò Barella, Alexis Sánchez (66' Roberto Gagliardini), Lautaro Martínez. Coach: Antonio Conte.
Goals: 3' Lautaro Martínez 0-1, 58', 84' Luis Suárez 1-1, 2-1.
Referee: Damir Skomina (SVN)   Attendance: 86,141.

23.10.19   Sinobo Stadium, Praha: SK Slavia Praha – FC Barcelona 1-2 (0-1)
SK Slavia Praha: Ondrej Kolár, Ondrej Kúdela, Jan Boril, Jaroslav Zeleny (46' Stanislav Tecl), Vladimír Coufal, David Hovorka, Nicolae Stanciu (77' Josef Husbauer), Lukás Masopust (76' Mick van Buren), Petr Sevcík, Peter Olayinka, Tomás Soucek. Coach: Jindrich Trpisovsky.
FC Barcelona: Marc-André ter Stegen, Piqué, Jordi Alba, Clément Lenglet, Nélson Semedo, Sergio Busquets (78' Arturo Vidal), Arthur (84' Ivan Rakitic), Frenkie de Jong, Lionel Messi, Luis Suárez, Antoine Griezmann (69' Ousmane Dembélé). Coach: Ernesto Valverde.
Goals: 3' Lionel Messi 0-1, 50' Jan Boril 1-1, 57' Peter Olayinka 1-2 (og).
Referee: Bobby Madden (SCO)   Attendance: 19,170.

23.10.19   Stadio Giuseppe Meazza, Milano: Internazionale – Borussia Dortmund 2-0 (1-0)
Internazionale: Samir Handanovic, Diego Godín, Kwadwo Asamoah (80' Cristiano Biraghi), Stefan de Vrij, Milan Skriniar, Antonio Candreva, Marcelo Brozovic, Roberto Gagliardini, Nicolò Barella, Romelu Lukaku (62' Sebastiano Esposito), Lautaro Martínez (90+1' Borja Valero). Coach: Antonio Conte.
Borussia Dortmund: Roman Bürki, Mats Hummels, Manuel Akanji (74' Jacob Bruun Larsen), Achraf Hakimi, Axel Witsel, Thomas Delaney (65' Mahmoud Dahoud), Nico Schulz, Julian Weigl, Jadon Sancho, Thorgan Hazard (84' Raphaël Guerreiro), Julian Brandt. Coach: Lucien Favre.
Goals: 22' Lautaro Martínez 1-0, 89' Antonio Candreva 2-0.
Referee: Anthony Taylor (ENG)   Attendance: 65,673.

Lautaro Martínez missed a penalty kick (82').

05.11.19   Camp Nou, Barcelona: FC Barcelona – SK Slavia Praha 0-0
FC Barcelona: Marc-André ter Stegen, Piqué, Jordi Alba (46' Sergi Roberto), Clément Lenglet, Nélson Semedo, Arturo Vidal, Sergio Busquets (68' Ivan Rakitic), Frenkie de Jong, Lionel Messi, Antoine Griezmann, Ousmane Dembélé (65' Ansu Fati). Coach: Ernesto Valverde.
SK Slavia Praha: Ondrej Kolár, Ondrej Kúdela, Michal Frydrych, Jan Boril, Vladimír Coufal, Nicolae Stanciu (63' Josef Husbauer), Lukás Masopust (82' Lukás Provod), Petr Sevcík, Peter Olayinka, Tomás Soucek, Ibrahim Traoré (57' Stanislav Tecl). Coach: Jindrich Trpisovsky.
Referee: Michael Oliver (ENG)   Attendance: 67,023.

05.11.19   Signal-Iduna-Park, Dortmund: Borussia Dortmund – Internazionale 3-2 (0-2)
Borussia Dortmund: Roman Bürki, Mats Hummels, Manuel Akanji, Achraf Hakimi, Axel Witsel, Mario Götze (64' Paco Alcácer), Nico Schulz, Julian Weigl, Jadon Sancho (82' Lukasz Piszczek), Thorgan Hazard (88' Raphaël Guerreiro), Julian Brandt. Coach: Lucien Favre.
Internazionale: Samir Handanovic, Diego Godín, Stefan de Vrij, Cristiano Biraghi (66' Valentino Lazaro), Milan Skriniar, Antonio Candreva, Matías Vecino (68' Stefano Sensi), Marcelo Brozovic, Nicolò Barella, Romelu Lukaku (73' Matteo Politano), Lautaro Martínez. Coach: Antonio Conte.
Goals: 5' Lautaro Martínez 0-1, 40' Matías Vecino 0-2, 51' Achraf Hakimi 1-2, 64' Julian Brandt 2-2, 77' Achraf Hakimi 3-2.
Referee: Danny Makkelie (HOL)   Attendance: 66,099.

27.11.19   Sinobo Stadium, Praha: SK Slavia Praha – Internazionale 1-3 (1-1)
SK Slavia Praha: Ondrej Kolár, Ondrej Kúdela, Michal Frydrych (83' Laco Takács), Jan Boril, Vladimír Coufal, Josef Husbauer (70' Jaroslav Zeleny), Nicolae Stanciu (58' Ibrahim Traoré), Lukás Masopust, Petr Sevcík, Peter Olayinka, Tomás Soucek. Coach: Jindrich Trpisovsky.
Internazionale: Samir Handanovic, Diego Godín, Stefan de Vrij, Cristiano Biraghi (76' Valentino Lazaro), Milan Skriniar, Antonio Candreva, Borja Valero (76' Roberto Gagliardini), Matías Vecino (80' Sebastiano Esposito), Marcelo Brozovic, Romelu Lukaku, Lautaro Martínez. Coach: Antonio Conte.
Goals: 19' Lautaro Martínez 0-1, 37' Tomás Soucek 1-1 (p), 81' Romelu Lukaku 1-2, 88' Lautaro Martínez 1-3.
Referee: Szymon Marciniak (POL)   Attendance: 19,370.

27.11.19   Camp Nou, Barcelona: FC Barcelona – Borussia Dortmund 3-1 (2-0)
FC Barcelona: Marc-André ter Stegen, Sergi Roberto, Samuel Umtiti, Clément Lenglet, Junior Firpo, Ivan Rakitic (78' Arturo Vidal), Sergio Busquets, Frenkie de Jong, Lionel Messi, Luis Suárez (90+1' Moussa Wagué), Ousmane Dembélé (26' Antoine Griezmann).
Coach: Ernesto Valverde.
Borussia Dortmund: Roman Bürki, Mats Hummels, Lukasz Piszczek (76' Dan-Axel Zagadou), Raphaël Guerreiro, Manuel Akanji, Achraf Hakimi, Axel Witsel, Nico Schulz (46' Jadon Sancho), Julian Weigl (85' Mario Götze), Marco Reus, Julian Brandt. Coach: Lucien Favre.
Goals: 29' Luis Suárez 1-0, 33' Lionel Messi 2-0, 67' Antoine Griezmann 3-0, 77' Jadon Sancho 3-1.
Referee: Clément Turpin (FRA)   Attendance: 90,071.

10.12.19   Stadio Giuseppe Meazza, Milano: Internazionale – FC Barcelona 1-2 (1-1)
Internazionale: Samir Handanovic, Diego Godín, Stefan de Vrij, Danilo D'Ambrosio (75' Matteo Politano), Cristiano Biraghi (69' Valentino Lazaro), Milan Skriniar, Borja Valero (77' Sebastiano Esposito), Matías Vecino, Marcelo Brozovic, Romelu Lukaku, Lautaro Martínez. Coach: Antonio Conte.
FC Barcelona: Neto, Samuel Umtiti, Clément Lenglet, Junior Firpo, Moussa Wagué, Jean-Clair Todibo, Ivan Rakitic (63' Frenkie de Jong), Arturo Vidal, Carles Aleñà, Antoine Griezmann (62' Luis Suárez), Carles Pérez (85' Ansu Fati). Coach: Ernesto Valverde.
Goals: 23' Carles Pérez 0-1, 44' Romelu Lukaku 1-1, 86' Ansu Fati 1-2.
Referee: Björn Kuipers (HOL)   Attendance: 71,818.

10.12.19 Signal-Iduna-Park, Dortmund: Borussia Dortmund – SK Slavia Praha 2-1 (1-1)
Borussia Dortmund: Roman Bürki, Mats Hummels, Raphaël Guerreiro, Manuel Akanji, Achraf Hakimi (83' Leonardo Balerdi), Dan-Axel Zagadou, Julian Weigl, Jadon Sancho (87' Mahmoud Dahoud), Marco Reus, Thorgan Hazard (83' Lukasz Piszczek), Julian Brandt.
Coach: Lucien Favre.
SK Slavia Praha: Ondrej Kolár, Ondrej Kúdela, Jan Boril, Vladimír Coufal, Laco Takács (83' Josef Husbauer), Nicolae Stanciu, Lukás Masopust (72' Ibrahim Traoré), Petr Sevcík, Peter Olayinka, Tomás Soucek, Milan Skoda (65' Abdulla Yusuf Helal).
Coach: Jindrich Trpisovsky.
Goals: 10' Jadon Sancho 1-0, 43' Tomás Soucek 1-1, 61' Julian Brandt 2-1.
Referee: Sergei Karasev (RUS)   Attendance: 65,079.
Sent off: 77' Julian Weigl.

GROUP G

17.09.19 Groupama Stadium, Décines-Charpieu:
              Olympique Lyonnais – Zenit Saint Petersburg 1-1 (0-1)
Olympique Lyonnais: Anthony Lopes, Marcelo, Léo Dubois, Youssouf Koné, Jason Denayer, Thiago Mendes, Lucas Tousart, Jeff Reine-Adélaïde (85' Martin Terrier), Bertrand Traoré (77' Maxwel Cornet), Memphis Depay, Moussa Dembélé. Coach: Sylvinho.
Zenit Saint Petersburg: Andrei Lunev, Branislav Ivanovic, Yaroslav Rakitskiy, Vyacheslav Karavaev (78' Oleg Shatov), Douglas Santos, Yordan Osorio, Yuriy Zhirkov (64' Daler Kuzyaev), Wilmar Barrios, Artem Dzyuba, Sardar Azmoun (47' Magomed Ozdoev), Sebastián Driussi. Coach: Sergey Semak.
Goals: 41' Sardar Azmoun 0-1, 51' Memphis Depay 1-1 (p).
Referee: Michael Oliver (ENG)   Attendance: 47,201.

17.09.19 Estádio do Sport Lisboa e Benfica, Lisboa: SL Benfica – RB Leipzig 1-2 (0-0)
SL Benfica: Odisseas Vlachodimos, Álex Grimaldo, Rúben Dias, "Ferro" Francisco Ferreira, Tomás Tavares, Adel Taarabt, Ljubomir Fejsa, Pizzi (76' Rafa Silva), Franco Cervi (76' Haris Seferovic), Raúl de Tomás, "Jota" João Filipe (67' David Tavares). Coach: Bruno Lage.
RB Leipzig: Péter Gulácsi, Marcel Halstenberg (83' Lukas Klostermann), Willi Orban, Nordi Mukiele, Ibrahima Konaté, Emil Forsberg (88' Christopher Nkunku), Diego Demme, Marcel Sabitzer, Konrad Laimer (39' Amadou Haïdara), Yussuf Poulsen, Timo Werner.
Coach: Julian Nagelsmann.
Goals: 69', 78' Timo Werner 0-1, 0-2, 84' Haris Seferovic 1-2.
Referee: Anastasios Sidiropoulos (GRE)   Attendance: 46,460.

02.10.19 Krestovsky Stadium, Saint Petersburg:
              Zenit Saint Petersburg – SL Benfica 3-1 (1-0)
Zenit Saint Petersburg: Andrei Lunev, Branislav Ivanovic, Igor Smolnikov (63' Yordan Osorio), Yaroslav Rakitskiy, Douglas Santos, Oleg Shatov (68' Vyacheslav Karavaev), Magomed Ozdoev, Wilmar Barrios, Artem Dzyuba, Sardar Azmoun (81' Aleksandr Erokhin), Sebastián Driussi. Coach: Sergey Semak.
SL Benfica: Odisseas Vlachodimos, Jardel, Álex Grimaldo, Rúben Dias, Tomás Tavares, Adel Taarabt, Ljubomir Fejsa (60' Caio Lucas), Pizzi (60' Carlos Vinícius), Gabriel, Rafa Silva, Haris Seferovic (81' Raúl de Tomás). Coach: Bruno Lage.
Goals: 22' Artem Dzyuba 1-0, 70' Rúben Dias 2-0 (og), 78' Sardar Azmoun 3-0, 85' Raúl de Tomás 3-1.
Referee: Carlos del Cerro Grande (ESP)   Attendance: 51,683.

02.10.19 Red Bull Arena, Leipzig: RB Leipzig – Olympique Lyonnais 0-2 (0-1)
RB Leipzig: Péter Gulácsi, Marcel Halstenberg, Willi Orban, Lukas Klostermann, Dayot Upamecano (66' Christopher Nkunku), Ibrahima Konaté (23' Nordi Mukiele), Marcel Sabitzer, Konrad Laimer, Amadou Haïdara (58' Emil Forsberg), Yussuf Poulsen, Timo Werner.
Coach: Julian Nagelsmann.
Olympique Lyonnais: Anthony Lopes, Marcelo, Fernando Marçal, Joachim Andersen, Léo Dubois, Youssouf Koné, Thiago Mendes, Lucas Tousart, Martin Terrier (69' Bertrand Traoré), Houssem Aouar (87' Jean Lucas), Memphis Depay (79' Moussa Dembélé). Coach: Sylvinho.
Goals: 11' Memphis Depay 0-1, 65' Martin Terrier 0-2.
Referee: Antonio Mateu Lahoz (ESP)   Attendance: 40,194.

23.10.19 Red Bull Arena, Leipzig: RB Leipzig – Zenit Saint Petersburg 2-1 (0-1)
RB Leipzig: Péter Gulácsi, Willi Orban, Lukas Klostermann, Nordi Mukiele, Dayot Upamecano, Emil Forsberg, Kevin Kampl, Marcel Sabitzer, Konrad Laimer (86' Diego Demme), Timo Werner (46' Matheus Cunha), Ademola Lookman (69' Yussuf Poulsen).
Coach: Julian Nagelsmann.
Zenit Saint Petersburg: Mikhail Kerzhalov, Branislav Ivanovic, Yaroslav Rakitskiy, Vyacheslav Karavaev, Douglas Santos, Oleg Shatov (65' Yordan Osorio), Magomed Ozdoev, Wilmar Barrios, Artem Dzyuba, Sardar Azmoun (75' Daler Kuzyaev), Sebastián Driussi (82' Róbert Mak). Coach: Sergey Semak.
Goals: 25' Yaroslav Rakitskiy 0-1, 49' Konrad Laimer 1-1, 59' Marcel Sabitzer 2-1.
Referee: Ali Palabiyik (TUR)   Attendance: 41,058.

23.10.19 Estádio do Sport Lisboa e Benfica, Lisboa:
            SL Benfica – Olympique Lyonnais 2-1 (1-0)
SL Benfica: Odisseas Vlachodimos, Álex Grimaldo, Rúben Dias, "Ferro" Francisco Ferreira, Tomás Tavares, Gabriel, Rafa Silva (20' Pizzi), Franco Cervi (78' Raúl de Tomás), Gedson Fernandes, Florentino Luís, Haris Seferovic (59' Carlos Vinícius). Coach: Bruno Lage.
Olympique Lyonnais: Anthony Lopes, Marcelo, Léo Dubois, Youssouf Koné, Jason Denayer, Lucas Tousart, Martin Terrier (56' Thiago Mendes), Houssem Aouar (88' Jeff Reine-Adélaïde), Memphis Depay, Maxwel Cornet (66' Bertrand Traoré), Moussa Dembélé.
Coach: Rudi Garcia.
Goals: 4' Rafa Silva 1-0, 70' Memphis Depay 1-1, 86' Pizzi 2-1.
Referee: Ivan Kruzliak (SVK)   Attendance: 53,035.

05.11.19 Krestovsky Stadium, Saint Petersburg:
            Zenit Saint Petersburg – RB Leipzig 0-2 (0-1)
Zenit Saint Petersburg: Mikhail Kerzhalov, Branislav Ivanovic (70' Sebastián Driussi), Igor Smolnikov (46' Vyacheslav Karavaev), Yaroslav Rakitskiy, Douglas Santos, Yordan Osorio, Aleksandr Erokhin (85' Daler Kuzyaev), Magomed Ozdoev, Wilmar Barrios, Artem Dzyuba, Sardar Azmoun. Coach: Sergey Semak.
RB Leipzig: Péter Gulácsi, Marcel Halstenberg (46' Kevin Kampl), Lukas Klostermann, Nordi Mukiele, Dayot Upamecano, Emil Forsberg (76' Amadou Haïdara), Diego Demme, Marcel Sabitzer, Konrad Laimer, Christopher Nkunku (61' Timo Werner), Yussuf Poulsen.
Coach: Julian Nagelsmann.
Goals: 45+5' Diego Demme 0-1, 63' Marcel Sabitzer 0-2.
Referee: Orel Grinfeld (ISR)   Attendance: 50,452.

05.11.19 Groupama Stadium, Décines-Charpieu:
Olympique Lyonnais – SL Benfica 3-1 (2-0)
Olympique Lyonnais: Anthony Lopes, Joachim Andersen, Léo Dubois, Youssouf Koné, Jason Denayer, Thiago Mendes, Lucas Tousart, Jeff Reine-Adélaïde (73' Bertrand Traoré), Houssem Aouar (90+1' Marcelo), Memphis Depay (46' Maxwel Cornet), Moussa Dembélé.
Coach: Rudi Garcia.
SL Benfica: Odisseas Vlachodimos, Álex Grimaldo, Rúben Dias, "Ferro" Francisco Ferreira (16' Jardel), Tomás Tavares, Gabriel, Franco Cervi (73' Pizzi), Chiquinho, Gedson Fernandes (46' Haris Seferovic), Florentino Luís, Carlos Vinícius. Coach: Bruno Lage.
Goals: 4' Joachim Andersen 1-0, 33' Memphis Depay 2-0, 76' Haris Seferovic 2-1, 89' Bertrand Traoré 3-1.
Referee: Björn Kuipers (HOL)   Attendance: 51,077.

27.11.19 Krestovsky Stadium, Saint Petersburg:
Zenit Saint Petersburg – Olympique Lyonnais 2-0 (1-0)
Zenit Saint Petersburg: Mikhail Kerzhalov, Branislav Ivanovic, Yaroslav Rakitskiy, Vyacheslav Karavaev, Douglas Santos, Magomed Ozdoev, Wilmar Barrios, Daler Kuzyaev (90+2' Aleksey Sutormin), Artem Dzyuba, Sardar Azmoun (83' Aleksandr Erokhin), Sebastián Driussi (81' Yuriy Zhirkov). Coach: Sergey Semak.
Olympique Lyonnais: Anthony Lopes, Marcelo, Fernando Marçal (58' Youssouf Koné), Joachim Andersen (83' Amine Gouiri), Léo Dubois, Jason Denayer, Lucas Tousart, Jeff Reine-Adélaïde, Bertrand Traoré, Maxwel Cornet (75' Mathis Rayan Cherki), Moussa Dembélé.
Coach: Rudi Garcia.
Goals: 42' Artem Dzyuba 1-0, 84' Magomed Ozdoev 2-0.
Referee: Daniele Orsato (ITA)   Attendance: 51,183.

27.11.19 Red Bull Arena, Leipzig: RB Leipzig – SL Benfica 2-2 (0-1)
RB Leipzig: Péter Gulácsi (64' Yvon Mvogo), Lukas Klostermann, Dayot Upamecano, Ethan Ampadu (56' Nordi Mukiele), Emil Forsberg, Diego Demme, Marcel Sabitzer, Konrad Laimer, Christopher Nkunku, Marcelo Saracchi (70' Patrik Schick), Timo Werner.
Coach: Julian Nagelsmann.
SL Benfica: Odisseas Vlachodimos, André Almeida, Álex Grimaldo, Rúben Dias, "Ferro" Francisco Ferreira, Adel Taarabt, Pizzi (90+3' Caio Lucas), Gabriel, Franco Cervi (90+8' "Jota" João Filipe), Chiquinho, Carlos Vinícius (82' Raúl de Tomás). Coach: Bruno Lage.
Goals: 20' Pizzi 0-1, 59' Carlos Vinícius 0-2, 90', 90+6' Emil Forsberg 1-2 (p), 2-2.
Referee: Jesús Gil Manzano (ESP)   Attendance: 38,339.

10.12.19 Estádio do Sport Lisboa e Benfica, Lisboa:
SL Benfica – Zenit Saint Petersburg 3-0 (0-0)
SL Benfica: Odisseas Vlachodimos, Álex Grimaldo, Rúben Dias, "Ferro" Francisco Ferreira, Tomás Tavares, Adel Taarabt, Pizzi, Gabriel (81' Andreas Samaris), Franco Cervi (81' Haris Seferovic), Chiquinho, Carlos Vinícius (89' Caio Lucas). Coach: Bruno Lage.
Zenit Saint Petersburg: Mikhail Kerzhalov, Branislav Ivanovic, Vyacheslav Karavaev, Douglas Santos, Yordan Osorio, Oleg Shatov (90' Róbert Mak), Aleksandr Erokhin (65' Aleksey Sutormin), Magomed Ozdoev (60' Igor Smolnikov), Wilmar Barrios, Artem Dzyuba, Sardar Azmoun. Coach: Sergey Semak.
Goals: 47' Franco Cervi 1-0, 58' Pizzi 2-0 (p), 79' Sardar Azmoun 3-0 (og).
Referee: Antonio Mateu Lahoz (ESP)   Attendance: 40,232.
Sent off: 56' Douglas Santos.

10.12.19   Groupama Stadium, Décines-Charpieu:
Olympique Lyonnais – RB Leipzig 2-2 (0-2)
Olympique Lyonnais: Anthony Lopes, Rafael (73' Fernando Marçal), Kenny Tete, Joachim Andersen, Jason Denayer, Thiago Mendes, Lucas Tousart (64' Jeff Reine-Adélaïde), Martin Terrier (87' Marcelo), Houssem Aouar, Memphis Depay, Moussa Dembélé.
Coach: Rudi Garcia.
RB Leipzig: Péter Gulácsi, Lukas Klostermann, Nordi Mukiele, Dayot Upamecano (55' Ethan Ampadu), Emil Forsberg, Diego Demme, Christopher Nkunku (75' Konrad Laimer), Marcelo Saracchi, Amadou Haïdara, Yussuf Poulsen, Timo Werner (55' Matheus Cunha).
Coach: Julian Nagelsmann.
Goals: 9' Emil Forsberg 0-1 (p), 33' Timo Werner 0-2 (p), 50' Houssem Aouar 1-2, 82' Memphis Depay 2-2.
Referee: Anthony Taylor (ENG)   Attendance: 53,288.

GROUP H

17.09.19   Johan Cruijff Arena, Amsterdam: AFC Ajax – Lille OSC 3-0 (1-0)
AFC Ajax: André Onana, Daley Blind, Nicolás Tagliafico, Joël Veltman, Edson Álvarez, Lisandro Martínez (88' Jurgen Ekkelenkamp), Sergiño Dest, Hakim Ziyech (77' Noa Lang), Dusan Tadic, Quincy Promes, David Neres (83' Klaas Jan Huntelaar). Coach: Erik ten Hag.
Lille OSC: Mike Maignan, José Fonte, Mehmet Çelik, Gabriel, Domagoj Bradaric, Benjamin André, Renato Sanches (63' Luiz Araujo), Jonathan Ikoné (63' Yusuf Yazici), Boubakary Soumaré (77' Xeka), Jonathan Bamba, Victor Osimhen. Coach: Christophe Galtier.
Goals: 18' Quincy Promes 1-0, 50' Edson Álvarez 2-0, 62' Nicolás Tagliafico 3-0.
Referee: Srdjan Jovanovic (SRB)   Attendance: 51,441.

17.09.19   Stamford Bridge, London: Chelsea FC – Valencia CF 0-1 (0-0)
Chelsea FC: Kepa, Azpilicueta, Marcos Alonso, Kurt Zouma (73' Olivier Giroud), Andreas Christensen, Fikayo Tomori, Mateo Kovacic (80' Ross Barkley), Jorginho, Mason Mount (16' Pedro), Willian, Tammy Abraham. Coach: Frank Lampard.
Valencia CF: Jasper Cillessen, Ezequiel Garay, Gabriel Paulista, Gayà, Daniel Wass, Dani Parejo, Francis Coquelin, Denis Cheryshev (90+2' Mouctar Diakhaby), Geoffrey Kondogbia, Kevin Gameiro (70' Maximiliano Gómez), Rodrigo (90' Lee Kang-In). Coach: Celades.
Goal: 74' Rodrigo 0-1.
Referee: Cüneyt Çakir (TUR)   Attendance: 39,469.

Ross Barkley missed a penalty kick (87').

02.10.19   Estadio de Mestalla, Valencia: Valencia CF – AFC Ajax 0-3 (0-2)
Valencia CF: Jasper Cillessen, Ezequiel Garay, Jaume Costa, Gabriel Paulista, Daniel Wass, Dani Parejo, Francis Coquelin (70' Thierry Correia), Gonçalo Guedes, Ferrán Torres (76' Denis Cheryshev), Rodrigo, Maximiliano Gómez (57' Lee Kang-In). Coach: Celades.
AFC Ajax: André Onana, Daley Blind, Nicolás Tagliafico, Joël Veltman, Edson Álvarez, Lisandro Martínez, Sergiño Dest, Hakim Ziyech (85' Klaas Jan Huntelaar), Donny van de Beek (88' Siem de Jong), Dusan Tadic, Quincy Promes (81' David Neres).
Coach: Erik ten Hag.
Goals: 8' Hakim Ziyech 0-1, 34' Quincy Promes 0-2, 67' Donny van de Beek 0-3.
Referee: Daniele Orsato (ITA)   Attendance: 44,659.

Dani Parejo missed a penalty kick (25').

02.10.19 Stade Pierre-Mauroy, Villeneuve-d'Ascq: Lille OSC – Chelsea FC 1-2 (1-1)
Lille OSC: Mike Maignan, José Fonte, Reinildo, Mehmet Çelik, Gabriel, Benjamin André (69' Renato Sanches), Jonathan Ikoné (62' Yusuf Yazici), Boubakary Soumaré, Luiz Araujo (75' Xeka), Jonathan Bamba, Victor Osimhen. Coach: Christophe Galtier.
Chelsea FC: Kepa, Azpilicueta, Marcos Alonso, Kurt Zouma, Fikayo Tomori, Reece James (67' Callum Hudson-Odoi), Jorginho, N'Golo Kanté, Mason Mount (87' Mateo Kovacic), Willian (85' Pedro), Tammy Abraham. Coach: Frank Lampard.
Goals: 22' Tammy Abraham 0-1, 33' Victor Osimhen 1-1, 78' Willian 1-2.
Referee: Aleksei Kulbakov (BLS)   Attendance: 48,523.

23.10.19 Johan Cruijff Arena, Amsterdam: AFC Ajax – Chelsea FC 0-1 (0-0)
AFC Ajax: André Onana, Daley Blind, Nicolás Tagliafico, Joël Veltman (89' Klaas Jan Huntelaar), Edson Álvarez (89' Siem de Jong), Lisandro Martínez, Sergiño Dest, Hakim Ziyech, Donny van de Beek, Dusan Tadic, Quincy Promes (74' David Neres).
Coach: Erik ten Hag.
Chelsea FC: Kepa, Azpilicueta, Marcos Alonso, Kurt Zouma, Fikayo Tomori, Mateo Kovacic, Jorginho, Mason Mount, Willian (66' Christian Pulisic), Tammy Abraham (71' Michy Batshuayi), Callum Hudson-Odoi (90' Reece James). Coach: Frank Lampard.
Goal: 86' Michy Batshuayi 0-1.
Referee: Ovidiu Hategan (ROM)   Attendance: 52,482.

23.10.19 Stade Pierre-Mauroy, Villeneuve-d'Ascq: Lille OSC – Valencia CF 1-1 (0-0)
Lille OSC: Mike Maignan, José Fonte, Mehmet Çelik, Gabriel, Tiago Djaló (87' Jonathan Bamba), Domagoj Bradaric, Benjamin André, Boubakary Soumaré, Yusuf Yazici (71' Loïc Rémy), Luiz Araujo (65' Jonathan Ikoné), Victor Osimhen. Coach: Christophe Galtier.
Valencia CF: Jasper Cillessen, Jaume Costa, Gabriel Paulista, Mouctar Diakhaby, Daniel Wass, Dani Parejo, Francis Coquelin, Denis Cheryshev (87' Ezequiel Garay), Geoffrey Kondogbia (46' Carlos Soler), Kevin Gameiro (65' Lee Kang-In), Maximiliano Gómez. Coach: Celades.
Goals: 63' Denis Cheryshev 0-1, 90+5' Jonathan Ikoné 1-1.
Referee: Deniz Aytekin (GER)   Attendance: 47,488.
Sent off: 84' Mouctar Diakhaby.

05.11.19 Estadio de Mestalla, Valencia: Valencia CF – Lille OSC 4-1 (0-1)
Valencia CF: Jasper Cillessen, Ezequiel Garay, Gabriel Paulista, Gayà, Daniel Wass, Dani Parejo, Denis Cheryshev (30' Ferrán Torres), Geoffrey Kondogbia, Lee Kang-In (54' Manu Vallejo), Rodrigo (90+3' Kevin Gameiro), Maximiliano Gómez. Coach: Celades.
Lille OSC: Mike Maignan, José Fonte, Adama Soumaoro (89' Jonathan Bamba), Mehmet Çelik, Gabriel, Domagoj Bradaric, Benjamin André (80' Luiz Araujo), Boubakary Soumaré, Yusuf Yazici (74' Renato Sanches), Loïc Rémy, Victor Osimhen. Coach: Christophe Galtier.
Goals: 25' Victor Osimhen 0-1, 66' Dani Parejo 1-1 (p), 82' Adama Soumaoro 2-1 (og), 84' Geoffrey Kondogbia 3-1, 90' Ferrán Torres 4-1.
Referee: Sergei Karasev (RUS)   Attendance: 38,252.

05.11.19   Stamford Bridge, London: Chelsea FC – AFC Ajax 4-4 (1-3)
Chelsea FC: Kepa, Azpilicueta, Marcos Alonso (46' Reece James), Kurt Zouma, Fikayo Tomori, Mateo Kovacic (87' Michy Batshuayi), Jorginho, Mason Mount (60' Callum Hudson-Odoi), Christian Pulisic, Willian, Tammy Abraham. Coach: Frank Lampard.
AFC Ajax: André Onana, Daley Blind, Nicolás Tagliafico, Joël Veltman, Noussair Mazraoui, Lisandro Martínez, Hakim Ziyech (72' Edson Álvarez), Donny van de Beek, Dusan Tadic, Quincy Promes, David Neres (72' Perr Schuurs). Coach: Erik ten Hag.
Goals: 2' Tammy Abraham 0-1 (og), 5' Jorginho 1-1 (p), 20' Quincy Promes 1-2, 35' Kepa 1-3 (og), 55' Donny van de Beek 1-4, 63' Azpilicueta 2-4, 71' Jorginho 3-4 (p), 74' Reece James 4-4.
Referee: Gianluca Rocchi (ITA)   Attendance: 39,132.
Sent-off: 68' Daley Blind, 69' Joël Veltman.

27.11.19   Estadio de Mestalla, Valencia: Valencia CF – Chelsea FC 2-2 (1-1)
Valencia CF: Jasper Cillessen, Ezequiel Garay, Jaume Costa (67' Kevin Gameiro), Gabriel Paulista, Gayà, Daniel Wass, Dani Parejo, Carlos Soler (78' Lee Kang-In), Ferrán Torres (74' Francis Coquelin), Rodrigo, Maximiliano Gómez. Coach: Celades.
Chelsea FC: Kepa, Azpilicueta, Kurt Zouma, Andreas Christensen, Reece James, Mateo Kovacic, Jorginho (72' Emerson), N'Golo Kanté, Christian Pulisic, Willian (80' Mason Mount), Tammy Abraham (46' Michy Batshuayi). Coach: Frank Lampard.
Goals: 40' Carlos Soler 1-0, 41' Mateo Kovacic 1-1, 50' Christian Pulisic 1-2, 82' Daniel Wass 2-2.
Referee: Felix Zwayer (GER)   Attendance: 43,486.

Dani Parejo missed a penalty kick (64').

27.11.19   Stade Pierre-Mauroy, Villeneuve-d'Ascq: Lille OSC – AFC Ajax 0-2 (0-1)
Lille OSC: Mike Maignan, Reinildo, Mehmet Çelik, Gabriel, Tiago Djaló, Benjamin André (77' Renato Sanches), Jonathan Ikoné, Boubakary Soumaré, Yusuf Yazici (82' Loïc Rémy), Jonathan Bamba (72' Luiz Araujo), Victor Osimhen. Coach: Christophe Galtier.
AFC Ajax: André Onana, Nicolás Tagliafico, Noussair Mazraoui (46' Edson Álvarez), Perr Schuurs, Lisandro Martínez, Sergiño Dest, Zakaria Labyad (45+2' Noa Lang), Hakim Ziyech (85' Siem de Jong), Donny van de Beek, Dusan Tadic, Quincy Promes. Coach: Erik ten Hag.
Goals: 2' Hakim Ziyech 0-1, 59' Quincy Promes 0-2.
Referee: Felix Brych (GER)   Attendance: 48,612.

10.12.19   Johan Cruijff Arena, Amsterdam: AFC Ajax – Valencia CF 0-1 (0-1)
AFC Ajax: André Onana, Daley Blind, Nicolás Tagliafico (89' Siem de Jong), Joël Veltman, Noussair Mazraoui, Edson Álvarez (46' Sergiño Dest), Lisandro Martínez, Hakim Ziyech, Donny van de Beek, Noa Lang (70' Klaas Jan Huntelaar), Dusan Tadic. Coach: Erik ten Hag.
Valencia CF: Jaume Doménech, Gabriel Paulista, Gayà, Mouctar Diakhaby, Daniel Wass, Dani Parejo, Francis Coquelin, Carlos Soler, Ferrán Torres (90+5' Eliaquim Mangala), Kevin Gameiro (54' Manu Vallego), Rodrigo. Coach: Celades.
Goal: 24' Rodrigo 0-1.
Referee: Clément Turpin (FRA)   Attendance: 51,931.
Sent off: 90+3' Gabriel Paulista.

10.12.19 Stamford Bridge, London: Chelsea FC – Lille OSC 2-1 (2-0)
Chelsea FC: Kepa, Azpilicueta, Kurt Zouma, Emerson, Antonio Rüdiger, Mateo Kovacic (82'
Mason Mount), Jorginho, N'Golo Kanté, Christian Pulisic (62' Callum Hudson-Odoi), Willian,
Tammy Abraham (72' Michy Batshuayi). Coach: Frank Lampard.
Lille OSC: Mike Maignan (72' Léo Jardim), Jérémy Pied, Mehmet Çelik, Gabriel, Tiago
Djaló, Thiago Maia (66' Jonathan Bamba), Xeka, Boubakary Soumaré, Yusuf Yazici, Loïc
Rémy, Luiz Araujo (82' Renato Sanches). Coach: Christophe Galtier.
Goals: 19' Tammy Abraham 1-0, 35' Azpilicueta 2-0, 78' Loïc Rémy 2-1.
Referee: Anastasios Sidiropoulos (GRE)   Attendance: 40,016.

KNOCKOUT PHASE
ROUND OF 16

18.02.20 Signal-Iduna-Park, Dortmund: Borussia Dortmund – Paris Saint-Germain 2-1 (0-0)
Borussia Dortmund: Roman Bürki, Mats Hummels, Lukasz Piszczek, Raphaël Guerreiro,
Achraf Hakimi, Dan-Axel Zagadou, Axel Witsel, Emre Can, Jadon Sancho (90+1' Marcel
Schmelzer), Thorgan Hazard (67' Giovanni Reyna), Erling Håland. Coach: Lucien Favre.
Paris Saint-Germain: Keylor Navas, Thiago Silva, Thomas Meunier, Layvin Kurzawa,
Marquinhos, Presnel Kimpembe, Ángel Di María (76' Pablo Sarabia), Marco Verratti, Idrissa
Gueye, Neymar, Kylian Mbappé. Coach: Thomas Tuchel.
Goals: 69' Erling Håland 1-0, 75' Neymar 1-1, 77' Erling Håland 2-1.
Referee: Antonio Mateu Lahoz (ESP)   Attendance: 66,099.

18.02.20 Estadio Wanda Metropolitano, Madrid:
Atlético Madrid – Liverpool FC 1-0 (1-0)
Atlético Madrid: Jan Oblak, Sime Vrsaljko, Stefan Savic, Felipe Monteiro, Renan Lodi, Saúl,
Koke, Thomas Lemar (46' Marcos Llorente), Thomas Partey, Álvaro Morata (70' Vitolo),
Ángel Correa (77' Diego Costa). Coach: Diego Simeone.
Liverpool FC: Alisson, Virgil van Dijk, Andrew Robertson, Joe Gomez, Trent Alexander-
Arnold, Georginio Wijnaldum, Jordan Henderson (80' James Milner), Fabinho, Roberto
Firmino, Mohamed Salah (72' Alex Oxlade-Chamberlain), Sadio Mané (46' Divock Origi).
Coach: Jürgen Klopp.
Goal: 4' Saúl 1-0.
Referee: Szymon Marciniak (POL)   Attendance: 67,443.

19.02.20 Stadio Giuseppe Meazza, Milan: Atalanta Bergamo – Valencia CF 4-1 (2-0)
Atalanta Bergamo: Pierluigi Gollini, Rafael Tolói, José Palomino, Hans Hateboer, Mattia
Caldara (75' Duván Zapata), Robin Gosens, Papu Gómez (81' Ruslan Malinovskiy), Josip
Ilicic, Marten van Roon, Remo Freuler, Mario Pasalic (90+2' Adrien Tameze).
Coach: Gian Piero Gasperini.
Valencia CF: Jaume Doménech, Eliaquim Mangala, Gayà, Mouctar Diakhaby, Daniel Wass,
Dani Parejo, Geoffrey Kondogbia, Gonçalo Guedes (64' Denis Cheryshev), Carlos Soler,
Ferrán Torres, Maximiliano Gómez (73' Kevin Gameiro). Coach: Celades.
Goals: 16' Hans Hateboer 1-0, 42' Josip Ilicic 2-0, 57' Remo Freuler 3-0,
62' Hans Hateboer 4-0, 66' Denis Cheryshev 4-1.
Referee: Michael Oliver (ENG)   Attendance: 44,236.

19.02.20   Tottenham Hotspur Stadium, London: Tottenham Hotspur – RB Leipzig 0-1 (0-0)
Tottenham Hotspur: Hugo Lloris, Toby Alderweireld, Serge Aurier, Ben Davies, Davinson Sánchez, Lucas Moura, Dele Alli (64' Érik Lamela), Harry Winks, Gedson Fernandes (64' Tanguy NDombèlé), Giovani Lo Celso, Steven Bergwijn. Coach: José Mourinho.
RB Leipzig: Péter Gulácsi, Marcel Halstenberg, Lukas Klostermann, José Angeliño, Nordi Mukiele, Ethan Ampadu, Marcel Sabitzer, Konrad Laimer (83' Emil Forsberg), Christopher Nkunku (74' Amadou Haïdara), Timo Werner, Patrik Schick (77' Yussuf Poulsen).
Coach: Julian Nagelsmann.
Goal: 58' Timo Werner 0-1 (p).
Referee: Cüneyt Çakir (TUR)   Attendance: 60,095.

25.02.20   Stamford Bridge, London: Chelsea FC – FC Bayern München 0-3 (0-0)
Chelsea FC: Willy Caballero, Azpilicueta (73' Pedro), Marcos Alonso, Antonio Rüdiger, Andreas Christensen, Reece James, Ross Barkley (61' Willian), Mateo Kovacic, Jorginho, Mason Mount, Olivier Giroud (61' Tammy Abraham). Coach: Frank Lampard.
FC Bayern München: Manuel Neuer, Jérôme Boateng, David Alaba, Joshua Kimmich, Benjamin Pavard, Thiago Alcântara (90' Leon Goretzka), Serge Gnabry (85' Corentin Tolisso), Kingsley Coman (66' Philippe Coutinho), Alphonso Davies, Thomas Müller, Robert Lewandowski. Coach: Hansi Flick.
Goals: 51', 54' Serge Gnabry 0-1, 0-2, 76' Robert Lewandowski 0-3.
Referee: Clément Turpin (FRA)   Attendance: 36,761.
Sent off: 83' Marcos Alonso.

25.02.20   Stadio San Paolo, Naples: SSC Napoli – FC Barcelona 1-1 (1-0)
SSC Napoli: David Ospina, Kostas Manolas, Nikola Maksimovic, Mário Rui, Giovanni Di Lorenzo, Diego Demme (80' Allan), Piotr Zielinski, Fabián Ruiz, Dries Mertens (54' Arkadiusz Milik), José Callejón (74' Matteo Politano), Lorenzo Insigne.
Coach: Gennaro Gattuso.
FC Barcelona: Marc-André ter Stegen, Piqué (90+3' Clément Lenglet), Samuel Umtiti, Nélson Semedo, Junior Firpo, Ivan Rakitic (56' Arthur), Arturo Vidal, Busquets, Frenkie de Jong, Lionel Messi, Antoine Griezmann (87' Ansu Fati). Coach: Quique Setién.
Goals: 30' Dries Mertens 1-0, 57' Antoine Griezmann 1-1.
Referee: Dr. Felix Brych (GER)   Attendance: 44,388.
Sent off: 89' Arturo Vidal.

26.02.20   Estadio Santiago Bernabéu, Madrid: Real Madrid CF – Manchester City 1-2 (0-0)
Real Madrid CF: Thibaut Courtois, Sergio Ramos, Dani Carvajal, Raphaël Varane, Ferland Mendy, Luka Modric (84' Lucas Vázquez), Casemiro, Isco (84' Luka Jovic), Federico Valverde, Karim Benzema, Vinicíus Júnior (75' Gareth Bale). Coach: Zinédine Zidane.
Manchester City: Ederson Moraes, Nicolás Otamendi, Kyle Walker, Benjamin Mendy, Aymeric Laporte (33' Fernandinho), Ilkay Gündogan, Kevin De Bruyne, Bernardo Silva (73' Raheem Sterling), Rodri Hernández, Riyad Mahrez, Gabriel Jesus. Coach: Pep Guardiola.
Goals: 60' Isco 1-0, 78' Gabriel Jesus 1-1, 83' Kevin De Bruyne 1-2 (p).
Referee: Daniele Orsato (ITA)   Attendance: 75,615.
Sent off: 86' Sergio Ramos.

26.02.20   Groupama Stadium, Décines-Charpieu:
           Olympique Lyonnais – Juventus 1-0 (1-0)
Olympique Lyonnais: Anthony Lopes, Marcelo, Fernando Marçal, Léo Dubois (78' Kenny Tete), Jason Denayer, Lucas Tousart, Bruno Guimarães, Houssem Aouar, Karl Toko Ekambi (66' Martin Terrier), Maxwel Cornet (81' Joachim Andersen), Moussa Dembélé.
Coach: Rudi García.
Juventus: Wojciech Szczesny, Leonardo Bonucci, Danilo, Alex Sandro, Matthijs de Ligt, Miralem Pjanic (62' Aaron Ramsey), Juan Cuadrado (70' Gonzalo Higuaín), Adrien Rabiot (78' Federico Bernardeschi), Rodrigo Bentancur, Cristiano Ronaldo, Paulo Dybala.
Coach: Maurizio Sarri.
Goal: 31' Lucas Tousart 1-0.
Referee: Jesús Gil Manzano (ESP)   Attendance: 57,335.

10.03.20   Estadio de Mestalla, Valencia: Valencia CF – Atalanta Bergamo 3-4 (1-2)
Valencia CF: Jasper Cillessen, Gayà, Mouctar Diakhaby (46' Gonçalo Guedes), Daniel Wass, Dani Parejo, Francis Coquelin (74' Denis Cheryshev), Geoffrey Kondogbia, Carlos Soler, Ferrán Torres, Kevin Gameiro, Rodrigo (79' Alessandro Florenzi). Coach: Celades.
Atalanta Bergamo: Marco Sportiello, José Palomino, Berat Djimsiti, Hans Hateboer, Mattia Caldara, Robin Gosens, Papu Gómez (78' Ruslan Malinovskiy), Josip Ilicic, Marten van Roon (45' Duván Zapata), Remo Freuler, Mario Pasalic (83' Adrien Tameze). Coach: Gian Piero Gasperini.
Goals: 3' Josip Ilicic 0-1 (p), 21' Kevin Gameiro 1-1, 43' Josip Ilicic 1-2 (p), 51' Kevin Gameiro 2-2, 67' Ferrán Torres 3-2, 71', 82' Josip Ilicic 3-3, 3-4.
Referee: Ovidiu Hategan (ROM)

Match was played behind closed doors due to a pandemic of COVID-19 in Spain.

10.03.20   Red Bull Arena, Leipzig: RB Leipzig – Tottenham Hotspur 3-0 (2-0)
RB Leipzig: Péter Gulácsi, Marcel Halstenberg, Lukas Klostermann, José Angeliño, Nordi Mukiele (56' Tyler Adams), Dayot Upamecano, Marcel Sabitzer (87' Emil Forsberg), Konrad Laimer, Christopher Nkunku (59' Amadou Haïdara), Timo Werner, Patrik Schick.
Coach: Julian Nagelsmann.
Tottenham Hotspur: Hugo Lloris, Toby Alderweireld, Serge Aurier (90+1' Malachi Fagan-Walcott), Japhet Tanganga, Érik Lamela, Lucas Moura, Dele Alli, Eric Dier, Harry Winks, Giovani Lo Celso (80' Gedson Fernandes), Ryan Sessegnon. Coach: José Mourinho.
Goals: 10', 21' Marcel Sabitzer 1-0, 2-0, 87' Emil Forsberg 3-0.
Referee: Carlos del Cerro Grande (ESP)   Attendance: 42,146.

11.03.20   Parc des Princes, Paris: Paris Saint-Germain – Borussia Dortmund 2-0 (2-0)
Paris Saint-Germain: Keylor Navas, Marquinhos, Juan Bernat, Presnel Kimpembe, Thilo Kehrer, Ángel Di María (79' Layvin Kurzawa), Idrissa Gueye, Pablo Sarabia (64' Kylian Mbappé), Leandro Paredes (90+2' Nianzou Kouassi), Edinson Cavani, Neymar.
Coach: Thomas Tuchel.
Borussia Dortmund: Roman Bürki, Mats Hummels, Lukasz Piszczek, Raphaël Guerreiro, Achraf Hakimi (87' Mario Götze), Dan-Axel Zagadou, Axel Witsel (71' Giovanni Reyna), Emre Can, Jadon Sancho, Thorgan Hazard (69' Julian Brandt), Erling Håland.
Coach: Lucien Favre.
Goals: 28' Neymar 1-0, 45+1' Juan Bernat 2-0.
Referee: Anthony Taylor (ENG)
Sent off: 89' Emre Can.

Match was played behind closed doors due to a pandemic of COVID-19 in France.

11.03.20 Anfield Road, Liverpool: Liverpool FC – Atlético Madrid 2-3 (1-0, 1-0) (a.e.t.)
Liverpool FC: Adrián, Virgil van Dijk, Andrew Robertson, Joe Gomez, Trent Alexander-Arnold, Georginio Wijnaldum (105' Divock Origi), Jordan Henderson (105' Fabinho), Alex Oxlade-Chamberlain (82' James Milner), Roberto Firmino (113' Takumi Minamino), Mohamed Salah, Sadio Mané. Coach: Jürgen Klopp.
Atlético Madrid: Jan Oblak, Stefan Savic, Kieran Trippier (91' Sime Vrsaljko), Felipe Monteiro, Renan Lodi, Saúl, Koke, Thomas Partey, Diego Costa (56' Marcos Llorente), Ángel Correa (105' José Giménez), João Félix (103' Álvaro Morata). Coach: Diego Simeone.
Goals: 43' Georginio Wijnaldum 1-0, 94' Roberto Firmino 2-0, 97', 105+1' Marcos Llorente 2-1, 2-2, 120+1' Álvaro Morata 2-3.
Referee: Danny Makkelie (HOL)   Attendance: 52,267.

Atlético Madrid won after extra time.

Due to the effects of the COVID-19 pandemic, the competition was postponed in mid-March, and play did not resume until August 2020.

07.08.20 Etihad Stadium, Manchester: Manchester City – Real Madrid 2-1 (1-1)
Manchester City: Ederson Moraes, Kyle Walker, João Cancelo, Aymeric Laporte, Fernandinho, Ilkay Gündogan, Kevin De Bruyne, Rodri Hernández (89' Nicolás Otamendi), Phil Foden (67' Bernardo Silva), Raheem Sterling (81' David Silva), Gabriel Jesus. Coach: Pep Guardiola.
Real Madrid CF: Thibaut Courtois, Dani Carvajal (83' Lucas Vázquez), Raphaël Varane, Ferland Mendy, Éder Militão, Luka Modric (83' Federico Valverde), Toni Kroos, Casemiro, Karim Benzema, Eden Hazard (83' Luka Jovic), Rodrygo (61' Marco Asensio). Coach: Zinédine Zidane.
Goals: 9' Raheem Sterling 1-0, 28' Karim Benzema 1-1, 68' Gabriel Jesus 2-1.
Referee: Dr. Felix Brych (GER)

07.08.20 Allianz Stadium, Torino: Juventus – Olympique Lyonnais 2-1 (1-1)
Juventus: Wojciech Szczesny, Leonardo Bonucci, Alex Sandro, Matthijs de Ligt, Miralem Pjanic (60' Aaron Ramsey), Juan Cuadrado (70' Danilo), Adrien Rabiot, Rodrigo Bentancur, Cristiano Ronaldo, Gonzalo Higuaín, Federico Bernardeschi (71' Paulo Dybala, 84' Marco Olivieri). Coach: Maurizio Sarri.
Olympique Lyonnais: Anthony Lopes, Marcelo, Fernando Marçal, Léo Dubois (90+1' Kenny Tete), Jason Denayer (61' Joachim Andersen), Bruno Guimarães, Houssem Aouar (90+1' Thiago Mendes), Maxence Caqueret, Memphis Depay (67' Moussa Dembélé), Karl Toko Ekambi (67' Jeff Reine-Adélaïde), Maxwel Cornet. Coach: Rudi García.
Goals: 12' Memphis Depay 0-1 (p), 43', 60' Cristiano Ronaldo 1-1 (p), 2-1.
Referee: Felix Zwayer (GER)

Olympique Lyonnais won on away goals.

08.08.20   Allianz Arena, München: FC Bayern München – Chelsea FC 4-1 (2-1)
FC Bayern München: Manuel Neuer, Jérôme Boateng (63' Niklas Süle), David Alaba, Joshua Kimmich (71' Odriozola), Ivan Perisic (64' Philippe Coutinho), Thiago Alcântara (70' Corentin Tolisso), Leon Goretzka, Serge Gnabry (81' Javi Martínez), Alphonso Davies, Thomas Müller, Robert Lewandowski. Coach: Hansi Flick.
Chelsea FC: Willy Caballero, Kurt Zouma, Emerson, Andreas Christensen, Reece James, Ross Barkley, Mateo Kovacic, N'Golo Kanté, Mason Mount, Tammy Abraham (81' Olivier Giroud), Callum Hudson-Odoi. Coach: Frank Lampard.
Goals: 10' Robert Lewandowski 1-0 (p), 24' Ivan Perisic 2-0, 44' Tammy Abraham 2-1, 76' Corentin Tolisso 3-1, 83' Robert Lewandowski 4-1.
Referee: Ovidiu Hategan (ROM)

08.08.20   Camp Nou, Barcelona: FC Barcelona – SSC Napoli 3-1 (3-1)
FC Barcelona: Marc-André ter Stegen, Piqué, Jordi Alba, Sergi Roberto, Clément Lenglet, Nélson Semedo, Ivan Rakitic, Frenkie de Jong, Lionel Messi, Luis Suárez (90+2' Junior Firpo), Antoine Griezmann (84' Monchu). Coach: Quique Setién.
SSC Napoli: David Ospina, Kostas Manolas, Mário Rui, Kalidou Koulibaly, Giovanni Di Lorenzo, Diego Demme (46' Stanislav Lobotka), Piotr Zielinski (70' Hirving Lozano), Fabián Ruiz (79' Eljif Elmas), Dries Mertens, José Callejón (70' Matteo Politano), Lorenzo Insigne (79' Arkadiusz Milik). Coach: Gennaro Gattuso.
Goals: 10' Clément Lenglet 1-0, 23' Leonel Messi 2-0, 45+1' Luis Suárez 3-0 (p), 45+5' Lorenzo Insigne 3-1 (p).
Referee: Cüneyt Çakir (TUR)

QUARTER-FINALS

Due to the ongoing COVID-19 pandemic, all the ties from the quarter-finals onwards were played at neutral venues in Lisbon, Portugal as single-match knock-out games. No spectators were allowed at any of these matches.

12.08.20   Estádio do Sport Lisboa e Benfinca, Lisboa:
                    Atalanta Bergamo – Paris Saint-Germain 1-2 (1-0)
Atalanta Bergamo: Marco Sportiello, Rafael Tolói, Berat Djimsiti (60' José Palomino), Hans Hateboer, Mattia Caldara, Robin Gosens (82' Timothy Castagne), Papu Gómez (59' Ruslan Malinovskiy), Marten van Roon, Remo Freuler, Mario Pasalic (70' Luis Muriel), Duván Zapata (82' Jacopo Da Riva). Coach: Gian Piero Gasperini.
Paris Saint-Germain: Keylor Navas (79' Sergio Rico), Thiago Silva, Marquinhos, Juan Bernat, Presnel Kimpembe, Thilo Kehrer, Ander Herrera (72' Julian Draxler), Idrissa Gueye (72' Leandro Paredes), Pablo Sarabia (60' Kylian Mbappé), Neymar, Mauro Icardi (79' Eric Maxim Choupo-Moting). Coach: Thomas Tuchel.
Goals: 27' Mario Pasalic 1-0, 90' Marquinhos 1-1, 90+3' Eric Maxim Choupo-Moting 1-2.
Referee: Anthony Taylor (ENG)

13.08.20   Estádio José Alvalade, Lisboa: RB Leipzig – Atlético Madrid 2-1 (0-0)
RB Leipzig: Péter Gulácsi, Marcel Halstenberg, Lukas Klostermann, José Angeliño, Dayot Upamecano, Kevin Kampl, Marcel Sabitzer (90+2' Nordi Mukiele), Konrad Laimer (72' Tyler Adams), Christopher Nkunku (83' Amadou Haïdara), Daniel Olmo (83' Patrik Schick), Yussuf Poulsen. Coach: Julian Nagelsmann.
Atlético Madrid: Jan Oblak, Stefan Savic, Kieran Trippier, José Giménez, Renan Lodi, Héctor Herrera (58' João Félix), Saúl, Koke (90+2' Felipe Monteiro), Yannick Carrasco, Marcos Llorente, Diego Costa (72' Álvaro Morata). Coach: Diego Simeone.
Goals: 51' Daniel Olmo 1-0, 71' João Félix 1-1 (pen), 88' Tyler Adams 2-1.
Referee: Szymon Marciniak (POL)

14.08.20   Estádio do Sport Lisboe e Benfica, Lisboa:
              FC Barcelona – FC Bayern München 2-8 (1-4)
FC Barcelona: Marc-André ter Stegen, Piqué, Jordi Alba, Sergi Roberto (46' Antoine Griezmann), Clément Lenglet, Nélson Semedo, Arturo Vidal, Busquets (70' Ansu Fati), Frenkie de Jong, Lionel Messi, Luis Suárez. Coach: Quique Setién.
FC Bayern München: Manuel Neuer, Jérôme Boateng (76' Niklas Süle), David Alaba, Joshua Kimmich, Ivan Perisic (67' Kingsley Coman), Thiago Alcântara, Leon Goretzka (84' Corentin Tolisso), Serge Gnabry (75' Philippe Coutinho), Alphonso Davies (84' Lucas Hernández), Thomas Müller, Robert Lewandowski. Coach: Hansi Flick.
Goals: 4' Thomas Müller 0-1, 7 David Alaba 1-1 (og), 22' Ivan Perisic 1-2,
27' Serge Gnaby 1-3, 31' Thomas Müller 1-4, 57' Luis Suárez 2-4, 63' Joshua Kimmich 2-5, 82' Robert Lewandowski 2-6, 85', 89' Philippe Coutinho 2-7, 2-8.
Referee: Damir Skomina (SVN)

15.08.20   Estádio José Alvalade, Lisboa: Manchester City – Olympique Lyonnais 1-3 (0-1)
Manchester City: Ederson Moraes, Kyle Walker, João Cancelo, Aymeric Laporte, Eric Gacía, Fernandinho (56' Riyad Mahrez), Ilkay Gündogan, Kevin De Bruyne, Rodri Hernández (84' David Silva), Raheem Sterling, Gabriel Jesus. Coach: Pep Guardiola.
Olympique Lyonnais: Anthony Lopes, Marcelo, Fernando Marçal, Léo Dubois (74' Kenny Tete), Jason Denayer, Bruno Guimarães (70' Thiago Mendes), Houssem Aouar, Maxence Caqueret, Memphis Depay (75' Moussa Dembélé), Karl Toko Ekambi (87' Jeff Reine-Adélaïde), Maxwel Cornet. Coach: Rudi García.
Goals: 24' Maxwel Cornet 0-1, 69' Kevin De Bruyne 1-1, 79', 87' Moussa Dembélé 1-2, 1-3.
Referee: Danny Makkelie (HOL)

SEMI-FINALS

18.08.20   Estádio do Sport Lisboe e Benfica, Lisboa:
           RB Leipzig – Paris Saint-Germain 0-3 (0-2)
RB Leipzig: Péter Gulácsi, Lukas Klostermann (82' Willi Orban), José Angeliño, Nordi Mukiele, Dayot Upamecano, Kevin Kampl (64' Tyler Adams), Marcel Sabitzer, Konrad Laimer (62' Marcel Halstenberg), Christopher Nkunku (46' Emil Forsberg), Daniel Olmo (46' Patrik Schick), Yussuf Poulsen. Coach: Julian Nagelsmann.
Paris Saint-Germain: Sergio Rico, Thiago Silva, Marquinhos, Juan Bernat, Presnel Kimpembe, Thilo Kehrer, Ángel Di María (87' Pablo Sarabia), Ander Herrera (83' Marco Verratti), Leandro Paredes (83' Julian Draxler), Neymar, Kylian Mbappé (86' Eric Maxim Choupo-Moting). Coach: Thomas Tuchel.
Goals: 13' Marquinhos 0-1, 42' Ángel Di Maria 0-2, 56' Juan Bernat 0-3.
Referee: Björn Kuipers (HOL)

19.08.20   Estádio José Alvalade, Lisboa:
           Olympique Lyonnais – FC Bayern München 0-3 (0-2)
Olympique Lyonnais: Anthony Lopes, Marcelo, Fernando Marçal (73' Mathis Rayan Cherki), Léo Dubois (67' Kenny Tete), Jason Denayer, Bruno Guimarães (46' Thiago Mendes), Houssem Aouar, Maxence Caqueret, Memphis Depay (58' Moussa Dembélé), Karl Toko Ekambi (67' Jeff Reine-Adélaïde), Maxwel Cornet. Coach: Rudi García.
FC Bayern München: Manuel Neuer, Jérôme Boateng (46' Niklas Süle), David Alaba, Joshua Kimmich, Ivan Perisic (63' Kingsley Coman), Thiago Alcântara (82' Corentin Tolisso), Leon Goretzka (82' Benjamin Pavard), Serge Gnabry (75' Philippe Coutinho), Alphonso Davies, Thomas Müller, Robert Lewandowski. Coach: Hansi Flick.
Goals: 18', 33' Serge Gnabry 0-1, 0-2, 88' Robert Lewandowski 0-3.
Referee: Antonio Mateu Lahoz (ESP)

FINAL

23.08.20   Estádio do Sport Lisboe e Benfica, Lisboa:
           Paris Saint-Germain – FC Bayern München 0-1 (0-0)
Paris Saint-Germain: Keylor Navas, Thiago Silva, Marquinhos, Juan Bernat (80' Layvin Kurzawa), Presnel Kimpembe, Thilo Kehrer, Ángel Di María (80' Eric Maxim Choupo-Moting), Ander Herrera (72' Julian Draxler), Leandro Paredes (65' Marco Verratti), Neymar, Kylian Mbappé. Coach: Thomas Tuchel.
FC Bayern München: Manuel Neuer, Jérôme Boateng (25' Niklas Süle), David Alaba, Joshua Kimmich, Thiago Alcântara (86' Corentin Tolisso), Leon Goretzka, Serge Gnabry (68' Philippe Coutinho), Kingsley Coman (68' Ivan Perisic), Alphonso Davies, Thomas Müller, Robert Lewandowski. Coach: Hansi Flick.
Goal: 59' Kingsley Coman 0-1.
Referee: Daniele Orsato (ITA)

UEFA CHAMPIONS LEAGUE 2020-2021

PRELIMINARY ROUND
SEMI-FINAL ROUND

08.08.20 Centre sportif de Colovray, Nyon (SUI): SP Tre Fiori – Linfield FC 0-2 (0-0)
SP Tre Fiori: Aldo Sioncini, Alessandro D'Addario, Peda Misimovic, Davide Simoncini (89' Luca Angelini), Angelo Gregorio, Louseny Kalissa (70' Pier Figone), Nicholas Santoni, Francesco Lunardini, Giacomo Pracucci, Bojan Gjurchinoski, Joel Hijuelos (76' Adriano Marzeglia). Coach: Matteo Cechetti.
Linfield FC: Christopher Johns, Ross Larkin, Jimmy Callacher, Ethan Boyle, Niall Quinn, Navid Nasseri (65' Andrew Waterworth), Daniel Kearns, Jamie Mulgrew, Kirk Millar, Shayne Lavery (65' Bastien Héry), Kyle McClean (65' Christy Manzinga). Coach: David Healy.
Goals: 71' Bastien Héry 0-1, 83' Christy Manzinga 0-2.
Referee: Balász Berke (HUN)
Sent off: 86' Giacomo Pracucci.

08.08.20 Centre sportif de Colovray, Nyon (SUI):
Drita Gjilan – Inter Club d'Escaldes 2-1 (2-1)
Drita Gjilan: Faton Maloku, Ardian Limani, Ardijan Cuculi, Ilir Blakçori, Hamdi Namani, Erjon Vuçaj, Astrit Fazliu (82' Albin Krasniqi), Xhevdet Shabani, Bunjamin Shabani, Almir Ajzeraj (89' Drilon Islami), Kastriot Rexha (73' Betim Haxhimusa). Coach: Ardijan Nuhiji.
Inter Club d'Escaldes: Josep Gómes, Federico Bessone, Emili García, Óscar Reyes, Toni Lao (61' Ludovic Clemente), Feher, Genís, Bruninho (72' Jordi Betriu), Jordi Roca, Sergi Moreno (90' Andrés Briñez), Bruno Lemiechevsky. Coach: Baines.
Goals: 21' Xhevdet Shabani 1-0, 29' Emili García 1-1, 45+3' Hamdi Namani 2-1.
Referee: Robert Jenkins (WAL)

PRELIMINARY ROUND
FINAL ROUND

11.08.20 Centre sportif de Colovray, Nyon (SUI): Drita Gjilan – Linfield FC 0-3
Referee: Ioannis Papadopoulos (GRE)

This match could not be played as two players from Drita Gjilan tested positive for SARS-2 coronavirus so the whole team was put into quarantine by the Swiss authorities.

Linfield FC were subsequently awarded a technical 3-0 victory by UEFA according to the regulations related to COVID-19.

FIRST QUALIFYING ROUND

18.08.20   Tofiq Bahramov adina Respublika stadionu, Baku:
     Qarabag FK – Sileks Kratovo 4-0 (2-0)
Qarabag FK: Sahrudin Mahammadaliyev, Maksim Medvedev (79' Abbas Hüseynov), Badavi Hüseynov, Kevin Medina, Jaime Romero (83' Elvin Dzhafarquliyev), Uros Matic, Filip Ozobic, Wilde-Donald Guerrier, Abdellah Zoubir (72' Owusu Kwabena), Ismayil Ibrahimli, Mahir Emreli. Coach: Qurban Qurbanov.
Sileks Kratovo: Daniel Bozinovski, Srdjan Draskovic, Hristijan Grozdanoski, Denis Ristov (59' Milos Zeravica), Angelce Timovski, Burhan Mustafov (84' Bojan Spirkoski), Dejan Tanturovski (74' Kristijan Kostovski), Viktor Serafimovski, Daniel Karceski, Pepi Gorgiev, Ivan Ivanovski. Coach: Goran Simov.
Goals: 11' Jaime Romero 1-0, 40', 51' Wilde-Donald Guerrier 2-0, 3-0, 80' Mahir Emreli 4-0.
Referee: Yaroslav Kozyk (UKR)

Qarabag FK played their home match at Tofiq Bahramov adina Respublika stadionu, Baku, instead of their regular stadium Azersun Arena, Baku, which did not meet UEFA requirements.

18.08.20   Stadion Wojska Polskiego, Warszawa: Legia Warszawa – Linfield FC 1-0 (1-0)
Legia Warszawa: Artur Boruc, Artur Jedrzejczyk, Filip Mladenovic, Mateusz Wieteska, Michal Karbownik, Domagoj Antolic, Pawel Wszolek, Valeriane Gvilia, Bartosz Slisz (46' Maciej Rosolek), Luquinhas, Tomás Pekhart (70' José Kanté). Coach: Aleksandar Vukovic.
Linfield FC: Christopher Johns, Matthew Clarke, Mark Stafford, Ross Larkin, Niall Quinn (84' Navid Nasseri), Ethan Boyle, Jamie Mulgrew, Kirk Millar, Bastien Héry (79' Conor Pepper), Stephen Fallon, Shayne Lavery (76' Christy Manzinga). Coach: David Healy.
Goal: 82' José Kanté 1-0.
Referee: Nicolas Laforge (BEL)
Sent off: 75' Kirk Millar.

18.08.20   Stadion Stadyen DASK Brestki, Brest: Dynamo Brest – FK Astana 6-3 (4-1)
Dynamo Brest: Sergey Ignatovich, Yevhen Khacheridi, Kirill Pechenin, Gaby Kiki, Sergey Kislyak (73' Sergey Krivets), Roman Yuzepchuk, Pavel Sedko, David Tweh, Artem Milevskiy (86' Artem Bykov), Mikhail Gordeychuk (73' Pavel Savitskiy), Abdoulaye Diallo. Coach: Sergey Kovalchuk.
FK Astana: Dmytro Nepogodov, Abzal Beysebekov, Uros Radakovic, Luka Simunovic, Marin Tomasov, Dmitriy Shomko, Ivan Maevski, Yuri Pertsukh (34' Tigran Barseghyan), Maks Ebong, Aleksey Shchetkin (34' Dorin Rotariu), Pieros Soteriou. Coach: Michal Bílek
Goals: 16' Mikhail Gordeychuk 1-0, 17' Kirill Pechenin 2-0, 22' Mikhail Gordeychuk 3-0, 37' Pavel Sedko 4-0, 45' Marin Tomasov 4-1, 53' Dorin Rotariu 4-2, 55' Abdoulaye Diallo 5-2, 87' Abzal Beysebekov 5-3, 90' Abdoulaye Diallo 6-3.
Referee: Novak Simovic (SRB)

18.08.20   Celtic Park, Glasgow: Celtic FC – KR Reykjavík 6-0 (3-0)
Celtic FC: Vassilis Barkas, Hatem Abd Elhamed, Christopher Jullien, Greg Taylor, Scott Brown (62' Olivier Ntcham), Nir Bitton, James Forrest, Callum McGregor, Mohamed Elyounoussi, Ryan Christie (72' Patryk Klimala), Odsonne Édouard (72' Albian Ajeti). Coach: Neil Lennon.
KR Reykjavík: Beitir Ólafsson, Arnór Adalsteinsson, Kristinn Jónsson (46' Atli Sigurjónsson) Finnur Tómas Pálmason, Pálmi Pálmason, Finnur Margeirsson, Arnthór Ingi Kristinsson, Pablo Punyed, Óskar Hauksson (73' Alex Freyr Hilmarsson), Kennie Chopart, Kristján Finnbogason (73' Ægir Jónasson). Coach: Rúnar Kristinsson.
Goals: 6' Mohamed Elyounoussi 1-0, 17' Arnór Adalsteinsson 2-0 (og), 31' Christopher Jullien 3-0, 46' Greg Taylor 4-0, 72' Odsonne Édouard 5-0, 90+1' Mohamed Elyounoussi 6-0.
Referee: Sebastian Gishamer (AUT)

18.08.20   Stadion Rajko Mitic, Beograd: Crvena Zvezda Beograd – Europa FC 5-0 (2-0)
Crvena Zvezda Beograd: Milan Borjan, Nemanja Milunovic, Milan Rodic (46' Milan Gajic), Milos Degenek, Marko Gobeljic, Aleksandar Katai, Srdjan Spiridonovic (68' Tómané), Sékou Sanogo (74' Milos Vulic), Guélor Kanga, Mirko Ivanic, El Fardou Ben Nabouhane. Coach: Dejan Stankovic.
Europa FC: Javi Muñoz, Olmo González, Jayce Olivero, Juampe Rico, Liam Walker, Willy (64' Polaco), Blas Álvarez (70' Álex Quillo), Marco Rosa, Ale Carrascal, Mohamed Badr Hassan, Adrián Gallardo (60' Manu Dimas). Coach: Rafael Escobar.
Goals: 35', 44', 52' El Fardou Ben Nabouhane 1-0, 2-0, 3-0, 78', 87' Mirko Ivanic 4-0, 5-0.
Referee: Volen Chinkov (BUL)

19.08.20   Stadion Yerevan Football Academy, Yerevan:
                    FC Ararat-Armenia – Omonia Nikosia 0-1 (0-0, 0-0) (a.e.t.)
FC Ararat-Armenia: Stefan Cupic, Alemão (85' Sargis Shahinyan), Sergiy Vakulenko, Ângelo Meneses (111' Aleksandar Damcevski), David Bollo, Yoan Gouffran (90+2' Armen Ambartsumyan), Kódjo Alphonse, Furdjel Narsingh, Yusuf Otubanjo (73' Zakaria Sanogo), Louis Ogana, Mailson. Coach: David Campaña.
Omonia Nikosia: Fabiano, Jan Lecjaks, Tomás Hubocan, Michael Lüftner, Ádam Lang, Jordi Gómez, Vítor Gomes (91' Ioannis Kousoulos), Charis Mavrias (81' Loizos Loizou), Michal Djuris (67' Éric Bauthéac), Thiago Santos (103' Marinos Tzionis), Andronikos Kakoullis. Coach: Henning Berg.
Goal: 94' Thiago Santos 0-1.
Referee: Viktor Shimusik (BLS)
Sent off: 97' David Bollo.

19.08.20   Aker Stadion, Molde: Molde FK – Kuopion PS 5-0 (2-0)
Molde FK: Andreas Linde, Kristoffer Haugen, Sheriff Sinyan, Magnus Eikrem (86' Tobias Christensen), Etzaz Hussain, Eirik Hestad, Fredrik Aursnes, Martin Ellingsen, Henry Wingo (74' Marcus Pedersen), Ola Brynhildsen (79' Erling Knudtzon), Ohi Omoijuanfo. Coach: Erling Moe.
Kuopion PS: Otso Virtanen, Juho Pirttijoki, Nuno Tomás (66' Joel Vartiainen), Luc Tabi Manga, Petteri Pennanen, Bismark Adjei-Boateng, Ilmari Niskanen, Urhu Nissilä, Saku Savolainen, Rangel (74' Aniekpeno Udoh), Usman Sale (74' Ats Purje). Coach: Arne Erlandsen.
Goals: 26' Eirik Hestad 1-0, 37' Magnus Eikrem 2-0, 69' Ohi Omoijuanfo 3-0, 90+1' Marcus Pedersen 4-0, 90+3' Erling Knudtzon 5-0.
Referee: Bryn Markham-Jones (WAL)

19.08.20   A. Le Coq Arena, Tallinn: FC Flora – FK Sūduva 1-1 (0-0, 1-1) (a.e.t.)
FC Flora: Matvei Igonen, Ken Kallaste (106' Henri Järvelaid), Märten Kuusk, Henrik Pürg, Michael Lilander, Konstatin Vassiljev, Martin Miller (62' Rauno Alliku), Markus Soomets, Vladislavs Kreida, Rauno Sappinen, Vlasiy Sinyavskiy (84' Frank Liivak).
Coach: Jürgen Henn.
FK Sūduva: Ivan Kardum, Vaidas Slavickas, Thomas Salamon (120' Valērijs Sabala), Aleksandar Zivanovic, Semir Kerla, Ivan Hladík, Evgen Efremov (72' Andro Svrljuga), Povilas Leimonas (37' Domagoj Pusic), Giedrius Matulevicius (61' Eligijus Jankauskas), Josip Tadic, Mihrit Topcagic. Coach: Saulius Sirmelis.
Goals: 49' Rauno Sappinen 1-0, 78' Mihret Topcagic 1-1 (p).
Referee: Nejc Kajtazovic (SVN)

FK Sūduva won 4-2 after penalties.
Penalties: Svrljuga 1-0, Vassiljev missed, Sabala 2-0, Sappinen 2-1, Tadic missed, Järvelaid 2-2, Pusic 3-2, Soomets missed, Topcagic 4-2.

19.08.20   Groupama Aréna, Budapest: Ferencvárosi TC – Djurgårdens IF 2-0 (1-0
Ferencvárosi TC: Dénes Dibusz, Endre Botka, Miha Blazic, Adnan Kovacevic, Eldar Civic, Somália, Igor Kharatin, Isael (75' Aïssa Laïdouni), Tokmac Nguen (63' Michal Skvarka), Franck Boli, Myrto Uzuni (84' Roland Varga). Coach: Serhiy Rebrov.
Djurgårdens IF: Per Bråtveit, Erik Berg, Jacob Une-Larsson, Jesper Nyholm, Aslak Witry, Jonathan Augustinsson, Fredrik Ulvestad, Jesper Karlström, Curtis Edwards (75' Haris Radetinac), Emmanuel Banda (18' Karl Holmberg), Emir Kujovic (46' Edward Chilufya).
Coach: Kim Bergstrand.
Goals: 33', 62' Tokmac Nguen 1-0, 2-0.
Referee: Fedayi San (SUI)

19.08.20   Bloomfield Stadium, Tel Aviv: Maccabi Tel Aviv – Riga FC 2-0 (0-0)
Maccabi Tel Aviv: Daniel Tenenbaum, Sheran Yeini, Eitan Tibi, Saborit, Maor Kandil, Avi Rikan, Dor Peretz (84' Itay Shechter), Dan Glazer, Eduardo Guerrero (46' Dan Bitton), Nick Blackman, Eylon Almog (82' Tal Ben Haim). Coach: Georgios Donis.
Riga FC: Roberts Ozols, Herdi Prenga, Antonijs Cernomordijs, Ritvars Rugins, Vyacheslav Sharpar, Jakub Hora (71' Dário Júnior), Felipe Brisola, Stefan Panic, Stênio Júnior (62' Jordan N'Kololo), Vladislavs Fjodorovs, Kule Mbombo (59' Roger). Coach: Oleg Komonov.
Goals: 58', 88' Nick Blackman 1-0 (p), 2-0 (p).
Referee: Igor Pajac (CRO)

19.08.20   Boris Paichadze Dinamo Arena, Tbilisi: Dinamo Tbilisi – KF Tiranë 0-2 (0-1)
Dinamo Tbilisi: Roin Kvaskhvadze, Nodar Iashvili, Luka Lochoshvili, Davit Kobouri (59' Giorgi Kimadze), Simon Gbegnon, Giorgi Papava, Bakar Kardava (67' Giorgi Kutsia), Akaki Shulaia, Irakli Bugridze (81' Giorgi Gabedava), Tornike Kapanadze, Pernambuco.
Coach: Kakhaber Chkhetiani.
KF Tiranë: Ilion Lika, Kristi Vangjeli, Kristijan Tosevski, Marsel Ismajlgeci, Filip Najdovski, Idriz Batha, Jurgen Çelhaka, Agustin Torassa (83' Gentian Muça), Elton Calé (71' Ardit Toli), Winful Cobbinah, Ernest Muçi (87' Albion Avdijaj). Coach: Ndubuisi Egbo.
Goals: 45+4' Agustin Torassa 0-1, 86' Marsel Ismajlgeci 0-2.
Referee: Roomer Tarajev (EST)

19.08.20   Szusza Ferenc Stadion, Budapest (HUN): NK Celje – Dundalk FC 3-0 (1-0)
NK Celje: Matjaz Rozman, Josip Calusic, Denis Marandici, Advan Kadusic, Zan Zaletel, Matic Vrbanec (86' Nino Pungarsek), Lan Stravs, Mitja Lotric, Dario Vizinger (90+3' Filip Dangubic), Ivan Bozic (82' Jakob Novak), Luka Kerin. Coach: Dusan Kosic.
Dundalk FC: Gary Rogers, Brian Gartland (76' Nathan Oduwa), Sean Gannon, Sean Hoare, Darragh Leahy, Chris Shields (82' David McMillan), Patrick McEleney, Jordan Flores (69' Sean Murray), Stefan Colovic, Patrick Hoban, Michael Duffy. Coach: Vinny Perth.
Goals: 43' Luka Kerin 1-0, 89' Dario Vizinger 2-0, 90+5' Filip Dangubic 3-0.
Referee: Vítor Ferreira (POR)

NK Celje played their home match at Szusza Ferenc Stadion, Budapest (HUN), instead of their regular stadium Stadion Z'dezele, Celje, due to travel restrictions related to the COVID-19 pandemic.

19.08.20   Stadion Krytyi futbolnyi Manesh, Tiraspol:
               FC Sheriff Tiraspol – CS Fola Esch 2-0 (1-0)
FC Sheriff Tiraspol: Dumitru Celeadnic, Andrei Peteleu, Ousmane N'Diaye, Faith Obilor, William Parra (90+3' Max Veloso), Cristiano, Charles Petro, Benedik Mioc, Gabrijel Boban (88' Andriy Bliznichenko), Anatole Abang, Frank Castañeda (67' Andrej Lukic). Coach: Zoran Zekic.
CS Fola Esch: Emmanuel Cabral, Julien Klein, Sylvio Ouassiero (80' Achraf Drif), Cédric Sacras, Rodrigue Dikaba (62' Zachary Hadji), Dejvid Sinani (82' Bruno Freire), Diogo Pimentel, Stefano Bensi, Gauthier Caron, Gilson Delgado, Jules Diallo.
Coach: Sébastian Grandjean.
Goals: 36' Anatole Abang 1-0, 81' Andrej Lukic 2-0.
Referee: Balász Berke (HUN)

19.08.20   Cardiff City Stadium, Cardiff: Connah's Quay Nomads – FK Sarajevo 0-2 (0-1)
Connah's Quay Nomads: Lewis Brass, George Horan, Danny Holmes, Callum Roberts, Pristley Parquharson, Danny Harrison (46' Sameron Dool), Aeron Edwards (78' John Disney), Callum Morris, Declan Poole (83' Jamie Insall), Michael Wilde, Craig Curran.
Coach: Andy Morrison.
FK Sarajevo: Vladan Kovacevic, Amer Dupovac, Dusan Hodzic, Andrej Djokanovic, Mirko Oremus, Hrvoje Milicevic, Amar Rahmanovic, Ivan Jukic, Mersudin Ahmetovic (81' Haris Handzic), Benjamin Tatar (71' Krste Velkoski), Djani Salcin (60' Selmir Pidro).
Coach: Vinko Marinovic
Goals: 16', 65' Benjamin Tatar 0-1, 0-2.
Referee: Jamie Robinson (NIR)

Connah's Quat Nomads played their home match at Cardiff City Stadium, Cardiff, instead of their regular stadium Deeside Stadium, Connah's Quay, which did not meet UEFA requirements.

19.08.20   Stadion Pod Goricom, Podgorica:
FK Buducnost Podgorica – PFC Ludogorets Razgrad 1-3 (1-2)
FK Buducnost Podgorica: Milos Dragojevic, Vladan Adzic, Luka Mirkovic, Igor Cukovic, Nemanja Sekulic, Milos Raickovic (82' Dejan Zarubica), Vasilije Terzic (75' Miomir Djurickovic), Petar Vukcevic, Igor Ivanovic, Panagiotis Moraitis, Ivan Bojovic (76' Aleksandar Vujacic). Coach: Mladen Milinkovic.
PFC Ludogorets Razgrad: Renan, Cosmin Moti, Dragos Grigore, Cicinho, Anton Nedyalkov, Mavis Tchibota (65' Dominik Yankov), Stéphane Badji, Cauly, Alex Santana, Higinio Marín (76' Claudiu Keserü), Bernard Tekpetey (85' Jorghinho). Coach: Pavel Vrba.
Goals: 12' Higinio Marín 0-1, 25' Mavis Tchibota 0-2, 31' Igor Cukovic 1-2, 90+3' Cauly 1-3.
Referee: Ferenc Karakó (HUN)

19.08.20   MFA Centenary Stadium, Ta'Qali: Floriana FC – CFR Cluj 0-2 (0-0)
Floriana FC: Ini Akpan, Enzo Ruiz, Alex Cini (69' Moustapha Beye), Jurgen Pisani (82' Brandon Paiber), Ryan Camenzuli, Diego Venancio, Nicola Leone, Matías García, Kristian Keqi, Flávio Carioca (67' Marcelo Dias), Tiago Adan. Coach: Vincenzo Potenza.
CFR Cluj: Cristian Balgradean, Paulo Vinícius, Camora, Mike Cestor, Andrei Burca, Ciprian Deac, Alexandru Chipciu (89' Catalin Golofca), Ovidiu Hoban, Mickaël Pereira (83' Mateo Susic), Catalin Itu (67' Luís Aurélio), Mário Rondón. Coach: Dan Petrescu.
Goals: 53' Mike Cestor 0-1, 90+7' Catalin Golofca 0-2.
Referee: Laurent Kopriwa (LUX)

21.08.20   Vid Djúpumýrar, Klaksvík: KÍ Klaksvík – Slovan Bratislava 3-0
Referee: Kristoffer Hagenes (NOR)

This match was originally scheduled to be played on 19th August 2020, at Vid Djúpumýrar, Klaksvík, but was postponed until 21st August 2020, after a staff member from Slovan Bratislava tested positive for SARS-2 coronavirus and the whole team was put into quarantine by the Faroese authorities.
On 21st August 2020 the match could not be played due to a player from Slovan Bratislava testing positive for SARS-2 coronavirus and the whole second team being put into quarantine by the Faroese authotities. KÍ Klaksvík were subsequently awarded a technical 3-0 victory by UEFA according to the regulations related to COVID-19.

SECOND QUALIFYING ROUND

25.08.20   Air Albania Stadium, Tirana: KF Tiranë – Crvena Zvezda Beograd 0-1 (0-0)
KF Tiranë: Ilion Lika, Kristi Vangjeli, Kristijan Tosevski, Erion Hoxhallari (76' Ardit Toli), Filip Najdovski, Idriz Batha, Jurgen Çelhaka, Agustin Torassa, Elton Calé (85' Albion Avdijaj), Winful Cobbinah (73 Jurgen Vrapi), Ernest Muçi. Coach: Ndubuisi Egbo.
Crvena Zvezda Beograd: Milan Borjan, Nemanja Milunovic, Milos Degenek (61' Milan Rodic), Marko Gobeljic, Radovan Pankov, Aleksandar Katai, Srdjan Spiridonovic (46' Mirko Ivanic), Sékou Sanogo, Guélor Kanga (83' Njegos Petrovic), Veljko Nikolic, Tómané. Coach: Dejan Stankovic.
Goal: 62' Tomané 0-1.
Referee: Kaspar Sjöberg (SWE)

KF Tiranë played their home match at Air Albania Stadium, Tirana, instead of their regular stadium Selman Stërmasi Stadium, Tirana.

25.08.20   Stadio Toumbas, Saloniki: PAOK Saloniki – Besiktas 3-1 (3-1)
PAOK Saloniki: Zivko Zivkovic, Fernando Varela, Sverrir Ingason, Rodrigo Alves (44' Dimitris Limnios), Dimitris Giannoulis, Giannis Michailidis, Omar El Kaddouri, Stefan Schwab, Dimitrios Pelkas (76' Anderson Esiti), Chuba Akpom, Christos Tzolis (84' Léo Jabá).
Coach: Abel Ferreira.
Besiktas: Ersin Destanoglu, Domagoj Vida, Fabrice N'Sakala (82' Umut Nayir), Wellinton Souza, Jeremain Lens, Atiba Hutchinson, Necip Uysal, Georges-Kévin N'Koudou, Bernard Mensah (69' Dorukhan Toköz), Tyler Boyd (46' Oguzhan Özyakup), Cyle Larin.
Coach: Sergen Yalçin.
Goals: 7', 24' Christos Tzolis 1-0, 2-0, 30' Dimitrios Pelkas 3-0, 37' Cyle Larin 3-1.
Referee: Daniele Doveri (ITA)

Chuba Akpom missed a penalty kick (41').

26.08.20   AFAS Stadion, Alkmaar: AZ Alkmaar – Viktoria Plzen 3-1 (0-0, 1-1) (a.e.t.)
AZ Alkmaar: Marco Bizot, Ron Vlaar (76' Ramon Leeuwin), Jonas Svensson, Owen Wijndal, Jordy Clasie (80' Ferdy Druijf), Fredrik Midtsjø, Dani de Wit, Teun Koopmeiners, Oussama Idrissi (93' Yukinari Sugawara), Myron Boadu, Calvin Stengs (64' Albert Gudmundsson).
Coach: Arne Slot.
Viktoria Plzen: Ales Hruska, David Limberský, Jakub Brabec, Lukás Hejda, Milan Havel, Jan Kopic (87' Jan Kovarík), Ales Cermák, Lukás Kalvach (105' Miroslav Kácer), Ondrej Mihálik (74' Adriel D'Avila Ba Loua), Pavel Bucha, Jean-David Beauguel (90+3' Ludek Pernica).
Coach: Adrián Gula.
Goals: 78' David Limberský 0-1, 90+5' Teun Koopmeiners 1-1 (p), 98',
118' Albert Gudmundsson 2-1, 3-1.
Referee: Luís Godinho (POR)

AZ Alkmaar won after extra time.

26.08.20   Hikvision arena, Marijampolé: FK Sūduva – Maccabi Tel Aviv 0-3 (0-1)
FK Sūduva: Ivan Kardum, Vaidas Slavickas, Thomas Salamon, Aleksandar Zivanovic, Semir Kerla, Ivan Hladík, Evgen Efremov (46' Andro Svrljuga), Povilas Leimonas (72' Renan Oliveira), Domagoj Pusic, Josip Tadic, Mihrit Topcagic (63 Eligijus Jankauskas).
Coach: Saulius Sirmelis.
Maccabi Tel Aviv: Daniel Tenenbaum, Sheran Yeini, Eitan Tibi, Ofir Davidzada, Saborit (76 Matan Baltaxa), Maor Kandil, Avi Rikan (81' Eylon Almog), Dor Peretz, Dan Glazer, Dan Bitton (88' Ben Bitton), Nick Blackman. Coach: Georgios Donis.
Goals: 30' Avi Rikan 0-1, 74' Nick Blackman 0-2, 90+2' Ofir Davidzada 0-3.
Referee: Rade Obrenovic (SLO)

26.08.20   Stadion Z'dezele, Celic: NK Celje – Molde FK 1-2 (1-0)
NK Celje: Matjaz Rozman, Josip Calusic, Denis Marandici, Advan Kadusic, Zan Zaletel, Matic Vrbanec, Lan Stravs (70' Nino Pungarsek), Mitja Lotric (84' Jakob Novak), Dario Vizinger, Ivan Bozic (85' Filip Dangubic), Luka Kerin. Coach: Dusan Kosic.
Molde FK: Andreas Linde, Kristoffer Haugen, Sheriff Sinyan, Marcus Pedersen, Magnus Eikrem (79' Tobias Christensen), Etzaz Hussain, Eirik Hestad (84' Ola Brynhildsen), Fredrik Aursnes, Martin Ellingsen, Erling Knudtzon (56' Ohi Omoijuanfo), Leke James.
Coach: Erling Moe.
Goals: 38' Mitja Lotric 1-0, 57' Etzaz Hussain 1-1, 74' Leke James 1-2.
Referee: Christopher Jäger (AUT)

26.08.20   Tofiq Bahramov adina Respublika stadionu, Baku:
            Qarabag FK – FC Sheriff Tiraspol 2-1 (1-0)
Qarabag FK: Sahrudin Mahammadaliyev, Maksim Medvedev, Qara Qarayev, Badavi Hüseynov, Kevin Medina, Jaime Romero (89' Owusu Kwabena), Uros Matic, Filip Ozobic (70' Ismayil Ibrahimli), Wilde-Donald Guerrier (90+4' Abbas Hüseynov), Abdellah Zoubir, Mahir Emreli. Coach: Qurban Qurbanov.
FC Sheriff Tiraspol: Dumitru Celeadnic, Andrei Peteleu, Ousmane N'Diaye, Faith Obilor (74' Keston Julien), Andrej Lukic, William Parra, Cristiano, Charles Petro, Benedik Mioc (46' Frank Castañeda), Gabrijel Boban (74' Richard Gadze), Anatole Abang. Coach: Zoran Zekic.
Goals: 22' Uros Matic 1-0 (p), 63' Mahir Emreli 2-0, 78' Frank Castañeda 2-1.
Referee: Mykola Balakin (UKR)
Sent off: 37' Anatole Abang.

Qarabag FK played their home match at Tofiq Bahramov adina Respublika stadionu, Baku, instead of their regular stadium Azersun Arena, Baku, which did not meet UEFA requirements.

28.08.20   Stadion Kranjceviceva, Zagreb: Lokomotiva Zagreb – Rapid Wien 0-1 (0-1)
Lokomotiva Zagreb: Krunoslav Hendija, Denis Kolinger, Stipo Markovic (61' Mario Budimir), Ivan Celikovic, Kemal Osmankovic, Marko Djira, Fran Karacic, Oliver Petrak (72' Sherif Kallaku), Dino Halilovic, Mario Cuze, Indrit Tuci (46' Jorge Sammir). Coach: Goran Tomic.
Rapid Wien: Richard Strebinger, Filip Stojkovic, Maximilian Hofmann, Maximilian Ullmann, Leo Greiml, Thomas Murg (64' Srdjan Grahovac), Dejan Petrovic, Dejan Ljubicic, Taxiarchis Fountas (86' Koya Kitagawa), Ercan Kara, Kelvin Arase (76' Thorsten Schick).
Coach: Dietmar Kühbauer.
Goal: 32' Ercan Kara 0-1.
Referee: Juan Martínez Munuera (ESP)

26.08.20   Huvepharma Arena, Razgrad: PFC Ludogorets Razgrad – FC Midtjylland 0-1 (0-0)
PFC Ludogorets Razgrad: Renan, Cosmin Moti, Dragos Grigore, Cicinho, Anton Nedyalkov, Anicet Andrianantenaina (55' Bernard Tekpetey), Mavis Tchibota (79' Jorghinho), Stéphane Badji, Cauly, Alex Santana, Claudiu Keserü (54' Higinio Marín). Coach: Pavel Vrba.
FC Midtjylland: Jesper Hansen, Erik Sviatchenko, Alexander Scholz, Joel Andersson, Paulinho, Awer Mabil, Bozhidar Kraev (65' Júnior Brumado), Anders Dreyer, Frank Onyeka, Jens Cajuste, Sory Kaba (75' Mikael Anderson). Coach: Brian Priske.
Goal: 78' Júnior Brumado 0-1.
Referee: Denys Shurman (UKR)

26.08.20   Stadionul Dr. Constantin Radulescu, Cluj-Napoca:
           CFR Cluj – Dinamo Zagreb 2-2 (0-1, 2-2) (a.e.t.)
CFR Cluj: Cristian Balgradean, Paulo Vinícius, Camora, Kévin Boli, Andrei Burca (82 Mateo Susic), Ciprian Deac, Alexandru Chipciu (46' Mário Rondón), Damjan Djokovic, Mickaël Pereira (68' Catalin Golofca), Mihai Bordeianu (113' Catalin Itu), Gabriel Debeljuh. Coach: Dan Petrescu.
Dynamo Zagreb: Dominik Livakovic, Marin Leovac, Kévin Théophile-Catherine, Emir Dilaver, Petar Stojanovic, Arijan Ademi, Amer Gojak, Luka Ivanusec (68' Bruno Petkovic), Lovro Majer (54' Lirim Kastrati), Mario Gavranovic (54' Josko Gvardiol), Mislav Orsic (108' Sadegh Moharrami). Coach: Zoran Mamic.
Goals: 14' Amer Gojak 0-1, 64' Mickaël Pereira 1-1, 78' Lirim Kastrati 1-2, 90+3' Gabriel Debeljuh 2-2.
Referee: António Nobre (POR)
Sent off: 51' Kévin Théophile-Catherine.

Ciprion Deac missed a penalty kick (52').

Dinamo Zagreb won 6-5 on penalties after extra time.
Penalties: Petkovic 1-0, Paulo Vinícius 1-1, Leovac 2-1, Djokovic 2-2, Ademi 3-2, Rondón 3-3, Stojanovic 4-3, Susic 4-4, Gojak missed, Golofca missed, Dilaver 5-4, Deac 5-5, Gvardiol 6-5, Boli missed.

26.08.20   Stadion Miejski Legii Warsawa im. Marszalka Józefa Pilsudskiego, Warszawa:
           Legia Warszawa – Omonia Nikosia 0-2 (0-0, 0-0) (a.e.t.)
Legia Warszawa: Artur Boruc, Artur Jedrzejczyk, Igor Lewczuk, Filip Mladenovic, Michal Karbownik, Domagoj Antolic, Valeriane Gvilia (60' Mateusz Wieteska, 108' André Martins), Bartosz Slisz, Luquinhas, Tomás Pekhart (70' José Kanté), Maciej Rosolek (79' Bartosz Kapustka). Coach: Aleksandar Vukovic.
Omonia Nikosia: Fabiano, Jan Lecjaks, Michael Lüftner, Ádam Lang, Ioannis Kousoulos, Jordi Gómez, Éric Bauthéac (91' Loizos Loizou), Vítor Gomes (103' Charis Mavrias), Marinos Tzionis (76' Ernest Asante), Michal Djuris, Thiago Santos (112' Kiko). Coach: Henning Berg.
Goals: 92' Jordi Gómes 0-1 (p), 107' Thiago Santos 0-2.
Referee: Nathan Verboomen (BEL)
Sent off: 56' Igor Lewczuk.

26.08.20   Stadven DASK Brestski, Brest: Dynamo Brest – FK Sarajevo 2-1 (1-1)
Dynamo Brest: Sergey Ignatovich, Yevhen Khacheridi, Kirill Pechenin, Gaby Kiki, Sergey Kislyak, Roman Yuzepchuk, Pavel Sedko (79' Pavel Savitskiy), David Tweh, Artem Milevskiy (86' Artem Bykov), Mikhail Gordeychuk (73' Sergey Krivets), Abdoulaye Diallo. Coach: Sergey Kovalchuk.
FK Sarajevo: Vladan Kovacevic, Amer Dupovac, Dusan Hodzic, Andrej Djokanovic (80' Haris Handzic), Mirko Oremus (90' Tino-Sven Susic), Hrvoje Milicevic, Amar Rahmanovic, Ivan Jukic (66' Matthias Fanimo), Mersudin Ahmetovic, Benjamin Tatar, Djani Salcin. Coach: Vinko Marinovic
Goals: 3' Mikhail Gordeychuk 1-0, 34' Andrej Djokanovic 1-1, 49' Abdoulaye Diallo 2-1.
Referee: Loukas Soteriou (CYP)

26.08.20   Stadion Wankdorf, Bern: BSC Young Boys – KÍ Klaksvík 3-1 (0-0)
BSC Young Boys: David von Ballmoos, Fabian Lustenberger, Jordan Lefort, Mohamed Camara, Quentin Maceiras (64' Ulisses Garcia), Miralem Sulejmani (64' Marvin Spielmann), Nicolas Moumi Ngamaleu, Christian Fassnacht, Vincent Sierro, Michel Aebischer (74' Christopher Martins), Jean-Pierre Nsamé. Coach: Gerardo Seoane.
KÍ Klaksvík: Kristian Joensen, Odmar Færø, Heini Vatnsdal, Jesper Brinck, Deni Pavlovic (77' Jonn Johanssen), Jákup Andreasen, Jóannes Bjartalid (89' Boris Dosljak), Jóannes Danielsen, Páll Klettskard, Patrik Johannesen, Ole Erik Midtskogen (90+2' Steinbjørn Olsen). Coach: Mikkjal Thomassen.
Goals: 51' Jean-Pierre Nsame 1-0, 57' Miralem Sulejmani 2-0, 79' Jonn Johannesen 2-1, 82' Nicolas Moumi Ngamaleu 3-1.
Referee: Athanasios Tzilos (GRE)

26.08.20   Celtic Park, Glasgow: Celtic FC – Ferencvárosi TC 1-2 (0-1)
Celtic FC: Vassilis Barkas, Hatem Abd Elhamed (78' Jeremie Frimpong), Christopher Jullien, Kristoffer Ajer, Greg Taylor, Scott Brown, James Forrest (78' Albian Ajeti), Callum McGregor, Mohamed Elyounoussi, Olivier Ntcham, Ryan Christie. Coach: Neil Lennon.
Ferencvárosi TC: Dénes Dibusz, Endre Botka, Miha Blazic, Adnan Kovacevic, Eldar Civic, Somália, Dávid Sigér, Igor Kharatin, Isael (71' Franck Boli), Tokmac Nguen (80' Michal Skvarka), Myrto Uzuni (86' Lasha Dvali). Coach: Serhiy Rebrov.
Goals: 7' Dávid Sigér 0-1, 53' Ryan Christie 1-1, 75' Tokmac Nguen 1-2.
Referee: Allard Lindhout (HOL)

THIRD QUALIFYING ROUND

15.09.20   NSK Olimpijs'kyj Stadium, Kyiv: Dynamo Kyiv – AZ Alkmaar 2-0 (0-0)
Dynamo Kyiv: Georgiy Bushchan, Tomasz Kedziora, Oleksandr Karavayev, Vitali Mykolenko, Illia Zabarnyi, Sergiy Sydorchuk, Vitaly Buyalskiy (79' Oleksandr Andrievsky), Carlos de Pena, Mykola Shaparenko (90+1' Bohdan Lyednyev), Gerson Rodrigues, Vladyslav Supriaha (74' Benjamin Verbic). Coach: Mircea Lucescu.
AZ Alkmaar: Marco Bizot, Ron Vlaar (80' Yukinari Sugawara), Jonas Svensson, Owen Wijndal, Jordy Clasie, Fredrik Midtsjø (66' Ferdy Druijf), Dani de Wit, Teun Koopmeiners, Albert Gudmundsson (58' Oussama Idrissi), Myron Boadu, Calvin Stengs. Coach: Arne Slot.
Goals: 49' Gerson Rodrigues 1-0, 86' Mykola Shaparenko 2-0.
Referee: Orel Grinfeld (ISR)

15.09.20   Stadio Toumbas, Saloniki: PAOK Saloniki – SL Benfica 2-1 (0-0)
PAOK Saloniki: Zivko Zivkovic, José Ángel Crespo, Fernando Varela, Sverrir Ingason, Dimitris Giannoulis, Giannis Michailidis, Omar El Kaddouri, Stefan Schwab, Dimitrios Pelkas (67' Andrija Zivkovic), Chuba Akpom (70' Karol Swiderski), Christos Tzolis (80' Anderson Esiti). Coach: Abel Ferreira.
SL Benfica: Odisseas Vlachodimos, Jan Vertonghen, André Almeida, Álex Grimaldo, Rúben Dias, Adel Taarabt (76' Rafa Silva), Pizzi, Julian Weigl, Éverton, Pedrinho (65' Darwin Núñez), Haris Seferovic (72' Carlos Vunícius). Coach: Jorge Jesus.
Goals: 64' Dimitris Giannoulis 1-0, 75' Andrija Zivkovic 2-0, 90+4' Rafa Silva 2-1.
Referee: Dr. Felix Brych (GER)

15.09.20 GHELAMCO-arena, Gent: KAA Gent – Rapid Wien 2-1 (1-0)
KAA Gent: Davy Roef, Dino Arslanagic, Michael Ngadeu-Ngadjui, Núrio Fortuna, Alessio Castro-Montes, Sven Kums, Niklas Dorsch (64' Vadis Odjidja-Ofoe), Elisha Owusu, Giorgi Chakvetadze (60' Roman Bezus), Laurent Depoitre, Roman Yaremchuk (89' Tim Kleindienst).
Coach: Wim De Decker.
Rapid Wien: Richard Strebinger, Filip Stojkovic, Maximilian Hofmann, Maximilian Ullmann, Leo Greiml, Thomas Murg, Dejan Petrovic (86' Srdjan Grahovac), Dejan Ljubicic, Taxiarchis Fountas, Ercan Kara (86' Koya Kitagawa), Kelvin Arase (73' Yusuf Demir).
Coach: Dietmar Kühbauer.
Goals: 36' Niklas Dorsch 1-0, 59' Roman Yaremchuk 2-0 (p), 90+3' Yusuf Demir 2-1.
Referee: Andreas Ekberg (SWE)

16.09.20 Neo GSP Stadium, Nicosia:
Omonia Nikosia – Crvena Zvezda Beograd 1-1 (1-1, 1-1) (a.e.t.)
Omonia Nikosia: Fabiano, Jan Lecjaks, Tomás Hubocan (90+3' Ioannis Kousoulos), Michael Lüftner, Ádam Lang, Jordi Gómez, Éric Bauthéac, Vítor Gomes, Thiago Santos (118' Ernest Asante), Fotis Papoulis (98' Loizos Loizou), Andronikos Kakoullis (65' Kaly Sene).
Coach: Henning Berg.
Crvena Zvezda Beograd: Milan Borjan, Nemanja Milunovic, Milan Rodic (106' Milan Gajic), Milos Degenek, Marko Gobeljic, Aleksandar Katai (101' Zeljko Gavric), Sékou Sanogo, Guélor Kanga, Mirko Ivanic (81' Dusan Jovancic), El Fardou Ben Nabouhane, Aleksa Vukanovic (89' Diego Falcinelli). Coach: Dejan Stankovic.
Goals: 31' Michael Lüftner 1-0, Mirko Ivanic 1-1.
Referee: Chris Kavanagh (ENG)

Omonia Nikosia won 4-2 on penalties after extra time.
Penalties: Gavric 1-0, Jordi Gómez 1-1, Ben Nabouhane 2-1, Vítor Gomes 2-2,
Falcinelli missed, Asante 2-3, Degenek missed, Lejaks 2-4

16.09.20 Groupama Aréna, Budapest: Ferencvárosi TC – Dinamo Zagreb 2-1 (1-1)
Ferencvárosi TC: Dénes Dibusz, Gergö Lovrencsics (25' Endre Botka), Miha Blazic, Adnan Kovacevic (73' Abraham Frimpong), Eldar Civic, Somália, Dávid Sigér, Igor Kharatin, Tokmac Nguen, Franck Boli (68' Isael), Myrto Uzuni. Coach: Serhiy Rebrov.
Dynamo Zagreb: Dominik Livakovic, Marin Leovac, Emir Dilaver, Petar Stojanovic, Josko Gvardiol, Arijan Ademi, Amer Gojak (71' Mario Gavranovic), Lovro Majer (60' Kristijan Jakic), Mislav Orsic (72' Luka Ivanusec), Bruno Petkovic, Lirim Kastrati.
Coach: Zoran Mamic.
Goals: 2' Gergö Lovrencsics 1-0, 23' Myrto Uzuni 1-1 (og), 65' Myrto Uzuni 2-1.
Referee: Tobias Stieler (GER)

16.09.20 AEK Arena – Georgios Karapatakis, Larnaca (CYP):
Qarabag FK – Molde FK 0-0 (a.e.t.)
Qarabag FK: Sahrudin Mahammadaliyev, Maksim Medvedev, Qara Qarayev (77' Ismayil Ibrahimli), Badavi Hüseynov, Kevin Medina, Uros Matic, Filip Ozobic (82' Patrick Andrade), Wilde-Donald Guerrier (114' Elvin Dzhafarquliyev), Abdellah Zoubir, Mahir Emreli (106' Abbas Hüseynov), Owusu Kwabena. Coach: Qurban Qurbanov.
Molde FK: Andreas Linde, Kristoffer Haugen, Stian Gregersen, Magnus Eikrem (79' Ohi Omoijuanfo), Etzaz Hussain (120' Tobias Christensen), Eirik Hestad, Fredrik Aursnes, Martin Ellingsen, Henry Wingo, Erling Knudtzon (69' Ola Brynhildsen), Leke James (99' Mathis Bolly). Coach: Erling Moe.
Referee: Srdjan Jovanovic (SRB)

Etzaz Hussein missed a penalty kick (102').

Molde FK won 6-5 on penalties (after extra time):
Penalties: Omoijuanfo 1-0, Matic 1-1, Aursnes 2-1, Medvedev 2-2, Hestad 3-2, Patrick Andrade 3-3, Christensen 4-3, Medina 4-4, Ellingsen 5-4, Mahammadaliyev 5-5, Haugen 6-5, Badavi Hüseynov missed.

Qarabag FK played their home match at AEK Arena – Georgios Karapatakis, Larnaca (Cyprus), instead of their regular stadium Azersun Arena, Baku, due to travel restrictions related to the COVID-19 pandemic between Azerbaijan and Norway.

16.09.20 Bloomfield Stadium, Tel Aviv: Maccabi Tel Aviv – Dynamo Brest 1-0 (0-0)
Maccabi Tel Aviv: Daniel Tenenbaum, Sheran Yeini, Eitan Tibi, Ofir Davidzada, Saborit, Maor Kandil, Eyal Golasa (65' Avi Rikan), Dor Peretz, Dan Glazer, Dan Bitton (82' Yonathan Cohen), Itay Shechter (57' Nick Blackman. Coach: Georgios Donis.
Dynamo Brest: Sergey Ignatovich, Yevhen Khacheridi (62' Aleksandr Pavlovets), Kirill Pechenin, Gaby Kiki, Sergey Kislyak, Roman Yuzepchuk, Pavel Sedko, David Tweh, Artem Milevskiy (86' Artem Bykov), Mikhail Gordeychuk (70' Pavel Savitskiy), Abdoulaye Diallo. Coach: Sergey Kovalchuk.
Goal: 50' Dan Bitton 1-0 (p).
Referee: Davide Massa (ITA)

16.09.20 MCH Arena, Herning: FC Midtjylland – BSC Young Boys 3-0 (0-0)
FC Midtjylland: Jesper Hansen, Erik Sviatchenko, Alexander Scholz, Joel Andersson, Paulinho, Awer Mabil, Bozhidar Kraev (62' Pione Sisto), Anders Dreyer (84' Evander), Frank Onyeka, Jens Cajuste, Sory Kaba (78' Júnior Brumado). Coach: Brian Priske.
BSC Young Boys: David von Ballmoos, Fabian Lustenberger, Jordan Lefort, Silvan Hefti, Mohamed Camara, Miralem Sulejmani (66' Marvin Spielmann), Christopher Martins, Nicolas Moumi Ngamaleu (66' Theoson Siebatcheu), Christian Fassnacht (82' Felix Mambimbi), Michel Aebischer, Jean-Pierre Nsamé. Coach: Gerardo Seoane.
Goals: 51' Jordan Lefort 1-0 (og), 61' Anders Dreyer 2-0, 84' Awer Mabil 3-0.
Referee: Georgi Kabakov (BUL)

PLAY-OFF ROUND

22.09.20   Sinobo Stadium, Praha: Slavia Praha – FC Midtjylland 0-0
Slavia Praha: Ondrej Kolár, Jan Boril, Vladimír Coufal, Tomás Holes, David Hovorka, David Zima, Nicolae Stanciu (90+1' Laco Takács), Lukás Masopust (71' Lukás Provod), Petr Sevcík, Peter Olayinka, Stanislav Tecl (59' Petar Musa). Coach: Jindrich Trpisovský.
FC Midtjylland: Jesper Hansen, Erik Sviatchenko, Alexander Scholz, Joel Andersson, Paulinho, Awer Mabil, Anders Dreyer (67' Pione Sisto), Evander (76' Mikael Anderson), Frank Onyeka, Jens Cajuste, Sory Kaba (89' Júnior Brumado). Coach: Brian Priske.
Referee: Cüneyt Çakir (TUR)

22.09.20   Bloomfield Stadium, Tel Aviv: Maccabi Tel Aviv – Red Bull Salzburg 1-2 (1-0)
Maccabi Tel Aviv: Daniel Tenenbaum, Sheran Yeini, Eitan Tibi, Ofir Davidzada, Ben Bitton, Eyal Golasa, Roslan Barsky (61' Tal Ben Haim), Matan Baltaxa (82' Matan Hozez), Dan Bitton, Eden Karzev (71' Itay Shechter), Eylon Almog. Coach: Georgios Donis.
Red Bull Salzburg: Cican Stankovic, Andreas Ulmer, André Ramalho, Max Wöber, Rasmus Kristensen, Masaya Okugawa (76' Noah Okafor), Antoine Bernède, Dominik Szoboszlai (86' Mohamed Camara), Enock Mwepu, Mërgim Berisha (46' Sékou Koïta), Patson Daka. Coach: Jesse Marsch.
Goals: 9' Dan Bitton 1-0, 49' Dominik Szoboszlai 1-1 (p), 57' Masaya Okugawa 1-2.
Referee: Michael Oliver (ENG)

22.09.20   Stadion FK Krasnodar, Krasnodar: FK Krasnodar – PAOK Saloniki 2-1 (1-1)
FK Krasnodar: Matvey Safonov, Sergey Petrov, Cristian Ramírez, Egor Sorokin, Rémy Cabella (81' Daniil Utkin), Victor Claesson, Tonny Vilhena, Kristoffer Olsson, Kaio Pantaleão, Marcus Berg, Wanderson (86' Magomed Suleymanov). Coach: Murad Musaev.
PAOK Saloniki: Zivko Zivkovic, José Ángel Crespo, Fernando Varela, Sverrir Ingason, Dimitris Giannoulis, Giannis Michailidis, Omar El Kaddouri, Stefan Schwab, Andrija Zivkovic, Dimitrios Pelkas (79' Diego Biseswar), Christos Tzolis (84' Karol Swiderski). Coach: Abel Ferreira.
Goals: 32' Dimitrios Pelkas 0-1, 39' Victor Claesson 1-1 (p), 70' Rémy Cabella 2-1.
Referee: Clément Turpin (FRA)

Dimitrios Pelkas missed a penalty kick (7').

23.09.20   Stadio Georgios Karaiskáki, Piraeus:
            Olympiakos Piraeus – Omonia Nikosia 2-0 (0-0)
Olympiakos Piraeus: José Sá, Rafinha, José Holebas, Rúben Semedo, Ousseynou Ba, Mathieu Valbuena, Kostas Fortounis (59' Youssef El-Arabi), Andreas Bouchalakis, Georgios Masouras (59' Lazar Randjelovic), Mady Camara, Koka (76' Yann M'Vila). Coach: Pedro Martins.
Omonia Nikosia: Fabiano, Jan Lecjaks, Tomás Hubocan, Michael Lüftner, Ádam Lang, Jordi Gómez, Éric Bauthéac (87' Loizos Loizou), Vítor Gomes, Thiago Santos, Fotis Papoulis (81' Ernest Asante), Kaly Sene (46' Michal Duris). Coach: Henning Berg.
Goals: 69' Mathieu Valbuena 1-0 (p), 90+2' Youssef El-Arabi 2-0.
Referee: Danny Makkelie (HOL)

23.09.20   Aker Stadion, Molde: Molde FK – Ferencvárosi TC 3-3 (0-1)
Molde FK: Andreas Linde, Kristoffer Haugen, Stian Gregersen, Magnus Eikrem (81 Ohi Omoijuanfo), Etzaz Hussain, Eirik Hestad, Fredrik Aursnes, Martin Ellingsen, Henry Wingo, Erling Knudtzon (57' Ola Brynhildsen), Leke James (89' Mathis Bolly). Coach: Erling Moe.
Ferencvárosi TC: Dénes Dibusz, Endre Botka, Miha Blazic, Abraham Frimpong, Eldar Civic, Somália (71' Dávid Sigér), Igor Kharatin, Aïssa Laïdouni, Tokmac Nguen (88' Isael), Franck Boli (73' Oleksandr Zubkov), Myrto Uzuni. Coach: Serhiy Rebrov.
Goals: 7' Franck Boli 0-1, 52' Myrto Uzumi 0-2, 55' Leke James 1-2, 65' Magnus Eikrem 2-2, 83' Martin Ellingsen 3-2, 87' Igor Kharatin 3-3 (p).
Referee: Carlos Del Cerro Grande (ESP)

23.09.20   GHELAMCO-arena, Gent: KAA Gent – Dynamo Kyiv 1-2 (1-1)
KAA Gent: Davy Roef, Igor Plastun, Michael Ngadeu-Ngadjui, Núrio Fortuna, Alessio Castro-Montes, Vadis Odjidja-Ofoe (62' Jordan Botaka), Roman Bezus, Niklas Dorsch, Elisha Owusu, Laurent Depoitre (72' Milad Mohammadi), Roman Yaremchuk (23' Tim Kleindienst). Coach: Wim De Decker.
Dynamo Kyiv: Georgiy Bushchan, Tomasz Kedziora, Oleksandr Karavayev, Vitali Mykolenko, Illia Zabarnyi, Sergiy Sydorchuk, Vitaly Buyalskiy, Carlos de Pena, Mykola Shaparenko (82' Volodymyr Shepelyev), Gerson Rodrigues (59' Viktor Tsygankov), Vladyslav Supriaha (66' Benjamin Verbic). Coach: Mircea Lucescu.
Goals: 9' Vladyslav Supriaha 0-1, 41' Tim Kleindienst 1-1, 79' Carlos de Pena 1-2.
Referee: Ovidiu Alin Hategan (ROM)
Sent off: 53' Roman Bezus.

29.09.20   Neo GSP Stadium, Nicosia: Omonia Nikosia – Olympiakos Piraeus 0-0
Omonia Nikosia: Fabiano, Jan Lecjaks, Tomás Hubocan, Michael Lüftner, Ádam Lang, Ioannis Kousoulos, Éric Bauthéac, Vítor Gomes, Marinos Tzionis (84' Kaly Sene), Michal Duris (70' Andronikos Kakoullis), Fotis Papoulis (70' Ernest Asante). Coach: Henning Berg.
Olympiakos Piraeus: José Sá, Rafinha, José Holebas, Rúben Semedo, Ousseynou Ba, Mathieu Valbuena (90+2' Kostas Fortounis), Yann M'Vila, Andreas Bouchalakis, Lazar Randjelovic (75' Georgios Masouras), Mady Camara (90+2' Cafú), Youssef El-Arabi.
Coach: Pedro Martins.
Referee: Antonio Miguel Mateu Lahoz (ESP)

29.09.20   Groupama Aréna, Budapest: Ferencvárosi TC – Molde FK 0-0
Ferencvárosi TC: Dénes Dibusz, Gergö Lovrencsics, Marcel Heister, Endre Botka, Miha Blazic, Somália (87' Abraham Frimpong), Dávid Sigér (79' Aïssa Laïdouni), Igor Kharatin, Tokmac Nguen (79' Isael), Oleksandr Zubkov, Myrto Uzuni. Coach: Serhiy Rebrov.
Molde FK: Andreas Linde, Kristoffer Haugen, Stian Gregersen, Magnus Pedersen, Magnus Eikrem, Etzaz Hussain (83' Ohi Omoijuanfo), Eirik Hestad, Fredrik Aursnes, Martin Ellingsen, Erlind Knudtzon (64' Ola Brynhildsen), Leke James. Coach: Erling Moe.
Referee: Björn Kuipers (HOL)

Ferencvárosi TC won on away goals.

29.09.20   NSK Olimpijs'kyj Stadium, Kyiv: Dynamo Kyiv – KAA Gent 3-0 (2-0)
Dynamo Kyiv: Georgiy Bushchan, Tomasz Kedziora, Oleksandr Karavayev, Vitali Mykolenko, Illia Zabarnyi, Sergiy Sydorchuk, Vitaly Buyalskiy, Carlos de Pena (59' Benjamin Verbic), Mykola Shaparenko (77' Oleksandr Andrievsky), Gerson Rodrigues (60' Viktor Tsygankov), Vladyslav Supriaha. Coach: Mircea Lucescu.
KAA Gent: Davy Roef, Igor Plastun, Michael Ngadeu-Ngadjui, Núrio Fortuna, Alessio Castro-Montes (65' Jordan Botaka), Niklas Dorsch, Elisha Owusu (54' Sulayman Marreh), Laurent Depoitre (74' Matisse Samoise), Tim Kleindienst, Anderson Niangbo, Osman Bukari.
Coach: Wim De Decker.
Goals: 9' Vitaly Buyalskiy 1-0, 36' Carlos de Pena 2-0 (p), Gerson Rodrigues 3-0 (p).
Referee: Szymon Marciniak (POL)

30.09.20   MCH Arena, Herning: FC Midtjylland – Slavia Praha 4-1 (0-1)
FC Midtjylland: Jesper Hansen, Erik Sviatchenko, Alexander Scholz, Joel Andersson, Paulinho, Pione Sisto (58' Anders Dreyer), Awer Mabil (90+2' Mikael Anderson), Evander (58' Bozhidar Kraev), Frank Onyeka, Jens Cajuste, Sory Kaba. Coach: Brian Priske.
Slavia Praha: Ondrej Kolár, Ondrej Kúdela, Jan Boril, Vladimír Coufal, Tomás Holes, David Hovorka, Nicolae Stanciu (68' Ibrahim Traoré), Lukás Masopust (73' Petar Musa), Petr Sevcík, Peter Olayinka (84' Jan Kuchta), Lukás Provod. Coach: Jindrich Trpisovský.
Goals: 3' Peter Olayinka 0-1, 65' Sory Kaba 1-1, 84' Alexander Scholz 2-1 (p), 88' Frank Onyeka 3-1, 90+1' Andres Dreyer 4-1.
Referee: Damir Skomina (SVK)

Sory Kaba missed a penalty kick (81').

30.09.20   Red Bull Arena, Wals-Siezenheim:
           Red Bull Salzburg – Maccabi Tel Aviv 3-1 (2-1)
Red Bull Salzburg: Cican Stankovic, Andreas Ulmer, André Ramalho, Albert Vallci, Max Wöber, Masaya Okugawa (82' Noah Okafor), Dominik Szoboszlai, Enock Mwepu, Mohamed Camara (74' Zlatko Junuzovic), Patson Daka, Sékou Koïta (66' Mërgim Berisha).
Coach: Jesse Marsch.
Maccabi Tel Aviv: Daniel Tenenbaum, Sheran Yeini, Eitan Tibi, Ben Bitton (65' Matan Hozez), Maor Kandil (74' Amit Glazer), Eyal Golasa, Matan Baltaxa, Dan Bitton, Eden Karzev, Itay Shechter, Eylon Almog (75' Ronen Hanzis). Coach: Georgios Donis.
Goals: 16' Patson Daka 1-0, 30' Eden Karzev 1-1, 45+4' Dominik Szoboszlai 2-1 (p), 68' Patson Daka 3-1.
Referee: Dr. Felix Brych (GER)

30.09.20   Stadio Toumbas, Saloniki: PAOK Saloniki – FK Krasnodar 1-2 (0-0)
PAOK Saloniki: Zivko Zivkovic, José Ángel Crespo (59' Moussa Wagué), Fernando Varela (76' Karol Swiderski)), Sverrir Ingason, Dimitris Giannoulis, Giannis Michailidis, Omar El Kaddouri, Stefan Schwab, Andrija Zivkovic, Dimitrios Pelkas (59' Antonio Colak), Christos Tzolis. Coach: Abel Ferreira.
FK Krasnodar: Matvey Safonov, Aleksandr Martynovich, Sergey Petrov, Cristian Ramírez, Rémy Cabella (85' Magomed Suleymanov), Yuri Gazinskiy (83' Ruslan Kambolov), Victor Claesson, Tonny Vilhena, Kaio Pantaleão, Daniil Utkin (58' Igor Smolnikov), Marcus Berg.
Coach: Murad Musaev.
Goals: 73' Giannis Michailidis 0-1 (og), 77' Omar El Kaddouri 1-1, 77' Rémy Cabella 1-2.
Referee: Daniele Orsato (ITA)

GROUP STAGE

GROUP A

FC Bayern München	6	5	1	0	18 -	5	16
Atlético Madrid	6	2	3	1	7 -	8	9
Red Bull Salzburg	6	1	1	4	10 -	17	4
Lokomotiv Moscow	6	0	3	3	5 -	10	3

GROUP B

Real Madrid CF	6	3	1	2	11 -	9	10
Borussia Mönchengladbach	6	2	2	2	16 -	9	8
Shakhtar Donetsk	6	2	2	2	5 -	12	8
Internazionale	6	1	3	2	7 -	9	6

GROUP C

Manchester City	6	5	1	0	13 -	1	16
FC Porto	6	4	1	1	10 -	3	13
Olympiakos Piraeus	6	1	0	5	2 -	10	3
Olympique Marseille	6	1	0	5	2 -	13	3

GROUP D

Liverpool FC	6	4	1	1	10 -	3	13
Atalanta Bergamo	6	3	2	1	10 -	8	11
AFC Ajax	6	2	1	3	7 -	7	7
FC Midtjylland	6	0	2	4	4 -	13	2

GROUP E

Chelsea FC	6	4	2	0	14 -	2	14
Sevilla CF	6	4	1	1	9 -	8	13
FK Krasnodar	6	1	2	3	6 -	11	5
Stade de Rennes	6	0	1	5	3 -	11	1

GROUP F

Borussia Dortmund	6	4	1	1	12 -	5	13
Lazio Roma	6	2	4	0	11 -	7	10
Club Brugge KV	6	2	2	2	8 -	10	8
Zenit Saint Petersburg	6	0	1	5	4 -	13	1

GROUP G

Juventus FC	6	5	0	1	14 -	4	15
FC Barcelona	6	5	0	1	16 -	5	15
Dynamo Kyiv	6	1	1	4	4 -	13	4
Ferencvárosi TC	6	0	1	5	5 -	17	1

GROUP H

Paris Saint-Germain	6	4	0	2	13	-	6	12
RB Leipzig	6	4	0	2	11	-	12	12
Manchester United	6	3	0	3	15	-	10	9
Istanbul Basaksehir	6	1	0	5	7	-	18	3

GROUP A

21.10.20 Red Bull Arena, Wals-Siezenheim:
Red Bull Salzburg – Lokomotiv Moscow 2-2 (1-1)
Red Bull Salzburg: Cican Stankovic, Andreas Ulmer, André Ramalho, Albert Vallci, Max Wöber, Zlatko Junuzovic (84' Noah Okafor), Dominik Szoboszlai, Enock Mwepu, Mohamed Camara (73' Masaya Okugawa), Patson Daka, Sékou Koïta (66' Mërgim Berisha). Coach: Jesse Marsch.
Lokomotiv Moscow: Guilherme, Vedran Corluka, Maciej Rybus, Dmitri Zhivoglyadov, Murilo Cerqueira, Grzegorz Krychowiak, Anton Miranchuk (69' Vitaliy Lisakovich), Daniil Kulikov, Fedor Smolov (62' Dmitry Rybchinsky), Éder (69' Zé Luís), Rifat Zhemaletdinov (63' François Kamano). Coach: Marko Nikolic.
Goals: 19' Éder 0-1, 45' Dominik Szoboszlai 1-1, 50' Zlatko Junuzovic 2-1, 75' Vitaliy Lisakovich 2-2.
Referee: Serdar Gözübüyük (HOL) Attendance: 3,000

21.10.20 Allianz Arena, München: FC Bayern München – Atlético Madrid 4-0 (2-0)
FC Bayern München: Manuel Neuer, David Alaba, Niklas Süle, Lucas Hernández, Benjamin Pavard (73' Bouna Sarr), Leon Goretzka (83' Javi Martínez), Corentin Tolisso, Joshua Kimmich, Thomas Müller (83' Alphonso Davies), Robert Lewandowski (83' Eric Maxim Choupo-Moting), Kingsley Coman (73' Douglas Costa). Coach: Hans Flick.
Atlético Madrid: Jan Oblak, Stefan Savic, Kieran Trippier, Felipe Monteiro, Renan Lodi, Héctor Herrera, Koke (79' Lucas Torreira), Yannick Carrasco (76' Vitolo), Marcos Llorente (79' Thomas Lemar), Luis Suárez (75' Ángel Correa), João Félix. Coach: Diego Simeone.
Goals: 28' Kingsley Coman 1-0, 41' Leon Goretzka 2-0, 66' Corentin Tolisso 3-0, 72' Kingsley Coman 4-0.
Referee: Michael Oliver (ENG)

27.10.20 RZD Arena, Moscow: Lokomotiv Moscow – FC Bayern München 1-2 (0-1)
Lokomotiv Moscow: Guilherme, Vedran Corluka (46' Slobodan Rajkovic), Maciej Rybus, Dmitri Zhivoglyadov, Murilo Cerqueira, Vladislav Ignatiev (76' Rifat Zhemaletdinov), Grzegorz Krychowiak, Anton Miranchuk, Daniil Kulikov (89' Vitaliy Lisakovich), Fedor Smolov (75' Dmitry Rybchinsky), Zé Luís. Coach: Marko Nikolic.
FC Bayern München: Manuel Neuer, David Alaba, Niklas Süle, Lucas Hernández, Benjamin Pavard, Leon Goretzka (46' Javi Martínez), Corentin Tolisso, Joshua Kimmich, Thomas Müller (46' Serge Gnaby), Robert Lewandowski, Kingsley Coman (69' Douglas Costa). Coach: Hans Flick.
Goals: 13' Leon Goretzka 0-1, 70' Anton Miranchuk 1-1, 79' Joshua Kimmich 1-2.
Referee: István Kovács (ROM) Attendance: 8,196

27.10.20   Estadio Wanda Metropolitano, Madrid:
Atlético Madrid – Red Bull Salzburg 3-2 (1-1)
Atlético Madrid: Jan Oblak, Stefan Savic, Kieran Trippier, Felipe Monteiro, Renan Lodi (82' Mario Hermoso), Héctor Herrera (82' Lucas Torreira), Koke, Marcos Llorente, Luis Suárez (82' Thomas Lemar), Ángel Correa, João Félix. Coach: Diego Simeone.
Red Bull Salzburg: Cican Stankovic, Andreas Ulmer, André Ramalho, Max Wöber (63' Jérôme Onguéné), Rasmus Kristensen, Zlatko Junuzovic (63' Majeed Ashimeru), Dominik Szoboszlai, Enock Mwepu, Mohamed Camara, Mërgim Berisha, Patson Daka (30' Sékou Koïta, 84' Noah Okafor). Coach: Jesse Marsch.
Goals: 29' Marcos Llorente 1-0, 40' Dominik Szobolszlai 1-1, 47' Felipe Monteiro 1-2 (og), 52', 85' João Félix 2-2, 3-2.
Referee: Ovidiu Alin Hategan (ROM)

03.11.20   RZD Arena, Moscow: Lokomotiv Moscow – Atlético Madrid 1-1 (1-1)
Lokomotiv Moscow: Guilherme, Slobodan Rajkovic, Maciej Rybus, Dmitri Zhivoglyadov, Murilo Cerqueira, Vladislav Ignatiev, Grzegorz Krychowiak, Anton Miranchuk (89' Dmitry Rybchinsky), Daniil Kulikov, Fedor Smolov (64' Rifat Zhemaletdinov), Zé Luís. Coach: Marko Nikolic.
Atlético Madrid: Jan Oblak, Stefan Savic, Kieran Trippier, José Giménez, Renan Lodi, Héctor Herrera, Saúl (46' Koke), Marcos Llorente (69' Vitolo, 78' Lucas Torreira), Luis Suárez, Ángel Correa, (69' Thomas Lemar) João Félix. Coach: Diego Simeone.
Goals: 18' José Giménez 0-1, 25' Anton Miranchuk 1-1 (p).
Referee: Benoît Bastien (FRA)   Attendance: 8,147

03.11.20   Red Bull Arena, Wals-Siezenheim:
Red Bull Salzburg – FC Bayern München 2-6 (1-2)
Red Bull Salzburg: Cican Stankovic, Andreas Ulmer, André Ramalho, Max Wöber, Rasmus Kristensen, Zlatko Junuzovic (65' Masaya Okugawa), Dominik Szoboszlai, Enock Mwepu, Mohamed Camara, Mërgim Berisha (76' Jérôme Onguéné), Sékou Koïta (65' Noah Okafor). Coach: Jesse Marsch.
FC Bayern München: Manuel Neuer, Jérôme Boateng, David Alaba, Lucas Hernández, Benjamin Pavard (74' Bouna Sarr), Corentin Tolisso (74' Javi Martínez), Joshua Kimmich, Thomas Müller (90+1' Jamal Musiala), Robert Lewandowski, Serge Gnaby (90+1' Douglas Costa), Kingsley Coman (74' Leroy Sané). Coach: Hans Flick.
Goals: 4' Mërgim Berisha 1-0, 21' Robert Lewandowski 1-1 (p), 44' R. Kristensen 1-2 (og), 66' Masaya Okugawa 2-2, 79' Jérôme Boateng 2-3, 83' Leroy Sané 2-4, 88' Robert Lewandowski 2-5, 90+2' Lucas Hernández 2-6.
Referee: Danny Makkelie (HOL)

25.11.20   Estadio Wanda Metropolitano, Madrid: Atlético Madrid – Lokomotiv Moscow 0-0
Atlético Madrid: Jan Oblak, Stefan Savic, Kieran Trippier, José Giménez, Renan Lodi (60' Mario Hermoso), Saúl, Koke, Yannick Carrasco (80' Sergio Camello), Marcos Llorente (60' Thomas Lemar), Ángel Correa, João Félix. Coach: Diego Simeone.
Lokomotiv Moscow: Guilherme, Vedran Corluka, Maciej Rybus, Dmitri Zhivoglyadov, Murilo Cerqueira, Vladislav Ignatiev, Grzegorz Krychowiak, Anton Miranchuk (76' Stanislav Magkeev), Daniil Kulikov, Zé Luís, François Kamano (76') Dmitry Rybchinsky). Coach: Marko Nikolic.
Referee: Slavko Vincic (SVN)

25.11.20   Allianz Arena, München: FC Bayern München – Red Bull Salzurg 3-1 (1-0)
FC Bayern München: Manuel Neuer, Jérôme Boateng, David Alaba, Benjamin Pavard (63'
Lucas Hernández), Chris Richards (79' Javi Martínez), Leon Goretzka, Marc Roca, Thomas
Müller, Robert Lewandowski, Serge Gnaby (62' Leroy Sané), Kingsley Coman (78' Douglas
Costa). Coach: Hans Flick.
Red Bull Salzburg: Cican Stankovic, Andreas Ulmer, André Ramalho, Max Wöber, Rasmus
Kristensen, Zlatko Junuzovic (71' Karim Adeyemi), Dominik Szoboszlai (71' Luka Sucic),
Enock Mwepu (72' Majeed Ashimeru), Mohamed Camara, Mërgim Berisha, Sékou Koïta.
Coach: Jesse Marsch.
Goals: 43' Robert Lewandowski 1-0, 52' Kingsley Coman 2-0, 68' Leroy Sané 3-0,
73' Mërgim Berisha 3-1.
Referee: Orel Grinfeld (ISR)
Sent off: 66' Marc Roca.

01.12.20   RZD Arena, Moscow: Lokomotiv Moscow – Red Bull Salzburg 1-3 (0-2)
Lokomotiv Moscow: Guilherme, Vedran Corluka, Slobodan Rajkovic (46' Vladislav Ignatiev),
Maciej Rybus, Vitaliy Lystsov (46' Anton Miranchuk), Dmitri Zhivoglyadov (84' Dmitry
Rybchinsky), Murilo Cerqueira, Stanislav Magkeev, Éder, Zé Luís (89' François Kamano),
Vitaliy Lisakovich (46' Maksim Mukhin). Coach: Marko Nikolic.
Red Bull Salzburg: Cican Stankovic, Andreas Ulmer, André Ramalho, Max Wöber, Rasmus
Kristensen, Zlatko Junuzovic, Dominik Szoboszlai (77' Patson Daka), Enock Mwepu,
Mohamed Camara (69' Luka Sucic), Mërgim Berisha (90+3' Jérôme Onguéné), Sékou Koïta
(70' Karim Adeyemi). Coach: Jesse Marsch.
Goals: 28', 41' Mërgim Berisha 0-1, 0-2, 79' Anton Miranchuk 1-2 (p),
81' Karim Adeyemi 1-3.
Referee: Ali Palabiyik (TUR)   Attendance: 6,759

01.12.20   Estadio Wanda Metropolitano, Madrid:
           Atlético Madrid – FC Bayern München 1-1 (1-0)
Atlético Madrid: Jan Oblak, Stefan Savic, Kieran Trippier, José Giménez (68' Felipe
Monteiro), Mario Hermoso, Saúl, Koke, Yannick Carrasco (87' Renan Lodi), Marcos Llorente,
Ángel Correa (80' Héctor Herrera), João Félix (87' Thomas Lemar). Coach: Diego Simeone.
FC Bayern München: Alexander Nübel, David Alaba, Bouna Sarr (62' Chris Richards), Niklas
Süle, Lucas Hernández, Bright Arrey-Mbi (61') Serge Gnabry, Javi Martínez (62' Thomas
Müller), Douglas Costa (86' Joshua Zirkzee), Jamal Musiala (76' Angelo Stiller), Eric Maxim
Choupo-Moting, Leroy Sané. Coach: Hans Flick.
Goals: 26' João Félix 1-0, 86' Thomas Müller 1-1 (p).
Referee: Clément Turpin (FRA)

09.12.20   Allianz Arena, München: FC Bayern München – Lokomotiv Moscow 2-0 (0-0)
FC Bayern München: Manuel Neuer, Jérôme Boateng (69' Chris Richards), Bouna Sarr, Niklas
Süle, Alphonso Davies (69' Lucas Hernández), Douglas Costa, Leon Goretzka (61' Jamal
Musiala), Marc Roca, Eric Maxim Choupo-Moting, Thomas Müller (46' Serge Gnabry), Leroy
Sané (84' Angelo Stiller). Coach: Hans Flick.
Lokomotiv Moscow: Guilherme, Vedran Corluka, Slobodan Rajkovic, Maciej Rybus, Dmitri
Zhivoglyadov, Stanislav Magkeev, Vladislav Ignatiev, Anton Miranchuk, Dmitry Rybchinsky
(88' Aleksandr Silyanov), Éder, François Kamano (76' Nikita Iosifov). Coach: Marko Nikolic.
Goals: 63' Niklas Süle 1-0, 80' Eric Maxim Choupo-Moting 2-0.
Referee: Sandro Schärer (SUI)

09.12.20   Red Bull Arena, Wals-Siezenheim: Red Bull Salzburg – Atlético Madrid 0-2 (0-1)
Red Bull Salzburg: Cican Stankovic, Andreas Ulmer, André Ramalho, Max Wöber (89'
Jérôme Onguéné), Rasmus Kristensen, Zlatko Junuzovic, Dominik Szoboszlai (89' Masaya
Okugawa), Enock Mwepu (89' Luka Sucic), Mërgim Berisha, Patson Daka (73' Noah Okafor),
Sékou Koïta (70' Karim Adeyemi). Coach: Jesse Marsch.
Atlético Madrid: Jan Oblak, Stefan Savic, Kieran Trippier, Felipe Monteiro, Mario Hermoso,
Saúl (64' Héctor Herrera), Koke, Yannick Carrasco (89' Thomas Lemar), Marcos Llorente
(90+1' Renan Lodi), Luis Suárez (64' Ángel Correa), João Félix (89' Lucas Torreira).
Coach: Diego Simeone.
Goals: 39' Mario Hermoso 0-1, 86' Yannick Carrasco 0-2.
Referee: Anthony Taylor (ENG)

GROUP B

21.10.20   Estadio Alfredo Di Stéfano, Madrid: Real Madrid CF – Shakhtar Donetsk 2-3 (0-3)
Real Madrid CF: Thibaut Courtois, Marcelo, Raphaël Varane, Ferland Mendy, Éder Militão,
Luka Modric (70' Toni Kroos), Casemiro, Federico Valverde, Luka Jovic (59' Vinícius
Júnior), Marco Asensio, Rodrygo (46' Karim Benzema). Coach: Zinédine Zidane.
Shakhtar Donetsk: Anatolii Trubin, Davit Khocholava, Valeriy Bondar, Dodô, Viktor
Kornienko, Dentinho (86' Heorhii Sudakov), Marlos, Manor Solomon (90+2' Vitão), Maycon,
Marcos Antônio (90+4' Bogdan Viunnik), Mateus Martins Tetê. Coach: Luís Castro.
Goals: 29' Mateus Martins Tetê 0-1, 33' Raphaël Varane 0-2 (og), 42' Manor Solomon 0-3,
54' Luka Modric 1-3, 59' Vinicíus Júnior 2-3.
Referee: Srdjan Jovanovic (SRB)

*Real Madrid CF played their home matches at Estadio Alfredo Di Stéfano, Madrid, instead of
their regular stadium Santiago Bernabéu, Madrid.*

21.10.20   Stadio Giuseppe Meazza, Milano:
           Internazionale – Borussia Mönchengladbach 2-2 (0-0)
Internazionale: Samir Handanovic, Matteo Darmian, Aleksandar Kolarov, Stefan de Vrij,
Danilo D'Ambrosio, Ivan Perisic (79' Alessandro Bastoni), Arturo Vidal, Christian Eriksen
(79' Marcelo Brozovic), Nicolò Barella, Alexis Sánchez (46' Lautaro Martínez), Romelu
Lukaku. Coach: Antonio Conte.
Borussia Mönchengladbach: Yann Sommer, Stefan Lainer, Matthias Ginter, Nico Elvedi,
Ramy Bensebaini, Christoph Kramer, Jonas Hofmann, Florian Neuhaus, Alassane Pléa (90'
Lars Stindl), Breel Embolo (74' Patrick Herrmann), Marcus Thuram (90+5' Hannes Wolf).
Coach: Marco Rose.
Goals: 49' Romelu Lukaku 1-0, 63' Ramy Bensebaini 1-1 (p), 84' Janos Hofmann 1-2,
90' Romelu Lukaku 2-2.
Referee: Björn Kuipers (HOL)   Attendance: 1,000

27.10.20 NSK Olimpijs'kyj Stadium, Kyiv: Shakhtar Donetsk – Internazionale 0-0
Shakhtar Donetsk: Anatolii Trubin, Davit Khocholava (62' Mykola Matvienko), Valeriy Bondar, Dodô, Viktor Kornienko, Dentinho (15' Taison), Marlos (88' Alan Patrick), Manor Solomon, Maycon, Marcos Antônio, Mateus Martins Tetê. Coach: Luís Castro.
Internazionale: Samir Handanovic, Ashley Young (85' Andrea Pinamonti), Stefan de Vrij, Danilo D'Ambrosio (80' Matteo Darmian), Achraf Hakimi, Alessandro Bastoni, Arturo Vidal (79' Christian Eriksen), Marcelo Brozovic, Nicolò Barella, Romelu Lukaku, Lautaro Martínez (72' Ivan Perisic). Coach: Antonio Conte.
Referee: Georgi Kabakov (BUL)   Attendance: 10,178

Shakhtar Donetsk played their home matches at NSK Olimpijs'kyj Stadium, Kyiv, instead of their regular stadium Donbass Arena, Donetsk, due to the war conditions in Eastern Ukraine.

27.10.20 Stadion im BORUSSIA-PARK, Mönchengladbach:
Borussia Mönchengladbach – Real Madrid CF 2-2 (1-0)
Borussia Mönchengladbach: Yann Sommer, Stefan Lainer, Matthias Ginter, Nico Elvedi, Ramy Bensebaini, Lars Stindl (79' Hannes Wolf), Christoph Kramer, Jonas Hofmann, Florian Neuhaus, Alassane Pléa (79' Breel Embolo), Marcus Thuram (71' Patrick Herrmann). Coach: Marco Rose.
Real Madrid CF: Thibaut Courtois, Sergio Ramos, Raphaël Varane, Ferland Mendy, Toni Kroos (71' Luka Modric), Casemiro, Lucas Vázquez, Federico Valverde, Karim Benzema, Marco Asensio, (84' Rodrygo), Vinícius Júnior (70' Eden Hazard). Coach: Zinédine Zidane.
Goals: 33', 58' Marcus Thuram 1-0, 2-0, 87' Karim Benzema 2-1, 90+3' Casemiro 2-2.
Referee: Orel Grinfeld (ISR)

03.11.20 NSK Olimpijs'kyj Stadium, Kyiv:
Shakhtar Donetsk – Borussia Mönchengladbach 0-6 (0-4)
Shakhtar Donetsk: Anatolii Trubin, Davit Khocholava, Valeriy Bondar, Dodô, Viktor Kornienko, Marlos (46' Viktor Kovalenko), Taison (46' Júnior Moraes), Manor Solomon, Maycon (69' Taras Stepanenko), Marcos Antônio (46' Alan Patrick), Mateus Martins Tetê. Coach: Luís Castro.
Borussia Mönchengladbach: Yann Sommer, Stefan Lainer (82' Michael Lang), Matthias Ginter, Nico Elvedi (82' Tony Jantschke), Ramy Bensebaini, Lars Stindl (69' Hannes Wolf), Christoph Kramer, Jonas Hofmann (75' Valentino Lazaro), Florian Neuhaus, Alassane Pléa (82' Ibrahima Traoré), Marcus Thuram. Coach: Marco Rose.
Goals: 8' Alassane Pléa 0-1, 17' Valeriy Bondar 0-2 (og), 26' Alassane Pléa 0-3, 44' Ramy Bensebaini 0-4, 65' Lars Stindl 0-5, 78' Alassane Pléa 0-6.
Referee: Serdar Güzübüyük (HOL)

03.11.20 Estadio Alfredo Di Stéfano, Madrid: Real Madrid CF – Internazionale 3-2 (2-1)
Real Madrid CF: Thibaut Courtois, Sergio Ramos, Raphaël Varane, Ferland Mendy, Toni Kroos (78' Luka Modric), Casemiro, Lucas Vázquez, Federico Valverde, Karim Benzema, Eden Hazard (64' Vinícius Júnior), Marco Asensio (64' Rodrygo). Coach: Zinédine Zidane.
Internazionale: Samir Handanovic, Ashley Young, Stefan de Vrij, Danilo D'Ambrosio, Achraf Hakimi, Alessandro Bastoni, Ivan Perisic (78' Alexis Sánchez), Arturo Vidal (87' Radja Nainggolan), Marcelo Brozovic, Nicolò Barella (78' Roberto Gagliardini), Lautaro Martínez. Coach: Antonio Conte.
Goals: 25' Karim Benzema 1-0, 33' Sergio Ramos 2-0, 35' Lautaro Martínez 2-1, 68' Ivan Perisic 2-2, 80' Rodrygo 3-2.
Referee: Clément Turpin (FRA)

25.11.20   Stadion im BORUSSIA-PARK, Mönchengladbach:
Borussia Mönchengladbach – Shakhtar Donetsk 4-0 (3-0)
Borussia Mönchengladbach: Yann Sommer, Oscar Wendt, Stefan Lainer, Matthias Ginter, Nico Elvedi, Lars Stindl (81' László Bénes), Christoph Kramer, Valentino Lazaro (69' Patrick Herrmann), Florian Neuhaus (69' Denis Zakaria), Breel Embolo (69' Alassane Pléa), Marcus Thuram (84') Ibrahima Traoré. Coach: Marco Rose.
Shakhtar Donetsk: Andriy Pyatov, Sergiy Kryvtsov, Mykola Matvienko, Valeriy Bondar, Dodô, Marlos (70' Marcos Antônio), Taras Stepanenko, Alan Patrick (81' Maycon), Manor Solomon (59' Fernando), Mateus Martins Tetê, Júnior Moraes. Coach: Luís Castro.
Goals: 17' Lars Stindl 1-0 (p), 34' Nico Elvedi 2-0, 45+1' Breel Embolo 3-0, 77' Oscar Wendt 4-0.
Referee: Cüneyt Çakir (TUR)

25.11.20   Stadio Giuseppe Meazza, Milano: Internazionale – Real Madrid CF 0-2 (0-1)
Internazionale: Samir Handanovic, Ashley Young, Stefan de Vrij, Milan Skriniar, Achraf Hakimi (63' Alexis Sánchez), Alessandro Bastoni (46' Danilo D'Ambrosio), Arturo Vidal, Roberto Gagliardini (78' Stefano Sensi), Nicolò Barella, Romelu Lukaku (86' Christian Eriksen), Lautaro Martínez (46' Ivan Perisic). Coach: Antonio Conte.
Real Madrid CF: Thibaut Courtois, Nacho, Dani Carvajal, Raphaël Varane, Ferland Mendy, Luka Modric, Toni Kroos, Lucas Vázquez, Martin Ødegaard (58' Casemiro), Eden Hazard (78' Vinícius Júnior), Mariano Díaz (58' Rodrygo). Coach: Zinédine Zidane.
Goals: 7' Eden Hazard 0-1 (p), 59' Achraf Hakimi 0-2 (og).
Referee: Anthony Taylor (ENG)
Sent off: 33' Arturo Vidal.

01.12.20   NSK Olimpijs'kyj Stadium, Kyiv: Shakhtar Donetsk – Real Madrid CF 2-0 (0-0)
Shakhtar Donetsk: Anatolii Trubin, Mykola Matvienko, Valeriy Bondar, Dodô, Vitão, Marlos (73' Maycon), Taras Stepanenko, Taison (74' Manor Solomon), Viktor Kovalenko (85' Alan Patrick), Mateus Martins Tetê, Júnior Moraes (25' Dentinho, 85' Fernando).
Coach: Luís Castro.
Real Madrid CF: Thibaut Courtois, Nacho, Raphaël Varane, Ferland Mendy, Luka Modric, Toni Kroos, Lucas Vázquez, Martin Ødegaard (77' Isco), Karim Benzema (77' Mariano Díaz), Marco Asensio, Rodrygo (77' Vinícius Júnior). Coach: Zinédine Zidane.
Goals: 57' Dentinho 1-0, 82' Manor Solomon 2-0.
Referee: Ovidio Alin Hategan (ROM)

01.12.20   Stadion im BORUSSIA-PARK, Mönchengladbach:
Borussia Mönchengladbach – Internazionale 2-3 (1-1)
Borussia Mönchengladbach: Yann Sommer, Oscar Wendt (78' Hannes Wolf), Tony Jantschke (46') Denis Zakaria, Stefan Lainer, Matthias Ginter, Lars Stindl (70' Breel Embolo), Christoph Kramer, Valentino Lazaro, Florian Neuhaus, Alassane Pléa, Marcus Thuram.
Coach: Marco Rose.
Internazionale: Samir Handanovic, Ashley Young (87' Ivan Perisic), Matteo Darmian (60' Achraf Hakimi), Stefan de Vrij, Milan Skriniar, Alessandro Bastoni, Marcelo Brozovic, Roberto Gagliardini, Nicolò Barella, Romelu Lukaku, Lautaro Martínez (71' Alexis Sánchez).
Coach: Antonio Conte.
Goals: 17' Matteo Darmian 0-1, 45+1' Alassane Pléa 1-1, 64', 73' Romelu Lukaku 1-2, 1-3, 76' Alassane Pléa 2-3.
Referee: Danny Makkelie (HOL)

09.12.20 Estadio Alfredo Di Stéfano, Madrid:
Real Madrid CF – Borussia Mönchengladbach 2-0 (2-0)
Real Madrid CF: Thibaut Courtois, Sergio Ramos, Raphaël Varane, Ferland Mendy, Luka Modric, Toni Kroos, Casemiro, Lucas Vázquez, Karim Benzema, Vinícius Júnior (74' Marco Asensio), Rodrygo (74' Sergio Arribas). Coach: Zinédine Zidane.
Borussia Mönchengladbach: Yann Sommer, Oscar Wendt (78' Valentino Lazaro), Stefan Lainer, Matthias Ginter, Nico Elvedi, Lars Stindl (85' Hannes Wolf), Christoph Kramer (85' László Bénes), Florian Neuhaus, Alassane Pléa, Breel Embolo (46' Denis Zakaria), Marcus Thuram (85' Patrick Herrmann). Coach: Marco Rose.
Goals: 9', 32' Karim Benzema 1-0, 2-0.
Referee: Björn Kuipers (HOL)

09.12.20 Stadio Giuseppe Meazza, Milano: Internazionale – Shakhtar Donetsk 0-0
Internazionale: Samir Handanovic, Ashley Young (68' Ivan Perisic), Stefan de Vrij, Milan Skriniar, Achraf Hakimi (85' Matteo Darmian), Alessandro Bastoni (85' Danilo D'Ambrosio), Marcelo Brozovic, Roberto Gagliardini (75' Alexis Sánchez), Nicolò Barella, Romelu Lukaku, Lautaro Martínez (85' Christian Eriksen). Coach: Antonio Conte.
Shakhtar Donetsk: Anatolii Trubin, Mykola Matvienko, Valeriy Bondar, Dodô, Vitão (36' Davit Khocholava), Marlos (64' Alan Patrick), Taras Stepanenko, Taison (86' Dentinho), Viktor Kovalenko, Maycon, Mateus Martins Tetê (65' Manor Solomon). Coach: Luís Castro.
Referee: Slavko Vinic (SVN)

GROUP C

21.10.20 Etihad Stadium, Manchester: Manchester City – FC Porto 3-1 (1-1)
Manchester City: Ederson Moraes, Kyle Walker, João Cancelo, Rúben Dias, Eric García, Ilkay Gündogan (68' Phil Foden), Bernardo Silva, Rodri Hernández (85' Fernandinho, 90+4' John Stones), Kun Agüero (68' Ferrán Torres), Riyad Mahrez, Raheem Sterling.
Coach: Pep Guardiola.
FC Porto: Agustin Marchesín, Pepe, Chancel Mbemba, Malang Sarr (80' Evanilson), Zaidu Sanusi (76' Shoya Nakajima), Sérgio Oliveira, Mateus Uribe, Fábio Vieira (77' Mehdi Taremi), Jesús Corona (77' Nanu), Moussa Marega, Luis Díaz (55' Wilson Manafá).
Coach: Sérgio Conceição.
Goals: 14' Luis Díaz 0-1, 20' Kun Agüero 1-1 (p), 65' Ilkay Gündogan 2-1, 73' Ferrán Torres 3-1.
Referee: Andris Treimanis (LVA)

21.10.20 Stadio Georgios Karaiskáki, Piraeus:
Olympiakos Piraeus – Olympique Marseille 1-0 (0-0)
Olympiakos Piraeus: José Sá, Rafinha, José Holebas, Rúben Semedo, Ousseynou Ba, Mathieu Valbuena (90+3' Pape Cissé), Yann M'Vila, Andreas Bouchalakis, Georgios Masouras (84' Ahmed Hassan "Koka"), Lazar Randjelovic (78' Kostas Fortounis), Youssef El-Arabi (90+3' Rúben Vinagre). Coach: Pedro Martins.
Olympique Marseille: Steve Mandanda, Hiroki Sakai, Álvaro González, Jordan Amavi, Duje Caleta-Car, Dimitri Payet (76' Nemanja Radonjic), Morgan Sanson (77' Michaël Cuisance), Valentin Rongier, Pape Alassane Gueye (85' Kevin Strootman), Dario Benedetto (77' Luis Henrique), Florian Thauvin (82' Valère Germain). Coach: André Villas-Boas.
Goal: 90+1' Ahmed Hassan "Koka" 1-0.
Referee: Daniele Orsato (ITA)

27.10.20   Estádio do Dragão, Porto: FC Porto – Olympiakos Piraeus 2-0 (1-0)
FC Porto: Agustin Marchesín, Pepe, Chancel Mbemba, Wilson Manafá, Zaidu Sanusi, Sérgio Oliveira (89' Romário Baró), Mateus Uribe, Otávio (70' Marko Grujic), Fábio Vieira (60' Shoya Nakajima), Jesús Corona (69' Evanilson), Moussa Marega. Coach: Sérgio Conceição.
Olympiakos Piraeus: José Sá, Rafinha, José Holebas (70' Rúben Vinagre), Rúben Semedo, Pape Cissé, Mathieu Valbuena (84' Ahmed Hassan "Koka"), Yann M'Vila, Andreas Bouchalakis (84' Pêpê Rodrigues), Georgios Masouras (53' Kostas Fortounis), Lazar Randjelovic (70' Bruma), Youssef El-Arabi. Coach: Pedro Martins.
Goals: 11' Fábio Vieira 1-0, 85' Sérgio Oliveira 2-0.
Referee: Daniels Siebert (GER)   Attendance: 2,450

27.10.20   Orange Vélodrome, Marseille: Olympique Marseille – Manchester City 0-3 (0-1)
Olympique Marseille: Steve Mandanda, Hiroki Sakai, Álvaro González, Jordan Amavi, Duje Caleta-Car, Boubacar Kamara, Leonardo Balerdi, Nemanja Radonjic (78' Dario Benedetto), Valentin Rongier (64' Morgan Sanson), Michaël Cuisance (85' Pape Alassane Gueye), Florian Thauvin (78' Dimitri Payet). Coach: André Villas-Boas.
Manchester City: Ederson Moraes, Kyle Walker, Aymeric Laporte (77' John Stones), Rúben Dias, Ilkay Gündogan (78' Bernardo Silva), Kevin De Bruyne (82' Cole Palmer), Oleksandr Zinchenko (68' João Cancelo), Rodri Hernández, Phil Foden, Raheem Sterling, Ferrán Torres (77' Riyad Mahrez). Coach: Pep Guardiola.
Goals: 18' Ferrán Torres 0-1, 76' Ilkay Gündogan 0-2, 81' Raheem Sterling 0-3.
Referee: Tobias Stieler (GER)

03.11.20   Etihad Stadium, Manchester: Manchester City – Olympiakos Piraeus 3-0 (1-0)
Manchester City: Ederson Moraes, Kyle Walker (82' João Cancelo), Nathan Aké, John Stones, Ilkay Gündogan, Kevin De Bruyne (85' Felix Nmecha), Oleksandr Zinchenko, Phil Foden (69' Rodri Hernández), Riyad Mahrez (69' Gabriel Jesus), Raheem Sterling (82' Bernardo Silva), Ferrán Torres. Coach: Pep Guardiola.
Olympiakos Piraeus: José Sá, Rafinha, José Holebas, Rúben Semedo, Pape Cissé, Mathieu Valbuena (85' El Arbi Soudani), Yann M'Vila, Andreas Bouchalakis (46' Pêpê Rodrigues), Lazar Randjelovic (46' Bruma), Mady Camara (73' Georgios Masouras), Youssef El-Arabi (76' Ahmed Hassan "Koka"). Coach: Pedro Martins.
Goals: 12' Ferrán Torres 1-0, 81' Gabriel Jesus 2-0, João Cancelo 3-0.
Referee: Carlos del Cerro Grande (ESP)

03.11.20   Estádio do Dragão, Porto: FC Porto – Olympique Marseille 3-0 (2-0)
FC Porto: Agustin Marchesín, Chancel Mbemba, Wilson Manafá, Malang Sarr, Zaidu Sanusi, Sérgio Oliveira (89' Marko Grujic), Mateus Uribe, Otávio (88' Mehdi Taremi), Jesús Corona (85' Fábio Vieira), Moussa Marega (88' Romário Baró), Luis Díaz (75' Shoya Nakajima). Coach: Sérgio Conceição.
Olympique Marseille: Steve Mandanda, Hiroki Sakai, Álvaro González, Jordan Amavi, Duje Caleta-Car, Boubacar Kamara (82' Kevin Strootman), Dimitri Payet (65' Luis Henríque), Morgan Sanson (65' Michaël Cuisance), Valentin Rongier, Dario Benedetto (77' Valère Germain), Florian Thauvin (82' Marley Aké). Coach: André Villas-Boas.
Goals: 4' Moussa Marega 1-0, 28' Sérgio Oliveira 2-0 (p), 69' Luis Díaz 3-0.
Referee: Antonio Miguel Mateu Lahoz (ESP)

Dimitri Payet missed a penalty kick (10').

25.11.20 Stadio Georgios Karaiskáki, Piraeus:
Olympiakos Piraeus – Manchester City 0-1 (0-1)
Olympiakos Piraeus: José Sá, Rafinha, Rúben Semedo, Mohamed Dräger (66' Marios Vrousai), Pape Cissé, Ousseynou Ba, Yann M'Vila, Kostas Fortounis, Pêpê Rodrigues (71' Andreas Bouchalakis), Georgios Masouras (78' El Arbi Soudani), Mady Camara.
Coach: Pedro Martins.
Manchester City: Ederson Moraes, João Cancelo, Benjamin Mendy (78' Oleksandr Zinchenko), John Stones, Rúben Dias, Ilkay Gündogan (86' Thomas Doyle), Bernardo Silva, Rodri Hernández (76' Fernandinho), Phil Foden, Raheem Sterling (76' Riyad Mahrez), Gabriel Jesus (78' Kun Agüero). Coach: Pep Guardiola.
Goal: 36' Phil Foden 0-1.
Referee: Davide Massa (ITA)

25.11.20 Orange Vélodrome, Marseille: Olympique Marseille – FC Porto 0-2 (0-1)
Olympique Marseille: Steve Mandanda, Hiroki Sakai, Álvaro González, Jordan Amavi, Boubacar Kamara (59' Michaël Cuisance), Leonardo Balerdi, Morgan Sanson (77' Yuto Nagatomo), Valentin Rongier, Valère Germain (59' Dario Benedetto), Florian Thauvin (78' Marley Aké), Luis Henríque (59' Dimitri Payet). Coach: André Villas-Boas.
FC Porto: Agustin Marchesín, Chancel Mbemba, Wilson Manafá, Malang Sarr, Zaidu Sanusi, Sérgio Oliveira (90' Mamadou Loum N'Diaye), Otávio, Marko Grujic, Jesús Corona (78' Mehdi Taremi), Moussa Marega (79' José Mário), Luis Díaz (79' Shoya Nakajima). Coach: Sérgio Conceição.
Goals: 39' Zaidu Sanusi 0-1, 72' Sérgio Oliveira 0-2 (p).
Referee: Andreas Ekberg (SWE)
Sent off: 67' Marko Grujic, 70' Leonardo Balerdi.

01.12.20 Orange Vélodrome, Marseille:
Olympique Marseille – Olympiakos Piraeus 2-1 (0-1)
Olympique Marseille: Steve Mandanda, Hiroki Sakai, Álvaro González, Jordan Amavi, Duje Caleta-Car, Boubacar Kamara, Dimitri Payet, Valentin Rongier (85' Pape Alassane Gueye), Michaël Cuisance (55' Morgan Sanson), Dario Benedetto (46' Valère Germain), Florian Thauvin (90+5' Marley Aké). Coach: André Villas-Boas.
Olympiakos Piraeus: José Sá, Rafinha, José Holebas, Rúben Semedo, Pape Cissé, Yann M'Vila (79' Georgios Masouras), Kostas Fortounis, Andreas Bouchalakis, Mady Camara, Youssef El-Arabi, Marios Vrousai (90+2' El Arbi Soudani). Coach: Pedro Martins.
Goals: 33' Mady Camara 0-1, 55', 75' Dimitri Payet 1-1 (p), 2-1 (p).
Referee: Jesús Gil Manzano (ESP)

01.12.20 Estádio do Dragão, Porto: FC Porto – Manchester City 0-0
FC Porto: Agustin Marchesín, Chancel Mbemba, Wilson Manafá (72' Nanu), Malang Sarr, Diogo Leite, Zaidu Sanusi, Sérgio Oliveira, Mateus Uribe, Otávio (87' Fábio Vieira), Jesús Corona (63' Luis Díaz), Moussa Marega (72' Evanilson). Coach: Sérgio Conceição.
Manchester City: Ederson Moraes, João Cancelo, Rúben Dias, Eric García, Fernandinho, Oleksandr Zinchenko, Bernardo Silva, Rodri Hernández, Phil Foden, Raheem Sterling, Ferrán Torres (71' Gabriel Jesus). Coach: Pep Guardiola.
Referee: Björn Kuipers (HOL)

09.12.20   Etihad Stadium, Manchester: Manchester City – Olympique Marseille 3-0 (0-0)
Manchester City: Zack Steffen, Kyle Walker, Aymeric Laporte, Nathan Aké, Eric García (28'
John Stones), Fernandinho, Ilkay Gündogan (46' Raheem Sterling), Bernardo Silva, Phil
Foden, Riyad Mahrez (67' Kun Agüero), Ferrán Torres. Coach: Pep Guardiola.
Olympique Marseille: Steve Mandanda, Yuto Nagatomo, Hiroki Sakai, Álvaro González,
Boubacar Kamara (66' Valentin Rongier), Leonardo Balerdi, Dimitri Payet (67' Michaël
Cuisance), Morgan Sanson, Pape Alassane Gueye (75' Kevin Strootman), Valère Germain (76'
Dario Benedetto), Florian Thauvin (75' Marley Aké). Coach: André Villas-Boas.
Goals: 48' Ferrán Torres 1-0, 77' Kun Agüero 2-0, 90' Álvaro González 3-0 (og).
Referee: Halil Umut Meler (TUR)

09.12.20   Stadio Georgios Karaiskáki, Piraeus: Olympiakos Piraeus – FC Porto 0-2 (0-1)
Olympiakos Piraeus: José Sá, Rafinha, José Holebas, Rúben Semedo, Pape Cissé, Yann
M'Vila, Andreas Bouchalakis, Georgios Masouras (46' Lazar Randjelovic), Mady Camara (35'
Kostas Fortounis), Youssef El-Arabi (81' Ousseynou Ba), Marios Vrousai (73' El Arbi
Soudani). Coach: Pedro Martins.
FC Porto: Diogo Costa, Chancel Mbemba, Nanu, Diogo Leite, Zaidu Sanusi, Otávio (79'
Malang Sarr), Marko Grujic, Romário Baró (64' Mateus Uribe), Felipe Anderson (63' Luis
Díaz), Toni Martínez (80' Evanilson), João Mário (72' Jesús Corona).
Coach: Sérgio Conceição.
Goals: 1-' Otávio 0-1 (p), 77' Mateus Uribe 0-2.
Referee: Dr. Felix Brych (GER)
Sent off: 79' Rúben Semedo.

GROUP D

21.10.20   Johan Cruijff ArenA, Amsterdam: AFC Ajax – Liverpool FC 0-1 (0-1)
AFC Ajax: André Onana, Daley Blind (83' Klaas Jan Huntelaar), Nicolás Tagliafico, Noussair
Mazraoui, Perr Schuurs (84' Lassina Traoré), Lisandro Martínez, Davy Klaassen (74' Jurgen
Ekkelenkamp), Ryan Gravenberch, Mohammed Kudus (9' Quincy Promes), Dusan Tadic,
David Neres (74' Zakaria Labyad). Coach: Erik ten Hag.
Liverpool FC: Adrián, Andrew Robertson, Joe Gomez, Trent Alexander-Arnold, James Milner
(90+2' Rhys Williams), Georginio Wijnaldum, Fabinho, Curtis Jones (46' Jordan Henderson),
Roberto Firmino (60' Diogo Jota), Mohamed Salah (60' Xherdan Shaqiri), Sadio Mané (60'
Takumi Minamino). Coach: Jürgen Klopp.
Goal: Nicolás Tagliafico 0-1 (og).
Referee: Dr. Felix Brych (GER)

21.10.20   MCH Arena, Herning: FC Midtjylland – Atalanta Bergamo 0-4 (0-3)
FC Midtjylland: Jesper Hansen, Erik Sviatchenko, Alexander Scholz, Joel Andersson,
Paulinho, Pione Sisto (87' Mikael Anderson), Awer Mabil (75' Lasse Vibe), Anders Dreyer,
Frank Onyeka (87' Bozhidar Kraev), Jens Cajuste (76' Nicolas Madsen), Sory Kaba (60'
Evander). Coach: Brian Priske.
Atalanta Bergamo: Marco Sportiello, Rafael Tolói, Berat Djimsiti, Hans Hateboer, Robin
Gosens, Cristian Romero (86' José Palomino), Papu Gómez (68' Mario Pasalic), Marten de
Roon, Remo Freuler (80' Matteo Pessina), Duván Zapata (80' Aleksey Miranchuk), Luis
Muriel (68' Josip Ilicic). Coach: Gian Piero Gasperini.
Goals: 26' Duván Zapata 0-1, 36' Papu Gómez 0-2, 42' Luis Muriel 0-3,
89' Aleksey Miranchuk 0-4.
Referee: Artur Manuel Ribeiro Soares Dias (POR)   Attendance: 132.

27.10.20   Anfield, Liverpool: Liverpool FC – FC Midtjylland 2-0 (0-0)
Liverpool FC: Alisson, Andrew Robertson, Joe Gomez, Trent Alexander-Arnold, James Milner, Jordan Henderson (46' Georginio Wijnaldum), Xherdan Shaqiri, Fabinho (30' Rhys Williams), Takumi Minamino (61' Mohamed Salah), Divock Origi (60' Sadio Mané), Diogo Jota (81' Roberto Firmino). Coach: Jürgen Klopp.
FC Midtjylland: Mikkel Andersen, Erik Sviatchenko, Alexander Scholz, Joel Andersson, Paulinho, Pione Sisto (72' Evander), Awer Mabil (66' Mikael Anderson), Anders Dreyer, Frank Onyeka, Jens Cajuste (81' Bozhidar Kraev), Sory Kaba (81' Luca Pfeiffer). Coach: Brian Priske.
Goals: 55' Diogo Jota 1-0, 90+3' Mohamed Salah 2-0 (p).
Referee: Pawel Raczkowski (POL)

27.10.20   Gewiss Stadium, Bergamo: Atalanta Bergamo – AFC Ajax 2-2 (0-2)
Atalanta Bergamo: Marco Sportiello, Rafael Tolói, Berat Djimsiti, Hans Hateboer, Robin Gosens, Cristian Romero, Papu Gómez (78' Luis Muriel), Josip Ilicic (79' Ruslan Malinovskyi), Remo Freuler, Mario Pasalic, Duván Zapata. Coach: Gian Piero Gasperini.
AFC Ajax: André Onana, Daley Blind, Nicolás Tagliafico, Noussair Mazraoui (56' Sean Klaiber), Perr Schuurs, Davy Klaassen, Ryan Gravenberch, Dusan Tadic, David Neres (69' Quincy Promes), Lassina Traoré, Antony (90+4' Zakaria Labyad). Coach: Erik ten Hag.
Goals: 30' Dusan Tadic 0-1 (p), 38' Lassina Traoré 0-2, 54', 60' Duván Zapata 2-1, 2-2.
Referee: Damir Skomina (SVN)

03.11.20   MCH Arena, Herning: FC Midtjylland – AFC Ajax 1-2 (1-2)
FC Midtjylland: Mikkel Andersen, Erik Sviatchenko, Alexander Scholz, Joel Andersson (64' Dion Cools), Paulinho, Pione Sisto, Awer Mabil, Anders Dreyer (75' Bozhidar Kraev), Frank Onyeka, Jens Cajuste (81' Evander), Sory Kaba (81' Lasse Vibe). Coach: Brian Priske.
AFC Ajax: André Onana, Daley Blind, Nicolás Tagliafico, Noussair Mazraoui (77' Sean Klaiber), Perr Schuurs (60' Edson Álvarez), Lisandro Martínez, Jurgen Ekkelenkamp (46' Davy Klaassen), Ryan Gravenberch, Dusan Tadic, Quincy Promes, Antony (90' Lassina Traoré.) Coach: Erik ten Hag.
Goals: 1' Antony 0-1, 13' Dusan Tadic 0-2, 18' Anders Dreyer 1-2.
Referee: Robert Madden (SCO)   Attendance: 132.

03.11.20   Gewiss Stadium, Bergamo: Atalanta Bergamo – Liverpool FC 0-5 (0-2)
Atalanta Bergamo: Marco Sportiello, Rafael Tolói, José Palomino, Johan Mojica (81' Matteo Ruggeri), Berat Djimsiti, Hans Hateboer (81' Fabio Depaoli), Papu Gómez (81' Sam Lammers), Remo Freuler, Mario Pasalic (63' Ruslan Malinovskyi), Duván Zapata, Luis Muriel (53' Matteo Pessina). Coach: Gian Piero Gasperini.
Liverpool FC: Alisson, Andrew Robertson (66'Naby Keïta), Joe Gomez, Trent Alexander-Arnold (82' Neco Williams), Rhys Williams, Georginio Wijnaldum (82' Kostas Tsimikas), Jordan Henderson (65' James Milner), Curtis Jones, Mohamed Salah, Sadio Mané, Diogo Jota (65' Roberto Firmino). Coach: Jürgen Klopp.
Goals: 16', 44' Diogo Jota 0-1, 0-2, 47' Mohamed Salah 0-3, 49' Sadio Mané 0-4, 54' Diogo Jota 0-5.
Referee: Ovidiu Alin Hategan (ROM)

25.11.20   Anfield, Liverpool: Liverpool FC – Atalanta Bergama 0-2 (0-0)
Liverpool FC: Alisson, Joel Matip (84' Takumi Minamino), Kostas Tsimikas (61' Andrew Robertson), Neco Williams, Rhys Williams, James Milner, Georginio Wijnaldum (61' Fabinho), Curtis Jones, Mohamed Salah (61' Roberto Firmino), Sadio Mané, Divock Origi (61' Diogo Jota). Coach: Jürgen Klopp.
Atalanta Bergamo: Pierluigi Gollini, Rafael Tolói, Berat Djimsiti, Hans Hateboer, Robin Gosens (75' Johan Mojica), Cristian Romero, Papu Gómez, Josip Ilicic (70' Duván Zapata), Marten de Roon, Remo Freuler, Matteo Pessina (85' Aleksey Miranchuk).
Coach: Gian Piero Gasperini.
Goals: 60' Josip Ilicic 0-1, 64' Robin Gosens 0-2.
Referee: Carlos del Cerro Grande (ESP)

25.11.20   Johan Cruijff ArenA, Amsterdam: AFC Ajax – FC Midtjylland 3-1 (0-0)
AFC Ajax: André Onana, Daley Blind (66' Lisandro Martínez), Nicolás Tagliafico, Noussair Mazraoui (82' Sean Klaiber), Perr Schuurs, Zakaria Labyad (81' Quincy Promes), Davy Klaassen (66' Edson Álvarez), Ryan Gravenberch, Dusan Tadic, David Neres (90+3' Jurgen Ekkelenkamp), Lassina Traoré. Coach: Erik ten Hag.
FC Midtjylland: Jesper Hansen, Erik Sviatchenko, Alexander Scholz, Paulinho (26' Joel Andersson), Dion Cools, Pione Sisto (81' Luka Pfeiffer), Awer Mabil, Anders Dreyer (82' Gustav Isaksen), Frank Onyeka, Nicolas Madsen (69' Mikael Anderson), Sory Kaba (69' Bozhidar Kraev). Coach: Brian Priske.
Goals: 47' Ryan Gravenberch 1-0, 49' Noussair Mazraoui 2-0, 66' David Neres 3-0, 80' Awer Mabil 3-1 (p).
Referee: Sergei Karasov (RUS)
Sent off: 90+1' Erik Sviatchenko.

01.12.20   Anfield, Liverpool: Liverpool FC – AFC Ajax 1-0 (0-0)
Liverpool FC: Caoimhin Kelleher, Joel Matip, Andrew Robertson, Neco Williams, Georginio Wijnaldum, Jordan Henderson, Fabinho, Curtis Jones, Mohamed Salah (90' Rhys Williams), Sadio Mané, Diogo Jota (68' Roberto Firmino). Coach: Jürgen Klopp.
AFC Ajax: André Onana, Daley Blind (86' Lisandro Martínez), Nicolás Tagliafico, Noussair Mazraoui (86' Klaas Jan Huntelaar), Perr Schuurs, Edson Álvarez (69' Zakaria Labyad), Davy Klaassen, Ryan Gravenberch, Dusan Tadic, David Neres (81' Lassina Traoré), Antony.
Coach: Erik ten Hag.
Goal: 58' Curtis Jones 1-0.
Referee: Tobias Stieler (GER)

01.12.20   Gewiss Stadium, Bergamo: Atalanta Bergamo – FC Midtjylland 1-1 (0-1)
Atalanta Bergamo: Marco Sportiello, José Palomino (68' Rafael Tolói), Berat Djimsiti, Hans Hateboer, Robin Gosens (86' Matteo Ruggeri), Cristian Romero, Papu Gómez (46' Josip Ilicic), Remo Freuler (68' Marten de Roon), Matteo Pessina, Duván Zapata, Luis Muriel (68' Amad Diallo Traoré). Coach: Gian Piero Gasperini.
FC Midtjylland: Jesper Hansen, Daniel Høegh, Alexander Scholz, Joel Andersson, Manjrekar James, Paulinho, Awer Mabil (67' Lasse Vibe), Anders Dreyer (82' Gustav Isaksen), Mikael Anderson, Frank Onyeka, Sory Kaba (82' Nicolas Madsen). Coach: Brian Priske.
Goals: 13' Alexander Scholz 0-1, 79' Cristian Romero 1-1.
Referee: Anastasios Sidiropoulos (GRE)

08.12.20 Johan Cruijff ArenA, Amsterdam: AFC Ajax – Atalanta Bergamo 0-1 (0-0)
AFC Ajax: André Onana, Nicolás Tagliafico (64' Klaas Jan Huntelaar), Noussair Mazraoui, Perr Schuurs, Lisandro Martínez (90+2' Jurriën Timber, 90+6' Edson Álvarez), Zakaria Labyad (63' Jurgen Ekkelenkamp), Davy Klaassen, Ryan Gravenberch, Dusan Tadic, Brian Brobbey (46' Quincy Promes), Antony. Coach: Erik ten Hag.
Atalanta Bergamo: Pierluigi Gollini, Rafael Tolói, Berat Djimsiti, Hans Hateboer, Robin Gosens (79' José Palomino), Cristian Romero, Papu Gómez, Marten de Roon, Remo Freuler, Matteo Pessina, Duván Zapata (79' Luis Muriel). Coach: Gian Piero Gasperini.
Goal: 85' Luis Muriel 0-1.
Referee: Carlos del Cerro Grande (ESP)
Sent off: 79' Ryan Gravenberch.

09.12.20 MCH Arena, Herning: FC Midtjylland – Liverpool FC 1-1 (0-1)
FC Midtjylland: Jesper Hansen, Erik Sviatchenko, Alexander Scholz, Paulinho, Dion Cools, Awer Mabil (63' Mikael Anderson), Anders Dreyer (76' Pione Sisto), Evander (90' Nicolas Madsen), Frank Onyeka (63' Gustav Isaksen), Jens Cajuste, Sory Kaba (90' Luca Pfeiffer). Coach: Brian Priske.
Liverpool FC: Caoimhin Kelleher, Kostas Tsimikas (61' Andrew Robertson), Trent Alexander-Arnold, Rhys Williams, Fabinho (46' Billy Koumetio), Naby Keïta (61' Jordan Henderson), Leighton Clarkson, Mohamed Salah, Takumi Minamino, Divock Origi (71' Roberto Firmino), Diogo Jota (87' Sadio Mané). Coach: Jürgen Klopp.
Goals: 1' Mohamed Salah 0-1, 62' Alexander Scholz 1-1 (p).
Referee: François Letexier (FRA)   Attendance: 147.

GROUP E

20.10.20 Stamford Bridge, London: Chelsea FC – Sevilla CF 0-0
Chelsea FC: Edouard Mendy, Thiago Silva, Kurt Zouma, Ben Chilwell, Reece James, Jorginho (65' Mateo Kovacic), N'Golo Kanté, Mason Mount (62' Hakim Ziyech), Christian Pulisic (90+1' Callum Hudson-Odoi), Kai Havertz, Timo Werner (90+1' Tammy Abraham). Coach: Frank Lampard
Sevilla CF: Yassine Bounou, Jesús Navas, Sergi Gómez (33' Joan Jordán), Diego Carlos, Ivan Rakitic (80' Franco Vázquez), Fernando, Nemanja Gudelj, Lucas Ocampos, Marcos Acuña, Suso (58' Óliver Torres), Luuk de Jong (80' Youssef En-Nesyri). Coach: Lopetegui.
Referee: Davide Massa (ITA)

20.10.20 Roazhon Park, Rennes: Stade de Rennes – FK Krasnodar 1-1 (0-0)
Stade de Rennes: Alfred Gomis, Damien Da Silva, Hamari Traoré, Dalbert Henrique (81' Adrien Truffert, Nayef Aguerd, Steven N'Zonzi, Benjamin Bourigeaud (69' Flavien Tait), Martin Terrier, Eduardo Camavinga (81' Adrien Hunou), Serhou Guirassy, Romain Del Castillo (62' Jérémy Doku). Coach: Julien Stéphan.
FK Krasnodar: Matvey Safonov, Igor Smolnikov, Sergey Petrov (72' Magomed Suleymanov), Cristian Ramírez, Evheniy Chernov, Egor Sorokin, Tonny Vilhena, Kristoffer Olsson, Kaio Pantaleão, Daniil Utkin (72' Yuri Gazinskiy), Marcus Berg. Coach: Murad Musaev.
Goals: 56' Serhou Guirassy 1-0 (p), 59' Cristian Ramírez 1-1.
Referee: Anastasios Sidiropoulos (GRE)   Attendance: 4,973.

28.10.20   Stadion FK Krasnodar, Krasnodar: FK Krasnodar – Chelsea FC 0-4 (0-1)
FK Krasnodar: Matvey Safonov, Igor Smolnikov, Aleksandr Martynovich, Cristian Ramírez, Evheniy Chernov, Yuri Gazinskiy, Tonny Vilhena, Kristoffer Olsson (82' Eduard Spertsyan), Kaio Pantaleão, Daniil Utkin (74' Magomed Suleymanov), Marcus Berg (87' Leon Sabua).
Coach: Murad Musaev.
Chelsea FC: Edouard Mendy, Azpilicueta, Kurt Zouma, Antonio Rüdiger, Ben Chilwell (81' Emerson), Mateo Kovacic (71' N'Golo Kanté), Jorginho (71' Mason Mount), Hakim Ziyech (80' Tammy Abraham), Kai Havertz, Callum Hudson-Odoi (71' Christian Pulisic), Timo Werner. Coach: Frank Lampard.
Goals: 37' Callum Hudson-Odoi 0-1, 76' Timo Werner 0-2 (p), 79' Hakim Ziyech 0-3, 90' Christian Pulisic 0-4.
Referee: Ali Palabiyik (TUR)   Attendance: 10,544.

Jorginho missed a penalty kick (14').

28.10.20   Estádio Ramón Sánchez Pizjuán, Sevilla: Sevilla CF – Stade de Rennes 1-0 (0-0)
Sevilla CF: Yassine Bounou, Jesús Navas, Diego Carlos, Jules Koundé, Fernando, Lucas Ocampos, Marcos Acuña, Óliver Torres (76' Ivan Rakitic), Joan Jordán (89' Nemanja Gudelj), Luuk de Jong (85' Youssef En-Nesyri), Munir (85' Franco Vázquez). Coach: Lopetegui.
Stade de Rennes: Alfred Gomis, Damien Da Silva, Daniele Rugani (17' Nayef Aguerd), Hamari Traoré, Brandon Soppy (77' Dalbert Henrique), Clément Grenier (77' Romain Del Castillo), Jonas Martin, Benjamin Bourigeaud (49' James Lea Siliki), Martin Terrier, Serhou Guirassy, Jérémy Doku. Coach: Julien Stéphan.
Goal: 55' Luuk de Jong 1-0.
Referee: Cüneyt Çakir (TUR)

04.11.20   Estádio Ramón Sánchez Pizjuán, Sevilla: Sevilla CF – FK Krasnodar 3-2 (1-2)
Sevilla CF: Tomáš Vaclík, Jesús Navas, Escudero (34' Marcos Acuña), Diego Carlos, Jules Koundé (34' Óscar Rodríguez), Ivan Rakitic, Nemanja Gudelj, Lucas Ocampos, Joan Jordán (60' Youssef En-Nesyri), Luuk de Jong (83' Karim Rekik), Munir (60' Fernando).
Coach: Lopetegui.
FK Krasnodar: Matvey Safonov, Aleksandr Martynovich, Cristian Ramírez (46' Egor Sorokin), Evheniy Chernov, Yuri Gazinskiy, Kristoffer Olsson, Kaio Pantaleão, Daniil Utkin (75' Wanderson), Leon Sabua (34' Eduard Spertsyan, 66' Victor Claesson), Marcus Berg, Magomed Suleymanov. Coach: Murad Musaev.
Goals: 17' Magomed Suleymanov 0-1, 21' Marcus Berg 0-2 (p), 42' Ivan Rakitic 1-2, 69', 72' Youssef En-Nesyri 2-2, 3-2.
Referee: Dr. Felix Brych (GER)
Sent off: 45+4' Jesús Navas.

04.11.20   Stamford Bridge, London: Chelsea FC – Stade de Rennes 3-0 (2-0)
Chelsea FC: Edouard Mendy, Thiago Silva (68' Antonio Rüdiger), Kurt Zouma, Ben Chilwell (81' Emerson), Reece James, Jorginho, N'Golo Kanté (62' Mateo Kovacic), Hakim Ziyech (75' Callum Hudson-Odoi), Mason Mount, Timo Werner, Tammy Abraham (63' Olivier Giroud). Coach: Frank Lampard.
Stade de Rennes: Alfred Gomis, Damien Da Silva, Hamari Traoré, Dalbert Henrique, Nayef Aguerd, Steven N'Zonzi (62' Clément Grenier), Benjamin Bourigeaud, James Lea Siliki (46' Adrien Truffert), Martin Terrier (62' Jérémy Doku), Yann Gboho (62' Romain Del Castillo), Serhou Guirassy (76' Adrian Hunou). Coach: Julien Stéphan.
Goals: 10', 41' Timo Werner 1-0 (p), 2-0 (p), 50' Tammy Abraham 3-0.
Referee: Felix Zwayer (GER)
Sent off: 40' Dalbert Henrique.

24.11.20   Stadion FK Krasnodar, Krasnodar: FK Krasnodar – Sevilla CF 1-2 (0-1)
FK Krasnodar: Evgeniy Gorodov, Igor Smolnikov, Aleksandr Martynovich, Cristian Ramírez, Rémy Cabella (85' Daniil Utkin), Yuri Gazinskiy, Victor Claesson (84' Evheniy Chernov), Kristoffer Olsson (67' Tonny Vilhena), Kaio Pantaleão, Marcus Berg (67' Ari), Magomed Suleymanov (46' Wanderson). Coach: Murad Musaev.
Sevilla CF: Tomás Vaclík, Escudero (61' Karim Rekik), Diego Carlos, Jules Koundé, Ivan Rakitic (61' Óliver Torres), Fernando, Nemanja Gudelj, Lucas Ocampos (72' Oussama Idrissi), Óscar Rodríguez (53' Joan Jordán), Luuk de Jong (72' Youssef En-Nesyri), Munir. Coach: Lopetegui.
Goals: 4' Ivan Rakitic 0-1, 56' Wanderson 1-1, 90+5' Munir 1-2.
Referee: Marco Guida (ITA)   Attendance: 10,554.

24.11.20   Roazhon Park, Rennes: Stade de Rennes – Chelsea FC 1-2 (0-1)
Stade de Rennes: Alfred Gomis, Damien Da Silva, Hamari Traoré, Gerzino Nyamsi, Adrien Truffert (86' Faitout Maouassa), Steven N'Zonzi, Benjamin Bourigeaud, James Lea Siliki (63' Romain Del Castillo), Eduardo Camavinga (78' Clément Grenier), Serhou Guirassy (86' M'Baye Niang), Jérémy Doku (86' Yann Gboho). Coach: Julien Stéphan.
Chelsea FC: Edouard Mendy, Thiago Silva, Azpilicueta, Kurt Zouma, Ben Chilwell, Mateo Kovacic (76' Kai Havertz), Jorginho, Mason Mount (68' N'Golo Kanté), Callum Hudson-Odoi (75' Hakim Ziyech), Timo Werner (90+2' Reece James), Tammy Abraham (69' Olivier Giroud). Coach: Frank Lampard.
Goals: 22' Callum Hudson-Odoi 0-1, 85' Serhou Guirassy 1-1, 90+1' Olivier Giroud 1-2.
Referee: Björn Kuipers (HOL)

02.12.20   Stadion FK Krasnodar, Krasnodar: FK Krasnodar – Stade de Rennes 1-0 (0-0)
FK Krasnodar: Matvey Safonov, Igor Smolnikov, Aleksandr Martynovich, Cristian Ramírez, Rémy Cabella, Yuri Gazinskiy (87' Ruslan Kambolov), Victor Claesson, Tonny Vilhena, Kaio Pantaleão, Marcus Berg (90+1' Ari), Wanderson (66' Magomed Suleymanov). Coach: Murad Musaev.
Stade de Rennes: Romain Salin, Damien Da Silva, Hamari Traoré, Gerzino Nyamsi, Adrien Truffert, Steven N'Zonzi, Benjamin Bourigeaud (73' Yann Gboho), James Lea Siliki (65' Clément Grenier), Eduardo Camavinga (82' Flavien Tait), Adrien Hunou (65' M'Baye Niang), Jérémy Doku. Coach: Julien Stéphan.
Goal: 71' Marcus Berg 1-0.
Referee: William Collum(SCO)   Attendance: 8,747.

02.12.20   Estádio Ramón Sánchez Pizjuán, Sevilla: Sevilla CF – Chelsea FC 0-4 (0-1)
Sevilla CF: Alfonso Pastor, Jesús Navas (59' Jules Koundé), Sergi Gómez, Karim Rekik, Diego Carlos, Ivan Rakitic (75' Óliver Torres), Franco Vásquez (66' Munir), Nemanja Gudelj, Óscar Rodríguez (60' Joan Jordán), Oussama Idrissi (59' Lucas Ocampos), Youssef En-Nesyri. Coach: Lopetegui.
Chelsea FC: Edouard Mendy, Azpilicueta, Emerson, Antonio Rüdiger, Andreas Christensen, Mateo Kovacic (67' Hakim Ziyech), Jorginho (85' Billy Gilmour), Christian Pulisic (67' Mason Mount), Kai Havertz (67' N'Golo Kanté), Callum Hudson-Odoi, Olivier Giroud (84' Timo Werner). Coach: Frank Lampard.
Goals: 8', 54', 74', 83' Olivier Giroud 0-1, 0-2, 0-3, 0-4 (p).
Referee: Artur Manuel Ribeiro Soares Dias (POR)

08.12.20 Stamford Bridge, London: Chelsea FC – FK Krasnodar 1-1 (1-1)
Chelsea FC: Kepa, Azpilicueta, Emerson, Antonio Rüdiger, Andreas Christensen, Mateo Kovacic (74' N'Golo Kanté), Jorginho, Kai Havertz (74' Timo Werner), Billy Gilmour, Faustino Anjorin (80' Olivier Giroud), Tammy Abraham. Coach: Frank Lampard.
FK Krasnodar: Evgeniy Gorodov, Igor Smolnikov, Aleksandr Martynovich, Cristian Ramírez, Rémy Cabella (80' Magomed Suleymanov), Victor Claesson, Tonny Vilhena, Kristoffer Olsson (80' Ruslan Kambolov), Kaio Pantaleão (74' Egor Sorokin), Marcus Berg (90' Evgeniy Markov). Wanderson (80' Evgeniy Chernov). Coach: Murad Musaev.
Goals: 24' Rémy Cabella 0-1, 28' Joginho 1-1 (p).
Referee: Pavel Královec (CZE)   Attendance: 2,000.

08.12.20 Roazhon Park, Rennes: Stade de Rennes – Sevilla CF 1-3 (0-2)
Stade de Rennes: Romain Salin, Damien Da Silva (70' Nayef Aguerd), Hamari Traoré, Dalbert Henrique, Brandon Soppy, Clément Grenier (79' Flavien Tait), Steven N'Zonzi, Faitout Maouassa (79' Adrien Truffert), Eduardo Camavinga, M'Baye Niang (70' Georginio Rutter), Jérémy Doku (79' Yann Gboho). Coach: Julien Stéphan.
Sevilla CF: Yassine Bounou, Sergi Gómez (76' Fernando), Karim Rekik, Diego Carlos, Jules Koundé, Ivan Rakitic, Nemanja Gudelj, Suso (76' Óscar Rodríguez), Óliver Torres (83' Franco Vásquez), Oussama Idrissi (72' Lucas Ocampos), Youssef En-Nesyri (83' Carlos Fernández). Coach: Lopetegui.
Goals: 32' Jules Koundé 0-1, 45+2', 81' Youssef En-Nesyri 0-2, 0-3, 86' Georginio Rutter 1-3 (p).
Referee: Bartosz Frankowski (POL)

GROUP F

20.10.20 Gazprom Arena, Saint Petersburg:
            Zenit Saint Petersburg – Club Brugge KV 1-2 (0-0)
Zenit Saint Petersburg: Mikhail Kerzhakov, Dejan Lovren, Yaroslav Rakitskiy, Vyacheslav Karavaev, Danil Krugovoy, Magomed Ozdoev (88' Aleksandr Erokhin), Wilmar Barrios, Daler Kuzyaev (72' Wendel), Artem Dzyaba, Sardar Azmoun, Sebastián Driussi (72' Andrey Mostovoy). Coach: Sergey Semak.
Club Brugge KV: Ethan Horvath, Eduard Sobol, Clinton Mata, Brandon Mechele, Federico Ricca, Ruud Vormer, Mats Rits, Hans Vanaken, Krépin Diatta (78' Noa Lang), Charles De Ketelaere, Emmanuel Dennis (82' Youssouph Badji). Coach: Philippe Clement.
Goals: 63' Emmanuel Dennis 0-1, 74' Ethan Horvath 1-1 (og), 90+3' Charles De Ketelaere 1-2.
Referee: Benoît Bastien (FRA)   Attendance: 16,682.

20.10.20   Stadio Olimpico, Roma: Lazio Roma – Borussia Dortmund 3-1 (2-0)
Lazio Roma: Thomas Strakosha, Francesco Acerbi, Patric, Adam Marusic, Luiz Felipe (51'
Wesley Hoedt), Lucas Leiva, Luis Alberto (80' Marco Parolo), Joaquín Correa (67' Vedat
Muriqi), Sergej Milinkovic-Savic (67' Jean-Daniel Akpa-Akpro), Mohamed Fares, Ciro
Immobile (80' Felipe Caicedo). Coach: Simone Inzaghi.
Borussia Dortmund: Marwin Hitz, Mats Hummels, Lukasz Piszczek (65' Julian Brandt),
Raphaël Guerreiro, Axel Witsel, Thomas Delaney, Thomas Meunier, Jadon Sancho, Jude
Bellingham (46' Giovanni Reyna), Marco Reus (78' Reinier), Erling Håland.
Coach: Lucien Favre.
Goals: 6' Ciro Immobile 1-0, 23' Marwin Hitz 2-0 (og), 71' Erling Håland 2-1,
76' Jean-Daniel Akpa-Akpro 3-1.
Referee: Clément Turpin (FRA)   Attendance: 1,000

28.10.20   Signal-Iduna-Park, Dortmund:
           Borussia Dortmund – Zenit Saint Petersburg 2-0 (0-0)
Borussia Dortmund: Roman Bürki, Mats Hummels, Raphaël Guerreiro, Manuel Akanji, Axel
Witsel, Thomas Meunier, Mahmoud Dahoud (66' Thorgan Hazard), Jadon Sancho (84'
Thomas Delaney), Giovanni Reyna (84' Jude Bellingham), Marco Reus (74' Julian Brandt),
Erling Håland. Coach: Lucien Favre.
Zenit Saint Petersburg: Mikhail Kerzhakov, Dejan Lovren, Yaroslav Rakitskiy, Vyacheslav
Karavaev, Douglas Santos, Aleksandr Erokhin, Wilmar Barrios (81' Aleksey Sutormin), Daler
Kuzyaev (71' Magomed Ozdoev), Wendel, Artem Dzyaba (46' Andrey Mostovoy), Sebastián
Driussi (74' Yuriy Zhirkov). Coach: Sergey Semak.
Goals: 78' Jadon Sancho 1-0 (p), 90+1' Erling Håland 2-0.
Referee: Björn Kuipers (HOL)

28.10.20   Jan Breydelstadion, Brugge: Club Brugge KV – Lazio Roma 1-1 (1-1)
Club Brugge KV: Simon Mignolet, Eduard Sobol, Clinton Mata, Simon Deli, Odilon
Kossounou, Ruud Vormer, Mats Rits, Hans Vanaken, Krépin Diatta, Charles De Ketelaere (84'
Noa Lang), Emmanuel Dennis (88' Michael Krmencík). Coach: Philippe Clement.
Lazio Roma: Pepe Reina, Francesco Acerbi, Patric (46' Andreas Pereira), Adam Marusic,
Wesley Hoedt, Marco Parolo, Jean-Daniel Akpa-Akpro, Joaquín Correa, Sergej Milinkovic-
Savic, Mohamed Fares (56' Vedat Muriqi), Felipe Caicedo (68' Szymon Czyz).
Coach: Simone Inzaghi.
Goals: 14' Joaquín Correa 0-1, 42' Hans Vanaken 1-1 (p).
Referee: Anthony Taylor (ENG)

04.11.20   Gazprom Arena, Saint Petersburg: Zenit Saint Petersburg – Lazio Roma 1-1 (1-0)
Zenit Saint Petersburg: Mikhail Kerzhakov, Dejan Lovren, Yaroslav Rakitskiy, Vyacheslav
Karavaev, Douglas Santos, Yuriy Zhirkov (78' Danil Krugovoy), Aleksandr Erokhin (61'
Andrey Mostovoy), Magomed Ozdoev (90+1' Aleksey Sutormin), Wilmar Barrios, Daler
Kuzyaev (90+1' Wendel), Artem Dzyaba. Coach: Sergey Semak.
Lazio Roma: Pepe Reina, Francesco Acerbi, Patric, Adam Marusic, Wesley Hoedt, Marco
Parolo (52' Danilo Cataldi), Jean-Daniel Akpa-Akpro, Joaquín Correa (85' Luiz Felipe), Sergej
Milinkovic-Savic, Mohamed Fares (59' Andreas Pereira), Vedat Muriqi (59' Felipe Caicedo).
Coach: Simone Inzaghi.
Goals: 32' Aleksandr Erokhin 1-0, 82' Felipe Caicedo 1-1.
Referee: Artur Manuel Ribeiro Soares Dias (POR)   Attendance: 17,427.

04.11.20 Jan Breydelstadion, Brugge: Club Brugge KV – Borussia Dortmund 0-3 (0-3)
Club Brugge KV: Simon Mignolet, Eduard Sobol, Clinton Mata, Simon Deli, Odilon Kossounou, Ruud Vormer (71' Éder Balanta), Mats Rits, Hans Vanaken (85' Siebe Schrijvers), Krépin Diatta, Emmanuel Dennis (85' Michael Krmencík), Noa Lang (76' Charles De Ketelaere). Coach: Philippe Clement.
Borussia Dortmund: Roman Bürki, Raphaël Guerreiro, Manuel Akanji, Axel Witsel, Thomas Delaney (72' Jude Bellingham), Thomas Meunier (84' Mateu Morey), Thorgan Hazard, Julian Brandt (72' Marco Reus), Mahmoud Dahoud, Giovanni Reyna (77' Felix Passlack), Erling Håland (84' Reinier). Coach: Lucien Favre.
Goals: 14' Thorgan Hazard 0-1, 18', 32' Erling Håland 0-2, 0-3.
Referee: Damir Skomina (SVN)

24.11.20 Stadio Olimpico, Roma: Lazio Roma – Zenit Saint Petersburg 3-1 (2-1)
Lazio Roma: Pepe Reina, Francesco Acerbi, Patric (60' Luiz Felipe), Adam Marusic, Wesley Hoedt, Lucas Leiva (68' Danilo Cataldi), Marco Parolo (60' Jean-Daniel Akpa-Akpro), Luis Alberto, Joaquín Correa, Manuel Lazzari (68' Mohamed Fares), Ciro Immobile (81' Vedat Muriqi). Coach: Simone Inzaghi.
Zenit Saint Petersburg: Mikhail Kerzhakov, Dejan Lovren, Yaroslav Rakitskiy, Douglas Santos (37' Aleksey Sutormin), Yuriy Zhirkov (73' Sardar Azmoun), Aleksandr Erokhin (74' Daniil Shamkin), Wilmar Barrios (59' Sebastián Driussi), Daler Kuzyaev, Andrey Mostovoy (59' Leon Musaev), Artem Dzyaba, Malcom. Coach: Sergey Semak.
Goals: 3' Ciro Immobile 1-0, 22' Marco Parolo 2-0, 25' Artem Dzyaba 2-1, 55' Ciro Immobile 3-1 (p).
Referee: Michael Oliver (ENG)

24.11.20 Signal-Iduna-Park, Dortmund: Borussia Dortmund – Club Brugge KV 3-0 (2-0)
Borussia Dortmund: Roman Bürki, Mats Hummels, Raphaël Guerreiro (80' Felix Passlack), Manuel Akanji, Thomas Delaney (72' Emre Can), Thomas Meunier (73' Mateu Morey), Thorgan Hazard, Jadon Sancho, Giovanni Reyna (81' Julian Brandt), Jude Bellingham, Erling Håland (81' Marco Reus). Coach: Lucien Favre.
Club Brugge KV: Simon Mignolet, Clinton Mata, Simon Deli, Odilon Kossounou, Ruud Vormer, Hans Vanaken, Éder Balanta (52' Mats Rits), Krépin Diatta (74' David Okereke), Charles De Ketelaere, Michael Krmencík (66' Youssouph Badji), Noa Lang (74' Siebe Schrijvers). Coach: Philippe Clement.
Goals: 18' Erling Håland 1-0, 45' Jadon Sancho 2-0, 60' Erling Håland 3-0.
Referee: Ivan Kruzliak (SVK)

02.12.20 Signal-Iduna-Park, Dortmund: Borussia Dortmund – Lazio Roma 1-1 (1-0)
Borussia Dortmund: Roman Bürki, Mats Hummels, Lukasz Piszczek, Raphaël Guerreiro (62' Nico Schulz), Manuel Akanji, Mateu Morey, Thomas Delaney, Thorgan Hazard (76' Julian Brandt), Giovanni Reyna, Jude Bellingham (88' Axel Witsel), Marco Reus (76' Jadon Sancho). Coach: Lucien Favre.
Lazio Roma: Pepe Reina, Francesco Acerbi, Patric, Adam Marusic, Wesley Hoedt, Lucas Leiva (70' Jean-Daniel Akpa-Akpro), Luis Alberto (79' Gonzalo Escalante), Joaquín Correa (70' Andreas Pereira), Sergej Milinkovic-Savic (79' Felipe Caicedo), Mohamed Fares (70' Manuel Lazzari), Ciro Immobile. Coach: Simone Inzaghi.
Goals: 44' Raphaël Guerreiro 1-0, 67' Ciro Immobile 1-1 (p).
Referee: Antonio Miguel Mateu Lahoz (ESP)

02.12.20   Jan Breydelstadion, Brugge: Club Brugge KV – Zenit Saint Petersburg 3-0 (1-0)
Club Brugge KV: Simon Mignolet, Clinton Mata (90+1' Thomas Van Den Deybus), Brandon Mechele, Federico Ricca, Odilon Kossounou, Ruud Vormer (88' Siebe Schrijvers), Hans Vanaken (87' Eduard Sobol), Éder Balanta, Charles De Ketelaere, Emmanuel Dennis, Noa Lang (87' David Okereke). Coach: Philippe Clement.
Zenit Saint Petersburg: Mikhail Kerzhakov, Yaroslav Rakitskiy (46' Danil Krugovoy), Douglas Santos, Danila Prokhin, Aleksandr Erokhin (46' Andrey Mostovoy), Wilmar Barrios, Daler Kuzyaev (65' Leon Musaev), Aleksey Sutormin, Sardar Azmoun, Sebastián Driussi (46' Magomed Ozdoev), Malcom (75' Daniil Shamkin). Coach: Sergey Semak.
Goals: 33' Charles De Ketelaere 1-0, 58' Hans Vanaken 2-0 (p), 73' Noa Lang 3-0.
Referee: Serdar Gözübüyük (HOL)

08.12.20   Gazprom Arena, Saint Petersburg:
        Zenit Saint Petersburg – Borussia Dortmund 1-2 (1-0)
Zenit Saint Petersburg: Mikhail Kerzhakov, Yaroslav Rakitskiy (67' Dejan Lovren), Douglas Santos, Danila Prokhin, Magomed Ozdoev (79' Danil Krugovoy), Wilmar Barrios, Daler Kuzyaev (60' Wendel), Aleksey Sutormin, Sardar Azmoun, Sebastián Driussi (60' Artem Dzyuba), Malcom (79' Vyacheslav Karavaev). Coach: Sergey Semak.
Borussia Dortmund: Marwin Hitz, Mats Hummels (72' Jadon Sancho), Lukasz Piszczek (72' Dan-Axel Zagadou), Nico Schulz, Axel Witsel, Thorgan Hazard (83' Ansgar Knauff), Emre Can, Julian Brandt (58' Giovanni Reyna), Felix Passlack (58' Youssoufa Moukoko), Jude Bellingham, Marco Reus. Coach: Lucien Favre.
Goals: 16' Sebastián Driussi 1-0, 68' Felix Passlack 1-1, 78' Axel Witsel 1-2.
Referee: István Kovács (ROM)   Attendance: 10,860.

08.12.20   Stadio Olimpico, Roma: Lazio Roma – Club Brugge KV 2-2 (2-1)
Lazio Roma: Pepe Reina, Francesco Acerbi, Adam Marusic, Wesley Hoedt (46' Stefan Radu), Luis Felipe, Lucas Leiva (75' Gonzalo Escalante), Luis Alberto (75' Jean-Daniel Akpa-Akpro), Joaquín Correa (86' Andreas Pereira), Manuel Lazzari, Sergej Milinkovic-Savic, Ciro Immobile (75' Felipe Caicedo). Coach: Simone Inzaghi.
Club Brugge KV: Simon Mignolet, Eduard Sobol, Clinton Mata (84' Ignace Van Der Brempt), Federico Ricca, Odilon Kossounou, Ruud Vormer, Hans Vanaken, Éder Balanta (73' Mats Rits), Krépin Diatta (84' David Okereke), Charles De Ketelaere, Noa Lang (42' Simon Deli). Coach: Philippe Clement.
Goals: 12' Joaquín Correa 1-0, 15' Ruud Vormer 1-1, 27' Ciro Immobile 2-1 (p),
76' Hans Vanaken 2-2.
Referee: Cüneyt Çakir (TUR)
Sent off: 39' Eduard Sobol.

GROUP G

20.10.20   NSK Olimpijs'kyj Stadium, Kyiv: Dynamo Kyiv – Juventus FC 0-2 (0-0)
Dynamo Kyiv: Georgiy Bushchan, Tomasz Kedziora, Oleksandr Karavayev (70' Denys Popov), Vitali Mykolenko, Illia Zabarnyi, Sergiy Sydorchuk, Vitaly Buyalskiy (89' Denys Garmash), Carlos de Pena (60' Gerson Rodrigues), Viktor Tsygankov (70' Benjamin Verbic), Mykola Shaparenko, Vladyslav Supriaha. Coach: Mircea Lucescu.
Juventus FC: Wojciech Szczesny, Leonardo Bonucci, Giorgio Chiellini (19' Merih Demiral), Danilo, Juan Cuadrado, Aaron Ramsey (79' Federico Bernardeschi), Adrien Rabiot, Rodrigo Bentancur (79' Arthur), Dejan Kulusevski (56' Paulo Dybala), Morata, Federico Chiesa. Coach: Andrea Pirlo.
Goals: 46', 84' Morata 0-1, 0-2.
Referee: Ovidiu Alin Hategan (ROM)   Attendance: 14,850.

20.10.20   Camp Nou, Barcelona: FC Barcelona – Ferencvárosi TC 5-1 (2-0)
FC Barcelona: Neto, Piqué, Sergi Roberto (62' Junior Firpo), Clément Lenglet, Sergiño Dest, Miralem Pjanic (76' Busquets), Philippe Coutinho (70' Ronald Araújo), Frenkie de Jong, Lionel Messi, Trincão (63' Ousmane Dembélé), Ansu Fati (62' Pedri).
Coach: Ronald Koeman.
Ferencvárosi TC: Dénes Dibusz, Endre Botka (77' Gergö Lovrencsics), Miha Blazic, Adrian Kovacevic, Eldar Civic (63' Marcel Heister), Dávid Sigér, Igor Kharatin, Aïssa Laïdouni (63' Somália), Isael, Tokmac Nguen (71' Franck Boli), Oleksandr Zubkov (71' Róbert Mak).
Coach: Serhiy Rebrov.
Goals: 27' Lionel Messi 1-0 (p), 42' Ansu Fati 2-0, 52' Philippe Coutinho 3-0, 70' Igor Kharatin 3-1 (p), 82' Pedri 4-1, 89' Ousmane Dembélé 5-1.
Referee: Sandro Schärer (SUI)
Sent off: 68' Piqué.

28.10.20   Allianz Stadium, Torino: Juventus FC – FC Barcelona 0-2 (0-1)
Juventus FC: Wojciech Szczesny, Leonardo Bonucci, Danilo, Merih Demiral, Juan Cuadrado, Adrien Rabiot (83' Federico Bernardeschi), Rodrigo Bentancur (83' Arthur), Dejan Kulusevski (75' Weston McKennie), Morata, Paulo Dybala, Federico Chiesa. Coach: Andrea Pirlo.
FC Barcelona: Neto, Jordi Alba, Sergi Roberto, Clément Lenglet, Ronald Araújo (46' Busquets), Miralem Pjanic, Frenkie de Jong, Lionel Messi, Antoine Griezmann (89' Junior Firpo), Ousmane Dembélé (66' Ansu Fati), Pedri (90+2' Martin Braithwaite).
Coach: Ronald Koeman.
Goals: 14' Ousmane Dembélé 0-1, Lionel Messi 0-2 (p).
Referee: Danny Makkelie (HOL)
Sent off: 85' Merih Demiral.

28.10.20   Groupama Aréna, Budapest: Ferencvárosi TC – Dynamo Kyiv 2-2 (0-2)
Ferencvárosi TC: Dénes Dibusz, Gergö Lovrencsics (86' Endre Botka), Marcel Heister, Miha Blazic, Adrian Kovacevic (86' Lasha Dvali), Somália, Dávid Sigér (73' Róbert Mak), Igor Kharatin (65' Aïssa Laïdouni), Isael (73 Franck Boli), Tokmac Nguen, Oleksandr Zubkov. Coach: Serhiy Rebrov.
Dynamo Kyiv: Denis Boyko, Tomasz Kedziora, Oleksandr Karavayev, Denys Popov, Illia Zabarnyi, Sergiy Sydorchuk, Vitaly Buyalskiy (82' Denys Garmash), Carlos de Pena, Viktor Tsygankov (90+3' Gerson Rodrigues), Mykola Shaparenko (89' Tudor Baluta), Vladyslav Supriaha (89' Benjamin Verbic). Coach: Mircea Lucescu.
Goals: 28' Viktor Tsygankov 0-1 (p), 41' Carlos de Pena 0-2, 59' Tokmac Nguen 1-2, 90' Franck Boli 2-2.
Referee: Ivan Kruzliak (SVK)   Attendance: 6,171.
Sent off: 86' Sergiy Sydorchuk.

04.11.20   Camp Nou, Barcelona: FC Barcelona – Dynamo Kyiv 2-1 (1-0)
FC Barcelona: Marc-André ter Stegen, Piqué, Jordi Alba, Sergiño Dest, Miralem Pjanic (60' Sergi Roberto), Busquets (74' Clément Lenglet), Frenkie de Jong, Lionel Messi, Antoine Griezmann (60' Ousmane Dembélé), Ansu Fati (74' Trincão), Pedri (83' Carles Aleñá). Coach: Ronald Koeman.
Dynamo Kyiv: Ruslan Neshcheret, Tomasz Kedziora, Artem Shabanov, Denys Popov, Illia Zabarnyi, Vitaly Buyalskiy (86' Bohdan Lednev), Oleksandr Andrievsky, Viktor Tsygankov, Volodymyr Shepelev, Gerson Rodrigues (71' Carlos de Pena), Vladyslav Supriaha (71' Benjamin Verbic). Coach: Mircea Lucescu.
Goals: 5' Lionel Messi 1-0 (p), 65' Piqué 2-0, 75' Viktor Tsygankov 2-1.
Referee: Michael Oliver (ENG)

04.11.20   Puskás Aréna, Budapest: Ferencvárosi FC – Juventus FC 1-4 (0-1)
Ferencvárosi TC: Dénes Dibusz, Gergö Lovrencsics, Endre Botka (68' Marcel Heister), Miha Blazic, Lasha Dvali, Somália, Dávid Sigér, Igor Kharatin, Isael (73' Franck Boli), Tokmac Nguen (73' Róbert Mak), Oleksandr Zubkov (80' Myrto Uzuni). Coach: Serhiy Rebrov.
Juventus FC: Wojciech Szczesny, Leonardo Bonucci, Giorgio Chiellini, Danilo, Juan Cuadrado (76' Gianluca Frabotta), Aaron Ramsey (53' Weston McKennie), Adrien Rabiot, Arthur (46' Rodrigo Bentancur), Cristiano Ronaldo, Morata (67' Paulo Dybala), Federico Chiesa (76' Federico Bernardeschi). Coach: Andrea Pirlo.
Goals: 7', 60' Morato 0-1, 0-2, 73' Paulo Dybala 0-3, 81' Lasha Dvali 0-4 (og), 90' Franck Boli 1-4.
Referee: Orel Grinfeld (ISR)   Attendance: 18,531.

Ferencvárosi FC played their home match at Puskás Aréna, Budapest, instead of their regular stadium Groupama Aréna, Budapest.

24.11.20   NSK Olimpijs'kyj Stadium, Kyiv: Dynamo Kyiv – FC Barcelona 0-4 (0-0)
Dynamo Kyiv: Georgiy Bushchan, Tomasz Kedziora, Oleksandr Karavayev (59' Denys Popov), Vitali Mykolenko, Illia Zabarnyi, Denys Garmash (59' Oleksandr Andrievsky), Vitaly Buyalskiy, Benjamin Verbic, Carlos de Pena (71' Vladyslav Supriaha), Mykola Shaparenko (71' Bohdan Lednev), Volodymyr Shepelev (83' Tudor Baluta). Coach: Mircea Lucescu.
FC Barcelona: Marc-André ter Stegen, Clément Lenglet (65' Jordi Alba), Junior Firpo, Óscar Mingueza, Sergiño Dest, Miralem Pjanic (65' Riqui Puig), Philippe Coutinho (65' Antoine Griezmann), Carles Aleñá, Martin Braithwaite, Trincão (83' Konrad de la Fuente), Pedri (73' Matheus Fernandes). Coach: Ronald Koeman.
Goals: 52' Sergiño Dest 0-1, 57', 70' Martin Braithwaite 0-2, 0-3 (p), 90+2' Antoine Griezmann 0-4.
Referee: Matej Jug (SVN)

24.11.20   Allainz Stadium, Torino: Juventus FC – Ferencvárosi TC 2-1 (1-1)
Juventus FC: Wojciech Szczesny, Danilo, Alex Sandro, Matthijs de Ligt, Juan Cuadrado, Arthur (82' Aaron Ramsey), Rodrigo Bentancur (83' Adrien Rabiot), Weston McKennie (62' Dejan Kulusevski), Cristiano Ronaldo, Paulo Dybala (62' Morata), Federico Bernardeschi (62' Federico Chiesa). Coach: Andrea Pirlo.
Ferencvárosi TC: Dénes Dibusz, Gergő Lovrencsics (75' Endre Botka), Marcel Heister, Miha Blazic, Abraham Frimpong, Lasha Dvali, Somália, Dávid Sigér (75' Aïssa Laïdouni), Tokmac Nguen (70' Franck Boli), Oleksandr Zubkov (70' Isael), Myrto Uzuni. Coach: Serhiy Rebrov.
Goals: 19' Myrto Uzuni 0-1, 35' Cristiano Ronaldo 1-1, 90+2' Morata 2-1.
Referee: Daniel Siebert (GER)

02.12.20   Allainz Stadium, Torino: Juventus FC – Dynamo Kyiv 3-0 (1-0)
Juventus FC: Wojciech Szczesny, Leonardo Bonucci (62' Danilo), Alex Sandro, Merih Demiral (69' Radu Dragusin), Matthijs de Ligt, Aaron Ramsey (62' Federico Bernardeschi), Rodrigo Bentancur (76' Arthur), Weston McKennie, Cristiano Ronaldo, Morata, Federico Chiesa (76' Dejan Kulusevski). Coach: Andrea Pirlo.
Dynamo Kyiv: Georgiy Bushchan, Tomasz Kedziora, Denys Popov, Vitali Mykolenko (84' Oleksandr Karavayev), Illia Zabarnyi, Sergiy Sydorchuk, Benjamin Verbic (72' Vladyslav Supriaha), Viktor Tsygankov (90+1' Bohdan Lednev), Mykola Shaparenko, Volodymyr Shepelev (72' Denys Garmash), Gerson Rodrigues (72' Carlos de Pena).
Coach: Mircea Lucescu.
Goals: 21' Federico Chiesa 1-0, 57' Cristiano Ronaldo 2-0, 66' Morata 3-0.
Referee: Stéphanie Frappart (FRA)

02.12.20   Puskás Aréna, Budapest: Ferencvárosi TC – FC Barcelona 0-3 (0-3)
Ferencvárosi TC: Dénes Dibusz, Marcel Heister (64' Gergő Lovrencsics), Endre Botka, Miha Blazic, Abraham Frimpong, Lasha Dvali, Somália (81' Igor Kharatin), Dávid Sigér (64' Aïssa Laïdouni), Isael, Tokmac Nguen (71' Róbert Mak), Myrto Uzuni (71' Roko Baturina).
Coach: Serhiy Rebrov.
FC Barcelona: Neto, Jordi Alba (46' Junior Firpo), Clément Lenglet (65' Carles Aleñá), Óscar Mingueza, Sergiño Dest, Miralem Pjanic, Busquets (46' Frenkie de Jong), Antoine Griezmann (65' Riqui Puig), Martin Braithwaite (80' Konrad de la Fuente), Ousmane Dembélé, Trincão.
Coach: Ronald Koeman.
Goals: 14' Antoine Griezmann 0-1, 21' Martin Braithwaite 0-2, 28' Ousmane Dembélé 0-3 (p).
Referee: Aleksei Kulbakov (BLS)

Ferencvárosi FC played their home match at Puskás Aréna, Budapest, instead of their regular stadium Groupama Aréna, Budapest.

08.12.20   Camp Nou, Barcelona: FC Barcelona – Juventus FC 0-3 (0-2)
FC Barcelona: Marc-André ter Stegen, Jordi Alba (55' Junior Firpo), Clément Lenglet (55' Samuel Umtiti), Ronald Araújo (82' Óscar Mingueza), Sergiño Dest, Miralem Pjanic, Frenkie de Jong, Lionel Messi, Antoine Griezmann, Trincão (46' Martin Braithwaite), Pedri (66' Riqui Puig). Coach: Ronald Koeman.
Juventus FC: Gianluigi Buffon, Leonardo Bonucci, Danilo, Alex Sandro, Matthijs de Ligt, Juan Cuadrado (85' Federico Bernardeschi), Aaron Ramsey (71' Adrien Rabiot), Arthur (71' Rodrigo Bentancur), Weston McKennie, Cristiano Ronaldo (90+2' Federico Chiesa), Morata (85' Paulo Dybala). Coach: Andrea Pirlo.
Goals: 12' Cristiano Ronaldo 0-1 (p), 20' Weston McKennie 0-2, 52' Cristiano Ronaldo 0-3 (p).
Referee: Tobias Stieler (GER)

08.12.20   NSK Olimpijs'kyj Stadium, Kyiv: Dynamo Kyiv – Ferencvárosi TC 1-0 (0-0)
Dynamo Kyiv: Georgiy Bushchan, Tomasz Kedziora, Denys Popov, Vitali Mykolenko, Illia Zabarnyi, Sergiy Sydorchuk (90+2' Oleksandr Andrievsky), Denys Garmash (70' Volodymyr Shepelev), Benjamin Verbic (86' Gerson Rodrigues), Carlos de Pena (70' Vladyslav Supriaha), Viktor Tsygankov (86' Bohdan Lednev), Mykola Shaparenko. Coach: Mircea Lucescu.
Ferencvárosi TC: Dénes Dibusz, Gergö Lovrencsics (80' Endre Botka), Marcel Heister, Miha Blazic, Lasha Dvali, Somália, Igor Kharatin (74' Isael), Aïssa Laïdouni, Tokmac Nguen (86' Franck Boli), Oleksandr Zubkov (80' Róbert Mak), Myrto Uzuni (73' Roko Baturina).
Coach: Serhiy Rebrov.
Goal: 60' Denys Popov 1-0.
Referee: Andreas Ekberg (SWE)

GROUP H

20.10.20   Parc des Princes, Paris: Paris Saint-Germain – Manchester United 1-2 (0-1)
Paris Saint-Germain: Keylor Navas, Layvin Kurzawa (86' Mitchel Bakker), Alessandro Florenzi (79' Colin Dagba), Presnel Kimpembe, Abdou Diallo, Ángel Di María (86' Pablo Sarabia), Ander Herrera (78' Rafinha), Idrissa Gueye (46' Moise Kean), Danilo Pereira, Neymar, Kylian Mbappé. Coach: Thomas Tuchel.
Manchester United: David de Gea, Alex Telles (67' Paul Pogba), Victor Lindelöf, Luke Shaw, Axel Tuanzebe, Aaron Wan-Bissaka, Fred, Bruno Fernandes (88' Donny van de Beek), Scott McTominay, Anthony Martial (88' Daniel James), Marcus Rashford.
Coach: Ole Gunnar Solskjær.
Goals: 23' Bruno Fernandes 0-1 (og), 55' Anthony Martial 1-1 (og), 87' Marcus Rashford 1-2.
Referee: Antonio Miguel Mateu Lahoz (ESP)

20.10.20   Red Bull Arena, Leipzig: RB Leipzig – Istanbul Basaksehir 2-0 (2-0)
RB Leipzig: Péter Gulácsi, Marcel Halstenberg, Willi Orban, José Angeliño, Nordi Mukiele, Dayot Upamecano (65' Ibrahima Konaté), Kevin Kampl (58' Tyler Adams), Christopher Nkunku (70' Justin Kluivert), Daniel Olmo (65' Benjamin Henrichs), Emil Forsberg (46' Hwang Hee-Chan), Yussuf Poulsen. Coach: Julian Nagelsmann.
Istanbul Basaksehir: Mert Günok, Martin Skrtel, Alexandru Epureanu, Rafael, Júnior Caiçara (30' Berkay Özcan), Boli Bolingoli-Mbombo, Mehmet Topal (66' Demba Ba), Edin Visca, Irfan Kahveci (83' Danijel Aleksic), Deniz Türüç (83' Giuliano), Enzo Crivelli.
Coach: Okan Buruk.
Goals: 16', 20' José Angeliño 1-0, 2-0.
Referee: Jesús Gil Manzano (ESP)   Attendance: 999.

28.10.20   Basaksehir Fatih Terim Stadyumu, Istanbul:
  Istanbul Basaksehir – Paris Saint-Germain 0-2 (0-0)
Istanbul Basaksehir: Mert Günok, Martin Skrtel, Alexandru Epureanu, Rafael, Boli Bolingoli-Mbombo (63' Hasan-Ali Kaldirim), Mehmet Topal (68' Demba Ba), Edin Visca, Irfan Kahveci, Deniz Türüç (81' Danijel Aleksic), Berkay Özcan, Enzo Crivelli (81' Giuliano). Coach: Okan Buruk.
Paris Saint-Germain: Keylor Navas, Layvin Kurzawa (87' Mitchel Bakker), Marquinhos, Alessandro Florenzi (73' Thilo Kehrer), Presnel Kimpembe, Ángel Di María (73' Rafinha), Ander Herrera (87' Idrissa Gueye), Danilo Pereira, Neymar (26' Pablo Sarabia), Kylian Mbappé, Moise Kean. Coach: Thomas Tuchel.
Goals: 64', 79' Moise Kean 0-1, 0-2.
Referee: Andreas Ekberg (SWE)   Attendance: 350.

28.10.20   Old Trafford, Manchester: Manchester United – RB Leipzig 5-0 (1-0)
Manchester United: David de Gea, Victor Lindelöf, Harry Maguire, Luke Shaw, Aaron Wan-Bissaka (81' Axel Tuanzebe), Nemanja Matic (63' Scott McTominay), Paul Pogba (81' Edinson Cavani), Fred, Donny van de Beek (68' Bruno Fernandes), Anthony Martial, Mason Greenwood (63' Marcus Rashford). Coach: Ole Gunnar Solskjær.
RB Leipzig: Péter Gulácsi, Marcel Halstenberg, Benjamin Henrichs (63' Marcel Sabitzer), José Angeliño, Dayot Upamecano, Ibrahima Konaté, Kevin Kampl (76' Justin Kluivert), Christopher Nkunku (65' Alexander Sorloth), Daniel Olmo, Emil Forsberg, Yussuf Poulsen. Coach: Julian Nagelsmann.
Goals: 21' Mason Greenwood 1-0, 74', 78' Marcus Rashford 2-0, 3-0,
87' Anthony Martial 4-0 (p), 90+2' Marcus Rashford 5-0.
Referee: Matej Jug (SVN)   Attendance: 577.

04.11.20   Basaksehir Fatih Terim Stadyumu, Istanbul:
  Istanbul Basaksehir – Manchester United 2-1 (2-1)
Istanbul Basaksehir: Mert Günok, Martin Skrtel, Alexandru Epureanu, Rafael, Boli Bolingoli-Mbombo, Danijel Aleksic, Edin Visca, Irfan Kahveci (90' Ponck), Deniz Türüç, Berkay Özcan (87' Mehmet Topal), Demba Ba (79' Fredrik Gulbrandsen).
Coach: Okan Buruk.
Manchester United: Dean Henderson, Harry Maguire, Luke Shaw, Axel Tuanzebe (46' Scott McTominay), Aaron Wan-Bissaka (76' Timothy Fosu-Mensah), Mata (61' Edinson Cavani), Nemanja Matic, Bruno Fernandes, Donny van de Beek (61' Paul Pogba), Anthony Martial, Marcus Rashford (76' Mason Greenwood). Coach: Ole Gunnar Solskjær.
Goals: 13' Demba Ba 1-0, 40' Edin Visca 2-0, 43' Anthony Martial 2-1.
Referee: Davide Massa (ITA)   Attendance: 350.

04.11.20 Red Bull Arena, Leipzig: RB Leipzig – Paris Saint-Germain 2-1 (1-1)
RB Leipzig: Péter Gulácsi, Willi Orban, José Angeliño, Nordi Mukiele (64' Benjamin Henrichs), Dayot Upamecano, Ibrahima Konaté, Marcel Sabitzer (90' Kevin Kampl), Christopher Nkunku, Daniel Olmo (64' Yussuf Poulsen), Amadou Haïdara (76' Tyler Adams), Emil Forsberg (76' Justin Kluivert). Coach: Julian Nagelsmann.
Paris Saint-Germain: Keylor Navas, Layvin Kurzawa (73' Mitchel Bakker), Marquinhos, Alessandro Florenzi (84' Rafinha), Presnel Kimpembe, Ángel Di María, Ander Herrera, Idrissa Gueye, Pablo Sarabia (73' Thilo Kehrer), Danilo Pereira, Moise Kean. Coach: Thomas Tuchel.
Goals: 6' Ángel Di María 0-1, 42' Christopher Nkunku 1-1, 57' Emil Forsberg 2-1 (p).
Referee: Szymon Marciniak (POL)
Sent off: 69' Idrissa Gueye, 90+5' Presnel Kimpembe.

Ángel Di María missed a penalty kick (16').

24.11.20 Old Trafford, Manchester: Manchester United – Istanbul Basaksehir 4-1 (3-0)
Manchester United: David de Gea, Alex Telles, Victor Lindelöf (46' Axel Tuanzebe), Harry Maguire, Aaron Wan-Bissaka (59' Brandon Williams), Fred, Bruno Fernandes (59' Mason Greenwood), Donny van de Beek, Edinson Cavani, Anthony Martial (82' Nemanja Matic), Marcus Rashford (59' Daniel James). Coach: Ole Gunnar Solskjær.
Istanbul Basaksehir: Mert Günok, Martin Skrtel (87' Ponck), Alexandru Epureanu, Rafael, Boli Bolingoli-Mbombo (74' Hasan-Ali Kaldirim), Nacer Chadli (61' Fredrik Gulbrandsen), Edin Visca, Irfan Kahveci (46' Mahmut Tekdemir), Deniz Türüç, Berkay Özcan (74' Giuliano), Demba Ba. Coach: Okan Buruk.
Goals: 7', 19' Bruno Fernandes 1-0, 2-0, 35' Marcus Rashford 3-0 (p), 75' Deniz Türüç 3-1, 90+2' Daniel James 4-1.
Referee: Ovidiu Alin Hategan (ROM)   Attendance: 545.

24.11.20 Parc des Princes, Paris: Paris Saint-Germain – RB Leipzig 1-0 (1-0)
Paris Saint-Germain: Keylor Navas, Marquinhos, Alessandro Florenzi, Abdou Diallo, Mitchel Bakker, Ángel Di María (64' Rafinha), Ander Herrera (83' Marco Verratti), Danilo Pereira, Leandro Paredes, Neymar (90' Pablo Sarabia), Kylian Mbappé (90' Moise Kean).
Coach: Thomas Tuchel.
RB Leipzig: Péter Gulácsi, José Angeliño, Nordi Mukiele (63' Willi Orban), Dayot Upamecano, Ibrahima Konaté, Marcel Sabitzer, Christopher Nkunku, Daniel Olmo (64' Justin Kluivert), Amadou Haïdara, Emil Forsberg (74' Alexander Sorloth), Yussuf Poulsen.
Coach: Julian Nagelsmann.
Goal: 11' Neymar 1-0 (p).
Referee: Danny Makkelie (HOL)

02.12.20 Basaksehir Fatih Terim Stadyumu, Istanbul:
         Istanbul Basaksehir – RB Leipzig 3-4 (1-2)
Istanbul Basaksehir: Mert Günok, Martin Skrtel (46' Alexandru Epureanu), Rafael, Boli Bolingoli-Mbombo (36' Nacer Chadli), Ponck, Edin Visca (64' Giuliano), Irfan Kahveci, Deniz Türüç, Berkay Özcan (46' Mahmut Tekdemir), Demba Ba, Fredrik Gulbrandsen (84' Enzo Crivelli). Coach: Okan Buruk.
RB Leipzig: Péter Gulácsi, José Angeliño, Nordi Mukiele, Dayot Upamecano, Ibrahima Konaté, Kevin Kampl (46' Tyler Adams), Marcel Sabitzer, Daniel Olmo (87' Justin Kluivert), Amadou Haïdara (90+4' Willi Orban), Emil Forsberg (65' Alexander Sorloth), Yussuf Poulsen. Coach: Julian Nagelsmann.
Goals: 26' Yussuf Poulsen 0-1, 43' Nordi Mukiele 0-2, 45+3' Irfan Kahveci 1-2, 66' Daniel Olmo 1-3, 72', 85' Irfan Kahveci 2-3, 3-3, 90+2' Alexander Sorloth 3-4.
Referee: Carlos del Cerro Grande (ESP)

02.12.20 Old Trafford, Manchester: Manchester United – Paris Saint-Germain 1-3 (1-1)
Manchester United: David de Gea, Alex Telles, Victor Lindelöf, Harry Maguire, Aaron Wan-Bissaka (90' Odion Ighalo), Fred, Bruno Fernandes, Scott McTominay, Edinson Cavani (79' Donny van de Beek), Anthony Martial (79' Mason Greenwood), Marcus Rashford (74' Paul Pogba). Coach: Ole Gunnar Solskjær.
Paris Saint-Germain: Keylor Navas, Marquinhos, Alessandro Florenzi (78' Thilo Kehrer), Presnel Kimpembe, Abdou Diallo (90' Idrissa Gueye), Marco Verratti (78' Rafinha), Danilo Pereira, Leandro Paredes (65' Ander Herrera), Neymar, Kylian Mbappé, Moise Kean (65' Mitchel Bakker). Coach: Thomas Tuchel.
Goals: 6' Neymar 0-1, 32' Marcus Rashford 1-1, 69' Marquinhos 1-2, 90+1' Neymar 1-3.
Referee: Daniele Orsato (ITA)   Attendance: 638.
Sent off: 70' Fred.

08.12.20 Red Bull Arena, Leipzig: RB Leipzig – Manchester United 3-2 (2-0)
RB Leipzig: Péter Gulácsi, Willi Orban, José Angeliño (87' Marcel Halstenberg), Nordi Mukiele, Ibrahima Konaté, Kevin Kampl (75' Tyler Adams), Marcel Sabitzer, Christopher Nkunku, Daniel Olmo (56' Justin Kluivert), Amadou Haïdara, Emil Forsberg (56' Yussuf Poulsen). Coach: Julian Nagelsmann.
Manchester United: David de Gea, Alex Telles (46' Donny van de Beek), Victor Lindelöf (77' Axel Tuanzebe), Harry Maguire, Luke Shaw (61' Brandon Williams), Aaron Wan-Bissaka (77' Timothy Fosu-Mensah), Nemanja Matic (61' Paul Pogba), Bruno Fernandes, Scott McTominay, Marcus Rashford, Mason Greenwood. Coach: Ole Gunnar Solskjær.
Goals: 2' José Angeliño 1-0, 13' Amadou Haïdara 2-0, 69' Justin Kluivert 3-0, 80' Bruno Fernandes 3-1 (p), 82' Ibrahima Konaté 3-2 (og).
Referee: Antonio Miguel Mateu Lahoz (ESP)

09.12.20 Parc des Princes, Paris: Paris Saint-Germain – Istanbul Basaksehir 5-1 (3-0)
Paris Saint-Germain: Keylor Navas, Marquinhos (67' Thilo Kehrer), Alessandro Florenzi (80' Timothée Pembele), Presnel Kimpembe (80' Abdou Diallo), Mitchel Bakker, Marco Verratti (80' Idrissa Gueye), Danilo Pereira, Leandro Paredes, Rafinha (46' Ángel Di María), Neymar, Kylian Mbappé. Coach: Thomas Tuchel.
Istanbul Basaksehir: Mert Günok, Hasan-Ali Kaldirim (68' Boli Bolingoli-Mbombo), Rafael (68' Giuliano), Ponck, Mehmet Topal, Mahmut Tekdemir (89' Nacer Chadli), Irfan Kahveci, Deniz Türüç, Berkay Özcan, Fredrik Gulbrandsen (80' Emre Kaplan), Enzo Crivelli (68' Demba Ba). Coach: Okan Buruk.
Goals: 21', 38' Neymar 1-0, 2-0, 42' Kylian Mbappé 3-0 (p), 50' Neymar 4-0, 57' Mehmet Topal 4-1, 62' Kylian Mbappé 5-1.
Referee: Ovidiu Alin Hategan (ROM) on 08.12.20 & Danny Makkelie (HOL) on 09.12.20.

On 8th December 2020 the match wa suspended after 14 minutes, with the score 0-0 as both teams left the pitch in protest after an alleged racist incident by a match official directed at the assistant manager of Istanbul Basaksehir. The match was resumed on 9th December 2020, with a new team of match officials.

KNOCKOUT PHASE
ROUND OF 16

16.02.21   Puskás Aréna, Budapest (HUN): RB Leipzig – Liverpool FC 0-2 (0-0)
RB Leipzig: Péter Gulácsi, Lukas Klostermann, José Angeliño, Nordi Mukiele (64' Willi Orban), Dayot Upamecano, Kevin Kampl (73' Hwang Hee-Chan), Marcel Sabitzer, Christopher Nkunku, Daniel Olmo, Tyler Adams, Amadou Haïdara (64' Yussuf Poulsen). Coach: Julian Nagelsmann.
Liverpool FC: Alisson, Andrew Robertson, Trent Alexander-Arnold, Ozan Kabak, Georginio Wijnaldum, Jordan Henderson, Thiago Alcântara (72' Alex Oxlade-Chamberlain), Curtis Jones, Roberto Firmino (72' Xherdan Shaqiri), Mohamed Salah (90' Neco Williams), Sadio Mané. Coach: Jürgen Klopp.
Goals: 53' Mohamed Salah 0-1, 58' Sadio Mané 0-2.
Referee: Slavko Vincic (SVN)

Match originally scheduled to be played at Red Bull Arena, Leipzig, was moved to Puskás Aréna, Budapest (Hungary), due to travel restrictions related to the COVID-19 pandemic.

16.02.21   Camp Nou, Barcelona: FC Barcelona – Paris Saint-Germain 1-4 (1-1)
FC Barcelona: Marc-André ter Stegen, Piqué (78' Riqui Puig), Jordi Alba, Clément Lenglet, Sergiño Dest (71' Óscar Mingueza), Busquets (79' Miralem Pjanic), Frenkie de Jong, Lionel Messi, Antoine Griezmann (85' Martin Braithwaite), Ousmane Dembélé, Pedri (79' Trincão). Coach: Ronald Koeman.
Paris Saint-Germain: Keylor Navas, Layvin Kurzawa, Marquinhos, Alessandro Florenzi (89' Thilo Kehrer), Presnel Kimpembe, Marco Verratti (73' Julian Draxler), Idrissa Gueye (46' Ander Herrera), Leandro Paredes, Mauro Icardi, Kylian Mbappé, Moise Kean (85' Danilo Pereira). Coach: Mauricio Pochettino.
Goals: 27' Lionel Messi 1-0 (p), 32', 65' Kylian Mbappé 1-1, 1-2, 70' Moise Kean 1-3, 85' Kylian Mbappé 1-4.
Referee: Björn Kuipers (HOL)

17.02.21   Estádio do Dragão, Porto: FC Porto – Juventus FC 2-1 (1-0)
FC Porto: Agustín Marchesín, Pepe, Chancel Mbemba, Wilson Manafá, Zaidu Sanusi, Sérgio Oliveira (90+1' Francisco Conceição), Mateus Uribe, Otávio (57' Luis Díaz), Jesús Corona (90+1' Mamadou Loum), Mehdi Taremi, Moussa Marega (66' Marko Grujic). Coach: Sérgio Conceição.
Juventus FC: Wojciech Szczesny, Giorgio Chiellini (35' Merih Demiral), Danilo, Alex Sandro, Matthijs de Ligt, Adrien Rabiot, Rodrigo Bentancur, Weston McKennie (63' Morata), Dejan Kulusevski (77' Aaron Ramsey), Cristiano Ronaldo, Federico Chiesa. Coach: Andrea Pirlo.
Goals: 2' Mehdi Taremi 1-0, 46' Moussa Marega 2-0, 82' Federico Chiesa 2-1.
Referee: Carlos Del Cerro Grande (ESP)

17.02.21   Estádio Ramón Sánchez Pizjuán, Sevilla: Sevilla CF – Borussia Dortmund 2-3 (1-3)
Sevilla CF: Yassine Bounou, Jesús Navas, Escudero, Diego Carlos, Jules Koundé, Ivan Rakitic (46' Nemanja Gudelj), Papu Gómez (60' Óliver Torres), Fernando, Suso (60' Luuk de Jong), Joan Jordán (72' Óscar Rodríguez), Youssef En-Nesyri (60' Munir). Coach: Lopetegui.
Borussia Dortmund: Marwin Hitz, Mats Hummels, Raphaël Guerreiro (76' Felix Passlack), Manuel Akanji, Mateu Morey, Emre Can, Mahmoud Dahoud (89' Thomas Meunier), Jadon Sancho, Jude Bellingham, Marco Reus (80' Julian Brandt), Erling Håland. Coach: Edin Terzic.
Goals: 7' Suso 1-0, 19' Mahmoud Dahoud 1-1, 27', 43' Erling Håland 1-2, 1-3, 84' Luuk de Jong 2-3.
Referee: Danny Makkelie (HOL)

23.02.21   Stadio Olimpico, Roma: Lazio Roma – FC Bayern München 1-4 (0-3)
Lazio Roma: Pepe Reina, Mateo Musacchio (31' Senad Lulic), Francesco Acerbi, Patric (53' Wesley Hoedt), Adam Marusic, Lucas Leiva (53' Gonzalo Escalante), Luis Alberto (81' Jean-Daniel Akpa-Akpro), Joaquín Correa, Manuel Lazzari, Sergej Milinkovic-Savic (81' Danilo Cataldi), Ciro Immobile. Coach: Simone Inzaghi.
FC Bayern München: Manuel Neuer, Jérôme Boateng, David Alaba, Niklas Süle, Alphonso Davies, Leon Goretzka (63' Javi Martínez), Joshua Kimmich, Jamal Musiala (90' Eric Maxim Choupo-Moting), Robert Lewandowski, Kingsley Coman (75' Lucas Hernández), Leroy Sané (90' Bouna Sarr). Coach: Hans Flick.
Goals: 9' Robert Lewandowski 0-1, 24' Jamal Musiala 0-2, 42' Leroy Sané 0-3, 47' Francesco Acerbi 0-4 (og), 49' Joaquín Correa 1-4.
Referee: Orel Grinfeld (ISR)

23.02.21   Arena Nationala, Bucharest (ROM): Atlético Madrid – Chelsea FC 0-1 (0-0)
Atlético Madrid: Jan Oblak, Stefan Savic, Felipe Monteiro, Mario Hermoso (84' Vitolo), Saúl (82' Lucas Torreira), Koke, Thomas Lemar, Marcos Llorente, Luis Suárez, Ángel Correa (82' Moussa Dembélé), João Félix (82' Renan Lodi). Coach: Diego Simeone.
Chelsea FC: Edouard Mendy, Azpilicueta, Marcos Alonso, Antonio Rüdiger, Andreas Christensen, Mateo Kovacic (74' Hakim Ziyech), Jorginho, Mason Mount (74' N'Golo Kanté), Olivier Giroud (87' Kai Havertz), Timo Werner (87' Christian Pulisic), Callum Hudson-Odoi (80' Reece James). Coach: Thomas Tuchel.
Goal: 68' Olivier Giroud 0-1.
Referee: Dr. Felix Brych (GER)

Match originally scheduled to be played at Metropolitano Stadium, Madrid, was moved to Arena Nationala, Bucharest (Romania), due to travel restrictions related to the COVID-19 pandemic.

24.02.21   Puskás Aréna, Budapest (HUN):
Borussia Mönchengladbach – Manchester City 0-2 (0-1)
Borussia Mönchengladbach: Yann Sommer, Stefan Lainer (63' Valentino Lazaro), Matthias Ginter, Nico Elvedi, Ramy Bensebaini, Lars Stindl (74' Breel Embolo), Christoph Kramer, Jonas Hofmann (87' Hannes Wolf), Florian Neuhaus, Denis Zakaria, Alassane Pléa (63' Marcus Thuram). Coach: Marco Rose.
Manchester City: Ederson Moraes, Kyle Walker, João Cancelo, Aymeric Laporte, Rúben Dias, Ilkay Gündogan, Bernardo Silva, Rodri, Phil Foden (80' Ferrán Torres), Raheem Sterling (69' Riyad Mahrez), Gabriel Jesus (80' Kun Agüero). Coach: Pep Guardiola.
Goals: 29' Bernardo Silva 0-1, 65' Gabriel Jesus 0-2.
Referee: Artur Manuel Ribeiro Soares Dias (POR)

Match originally scheduled to be played at Borussia-Park, Mönchengladbach, was moved to Puskás Aréna, Budapest (Hungary), due to travel restrictions related to the COVID-19 pandemic.

24.02.21   Gewiss Stadium, Bergamo: Atalanta Bergamo – Real Madrid CF 0-1 (0-0)
Atalanta Bergamo: Pierluigi Gollini, Rafael Tolói, Berat Djimsiti, Robin Gosens, Cristian Romero, Joakim Mæhle (86' José Palomino), Marten de Roon, Remo Freuler, Matteo Pessina, Duván Zapata (30' Mario Pasalic), Luis Muriel (56' Josip Ilicic, 86' Ruslan Malinovskyi). Coach: Gian Piero Gasperini.
Real Madrid CF: Thibaut Courtois, Nacho, Raphaël Varane, Ferland Mendy, Luka Modric, Toni Kroos, Casemiro, Isco (76' Hugo Duro), Lucas Vázquez, Marco Asensio (76' Sergio Arribas), Vinícius Júnior (57' Mariano Díaz). Coach: Zinédine Zidane.
Goal: 86' Ferland Mendy 0-1.
Referee: Tobias Stieler (GER)
Sent off: 17' Remo Freuler.

09.03.21   Allianz Stadium, Torino: Juventus FC – FC Porto 3-2 (0-1, 2-1) (a.e.t.)
Juventus FC: Wojciech Szczesny, Leonardo Bonucci (75' Matthijs de Ligt), Alex Sandro, Merih Demiral, Juan Cuadrado, Aaron Ramsey (75' Weston McKennie), Adrien Rabiot, Arthur (102' Dejan Kulusevski), Cristiano Ronaldo, Morata, Federico Chiesa (102' Federico Bernardeschi). Coach: Andrea Pirlo.
FC Porto: Agustín Marchesín, Pepe, Chancel Mbemba, Wilson Manafá, Zaidu Sanusi (71' Luis Díaz), Sérgio Oliveira (118' Mamadou Loum), Mateus Uribe (90' Marko Grujic), Otávio (62' Malang Sarr), Jesús Corona (118' Diogo Leite), Mehdi Taremi, Moussa Marega (106' Toni Martínez). Coach: Sérgio Conceição.
Goals: 19' Sérgio Oliveira 0-1 (p), 48', 63' Federico Chiesa 1-1, 2-1, 115' Sérgio Oliveira 2-2, 117' Adrien Rabiot 3-2.
Referee: Björn Kuipers (HOL)
Sent off: 54' Mehdi Taremi.

FC Porto won on away goals.

09.03.21 Signal-Iduna-Park, Dortmund: Borussia Dortmund – Sevilla CF 2-2 (1-0)
Borussia Dortmund: Marwin Hitz, Mats Hummels, Nico Schulz (89' Dan-Axel Zagadou), Mateu Morey (90+5' Thomas Meunier), Thomas Delaney, Thorgan Hazard (67' Felix Passlack), Emre Can, Mahmoud Dahoud, Jude Bellingham, Marco Reus, Erling Håland. Coach: Edin Terzic.
Sevilla CF: Yassine Bounou, Jesús Navas, Diego Carlos, Jules Koundé, Fernando (86' Ivan Rakitic), Lucas Ocampos (60' Luuk de Jong), Marcos Acuña, Suso (86' Munir), Joan Jordán (60' Papu Gómez), Óscar Rodríguez (79' Óliver Torres), Youssef En-Nesyri.
Coach: Lopetegui.
Goals: 35', 54' Erling Håland 1-0, 2-0 (p), 69', 90+6' Youssef En-Nesyri 2-1 (p), 2-2.
Referee: Cüneyt Çakir (TUR)

10.03.21 Puskás Aréna, Budapest (HUN): Liverpool FC – RB Leipzig 2-0 (0-0)
Liverpool FC: Alisson, Andrew Robertson (90' Kostas Tsimikas), Trent Alexander-Arnold, Nathaniel Phillips, Ozan Kabak, Georginio Wijnaldum (82' James Milner), Thiago Alcântara (72' Naby Keïta), Fabinho, Mohamed Salah, Sadio Mané (89' Alex Oxlade-Chamberlain), Diogo Jota (71' Divock Origi). Coach: Jürgen Klopp.
RB Leipzig: Péter Gulácsi, Lukas Klostermann, Nordi Mukiele, Dayot Upamecano, Kevin Kampl (46' Alexander Sørloth), Marcel Sabitzer, Christopher Nkunku, Daniel Olmo (72' Amadou Haïdara), Tyler Adams, Emil Forsberg (60' Justin Kluivert), Yussuf Poulsen (60' Hwang Hee-Chan). Coach: Julian Nagelsmann.
Goals: 70' Mohamed Salah 1-0, 74' Sadio Mané 2-0.
Referee: Clément Turpin (FRA)

Match originally scheduled to be played at Anfield, Liverpool, was moved to Puskás Aréna, Budapest (Hungary), due to travel restrictions related to the COVID-19 pandemic.

10.03.21 Parc des Princes, Paris: Paris Saint-Germain – FC Barcelona 1-1 (1-1)
Paris Saint-Germain: Keylor Navas, Layvin Kurzawa (46' Abdou Diallo), Marquinhos, Alessandro Florenzi (76' Colin Dagba), Presnel Kimpembe, Marco Verratti (84' Rafinha), Idrissa Gueye (60' Danilo Pereira), Leandro Paredes, Julian Draxler (59' Ángel Di María), Mauro Icardi, Kylian Mbappé. Coach: Mauricio Pochettino.
FC Barcelona: Marc-André ter Stegen, Jordi Alba, Clément Lenglet, Óscar Mingueza (35' Junior Firpo), Sergiño Dest (66' Trincão), Busquets (79' Ilaix Kourouma), Frenkie de Jong, Lionel Messi, Antoine Griezmann, Ousmane Dembélé (78' Martin Braithwaite), Pedri (78' Miralem Pjanic). Coach: Ronald Koeman.
Goals: 31' Kylian Mbappé 1-0 (p), 37' Lionel Messi 1-1.
Referee: Anthony Taylor (ENG)

Lionel Messi missed a penalty kick (45+3').

16.03.21 Puskás Aréna, Budapest (HUN):
Manchester City – Borussia Mönchengladbach 2-0 (2-0)
Manchester City: Ederson Moraes, Kyle Walker, João Cancelo (64' Oleksandr Zinchenko), John Stones, Rúben Dias (70' Aymeric Laporte), Ilkay Gündogan (70' Raheem Sterling), Kevin De Bruyne, Bernardo Silva (75' Kun Agüero), Rodri (63' Fernandinho), Phil Foden, Riyad Mahrez. Coach: Pep Guardiola.
Borussia Mönchengladbach: Yann Sommer, Stefan Lainer, Matthias Ginter, Nico Elvedi (88' Tony Jantschke), Ramy Bensebaini (88' Oscar Wendt), Lars Stindl (80' Ibrahima Traoré), Jonas Hofmann, Florian Neuhaus, Denis Zakaria, Breel Embolo (65' Hannes Wolf), Marcus Thuram (65' Alassane Pléa). Coach: Marco Rose.
Goals: 12' Kevin De Bruyne 1-0, 18' Ilkay Gündogan 2-0.
Referee: Sergey Karasev (RUS)

Match originally scheduled to be played at Etihad Stadium, Manchester, was moved to Puskás Aréna, Budapest (Hungary), due to travel restrictions related to the COVID-19 pandemic.

16.03.21 Estadio Alfredo Di Stéfano, Madrid: Real Madrid CF – Atalanta Bergamo 3-1 (1-0)
Real Madrid CF: Thibaut Courtois, Sergio Ramos (64' Éder Militão), Nacho, Raphaël Varane, Ferland Mendy, Luka Modric, Toni Kroos, Lucas Vázquez, Federico Valverde (82' Marco Asensio), Karim Benzema, Vinícius Júnior (69' Rodrygo). Coach: Zinédine Zidane.
Atalanta Bergamo: Marco Sportiello, Rafael Tolói (61' José Palomino), Berat Djimsiti, Robin Gosens (57' Josip Ilicic), Cristian Romero, Joakim Mæhle, Marten de Roon, Mario Pasalic (46' Duván Zapata), Ruslan Malinovskyi, Matteo Pessina (84' Mattia Caldara), Luis Muriel (84' Aleksey Miranchuk). Coach: Gian Piero Gasperini.
Goals: 34' Karim Benzema 1-0, 60' Sergio Ramos 2-0 (p), 83' Luis Muriel 2-1, 84' Marco Asensio 3-1.
Referee: Danny Makkelie (HOL)

17.03.21 Allianz Arena, München: FC Bayern München – Lazio Roma 2-1 (1-0)
FC Bayern München: Alexander Nübel, Jérôme Boateng (46' Niklas Süle), David Alaba, Lucas Hernández, Benjamin Pavard, Leon Goretzka (64' Alphonso Davies), Joshua Kimmich (77' Javi Martínez), Thomas Müller (71' Jamal Musiala), Robert Lewandowski (71' Eric Maxim Choupo-Moting), Serge Gnabry, Leroy Sané. Coach: Hans Flick.
Lazio Roma: Pepe Reina, Stefan Radu, Francesco Acerbi, Adam Marusic, Luis Alberto (75' Danilo Cataldi), Joaquín Correa, Gonzalo Escalante (84' Jean-Daniel Akpa-Akpro), Manuel Lazzari (57' Marco Parolo), Sergej Milinkovic-Savic, Mohamed Fares (46' Senad Lulic), Vedat Muriqi (56' Andreas Pereira). Coach: Simone Inzaghi.
Goals: 33' Robert Lewandowski 1-0 (p), 73' Eric Maxim Choupo-Moting 2-0, 82' Marco Parolo 2-1.
Referee: István Kovács (ROM)

17.03.21 Stamford Bridge, London: Chelsea FC – Atlético Madrid 2-0 (1-0)
Chelsea FC: Edouard Mendy, Azpilicueta, Marcos Alonso (90+4' Ben Chilwell), Kurt Zouma, Antonio Rüdiger, Reece James, Mateo Kovacic, N'Golo Kanté, Hakim Ziyech (77' Christian Pulisic), Kai Havertz (90+3' Emerson), Timo Werner (83' Callum Hudson-Odoi).
Coach: Thomas Tuchel.
Atlético Madrid: Jan Oblak, Stefan Savic, Kieran Trippier (69' Thomas Lemar), José Giménez, Rena Lodi (46' Mario Hermoso), Saúl, Koke, Yannick Carrasco (53' Moussa Dembélé), Marcos Llorente, Luis Suárez (59' Ángel Correa), João Félix. Coach: Diego Simeone.
Goals: 34' Hakim Ziyech 1-0, 90+4' Emerson 2-0.
Referee: Daniele Orsato (ITA)
Sent off: 81' Stefan Savic.

QUARTER-FINALS

06.04.21 Etihad Stadium, Manchester: Manchester City – Borussia Dortmund 2-1 (1-0)
Manchester City: Ederson Moraes, Kyle Walker, João Cancelo, John Stones, Rúben Dias, Ilkay Gündogan, Kevin De Bruyne, Bernardo Silva (59' Gabriel Jesus), Rodri, Phil Foden, Riyad Mahrez. Coach: Pep Guardiola.
Borussia Dortmund: Marwin Hitz, Mats Hummels, Raphaël Guerreiro, Manuel Akanji, Mateu Morey (81' Thomas Meunier), Emre Can, Mahmoud Dahoud (81' Thomas Delaney), Ansgar Knauff (63' Giovanni Reyna), Jude Bellingham, Marco Reus, Erling Håland.
Coach: Edin Terzic.
Goals: 19' Kevin De Bruyne 1-0, 84' Marco Reus 1-1, 90' Phil Foden 2-1.
Referee: Ovidia Alin Hategan (ROM)

06.04.21 Estadio Alfredo Di Stéfano, Madrid: Real Madrid CF – Liverpool FC 3-1 (2-0)
Real Madrid CF: Thibaut Courtois, Nacho, Ferland Mendy, Éder Militão, Luka Modric, Toni Kroos, Casemiro, Lucas Vázquez, Karim Benzema, Marco Asensio (70' Federico Valverde), Vinícius Júnior (85' Rodrygo). Coach: Zinédine Zidane.
Liverpool FC: Alisson, Andrew Robertson, Trent Alexander-Arnold, Nathaniel Phillips, Ozan Kabak (81' Roberto Firmino), Georginio Wijnaldum, Fabinho, Naby Keïta (42' Thiago Alcântara), Mohamed Salah, Sadio Mané, Diogo Jota (81' Xherdan Shaqiri).
Coach: Jürgen Klopp.
Goals: 27' Vinícius Júnior 1-0, 36' Marco Asension 2-0, 51' Mohamed Salah 2-1, 65' Vinícius Júnior 3-1.
Referee: Dr. Felix Brych (GER)

07.04.21   Estádio Ramón Sánchez Pizjuán, Sevilla (ESP): FC Porto – Chelsea FC 0-2 (0-1)
FC Porto: Agustín Marchesín, Pepe, Chancel Mbemba, Wilson Manafá (83' Francisco Conceição), Zaidu Sanusi, Mateus Uribe, Otávio (83' Fábio Vieira), Marko Grujic, Jesús Corona, Moussa Marega (83' Toni Martínez), Luis Díaz. Coach: Sérgio Conceição.
Chelsea FC: Edouard Mendy, Azpilicueta, Antonio Rüdiger, Andreas Christensen, Ben Chilwell, Reece James (80' Thiago Silva), Mateo Kovacic (90+2' Emerson), Jorginho, Mason Mount (80' N'Golo Kanté), Kai Havertz (65' Olivier Giroud), Timo Werner (65' Christian Pulisic). Coach: Thomas Tuchel.
Goals: 32' Mason Mount 0-1, 85' Ben Chilwell 0-2.
Referee: Slavko Vincic (SVN)

Match was played at Estádio Ramón Sánchez Pizjúan, Sevilla (Spain), due to travel restrictions related to the COVID-19 pandemic.

07.04.21   Allianz Arena, München: FC Bayern München – Paris Saint-Germain 2-3 (1-2)
FC Bayern München: Manuel Neuer, David Alaba, Niklas Süle (42' Jérôme Boateng), Lucas Hernández, Benjamin Pavard, Leon Goretzka (33' Alphonso Davies), Joshua Kimmich, Eric Maxim Choupo-Moting, Thomas Müller, Kingsley Coman, Leroy Sané. Coach: Hans Flick.
Paris Saint-Germain: Keylor Navas, Marquinhos (31'Ander Herrera), Presnel Kimpembe, Abdou Diallo (46' Mitchel Bakker), Colin Dagba, Ángel Di María (71' Moise Kean), Idrissa Gueye, Danilo Pereira, Julian Draxler, Neymar (90' Rafinha), Kylian Mbappé.
Coach: Mauricio Pochettino.
Goals: 3' Kylian Mbappé 0-1, 28' Marquinhos 0-2, 37' Eric Maxim Choupo-Moting 1-2, 60' Thomas Müller 2-2, 68' Kylian Mbappé 2-3.
Referee: Antonio Miguel Mateu Lahoz (ESP)

13.04.21   Estádio Ramón Sánchez Pizjuán, Sevilla (ESP): Chelsea FC – FC Porto 0-1 (0-0)
Chelsea FC: Edouard Mendy, Thiago Silva, Azpilicueta, Antonio Rüdiger, Ben Chilwell, Reece James, Jorginho, N'Golo Kanté, Mason Mount (86' Hakim Ziyech), Christian Pulisic, Kai Havertz (90+2' Olivier Giroud). Coach: Thomas Tuchel.
FC Porto: Agustín Marchesín, Pepe, Chancel Mbemba, Wilson Manafá (75' Nanu), Zaidu Sanusi, Sérgio Oliveira (84' Fábio Vieira), Mateus Uribe, Otávio, Marko Grujic (63' Mehdi Taremi), Jesús Corona (75' Luis Díaz), Moussa Marega (75' Evanilson).
Coach: Sérgio Conceição.
Goal: 90+4' Mehdi Taremi 0-1.
Referee: Clément Turpin (FRA)

Match was played at Estádio Ramón Sánchez Pizjúan, Sevilla (Spain), due to travel restrictions related to the COVID-19 pandemic between Portugal and the United Kingdom.

13.04.21 Parc des Princes, Paris: Paris Saint-Germain – FC Bayern München 0-1 (0-1)
Paris Saint-Germain: Keylor Navas, Presnel Kimpembe, Abdou Diallo (58' Mitchel Bakker), Colin Dagba, Ángel Di María (88' Ander Herrera), Idrissa Gueye, Danilo Pereira, Leandro Paredes, Julian Draxler (73' Moise Kean), Neymar, Kylian Mbappé.
Coach: Mauricio Pochettino.
FC Bayern München: Manuel Neuer, Jérôme Boateng, David Alaba, Lucas Hernández, Benjamin Pavard, Alphonso Davies (71' Jamal Musiala), Joshua Kimmich, Eric Maxim Choupo-Moting (85' Javi Martínez), Thomas Müller, Kingsley Coman, Leroy Sané.
Coach: Hans Flick.
Goal: 40' Eric Maxim Choupo-Moting 0-1.
Referee: Daniele Orsato (ITA)

Paris Saint-Germain won on away goals.

14.04.21 Signal-Iduna-Park, Dortmund: Borussia Dortmund – Manchester City 1-2 (1-0)
Borussia Dortmund: Marwin Hitz, Mats Hummels, Raphaël Guerreiro, Manuel Akanji, Mateu Morey (81' Steffen Tigges), Emre Can, Mahmoud Dahoud (76' Thorgan Hazard), Ansgar Knauff (68' Giovanni Reyna), Jude Bellingham (81' Julian Brandt), Marco Reus, Erling Håland. Coach: Edin Terzic.
Manchester City: Ederson Moraes, Kyle Walker, John Stones, Rúben Dias, Ilkay Gündogan, Kevin De Bruyne, Oleksandr Zinchenko, Bernardo Silva, Rodri, Phil Foden, Riyad Mahrez (88' Raheem Sterling). Coach: Pep Guardiola.
Goals: 15' Jude Bellingham 1-0, 55' Riyad Mahrez 1-1 (p), 75' Phil Foden 1-2.
Referee: Carlos del Cerro Grande (ESP)

14.04.21 Anfield, Liverpool: Liverpool FC – Real Madrid CF 0-0
Liverpool FC: Alisson, Andrew Robertson, Trent Alexander-Arnold, Nathaniel Phillips, Ozan Kabak (60' Diogo Jota), James Milner (60' Thiago Alcântara), Georginio Wijnaldum, Fabinho, Roberto Firmino (82' Xherdan Shaqiri), Mohamed Salah, Sadio Mané (82' Alex Oxlade-Chamberlain). Coach: Jürgen Klopp.
Real Madrid CF: Thibaut Courtois, Nacho, Ferland Mendy, Éder Militão, Luka Modric, Toni Kroos (72' Odriozola), Casemiro, Federico Valverde, Karim Benzema, Marco Asensio (82' Isco), Vinícius Júnior (72' Rodrygo). Coach: Zinédine Zidane.
Referee: Björn Kuipers (HOL)

SEMI-FINALS

27.04.21 Estadio Alfredo Di Stéfano, Madrid: Real Madrid CF – Chelsea FC 1-1 (1-1)
Real Madrid CF: Thibaut Courtois, Marcelo (77' Marco Asensio), Nacho, Dani Carvajal (77 Odriozola), Raphaël Varane, Éder Militão, Luka Modric, Toni Kroos, Casemiro, Karim Benzema (90+2' Rodrygo), Vinícius Júnior (66' Eden Hazard). Coach: Zinédine Zidane.
Chelsea FC: Edouard Mendy, Thiago Silva, Azpilicueta (66' Reece James), Antonio Rüdiger, Andreas Christensen, Ben Chilwell, Jorginho, N'Golo Kanté, Mason Mount, Christian Pulisic (66' Hakim Ziyech), Timo Werner (66' Kai Havertz). Coach: Thomas Tuchel.
Goals: 14' Christian Pulisic 0-1, 29' Karim Benzema 1-1.
Referee: Danny Makkelie (HOL)

28.04.21   Parc des Princes, Paris: Paris Saint-Germain – Manchester City 1-2 (1-0)
Paris Saint-Germain: Keylor Navas, Marquinhos, Alessandro Florenzi, Presnel Kimpembe, Mitchel Bakker, Ángel Di María (80' Danilo Pereira), Marco Verratti, Idrissa Gueye, Leandro Paredes (83' Ander Herrera), Neymar, Kylian Mbappé. Coach: Mauricio Pochettino.
Manchester City: Ederson Moraes, Kyle Walker, João Cancelo (61' Oleksandr Zinchenko), John Stones, Rúben Dias, Ilkay Gündogan, Kevin De Bruyne, Bernardo Silva, Rodri, Phil Foden, Riyad Mahrez. Coach: Pep Guardiola.
Goals: 15' Marquinhos 1-0, 64' Kevin De Bruyne 1-1, 71' Riyad Mahrez 1-2.
Referee: Dr. Felix Brych (GER)
Sent off: 77' Idrissa Gueye.

04.05.21   Etihad Stadium, Manchester: Manchester City – Paris Saint-Germain 2-0 (1-0)
Manchester City: Ederson Moraes, Kyle Walker, John Stones, Rúben Dias, Fernandinho, Ilkay Gündogan, Kevin De Bruyne (82' Gabriel Jesus), Oleksandr Zinchenko, Bernardo Silva (82' Raheem Sterling), Phil Foden (85' Kun Agüero), Riyad Mahrez. Coach: Pep Guardiola.
Paris Saint-Germain: Keylor Navas, Marquinhos, Alessandro Florenzi (75' Colin Dagba), Presnel Kimpembe, Abdou Diallo (82' Mitchel Bakker), Ángel Di María, Ander Herrera (62' Julian Draxler), Marco Verratti, Leandro Paredes (75' Danilo Pereira), Neymar, Mauro Icardi (62' Moise Kean). Coach: Mauricio Pochettino.
Goals: 11', 63' Riyad Mahrez 1-0, 2-0.
Referee: Björn Kuipers (HOL)
Sent off: 69' Ángel Di María.

05.05.21   Stamford Bridge, London: Chelsea FC – Real Madrid CF 2-0 (1-0)
Chelsea FC: Edouard Mendy, Thiago Silva, Azpilicueta (88' Reece James), Antonio Rüdiger, Andreas Christensen, Ben Chilwell, Jorginho, N'Golo Kanté, Mason Mount (88' Hakim Ziyech), Kai Havertz (90+4' Olivier Giroud), Timo Werner (67' Christian Pulisic).
Coach: Thomas Tuchel.
Real Madrid CF: Thibaut Courtois, Sergio Ramos, Nacho, Ferland Mendy (63' Federico Valverde), Éder Militão, Luka Modric, Toni Kroos, Casemiro (76' Rodrygo), Karim Benzema, Eden Hazard (89' Mariano Díaz), Vinícius Júnior (63' Marco Asensio).
Coach: Zinédine Zidane.
Goals: 28' Timo Werner 1-0, 85' Mason Mount 2-0.
Referee: Daniele Orsato (ITA)

FINAL

29.05.21   Estádio do Dragão, Porto (POR): Manchester City – FC Chelsea 0-1 (0-1)
Manchester City: Ederson Moraes, Oleksandr Zinchenko, Rúben Dias, John Stones, Kyle Walker, Phil Foden, Ilkay Gündogan, Bernardo Silva (64' Fernandinho), Raheem Sterling (77' Kun Agüero), Kevin De Bruyne (60' Gabriel Jesus), Riyad Mahrez. Coach: Pep Guardiola.
Chelsea FC: Edouard Mendy, Antonio Rüdiger, Thiago Silva (39' Andreas Christensen), Azpilicueta, Ben Chilwell, Jorginho, N'Golo Kanté, Reece James, Mason Mount (80' Mateo Kovacic), Kai Havertz, Timo Werner (66' Christian Pulisic). Coach: Thomas Tuchel.
Goal: 42' Kai Havertz 0-1.
Referee: Antonio Mateu Lahoz (ESP)   Attendance: 14,110

EUROPEAN CHAMPIONS CUP / CHAMPIONS LEAGUE WINNERS

1956	Real Madrid	Spain
1957	Real Madrid	Spain
1958	Real Madrid	Spain
1959	Real Madrid	Spain
1960	Real Madrid	Spain
1961	SL Benfica	Portugal
1962	SL Benfica	Portugal
1963	AC Milan	Italy
1964	Internazionale	Italy
1965	Internazionale	Italy
1966	Real Madrid	Spain
1967	Celtic FC	Scotland
1968	Manchester United	England
1969	AC Milan	Italy
1970	Feijenoord	Netherlands
1971	AFC Ajax	Netherlands
1972	AFC Ajax	Netherlands
1973	AFC Ajax	Netherlands
1974	Bayern München	Germany
1975	Bayern München	Germany
1976	Bayern München	Germany
1977	Liverpool FC	England
1978	Liverpool FC	England
1979	Nottingham Forest	England
1980	Nottingham Forest	England
1981	Liverpool FC	England
1982	Aston Villa	England
1983	Hamburger SV	Germany
1984	Liverpool FC	England
1985	Juventus	Italy
1986	FC Steaua Bucuresti	Romania
1987	FC Porto	Portugal
1988	PSV	Netherlands
1989	AC Milan	Italy
1990	AC Milan	Italy
1991	Crvena Zvezda Beograd	Serbia
1992	FC Barcelona	Spain
1993	Olympique Marseille	France
1994	AC Milan	Italy
1995	AFC Ajax	Netherlands
1996	Juventus	Italy
1997	Borussia Dortmund	Germany
1998	Real Madrid	Spain
1999	Manchester United	England
2000	Real Madrid	Spain
2001	Bayern München	Germany
2002	Real Madrid	Spain

2003	AC Milan	Italy
2004	FC Porto	Portugal
2005	Liverpool FC	England
2006	FC Barcelona	Spain
2007	AC Milan	Italy
2008	Manchester United	England
2009	FC Barcelona	Spain
2010	Internazionale	Italy
2011	FC Barcelona	Spain
2012	Chelsea FC	England
2013	Bayern München	Germany
2014	Real Madrid	Spain
2015	FC Barcelona	Spain
2016	Real Madrid	Spain
2017	Real Madrid	Spain
2018	Real Madrid	Spain
2019	Liverpool FC	England
2020	FC Bayern München	Germany
2021	Chelsea FC	England

ALL-TIME RECORD – CLUBS

Real Madrid	13
AC Milan	7
Bayern München	6
Liverpool FC	6
FC Barcelona	5
AFC Ajax	4
Internazionale	3
Manchester United	3
SL Benfica	2
Nottingham Forest	2
Juventus	2
FC Porto	2
Chelsea FC	2
Celtic FC	1
Feijenoord	1
Aston Villa	1
Hamburger SV	1
FC Steaua Bucuresti	1
PSV	1
Crvena Zvezda Beograd	1
Olympique Marseille	1
Borussia Dortmund	1

ALL-TIME RECORD – COUNTRIES

Spain	18
England	14
Italy	12
Germany	8
Netherlands	6
Portugal	4
Scotland	1
Romania	1
Serbia	1
France	1